SOVIET FIGHTERS

OF THE SECOND WORLD WAR

SOVIET FIGHTERS OF THE SECOND WORLD WAR

JASON NICHOLAS MOORE

FONTHILL

I dedicate this book to the brave women and men of the Soviet Union, both military and civilian, who sacrificed so much in their terrible war to defeat Nazi aggression.

Fonthill Media Language Policy

Fonthill Media publishes in the international English language market. One language edition is published worldwide. As there are minor differences in spelling and presentation, especially with regard to American English and British English, a policy is necessary to define which form of English to use. The Fonthill Policy is to use the form of English native to the author. Jason Nicholas Moore was born and educated in the United States, but prefers to write in British English; therefore, British English has been adopted in this publication.

Fonthill Media Limited
Fonthill Media LLC
www.fonthillmedia.com
office@fonthillmedia.com

First published in the United Kingdom and the United States of America 2021

British Library Cataloguing in Publication Data:
A catalogue record for this book is available from the British Library

ISBN 978-1-78155-825-6

Typeset in 10pt on 13pt Sabon
Printed and bound in England

Acknowledgements

I gratefully acknowledge the kind assistance of Viktor Kulikov for the fine photographs he provided. I would like to give a special thank you to my editor, Jay Slater, and to all the fine folk at Fonthill for your hard work in turning this manuscript into a presentable book). I would also like especially to thank Michal Sekula. Without Michal's fine and accurate work on the colour profiles, this book would have been very much the poorer, and no doubt his fine profiles will prove of interest to both aviation enthusiasts and aviation modellers alike. Moreover, I would like to thank my family for their moral support, financial assistance, and forbearance as I pursued this literary work. As with all my humble efforts, I hope that I have made them proud with it. Finally, any mistakes and errors in this work are my own.

Glossary

AA: Anti-aircraft artillery, sometimes abbreviated to 'AAA' or referred to as 'triple-A'. Another name for this is flak, the German name for it (which is the name I will normally use throughout this book—see entry for flak below). These were guns, ranging from rifle calibre guns to large cannons that were used against aircraft.

ADD (*Aviatsiya Dal'nevo Deystviya*): 'Long-range Aviation', which was under the direct control of the *Stavka*, the Soviet High Command (see further on). The ADD was dissolved in late 1944 and its aircraft absorbed into the Red Air Force (VVS) as the 18th Air Army (18th VA).

AVMF (*Aviatsionniy Voyenno Morskovo Flota*): the Naval Air Forces. These were separate from the Red Air Force, which was a part of the Red Army. Each major fleet had its own aerial assets, which were mainly the same aircraft that were also used by the Red Air Force. For example, the Naval Air Forces used the same fighter aircraft as the VVS. These aircraft were used both to support ground forces, such as the VVS would, and also to support maritime forces and attack enemy maritime assets.

Bakelite: the first synthetic plastic, formed from phenol formaldehyde resin and a filler such as wood, this was used by the Soviets for such items as switches and knobs on cockpit instruments. It was also used to strengthen wooden aeroplane elements, such as the fuselage longerons and spars on the LaGG-3, as well as the plywood skins on Yakovlev fighters.

Bezant: a synthetic leather that was used by the Soviets for, among other items, backseat cushions or to cover portions of the landing gear.

Blitzkrieg: 'Lightning War' in German. This was the name given to the German method of war, whereby the enemy was to be overwhelmed by speedy armoured columns striking deep through the enemy's lines, supported by infantry and the heavy use of aircraft, such as the dive-bombing Ju 87. It was this method of warfare that worked so well initially against the Soviets during Operation Barbarossa (see further on).

Bort: tactical or aircraft number. Most fighters bore some sort of aircraft number on the tail or fuselage (or, much more rarely, both). The numbers were typically red, white, or blue (or a combination of these) and they were normally one or two digits; style varied from regiment to regiment. These were not applied at the factory, but in the field by the regiments (*polks*). Although you may see it in colour profiles, yellow was rarely used during the Great Patriotic War as this was the Axis identification colour.

CAS: close air support, often referred to as ground attack; the main duty of the Il-2 (see further on), but one in which fighters were also involved. This consisted of support for the Red Army ground troops and tank divisions, which involved attacking the German units the Soviet troops were engaged with. Fighters were used for protecting the Tu-2s, Pe-2s, and Il-2s engaged in this activity. This and the terms 'ground attack' or 'ground support' are used interchangeably in this volume.

CMF: Black Sea Fleet. One of the Soviet naval fleets, based originally in Sevastopol. The fleet was based at Batumi and especially at Poti in Soviet Georgia during much of the Great Patriotic War after the fall of Sevastopol in 1942. Although the Soviets did not have aircraft carriers during the Great Patriotic War, ground-based aircraft units were attached to all the fleets. Sometimes you will see this as 'ChMF', from *Cherniy Morskovo Flota*, which is 'Black Sea Fleet' in Russian.

Combat turn: an aerial manoeuvre in which the aircraft would show how much altitude it could gain while turning 360 degrees. It was a measure of vertical manoeuvrability (and engine power).

Design Bureau: see OKB entry further on.

Dogfight: a reference to aerial combat, especially that which involved a great deal of manoeuvring. An aircraft participating in such combat was a 'dogfighter'. A good dogfighter would be a fighter that was good at manoeuvring combat.

Eskadrilya: a squadron. It constituted part of a *polk* (regiment; see entry further on).

Fighter: the most commonly used English term for an aeroplane designed to down other aeroplanes.

Fighter-bomber: a fighter that is used for attacking ground and marine targets, by using its guns, rockets, or bombs, or a combination of these.

Flak: a contraction of the German term *Flugzeugabwehrkanone*, or 'Aircraft Defence Cannon'. This is the same as anti-aircraft artillery (AAA) and is the term I will use throughout this book.

Frise-type aileron: this is an aileron that has the nose portion projecting ahead of the hinge (rotation) axis and a lower surface in line with the lower surface of the wing.

Frontal Aviation: used to describe the aviation units that operated close to the front lines in support of the ground troops. This included fighter, ground attack, and bomber units.

Frontal Fighter: a fighter that operated close to the front lines to provide support for the troops and the shturmoviks and bombers supporting them. These aircraft did not have to be particularly long ranged. Most Soviet fighters of the Second World War were used as frontal fighters.

Great Patriotic War (*Velikoiy Otechestvennoiy Voiyni* in Russian, or *BOB* in Cyrillic): the Soviet/Russian term for the war between Nazi Germany and the Soviet Union (22 June 1941–9 May 1945). This normally excludes the August 1945 campaign against the Japanese Kwantung Army in Manchuria (known by the Soviets as the 'Manchurian Strategic Offensive Operation'; see the entry for this further on).

Ground attack: see previous CAS entry. These terms will be used interchangeably throughout the text.

Guards: a designation for units that had distinguished themselves in combat (*Gvardiya* in Russian). In addition to receiving higher pay than normal Red Army units, they also were the first units to receive new equipment. These were considered elite units. Some fighter units were designated as Guards units.

Gunston: this refers to the noted Soviet aircraft historian Bill Gunston. I will sometimes use this in the text to refer to information from Mr Gunston's works. At other times, I will use 'Bill Gunston' to refer to Mr Gunston.

Heer: the official name for the German army under the Nazis though seldom used, as the term *Wehrmacht* (see further on) has supplanted it in common usage.

Hero of the Soviet Union (often abbreviated to 'HSU'): the highest military honour accorded to Soviet military personnel during the Great Patriotic War. Being awarded with this title was equivalent to winning the American Medal of Honor [*sic.*] or the British Victoria Cross. The medal that went along with the title consisted of a simple golden star suspended from a small red rectangle. Some fighter pilots were awarded this title multiple times.

IAD (*Istrebitelnaya Aviatsionnaya Divisiya*): fighter division. This referred to fighter aircraft divisions. A Guards division would be referred to as a GvIAD (in this case the Gv stood for *Gvardeiyskaya*, the Russian adjectival variant of Guards or *Gvardiya*).

IAK (*Istrebitelniy Aviatsionniy Korpus*): fighter corps. This referred to fighter aircraft corps. A Guards fighter corps would be referred to as a GvIAK (Gv for *Gvardeiyskiy* (m) or *Gvardeiyskaya* (f), meaning 'Guards'). This was normally the largest fighter unit, there being only one fighter air army (the 1st Fighter Air Army).

IAP (*Istrebitelniy Aviatsionniy Polk*): fighter regiment. This referred to fighter aircraft regiments. A Guards regiment would be referred to as a GvIAP.

Il-2: the main Soviet ground attack aircraft of the war, and the single most important aircraft in the Soviet inventory (see Shturmovik entry further on). One of the main duties of the fighters was to protect this vital aircraft on its missions.

Interceptor: a fighter that has been optimised to intercept other aircraft. An interceptor is often characterised by a high rate of climb, and sometimes by a high service ceiling.

Istrebitel: 'Destroyer' in Russian, this was the Soviet term for a fighter aircraft.

Izdeliye: 'Object' in Russian. Aircraft (and other products) were assigned an *Izdeliye* number by the appropriate design bureau or OKB (see further on for a definition of 'OKB'); for example, the I-200 (MiG-1) was initially the 'Izdeliye 61'; '61' being the *Izdeliye* number. Thus, the first I-200 was 'Object 61'.

KBF: Red Banner Fleet (or Baltic Fleet). One of the Soviet naval fleets, based in Leningrad and on Kronstadt Island in the Gulf of Finland. During the siege of Leningrad, its ships did not venture out into the Baltic Sea (other than submarines). The aircraft attached to the fleet were active in the Baltic Sea against Axis shipping and Axis ports, as well as providing ground support for Red Army troops, with fighters providing protection for the ground attack and bomber/torpedo aircraft.

Kriegsmarine: the German Navy. Although the war was fought mainly on land, the *Kriegsmarine* was very active in the Baltic and Black Seas during the Great Patriotic War. Along with the *Heer* (Army) and the *Luftwaffe* (Air Force), it formed the *Wehrmacht*.

LII (*Lyotno Isslydovatel'skiy Institut*): Flight Research Institute, based at Zhukovskiy, outside of Moscow. This was the flight-testing centre for the TsAGI (see entry further on).

Laminar flow wing: a wing with an aerofoil where the thickest part is moved aft, instead of the thickest part being towards the front of the wing. In addition, the wing aerofoil is symmetrical, as opposed to the asymmetry of most wing aerofoils. These wings, if designed, built, and maintained properly, can dramatically cut down on drag. This type of wing was used experimentally on some Soviet fighters during the Second World War but did not prove to be a success due to the manufacturing tolerances and maintenance involved in keeping the wing surface smooth enough to benefit from the laminar flow design.

Lavochkin, Semyon Sergeyevich (1900–60): the chief designer of the Lavochkin design bureau, or OKB (see entry further on), and the designer of the Lavochkin fighters used during the Great Patriotic War, which, along with the Yakovlev fighters (see entry further on), were the main fighters used by the Soviet Union during the war.

Lavochkins: the term, alongside 'Lavochkin fighters', that I will use throughout the text to refer to the Lavochkin fighters of the Great Patriotic War.

Luftwaffe: the German Air Force. It officially came into existence in 1935, in defiance of the Versailles Treaty of 1919. Unlike the Red Air Force or *VVS* (see entry further on) it was a separate service co-equal with the Army (*Heer*, although the term *Wehrmacht* is normally used) and Navy (*Kriegsmarine*).

Manchurian Strategic Offensive Operation: the 'Manchurian Operation', 'Manchurian Campaign', or the 'Manchurian Offensive' was the last major operation of the Second World War; this operation took place in August 1945 against the forces of Imperial Japan (the 'Kwantung Army'), ending with their defeat.

NII VVS (*Nauchno-issledovatel'skiy Institut Voyenno-vozdushnykh Seel*): Scientific Research Institute of the Red Air Force. The testing facility for the VVS (Red Air Force), located at Zhukovskiy, outside of Moscow.

NIPAV (*Nauchno-isptatel'niy Poligon Aviatsionnovo Vo'oruzheniya*): the scientific test range of aircraft armament.

NKAP (*Narkomaviaprom*; from *Narodniy Komissariat Aviatsionnoiy Promyshlennostiy*): the Soviet Air Ministry (literally 'People's Commissariat of the Aircraft Industry'). This was the ministry responsible for aircraft development. During the Great Patriotic War, it was headed by Aleksei Ivanovich Shakhurin (1904–75).

NKVD (*Narodniy Komissariat Vnutrennik Del*): People's Commissariat of Internal Affairs, the ministry that included the security or secret police, in addition to normal police and border guards. It was this ministry that arrested aviation specialists and imprisoned them in a special prison, or *sharashka* (see further on). It later became the MVD in 1946, when the 'People's Commissariats' (*Narodniy Komissariat*) became 'Ministries' (*Ministerstvo*). This was the precursor to the KGB of Cold War fame.

OKB (*Opitnoye Konstruktorskoye Byuro*): Russian for 'Experimental Design Bureau', 'OKB' being the acronym. A state-run research institute that was something like an engineering company tasked with the design of prototypes. These organisations were not intended for mass producing the aircraft they designed. However, they usually had the facilities and resources to construct prototypes. Designs accepted by the state were then assigned to a factory (*Zavod*) or factories for mass production. A bureau was officially identified by a number or an acronym (such as 'TsKB') and later by initials from its head designer's last name (such as 'La' for Lavochkin). Also known as a 'Design Bureau', the OKB was a collection of Soviet designers grouped around a single head designer, with the bureau being under the name of the head designer (from mid-December 1940 onwards). In the case of the Yak-9 fighter, the head designer was Aleksandr Sergeyevich Yakovlev (1906–89). Design bureaus would respond to (or be directed to respond to) government specifications for aircraft. In contrast to Western aircraft companies, Soviet design bureaus did not own their own production facilities, but factories were assigned to produce their designs as described above.

Operation Barbarossa: this operation, named after a twelfth-century German (Holy Roman Empire) king, was the name the Germans gave for their initial campaign against the Soviet Union. Commenced on 22 June 1941, this operation was designed to defeat the Soviet Union by the end of 1941, but failed ultimately, although at a huge loss to both sides.

PVO (*Protivo Vozdushniy Oborony*): 'Anti-Aerial Defence'. This branch of the Soviet military, as distinct from the VVS (Red Air Force), was responsible for air defence. Its assets included anti-aircraft artillery, early warning systems (including radar), searchlights, and fighter aircraft for intercepting enemy aircraft, and the personnel to operate this equipment. It was commanded by General Mikhail Stepanovich Gromadin (1899–1962) during the Great Patriotic War; from 1942, it was a separate service from the VVS. Even after the fall of the Soviet Union in 1991, it remained separate from the VVS under the Russian Federation (Russia) until it was merged with the VVS in 1998.

PARM (*Polevaya Aviaremontnaya Masterskaya*): 'Field Aircraft Repair Workshop'. These repair shops, in addition to repairing damaged aircraft, sometimes rebuilt the often poorly constructed aircraft that came directly from the factories, before releasing them to front-line units. Ironically, one of the reasons the fighters (and other Soviet aircraft) were often of poor manufacture is that the experienced machinists and mechanics were in the Red Army, and not on the production lines, where their place was often taken by semi-skilled and unskilled labourers.

Para: a pair of aeroplanes, two of which composed a *zveno* (flight).

Pe-2: the main Soviet dive-bomber during the Great Patriotic War, designed by Vladimir Mikhailovich Petlyakov (1891–1942). It was sometimes known as the *Peshka*, or 'Pawn' in Russian. The fighter version was designated as the 'Pe-3'. Post-war, the Pe-2 was known as the 'Buck' by NATO.

Polk: Regiment. As used in this book, it refers to an air regiment, the basic unit of the VVS, the AVMF, the ADD, and the PVO.

Ramjet: this is a simple type of jet with few or no moving parts (there are no turbines). The air is compressed by the forward speed of the aircraft, then ignited in the combustion chamber. The engine is very simple, but it has to already be moving forward at some speed before it can be operated. Engines of this sort were tested on various Soviet aircraft as a means of boosting the aircraft's speed.

RKKA (taken from the Cyrillic acronym for the 'Workers and Peasants Red Army', *Rabochye-Krestiyanskoy Krasnoy Armiy*; *PKKA* in Cyrillic): the Red Army. The Air Force was the 'VVS RKKA' (*BBC PKKA* in Cyrillic).

Red Air Force: Also known as the VVS. See further on for a definition of VVS. This term will be used interchangeably with VVS in this book. Note that after the war, it was often called the 'Soviet Air Force', but the term 'Red Air Force' continued to be used, as did the term VVS.

Red Army: the main fighting force of the Soviet Union, consisting of rifle (infantry), tanks, cavalry, and the Air Force (although not until 1944 the long-range bomber force, the *ADD*, which was until then under the direct command of the Soviet High Command: the *Stavka*). The name was officially changed to the Soviet Army in 1946, although it was still commonly referred to as the Red Army for a long time after the war. The Soviet Navy was a separate military arm from the Red Army.

SMF: Northern Fleet, based at Murmansk. This fleet was responsible for, among other things, providing protection to Allied convoys bringing Lend-Lease equipment to the Soviet Union.

Schrenk-type flap: this is a flap that is lowered from the bottom of the wing only, with the top being a fixed integral part of the wing.

Serial Number: applied at the factory, this number could consist of from six to ten digits and incorporated the *Zavod* number, such as '1660920', where *Zavod* 166 was the producing factory. Often, this number is referred to as the construction number, or 'c/n'.

Sharashka: special prisons organised by the NKVD (see previous entry) for special prisoners, such as scientists and engineers. These prisons had better conditions than the run-of-the-mill gulag prisons and the prisoners were allowed (or coerced) to continue their work, under NKVD supervision. Andrey Tupolev designed the Tu-2 in a *sharashka*, known as Zavod 156 or Z.156. Vladimir Petlyakov also designed his dive-bomber, the Pe-2 (originally the VI-100 fighter), in the same *sharashka* as Tupolev. Dmitriy Lyudvigovich Tomashevich designed his fighter (the '110') in this *sharashka*.

Shpon: plywood sheets layered cross-grain to each other in thin sheets of veneer. The Soviets often used this material in the construction of their aeroplanes.

Shturmovik: Russian for 'ground attack aeroplane' (Штурмовик); became synonymous with the Il-2 ground attack aircraft designed by Sergeiy Vladimirovich Ilyushin (1894–1977). Note that the accepted standard transliteration for this word into English is 'Shturmovik', not 'Sturmovik', 'Stormovik', or other variations you will see. This was the standard Soviet ground attack aircraft for the Red Air Force throughout the Great Patriotic War and was considered the single most important aeroplane in the Soviet inventory. Normally it will be referred to simply as the 'Il-2' in this book. If capitalised, as 'Shturmovik', it refers to the Il-2. If not capitalised, as 'shturmovik', it refers to ground attack aircraft in general, such as the Su-6 or Il-10.

Soviet Air Force: the post-war name for the Red Air Force.

Soviet Navy: a separate military arm from the Red Army, unlike the Red Air Force, which was part of the Red Army during the Second World War. The Soviet Navy included the AVMF (Naval Air Forces).

Soviet Union: this term, the shortened version of the 'Union of the Soviet Socialist Republics', to give its full name translated into English, will be used throughout this book instead of the commonly used, but inaccurate, especially in the context of the Second World War, 'Russia'. Likewise, 'Soviet' will be used instead of 'Russian'.

Stavka (*Shtab Glavno/Verkhovnovo Komandovaniya*): The Soviet High Command. The Stavka had direct control over the ADD (the Soviet strategic bomber force), as well as control over the Soviet military forces.

Taran: a ramming attack by a Soviet aircraft against the enemy. These often occurred when the pilot had run out of ammunition and had no other means of stopping an enemy aircraft. The pilot might ram the aircraft with one of his wingtips or get close enough to chop up the enemy aircraft's tail surfaces with his propeller. These were not supposed to be suicide attacks, and many pilots who attempted these attacks survived, either to land their damaged aircraft or to successfully bail-out.

TOF: the Pacific Fleet, based at Vladivostok. It did not see action during the Great Patriotic War, but it did see action during the Manchurian Operation.

TsAGI (*Tsentralniy Aerodynamitskiy i Gidrodynamitskiy Institut*): The Central Aerodynamic and Hydrodynamic Institute, which was the equivalent of the American NACA (the National Advisory Committee on Aeronautics—the precursor to NASA).

TsIAM (*Tsentralniy Institut Aviatsionnovo Motorostroyeniya*): The Central Aero Institute of Aero Engines, which was (and is) located in Moscow.

Top cover: one of the duties of the Red Air Force fighters was to provide 'top cover' for bombers and shturmoviks. This consisted of them flying above the bombers and shturmoviks to protect them from Axis fighters.

Tupolev: this refers to both the man, Andrey Nikolayevich Tupolev, and the OKB he founded. Andrey Tupolev was born in Pustomazovo, near Tver, on 10 November 1888 and died in Moscow on 23 December 1972. He was the most prolific and influential designer in Soviet aviation history, and some of his designs, such as the Tu-95 'Bear' strategic bomber, continue in use today. He was a pioneer in the use of all-metal aircraft, including all-metal fighters, such as the pre-war I-14, a competitor to the Polikarpov I-16.

VVS (*Voyenno-vozdushniye siliy*): the 'Military Air Forces' (Red Air Force), *BBC* in Cyrillic (Военно-воздушные силы). This acronym will be used interchangeably with the term 'Red Air Force' in this book. The head of the VVS from 1942 until after the war was Aleksandr Aleksandrovich Novikov (1900–76), who was replaced in 1946 by Konstantin Andreyevich Vershinin (1900–73).

Wehrmacht: the German Armed Forces under the Nazis (including the *Kriegsmarine* (Navy), and the Luftwaffe, in addition to the *Heer* (Army), although now often used to refer to the German Army alone. The actual German term for the army was *Heer*, but this is almost never used in historical books and will not be used in this work. Following convention, the term '*Wehrmacht*' will be used to refer to the German Army, and the *Kriegsmarine* and Luftwaffe will each be referred to as such.

YG: this refers to the noted Soviet aircraft historian Yefim Gordon. I will sometimes use this abbreviation in the text to refer to information from Mr Gordon's works. At other times I will use 'Yefim Gordon' or 'Gordon' to refer to Mr Gordon.

Yakovlev: refers to both the designer, Aleksandr Yakovlev, and the inline-engined fighter aircraft that he designed and produced. The Yakovlev fighters, often referred to simply as 'Yak' or 'Yaks', were the main Soviet fighters of the Great Patriotic War, along with the Lavochkin fighters. The Yak-1 through Yak-9 were produced in huge numbers, with more than 36,000 being produced during and after the Second World War. As with the Lavochkin fighters, one of the main duties of these fighters was in providing escort for bombers and ground attack aircraft. Yakovlev, in addition to being the head designer of the Yakovlev OKB, was also the vice-minister of the Aviation Industry (NKAP) from 1940–46, a position of some power, where he helped with the evacuation of aircraft industries to the East during the Great Patriotic War.

Zavod (pl. *Zavodi*): Russian for 'Factory' or 'Plant'. These factories were owned by the state, and design bureaus would be directed by the NKAP to use a particular *zavod* for a particular aeroplane. Zavodi could and did change which aeroplanes they built, for example, Zavod 381 at Nizhniy Tagil in 1942 went from producing single-seater Il-2s to producing Lavochkin fighters. I will use '*zavod*' and 'factory' interchangeably in the text.

Zveno: flight, composed of two *paras* ('Pairs' or *Pari* in Russian, plural) of aeroplanes, for a total of four aircraft. Copied from the Luftwaffe *Schwarm* or 'Finger-four' formation.

Note on transliteration: I have tried to use generally accepted norms for transliteration from Russian Cyrillic to English language Latin characters throughout this book. You will see the common Russian adjectival suffix 'ий', used both in proper names and adjectives, variously transliterated in different books as 'ii', 'iiy', 'y', 'yi' or 'iy'; I have attempted to consistently use 'iy'.

Note on names: traditionally, Russian names (names from the Second World War were generally recorded in the Russian style) were written with the *familiya* (family) name first, then the *imiya* (given name) followed by the *otchestvo* (patronymic, based upon the father's name). For example, Georgiy Konstantinovich Zhukov would be written as 'Zhukov Georgiy Konstantinovich'. I have generally followed the Western convention of writing the given name first, followed by the patronymic then the family name.

Preface

The definition of what constitutes a 'fighter' aircraft is rather simple; it is an aircraft that is designed to shoot down other aircraft. Purpose-built fighters were used for the initial time in the First World War (1914–1918), the 'Great War', where they were sometimes known as 'scouts' in reference to their original reconnaissance role. Fighters are used for other purposes as well; their high-speed enables them to perform reconnaissance missions over heavily defended targets. Escort fighters are used to escort and protect other aircraft, such as bombers, or in the case of the Soviet Union during the Great Patriotic War, also shturmoviks (ground attack aircraft), protecting them from enemy fighters.

Escort fighters are often long-ranged aircraft to enable them to stay with their charges. Interceptors are used to intercept other aircraft, and they often have a high rate of climb to enable them to quickly catch these aircraft, and they sometimes also have a high-altitude capability. Interceptors are frequently short ranged, being used to defend specific potential targets, or for 'point defence', such as a city or a factory. Fighters are also often used as an attack or bomber aircraft ('fighter-bombers'), using cannons, bombs, and rockets to attack ground (and marine) targets. Soviet fighters were regularly used in this capacity during the Great Patriotic War, given the paramount importance of the ground war. Ultimately, however, a fighter is first and foremost an aeroplane designed to engage and destroy other aeroplanes in aerial combat.

The Soviet fighters of the Second World War still remain relatively little known in the West, recognised mainly as names, although they greatly helped the Red Army achieve its historic victory over the forces of Nazi Germany and their allies. It is my sincere hope to correct that lack of knowledge with this reference work on these fighters. I will describe in detail the main Soviet-built fighters in use from 1939 to 1945. I will examine the design, history, and combat use of Soviet-built fighters, including single-engined fighter aircraft such as the Yakovlev fighters, and multi-engined fighters such as the Pe-3. The present book will not describe in detail the Western Allied-supplied Lend-Lease fighters used by the Soviet Union, as these will be covered fully in a later book.

A rather serious issue in dealing with some of the Soviet fighters of the Second World War is that only a few, or none (such as the LaGG-3, the La-5, and some lesser-known types such as the I-180), have survived the ravages of time (or the deliberate effort by the Soviet Union in the 1950s to scrap all aircraft considered obsolete) in more than fragmentary form. The development of these aircraft, therefore, must be determined by other means—from photographs, factory records, technical manuals, and contemporary descriptions, there being in some cases no extant aircraft to examine.

Some information is based upon interviews conducted decades after the war, upon that imperfect instrument the human memory. Due at least partly to this, I will of necessity use a term such as 'apparently' or a phrase like 'unclear from the record' much more than I would have preferred; it is difficult to be absolutely certain about changes or additions to certain aircraft types and exactly when they occurred due to gaps in the record and the lack of extant examples to scrutinise.

As the Soviets were locked in a pitiless life-or-death struggle with a remorseless enemy in Nazi Germany, they often had neither the time nor the inclination to fully document the many changes and revisions that were made to their aircraft. Mere survival was far more important than full documentation. To complicate matters further, some changes to aircraft designs were made at some factories but not implemented in other factories, or implemented at different times in different factories, and some changes were affected in the field as field modifications, and apparently not recorded at all, except through what can be gleaned from photographs.

As with all my books, a term you will not see me use in this book is 'Russia' to refer to the Soviet Union. Although this convention is unfortunately still used in nearly every English-language Soviet war history in addition to common colloquial usage, it is inaccurate. Russia, or the Russian Soviet Federative Socialist Republic, was the largest and most populous Soviet republic, but it was still just one of the constituent republics that together made up the Soviet Union. Although ethnic Russians made up a majority of the military, both in the field and especially in the officer corps, millions of non-Russians also served (and died) in the Red Army during the Great Patriotic War. For example, 1.5 million Ukrainian soldiers died fighting for the Soviet Union.

It should also be remembered that Josef Stalin, the head of the Soviet Union himself, was not Russian, but Georgian, from the Caucasus region. In addition, most of the Soviet civilian casualties occurred in the non-Russian republics of Byelorussia and Ukraine. It is no more accurate to refer to the members of the Red Army (or the Red Air Force) as 'Russians' or to their country as 'Russia' than it is to refer to the British and Commonwealth forces of the Second World War as 'English', or to the UK (and the Commonwealth) as 'England'. When I use the term 'Russia' in this book, it is to refer to a specific geographic region in the Soviet Union, not to the Soviet Union as a whole, and 'Russian' will refer to an ethnic Russian and not just act as a catch-all descriptor for any Soviet citizen.

Jason Nicholas Moore
Seguin, Texas
7 February 2021

Timeline

The list below is a timeline of the important or noteworthy occurrences throughout the development of Soviet fighters (and the Second World War in general). It is in strict chronological order:

29 April 1930: First flight of the Polikarpov I-5
30 December 1933: First flight of the TsKb-12bis (the prototype of the I-16, Polikarpov's first monoplane fighter)
1934: The I-16 enters service
January 1939: Soviet requirement for new monoplane fighters issued
1 September 1939: Beginning of the Second World War in Europe
22 December 1939: First flight of the VI-100 Fighter (was developed into the Pe-2 dive-bomber and Pe-3 heavy fighter)
13 January 1940: First flight of the I-26 (was developed into the Yak-1)
30 March 1940: First flight of the I-301 (was developed into the LaGG-3)
5 April 1940: First flight of the I-200 (MiG-1 – was developed into the MiG-3)
October 1940: Yak-1 enters service
29 October 1940: First flight of the I-200 fourth prototype (prototype of the MiG-3)
December 1940: First flight of production LaGG-3
20 December 1940: First flight of the MiG-3
22 June 1941: Invasion of the Soviet Union by Germany (Operation Barbarossa)
September 1941: Yak-7 enters service
5 December 1941: Beginning of the Soviet Winter Counteroffensive
5 April 1942: State tests begin on the LaGG-3 M-82, prototype of the La-5
20 June 1942: First delivery of production La-5 (LaG-5)
26 June 1942: Factory tests begin on the Yak-7DI, prototype of the Yak-9
November 1942: Yak-9 enters service
19 November 1942: Beginning of Operation Uranus (the encirclement of the 6th Army at Stalingrad)
5 July 1943: Beginning of Operation Citadel (the Battle of Kursk)

1 February 1944: First flight of La-5 1944 Etalon, prototype of the La-7
3 March 1944: First production Yak-3 flies
June 1944: First production La-7s delivered
23 June 1944: Beginning of Operation Bagration
16 April 1945: Beginning of the Berlin Strategic Offensive Operation (the Battle of Berlin)
9 May 1945: Victory Day (Official end of the European War for the Soviets)
8 August 1945: Beginning of the Manchurian Strategic Offensive Operation
2 September 1945: Official end of the Second World War
1948: Production of the Yak-9 (Yak-9P) ends

Contents

Introduction

This is certainly not the first book in English on Soviet fighters of the Second World War, as the noted Soviet aviation historian Yefim Gordon has already written some excellent books on these aircraft (listed in the bibliography), including a book on bombers that also includes twin-engined fighters and a fine book on the Yakovlev fighters. I myself have written a comprehensive guide to the Lavochkin fighters of the Second World War. It is, however, the first time, as far as I know, that a comprehensive reference work on all the Soviet-built fighters of the Second World War has been written by a native English speaker since the British aviation historian William Green's works in the 1960s and 1970s. Since that time, much more evidence has come to light regarding these fighters as wartime Soviet archives have opened up, and this book will include the most up-to-date research on these aircraft.

The basic layout of this book is simple enough. I will list, first by type, such as 'single-engined fighters', then in alphabetical order by OKB (Design Bureau) under each type, the Soviet-built fighters that saw service in the Second World War. Note that the most common designation will be listed first, with alternate names listed in parentheses after, such as 'I-28 (Yak-5)'. I shall also include, again in alphabetical order, an overview of the experimental fighters and some of the 'paper' fighters (unbuilt projects) that were designed during the Second World War. I will not describe in any great detail the Soviet use of foreign-built aircraft, such as Lend-Lease types like the P-39 Airacobra and Hawker Hurricane, since these shall be dealt with in a separate book devoted to Lend-Lease aircraft under Soviet use. Of historical necessity, these Lend-Lease aircraft will be mentioned mostly in passing in the combat history sections of this work.

This book will concentrate on the fighter aircraft of the Lavochkin, Mikoyan-Gurevich, Polikarpov, and Yakovlev design bureaus (especially the Lavochkin and Yakovlev fighters) as these were the main Soviet-built fighters of the war, but every Soviet-built fighter used in the Second World War will be covered, even if only comparatively briefly.

Besides describing the genesis of each fighter, I shall describe its service use and a technical description of the main fighter types. Although there is a section on Soviet colours and markings as generally used, each fighter has a section dealing with the colours and markings as used with that particular fighter. The strategy and tactics peculiar to the most important fighters are discussed, as is their use in combat. The combat usage of the Lavochkin fighters and the Yakovlev fighters will be discussed in some detail in their respective sections, as they were by far the most important Soviet fighters used during the Great Patriotic War. Although their combat use will be discussed, I make no attempt to cover all the action they or the other Soviet fighters saw, as this book is a general guide to Soviet Second World War fighters and is not intended as a complete operational history. What will be included is a selection of some characteristic combat actions for these aircraft.

Colour profiles of each service fighter are also included, to show typical camouflage and markings for each type, and some experimental types are also profiled.

One note should be mentioned about naming conventions—at times, you will see in Western accounts a Soviet aircraft described, for example, as the 'Yakovlev Yak-9'. This is not the usual Soviet or Russian usage as it is redundant; the OKB's name, in this instance 'Yakovlev', is already indicated in the service designation as 'Yak'. I have typically used the Soviet convention in this work.

1
Pre-Second World War Soviet Fighters

Before the Second World War, the Red Air Force was still mostly equipped with obsolete and obsolescent fighter aircraft. The Polikarpov biplanes, the I-15bis and I-153, and the monoplane I-16 are the main examples. These aircraft were still competitive fighters in the mid to late 1930s. However, by the beginning of the Second World War, they were obsolescent as despite being very manoeuvrable, they were relatively slow and usually armed only with machine guns.

Although these aircraft had been adequate against the scant and scattered air opposition the Red Air Force had faced early in the Second World War (with the exception of Finland), these aircraft would find a much tougher foe in Germany. They were easily outclassed by the Luftwaffe's faster and better-armed Bf 109 and Bf 110 fighters, for instance. In its newly introduced 'F' version (the 'Friedrich'), the Bf 109 was the best fighter aircraft in the world at that time (mid-1941), and even the earlier Bf 109E was better than any production fighter the Soviet Union possessed at the time of Operation Barbarossa.

When it first entered service with the Red Air Force in late 1934, the Polikarpov I-16 was a trendsetter, the first single-seat monoplane fighter with a retractable landing gear to go into service anywhere in the world. By the time of Operation Barbarossa (see further on), it was outdated. Its excellent manoeuvrability could not completely make up for its lack of speed compared to German fighters, and its biplane cousins, the I-15bis and I-153, were at an even greater disadvantage in terms of speed, despite being more manoeuvrable than the I-16 and the German fighters. It was imperative for the Red Air Force that these fighters be replaced as quickly as possible if the Soviet Union were to have any chance of contesting air superiority with the Luftwaffe, and air superiority was necessary if the Soviet Union hoped to defeat the Axis forces, in their upcoming conflict with Germany and her Axis allies.

Even before the Second World War, the leaders of the Red Air Force were not unaware of the obsolescence of their fighters and had started looking for modern replacements. It was this search that led in January 1939 to a meeting involving Josef Stalin, Minister of Defence Kliment Yefremovich Voroshilov (1881–1969), and heads of various OKBs. From this meeting came a request from Josef Stalin and the NKAP (Air Ministry) for new fighter designs. This request resulted in the development of the LaGG-3, the MiG-1 and its improved version the MiG-3, and the Yak-1 fighters, all of which were modern monoplane fighters, with most of the LaGG-3s and all the Yak-1s being equipped with cannons and machine guns. When it first entered service in 1941, the MiG-1 was the fastest fighter in the world, with a top speed of over 400 mph (644 kph), and its development, the MiG-3, had a top speed of over 390 mph (628 kph). The LaGG-3 was the last of these new Soviet monoplane fighters to go into service, with the Yak-1 being the first (and best) of the new fighters.

By the time of Operation Barbarossa, the new fighters had just started to go into service and equip front-line units.

2
Second World War Fighters

Single-Engined Fighters

An examination of Soviet single-engined fighters of the Second World War will reveal one characteristic to the observant; they were small. This had two advantages: it usually conferred manoeuvrability on these aircraft that would have been lacking in larger aircraft, and perhaps as an unintended benefit, the small size of Soviet fighters enabled the Soviet Union to build more of them. It also conserved precious resources such as aluminium, which was in short supply in the Soviet Union, especially during the Great Patriotic War. Even composite construction aircraft, such as the Yakovlev fighters (as opposed to mainly wooden aircraft such as the Lavochkin fighters), used relatively little aluminium, especially when compared to Western Allied aircraft or Axis aircraft.

Kocherigin DI-6I/DI-6Sh

This two-seat biplane with retractable landing-gear was designed by the Sergeiy A. Kocherigin 'brigade' of the TsKB-TsAGI. The actual designer was Vladimir Panfilovich Yatsenko (1892–1964), who later designed the I-28 monoplane fighter. The aircraft was designed as a two-seat fighter that would have a similar performance to a single-seat fighter. This is why retractable landing gear, one of the first to be planned for a combat aircraft, were to be used. The type flew for the first time on 30 September 1934.

The aircraft was built in two versions—the DI-6I ('DI' for *Dvukhmestniy Istrebitel'*, meaning 'two-seat fighter') and the DI-6Sh ('Sh' for *Shturmovik*, meaning 'attack aircraft'). The fighter version was armed with two ShKAS machine guns in the wings and a defensive gun for the gunner/observer. The ground attack version had the gun for the gunner/observer and four PV-1 machine guns in pods under the wings, two per wing. The pilot's cockpit was open and sat high on the fuselage, while the semi-enclosed position for the gunner was located below the level of the pilot's headrest. In all, 222 were built, with sixty being the ground attack version. The aircraft suffered from vibration problems and poor visibility for the rear gunner, as well as being limited by a small bomb load (110 lb (50 kg) of small bombs), so the type began to be withdrawn from service units in 1939.

It appears that references to the DI-6 fighting at the Khalkhin-Gol (Nomonhan Incident) against the Japanese in 1939 and during the Winter War with Finland in 1939–40 are probably untrue. Evidently, the only combat use of the DI-6 was during the Soviet invasion of Poland during September–October 1939. The DI-6Sh ground attack version was used by the 14th ShAP to support the Horse-Mechanised Group of the Byelorussian Front in Poland.

Oddly enough, German photographs from early in the Great Patriotic War show DI-6s apparently abandoned on airfields. In actuality, it appears that these were ground-instruction airframes that were used as decoys or dummy targets on airfields to entice the Germans to waste their bombs on these useless aircraft. Some of these DI-6s had their landing gear fixed, and some were even without engines. Other than this, the DI-6 saw no use, definitely not during the Great Patriotic War.

3

Lavochkin Fighters

The second-most produced family of Soviet-built fighters during the Second World War (after the Yakovlev fighters), the Lavochkin fighters ranged from the indifferent inline-engined LaGG-3 to the superb radial-engined La-7. In all, over 22,000 Lavochkin fighters from the LaGG-3 to the La-7 were produced.

LaGG-1 and LaGG-3

The last of the new monoplane fighters to enter service with the VVS in the early part of the Second World War was the LaGG-3 (the others were the MiG-3 and Yak-1). However, it was not the best as its mainly wooden structure proved overweight. Nonetheless, it was a tough aircraft, and it remained in production throughout much of the war; it saw action from the beginning of the Great Patriotic War through to the Manchurian Campaign. The design was also successfully adapted to use a radial engine (the Shvetsov M-82), as the La-5, but more on that further on in the La-5 section.

First of the Breed—I-301

The I-301, the prototype of the LaGG-3, first flew on 30 March 1940. Semyon Alekseyevich Lavochkin, born in Smolensk on 11 September 1900 (died 1960) to a family of Jewish teachers, was the main designer of the aeroplane. The OKB that built the LaGG-3, OKB-301, had been founded in 1939 at Zavod 301 in Khimki, a suburb of Moscow. This new OKB was headed by Vladimir Petrovich Gorbunov (1903–45), the head of the NKAP's technical department. In addition to Semyon Lavochkin, an engineer named Mikhail Ivanovich Gudkov (1904–83) was involved with the design of the aircraft. It was from the family names of these men, Lavochkin-Gorbunov-Gudkov, that the name for the new OKB, 'LaGG', was derived.

Vladimir Gorbunov had the idea for an all-wooden fighter in 1939. The new fighter was to have elements constructed out of a wood product newly invented by the engineer Leontiy I. Ryzhkov, called *Delta Drevresina* ('Delta Timber' or 'Delta Wood'). This

Semyon Alekseyevich Lavochkin. (*Viktor Kulikov's collection*)

phenol-formaldehyde-impregnated wood was both stronger and more resistant to fire than normal wood. It was a type of bakelised-wood product, or plasticised wood. *Delta drevresina* could be moulded to shape when heated, and it was heavier than normal wood or plywood. It was to be used for such items as the caps on the wing spars and the fuselage longerons that needed extra strength. *Delta drevresina* gave the I-301 great structural strength, but at the cost of being heavier than a conventional wooden aircraft; this extra weight would constantly come back to haunt the LaGG-3, the I-301's production version.

The I-301, initially known as the 'Type K', was approved by the NII VVS in January 1940. It derived its name from being a fighter aircraft (*Istrebitel'*, meaning 'Destroyer' in Russian) and was built by OKB-301. Although some older Western publications refer to the prototype as the 'I-22', it now appears that this designation was never used by the Soviets. The I-301 was powered by the Klimov M-105P engine ('P' apparently standing for *Pushka*, or 'Cannon' in Russian, which the M-105P was able to accommodate between its cylinder banks) and had a maximum rating of 1,100 hp.

That there were three designers on the project inevitably led to conflicts. For example, Gudkov wanted the tailplanes to be constructed of metal, not wood. In the end, they were built of wood, but no doubt with only grudging acceptance from Gudkov. Whatever their differences, the I-301 began to take shape as a modern, cantilever, low-wing monoplane, with fully retractable landing gear, an enclosed cockpit, and clean lines.

The I-301 was completed by March 1940, taking off for the first time on the 30th, flown by pilot-engineer Aleksey Ivanovich Nikashin (?–1943). With its highly polished red varnish finish, it was nicknamed the 'Piano'. Although Nikashin found the aircraft to be generally easy to fly, he had a few reservations—the cockpit became too hot (a problem that persisted with all subsequent Great Patriotic War Lavochkin fighters), the stick forces for the elevators and ailerons were excessive, and there was some longitudinal instability.

Blinded by the sun while attempting to land the I-301, Nikashin crash-landed on 11 August 1940, but the aircraft was repaired. On 2 October 1940, NKAP Order No. 521 was issued—a far-reaching requirement that all fighters had to have a range of at least 1,000 km (621 miles). To meet this requirement, the opportunity was taken to install two more fuel tanks (one in each outer wing) into the I-301. This addition, of course, made the aircraft heavier, but the requirement had to be met. The result was named the 'LaGG-3'.

LaGG-1

As this was the first aeroplane of the new Lavochkin-Gorbunov-Gudkov design bureau, the I-301 fighter was to be given the service designation of LaGG-1 (by 1940 in the Soviet Union, fighters were given odd numbers in their designation). There were plans to build the LaGG-1 for evaluation purposes (one source estimates as many as 100 were to be built), but in the end, the LaGG-3 was built instead.

LaGG-3

The team that had designed the I-301 was now split up, with Semyon Lavochkin and the majority of OKB-301 moving from Khimki to *Zavod* 21 at Gor'kiy (now once again Nizhniy Novgorod, its pre-Soviet name). Vladimir Gorbunov became the chief engineer of Zavod 31 at Taganrog, on the Sea of Azov (near the Black Sea) and was tasked with starting production of the LaGG-3 there. After the German advance, this *zavod* was moved to Tbilisi (Tiflis), the capital of Georgia. Mikhail Gudkov remained with OKB-301 in Moscow and was given the responsibility for building a 37-mm armed LaGG-3.

The first production LaGG-3 was manufactured at *Zavod* 23 (Z.23) in Leningrad and was flown by A. I. Nikashin in December 1940. Z.23 only produced a relative handful of LaGG-3s—about fifty-four in total—before the plant was evacuated to Novosibirsk (where it was incorporated into the huge Z.153) from the soon-to-be-surrounded Leningrad; it never produced another LaGG-3.

By January 1941, LaGG-3 production at Z.21 only occupied half of the available space as the other half was taken up by the production of the Polikarpov I-16, which the plant had previously wholly devoted itself to producing, namely the last of the I-16 *tip* 29s. The first Z.21-produced LaGG-3 did not fly until 23 January 1941, and it was used to complete the delayed state acceptance tests. From February to April 1941, tests were conducted on handling, the engine, and armament. It was found that the engine overheated, and the MP-6 23-mm cannon had a recoil 2.5 times greater than had been guaranteed by designers Yakov Grigorevich Taubin (?–1941) and Mikhail N. Baburin (?–1944), of OKB-16. Due to these problems with the cannon, it was replaced in the initial series of the LaGG-3 by a Berezin 12.7-mm (50-calibre) UB machine gun, fitted to fire through the spinner. This gave the aircraft a still quite respectable firepower of three Berezin 12.7-mm machine guns and two ShKAS 7.62-mm (30-calibre) machine guns.

By 4 April 1941, only forty-three LaGG-3s had entered service, with thirty-seven coming from Z.21, five from Z.23, and only one from Z.31 (still at Taganrog, before its

I-301-1, prototype of the LaGG-3 during manufacturer's flight tests in 1940. Note that the canopy has been removed to improve the pilot's view. (*G. F. Petrov's collection*)

move to Tbilisi). Z.21 was still having problems with standardising production of the LaGG-3, trying to ensure that all the subcontractors received the appropriate drawings.

There were issues with the production aircraft, such as a generally poor finish and signs of a haphazard and rushed construction; for example, unfastened bolts were left in the structure, and rags were reportedly even left in pipes. The poor surface finish, the addition of the aerial mast, and the fixed tailwheel (used on some series) together made the production aircraft slower than the I-301 prototype by as much as 31 mph (50 kph). The pilots' habit of flying with the canopy open, due to the heat in the cockpit and the poor clarity of the canopy, also added to the loss in speed (the canopy was also difficult to open in an emergency). In addition, the take-off run was increased from 1,164 feet (355 m) with the I-301 to 1,640 feet (500 m) with the production aircraft. There were also problems with severe vibrations occurring when the aircraft dived at speeds of more than 373 mph (600 kph).

The handling of the LaGG-3 left something to be desired, as it could flip into a vicious spin during steep banking turns, and it tended to nose up during a landing approach and even stall. The LaGG-3 was still an immature aeroplane, but with the very real possibility of war looming, the Soviets felt they had little choice but to continue with production and correct issues as they went along.

The situation was serious enough that the head of the Red Air Force, Pavel Fedorovich Zhigarev (1900–63), sent a letter to Stalin on 24 May 1941. Of the 593 aircraft that had been scheduled to have been accepted by the Red Air Force, he wrote, only 158 had been accepted. Of these, only thirty-nine had reached the *polks*, the rest needing modifications of various sorts. A total of sixty-six pilots were flying LaGG-3s as of this date.

Zavod 31 had started production of the LaGG-3, delivering its first aircraft in March 1941, and by August 1941, it had delivered 130 aircraft in that month alone. A *polk* was formed to test these LaGG-3s in combat over Rostov-on-Don (Rostov-na-Donu). Colonel Ye. Kondrat, who had formed the *polk*, was able to shoot down a reconnaissance Ju 88.

This early series was used by the NII VVS to test the spinning characteristics of the LaGG-3. This explains the missing lower rudder balance, as sometimes, a spin-recovery parachute was attached here during trials. This aircraft is also equipped with wing slats, which were used on the later series LaGG-3s. (*Viktor Kulikov's collection*)

By the end of 1941, 2,463 LaGG-3s had rolled off various assembly lines, which was more than twice as many as the Yak-1, its main fighter competitor. Some 2,141 LaGG-3s alone were built in the six months after the German invasion. More than half of the 2,463 LaGG-3s were produced at Z.21 in Gor'kiy (1,659), which was the main *zavod* for the Lavochkin OKB. Z.31 produced 474, Z.153 produced 265, and Z.23 produced either fifty-four or sixty-five (sources differ on this). Its higher production rate and ready availability meant that the LaGG-3 often replaced the Yak-1 at the Front out of expediency, even though the Yak-1 was a superior fighter.

The number of LaGG-3s planned for construction by the end of 1941 was 2,960, so the number built, 2,463, was over 83 per cent of this figure—no small achievement considering the momentous events of 1941, which included the large-scale evacuation of factories and other material to the east. Whereas much of the rest of the aeronautical industry was evacuated, the Gor'kiy plant was not evacuated, and this accounted for LaGG-3 production in such relatively large numbers. Indeed, by early 1942, the LaGG-3 was the most numerous fighter in the Red Air Force, as Gor'kiy continued to produce them; by May 1942, LaGG-3s constituted a full one-third of all Soviet fighters.

Combat Tactics

The LaGG-3 was inferior to the German Bf 109 and Fw 190. Consequently, tactics had to be devised to minimise its weaknesses and maximise its strengths. Chief among its weaknesses in aerial combat were a lack of horizontal speed and a lack of vertical manoeuvrability. On the other hand, it had good horizontal manoeuvrability and could execute a 360-degree turn in under twenty seconds in some versions (the series 66 with its slat-equipped wings was noted for its horizontal-turning capabilities). Therefore, the LaGG-3s tried to engage the German fighters in turning contests, while the Germans tried to engage them in the vertical plane. Unfortunately for the LaGG-3s, as they were overweight, they tended to bleed off speed in turns, and this was a major factor in their poor vertical manoeuvrability. Their inferior speed also allowed the Germans to break off combat at will, and there was nothing the LaGG-3 could do to counter this advantage.

Combat Use

Operation Barbarossa

Despite the signing of the Non-Aggression Pact between Germany and the Soviet Union on 23 August 1939, war had always been in sight. Hitler's own personal views included the necessity at the very least of annexing the western portions of the Soviet Union as *Lebensraum* ('Living Room', meaning space for expansion) for the German people. Not only would this area be colonised by the Germans in the long term, but in the short term, the factories and resources of the western Soviet Union were considered essential if Germany were to become completely self-sufficient, with no need for overseas resources or trade. This seemed especially important as long as the British Empire remained hostile and controlled the seas; even before the Battle of Britain, the United Kingdom had shown no willingness to negotiate with the Nazi regime. After the Luftwaffe's failure in the Battle of Britain and the cancellation of the plan to invade the United Kingdom (*Unternehmen Seelowe*, 'Operation Sea Lion'),

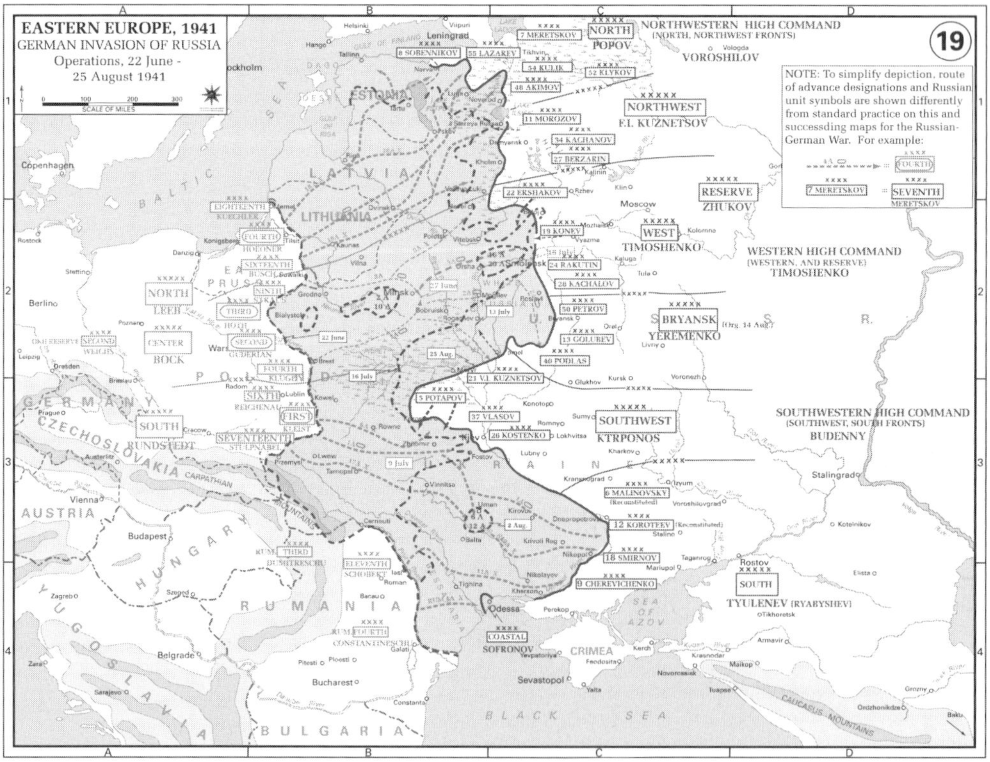

The Battle of the Frontiers (Operation Barbarossa). (*History Department of the United States Military Academy*)

this occupation of the western Soviet Union became even more imperative. Accordingly, plans were drawn up for the largest invasion in history.

The LaGG-3 was already in limited service by 22 June 1941, the opening day of Operation Barbarossa. It saw combat during the initial phases, though not on the very first days. Many LaGG-3s had been sent to the Far East, where Japan was still eyed with great suspicion despite its non-aggression pact with the Soviet Union (signed on 13 April 1941), or to air defence units in the north, like PVO units around Leningrad, where the 19th IAP was the first service unit to receive LaGG-3s. In addition, some were sent to the 24th and 157th IAPs of the Moscow PVO Zone.

It was not in service in the border districts, however, so it did not see action on that first disastrous day of the Great Patriotic War—a blessing in disguise. Unlike so many of the aircraft in the border districts, the LaGG-3s survived to fight another day. They soon streamed to the front to replace aircraft like the I-16 and the I-153, which had been destroyed in great numbers during the initial phases of the Great Patriotic War. By July, they were in the thick of the fighting to stop the seemingly inexorable German attack, strafing advancing columns.

As a ground attack aircraft, the early LaGG-3s could call on a reasonably heavy fixed armament; most LaGG-3s from the series 11 onwards could carry six RS-82s or the larger RS-132s (from early 1942) unguided rockets on rails under the wings (some carried up to eight, although these may have been experimental installations or field modifications). The 'RS' stood for *Reactivniy Snaryad*, or 'Rocket-Powered Projectile', with the '82' or '132' being the diameter in millimetres. In addition, the LaGG-3s from the series 11 onwards could carry two small bombs, one under each wing. A few LaGG-3s were fitted with 37-mm cannons firing through the spinner, which proved useful in attacking ground targets (as well as enemy bombers). Despite its great structural strength, the aircraft was vulnerable in ground attack operations due to its unprotected inline engine, which was susceptible to ground fire (like most inline engines).

A LaGG-3 taking off from a snowy field with six rockets in total under the wings. (*Viktor Kulikov's collection*)

BATTLE OF MOSCOW

By October 1941, the Germans were ready for the assault on Moscow, having once again accomplished huge encirclements of the Soviet forces, this time at Bryansk and Vyazma. Operation Typhoon (*Unternehmen Taifun* in German) started in October, when the Germans were able to retrieve some of their forces sent south to deal with the capture of Kiev (it fell on 19 September 1941). On 2 October 1941, the 9th Army launched Operation Typhoon under the command of Field Marshal Fedor von Bock (1880–1945). The Battle of Moscow had begun. At this time, the Soviets had 1,368 aircraft defending Moscow, of which 708 were fighters. However, not all were operational nor modern. As time went on, more of the new fighters such as the LaGG-3, MiG-3, and the Yak-1 were employed.

Regardless of their vulnerability, the LaGG-3s were heavily used in a ground attack role from late 1941 to early 1942, in particular, the Kalinin area during the Battle of Moscow. Here, the 129th IAP became the 5th GvIAP on 6 December 1941 for its successes in battle. After the Germans started bombing Moscow, the LaGG-3s reverted to their original fighter role for use against the German bombers.

There is an oft-repeated story—that pilots stated 'LaGG' referred to the Russian phrase *Lakirovanniy Grantirovanniy Grob*, or 'Guaranteed Lacquered Coffin'. I believe this is somewhat dubious because to openly question the effectiveness of any Soviet weapon during the Great Patriotic War was considered defeatism—a serious crime that could even earn you a one-way trip to a penal battalion or other punishment. I am also sceptical about the LaGG-3 being called 'the Mortician's Mate', another supposed nickname, for the same reason. These terms may possibly have been used occasionally, by brave or foolhardy pilots or ground crew, but I doubt that they would have been common expressions. The situation where pilots openly questioned their aircraft, like American naval aviators referring to the Curtiss SB2C Helldiver dive-bomber as the 'Beast' or 'Son of a Bitch, Second Class', was not duplicated in the Soviet military. Another factor to consider is this: pilots, like many soldiers, are often a superstitious lot—as a pilot, do you really want to habitually be referring to your aircraft as a 'coffin'? It is not something that you want to become a self-fulfilling sobriquet.

If nothing else, pilots appreciated the LaGG-3's toughness. One pilot who owed his life to the LaGG-3's durability was twice Hero of the Soviet Union Pavel Yakovlevich Golovachev, who survived an encounter with a Bf 109 in the summer of 1941, in which his aeroplane was badly shot up. Despite having his canopy blown off and his instrument panel smashed, Golovachev survived and was able to land at his base after lowering his damaged landing gear with the emergency manual landing gear extension winch. In another instance, a LaGG-3 was able to return to its base with seventy-five cannon and bullet holes, and both the instrument panel and cockpit canopy shattered. It was repaired and back in service the next day, showing both the sturdiness of the LaGG-3 and the efficiency and speed of the Soviet mechanics, who often performed near-miracles in keeping their aircraft flying.

The highest-scoring ace on the LaGG-3 was Andrei Kulagin, who was sent to the front in July 1942 after graduating from flight school in the spring. Kulagin was sent to the LaGG-3-equipped 249th IAP (163rd GvIAP from 5 February 1944).

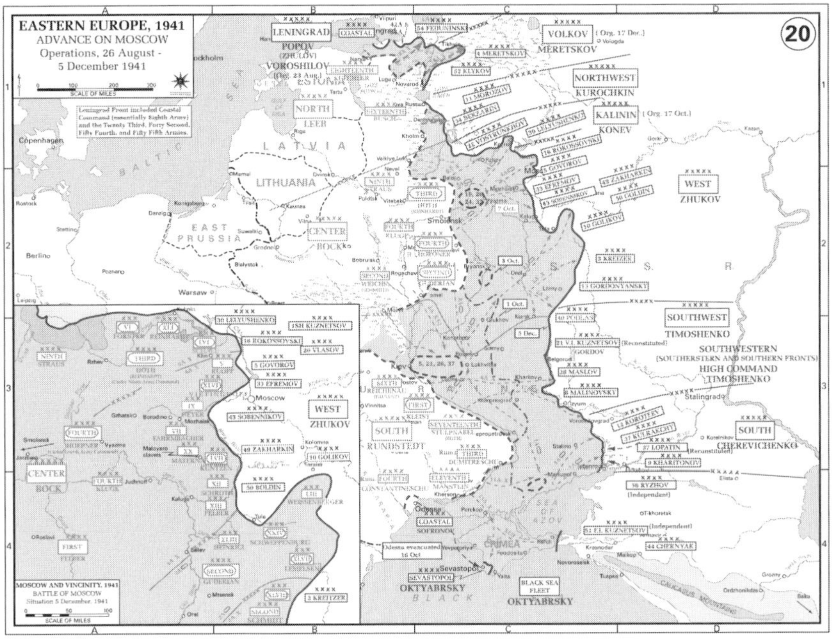

Above: The German advance on Moscow. (*History Department of the United States Military Academy*)

Below: Close-up of the Soviet Winter Offensive near Moscow. (*History Department of the United States Military Academy*)

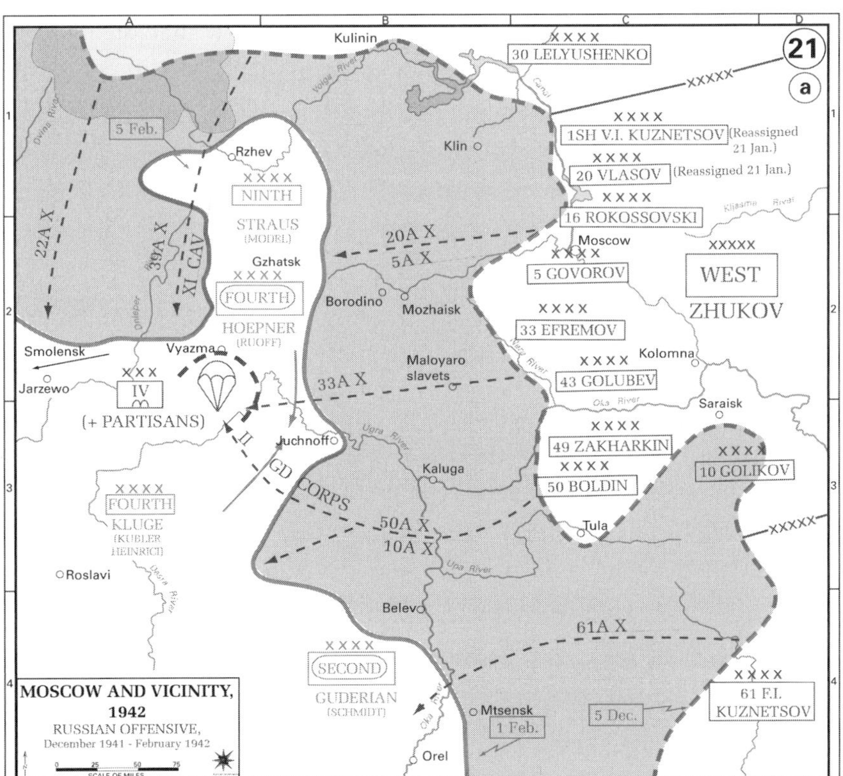

A LaGG-3 preparing to take off from a snow-covered field. Note the winter-camouflaged example in the background with a ski in place of the tailwheel. This is probably a ski-equipped LaGG-3, seen in the winter of 1941–42. (*Viktor Kulikov's collection*)

Two early LaGG-3s (note the two rudder balances on the nearest aircraft) taking off. This aircraft has the sliding canopy removed, which was often done in the field with early LaGG-3s because of the poor canopy visibility and difficulty in sliding the canopy back when bailing out. The black and green camouflage scheme shows up well here. (*Viktor Kulikov's collection*)

Shortly before attaining its Guards' status, the *polk* had been given the difficult task of night-interception, made even more difficult by the fact that the LaGG-3 had no radar. However, techniques to vector radar-less aircraft onto enemy aircraft had been used successfully by both the *Wilde Sau* ('Wild Sow') units of the Luftwaffe and by night fighter units of the RAF. These involved directing fighters into the general vicinity of the enemy by ground-control radar, then a combination of good eyesight and searchlights were used to find the enemy aircraft. That was the theory, anyway, and it worked well enough for Kulagin; he claimed seven He 111 bombers shot down by this method. By February 1944, he had completed 320 combat sorties and had twenty-two individual and four shared victories to his credit, claimed in 106 aerial engagements. He was awarded the Hero of the Soviet Union title on 1 July 1944.

A note about how Soviet victories were confirmed and recorded would be useful. For a claimed victory to be confirmed, it had to have been witnessed by at least one other person, either in the air or on the ground. Unlike the RAF and the USAAF, the VVS did not apportion partial victories; instead, these were considered shared victories, shared among all the aircraft in the *polk*. In the previous example, Andrei Kulagin had four shared victories in addition to the twenty-two that were granted to him as an individual. The concept of shared victories probably owed something to the collectivism of Communist ideology; that was the theory.

By the end of the war, having switched to the La-5 (in late 1944 the 163rd GvIAP finally traded in their LaGG-3s for La-5s), Andrei Kulagin had flown an impressive total of 766 combat sorties, and had thirty-two individual and seven shared victories to his name, gained in 146 combats. Of these, twenty-six were recorded with the LaGG-3, making him the most successful of all the LaGG-3 pilots. Kulagin was also the highest-scoring Soviet night fighter pilot.

The 163rd GvIAP (249th IAP) was not the only unit to use the LaGG-3 well into 1944. Another such unit was the 88th IAP, which saw action over the North Caucasus and southern Ukraine. It received its first LaGG-3s in November 1942 and did not receive La-5s until May 1944, after having been designated as a Guard's unit, 159th GvIAP, on 5 February 1944. Despite having used the supposedly inferior LaGG-3 for so long, the unit boasted nine Heroes of the Soviet Union and at least fifteen aces.

One of the most interesting of its aces was Kubati Kardanov, who was a Kabardian, a small ethnic group from the Caucasus (an example of the contribution of non-Russian ethnicities towards Soviet victory). He was awarded the Hero of the Soviet Union title on 24 August 1943. His flight numbers by the end of the war were over 700 combat sorties, during which he had downed seventeen aircraft individually and twelve shared. In addition to his aerial combats, he was credited with hitting two tanks, seven artillery pieces, thirteen flak units, and 127 trucks in a ground attack role.

The most successful LaGG-3 ace after Andrei Kulagin was Pavel Kamozin, who had completed his flight training as early as 1938 and became a flight instructor. By the time he was transferred to the P-39-equipped 66th IAP where he was a squadron commander, he had flown more than 100 combat sorties in the LaGG-3, in which he was credited with seventeen individual victories and seven shared victories. These seventeen victories on the LaGG-3 were second only behind Andrei Kulagin's twenty-six. Kamozin was made a Hero of the Soviet Union on 1 May 1943 and finished the war with more than 200 sorties, credited with thirty-five individual and thirteen shared victories in seventy aerial engagements.

Battle of the Kuban and the Crimea

After the defeat at Stalingrad, the *Wehrmacht* continued its retreat westwards across the steppes of Southern Russia, abandoning all of its captured territories south and east of the Don River, except for the Taman Peninsula, opposite the Kerch Peninsula of the Crimea, where they established a defensive position called the Blue Line. The Taman Peninsula was first held to allow German Army Group A in the Caucasus to retreat and then continued to be held as a launching point for a possible future offensive back into the Caucasus region and its oilfields, which Hitler still hoped to conquer. The fighting raged here for much of 1943 (from June to October), along and around the Kuban River, after which the fighting takes its name.

Most of the improved later versions of the LaGG-3 (characterised by the series 35 and series 66 aircraft) that were manufactured in 1943 by Z.31 were used in the North Caucasus district. Here they were used by the 4th VA (Air Army) at the Battle of the Kuban. One of the regiments involved, the 979th IAP, even achieved some successes against Bf 109Gs. These improved, lightened LaGG-3s were apparently not markedly inferior to the Bf 109Gs they faced, at least at low altitudes, and in one instance even downed three of the German aircraft without loss to themselves. Another *polk* involved, the 88th IAP, was composed of series 66 LaGG-3s that had been purchased by the people of Georgia. Although from 1943 on most LaGG-3s served with units of lower status, some Guards units continued to operate the LaGG-3 into 1944.

The LaGG-3 also fought in the successful Soviet offensive to retake the Crimea in 1944. As they were in production for longer, the later LaGG-3s outlived their supposed replacement, the raised fuselage deck or 'high-back' La-5, production of which ended during 1943. It is unclear from the records how much the LaGG-3 was used on the Eastern Front after 1944, although they were apparently still serving in Courland (Kurland) in 1945. They certainly served in the Far East well into 1945.

Manchurian Strategic Offensive Operation

Perhaps surprisingly, the LaGG-3 survived in service in the Far East long enough to take part in the Manchurian Strategic Offensive Operation, the last Soviet action of the war, in August 1945 when the Soviets attacked the Japanese Kwantung Army in Japanese-held Manchuria (the puppet state of Manchukuo). This was the last large action of the Second World War. Although I have found no definitive information regarding when the LaGG-3 was finally retired from service, it is doubtful whether the LaGG-3 survived in service for very long after the Pacific War ended. No LaGG-3s have survived to the present day.

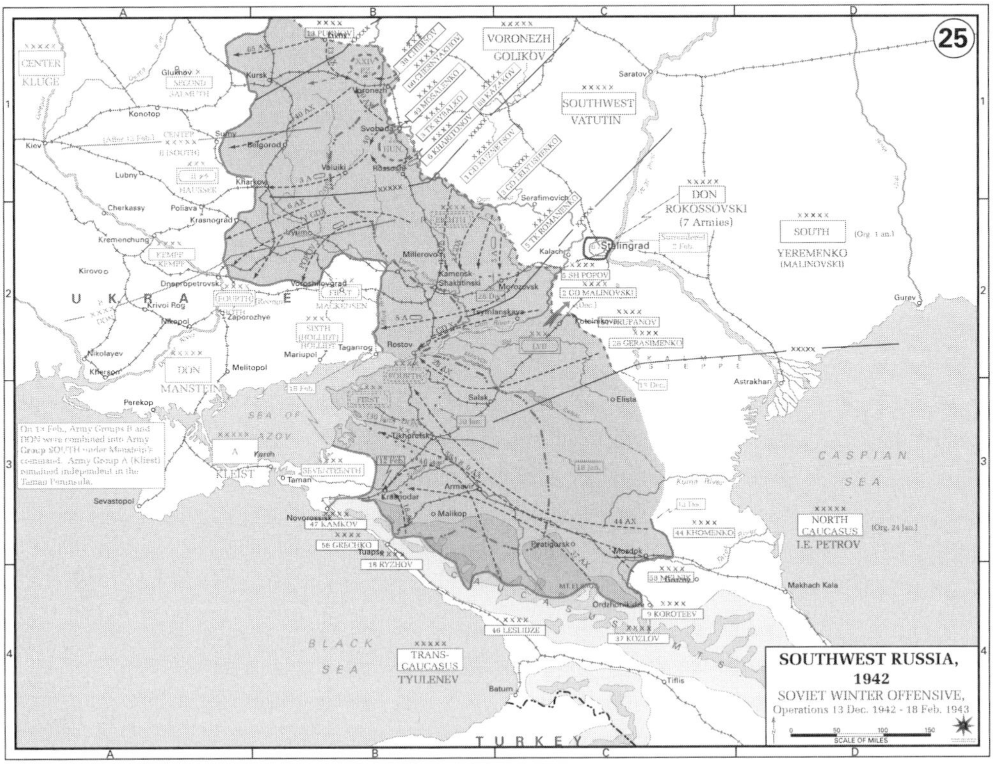

Operation Little Saturn and the German withdrawal from the Caucasus. Note how the Germans still hold onto the Taman Peninsula opposite the Crimea. (*History Department of the United States Military Academy*)

LaGG-3s of the 9th GvIAP of the CMF (Black Sea Fleet) at Novorossiysk during the spring of 1944. These aircraft appear to be series 66 versions with the two-grey camouflage scheme. Note the quick recognition markings on the tail, which were common in the last year or so of the Great Patriotic War. (*Viktor Kulikov's collection*)

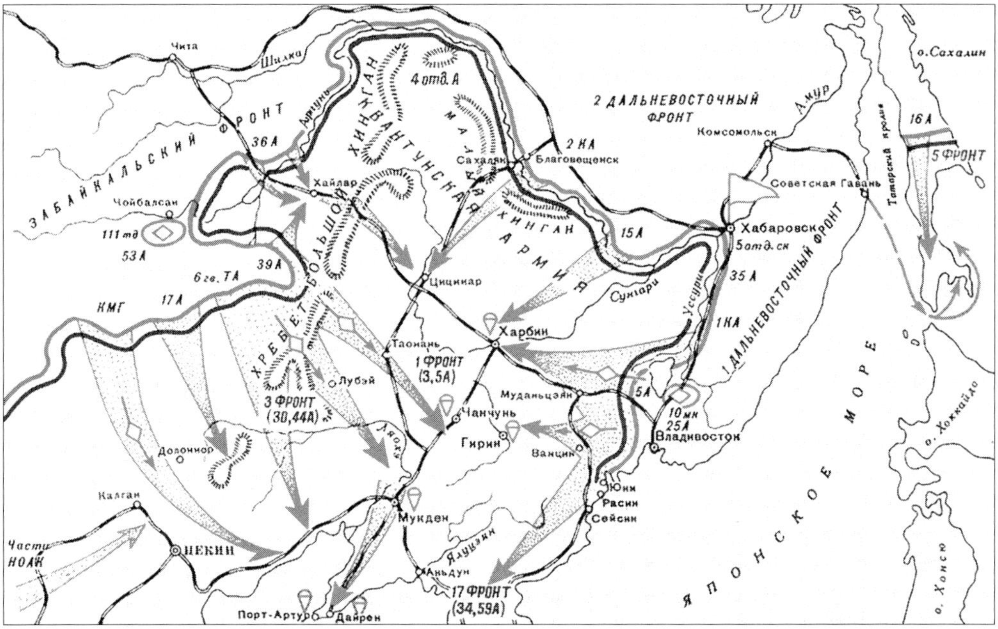

The Manchurian Strategic Offensive Operation. (*Wikimedia*)

The Photoreconnaissance Version

With a camera installed in the lower rear fuselage, the LaGG-3 engaged in photoreconnaissance. The camera fitted was an AFA-I (*Aerofotoapparat Istrebitelya*: 'Aerial Camera for Fighters'); it had two focal length lenses, one of 300 mm and one of 500 mm. The aircraft still retained its normal fixed armament. The records do not indicate how many LaGG-3s were thus equipped. No doubt, some were modified in the field.

LaGG-3-37 (series 34 LaGG-3)/K-37

When the original OKB-301 was split up, Mikhail Gudkov remained in Moscow to work on the development of a LaGG-3 fitted with a Sh-37 37-mm cannon. Boris Gavriilovich Shpital'niy (1902–72), one of the designers of the ShVAK 20-mm cannon and the ShKAS 7.62-mm (30-calibre) machine gun along with Irinarkh Andreyevich Komaritskiy, created this 37-mm cannon, which could fire through the spinner, like the ShVAK cannon. A LaGG-3 fitted with this powerful cannon was tested at the NII VVS, and in early 1942, a batch of twenty fighters fitted with the Sh-37 was produced. These aircraft—sometimes referred to as the 'K-37'—completed successful combat trials at the Bryansk Front, but large-scale production was not forthcoming due to the unreliability of the Sh-37 cannon. The 'K' in the name 'K-37' may have come from *Krupnokalibernaya* ('Large Calibre (Cannon)').

A further batch of LaGG-3s was fitted with the superior Nudelman-Suranov NS-37 cannon (originally known as the '11P37'), and these aircraft were produced in December 1942 as the 'LaGG-3-37'. Some were used by the famous French-manned Normandie-Niemen regiment. These aircraft were also apparently designated as the 'series 34 LaGG-3'. The aircraft not only proved useful against ground targets, as the NS-37 was able to penetrate nearly 50 mm of armour from a distance of 656 feet (200 m), but they also proved very capable of downing enemy aircraft, including bombers. Armour-piercing shells were used for ground targets, while high-explosive shells were used against aerial targets. One hit from a 37-mm high-explosive shell was normally enough to destroy an aircraft. The records do not specify exactly how many of these aircraft were produced, but the number was evidently not great. This aircraft reintroduced the retractable tailwheel present on the earliest LaGG-3s.

For attacking ground targets, the LaGG-3-37s were superseded by the 37-mm armed straight-winged two-seater Il-2s (Il-2-37), which featured two of these cannons in underwing gondolas. In the air-to-air role, they were superseded by the 37-mm armed Yak-9T (described further on), which was faster and had better handling.

Naval Service

In addition to serving with VVS units, the LaGG-3 also served with units of the various Soviet Fleets. Such a unit was the 5th IAP of the Red Banner (Baltic) Fleet. One of its most successful pilots was Georgiy Dimitriyevich Kostylev, who shot down four aircraft during the Winter War with Finland in 1939–40. He received his LaGG-3 in August 1941. He was awarded the Hero of the Soviet Union title on 23 October 1942. By April 1943, he had flown 233 combat sorties, fought the enemy fifty-nine times, and been credited with nine individual and thirty-four shared victories.

Kostylev was appointed chief of the inspectorate of the Fighter Aviation VVS-KBF (Air Force of the Red Banner Fleet) and was promoted to major in October 1943. By the end of the war, Georgiy Kostylev had flown in 418 sorties and engaged the enemy in combat 112 times. During these sorties, he was credited with destroying twenty-two enemy aircraft and having thirty-four shared kills. He often shared kills or gave them to other pilots, so it is not clear exactly how many aircraft he actually shot down.

A brief note about the Air Force Inspectorate, of which Georgiy Kostylev became a part, is in order here. When General Aleksandr Novikov became the Red Air Force chief in 1942, as part of his efforts to reorganise and improve this force, he revitalised the office of the Air Force Inspectorate. Officers assigned to the inspectorate were experienced pilots who were expected to fly with the pilots of the units to which they were temporarily assigned, evaluating their skills and helping to improve their tactics. They would travel to front-line units to deal with operational problems and assist with the proper training of pilots. Their duty was to make sure that the frontal units were operating at peak efficiency.

Another ace from Kostylev's 5th IAP was Igor Kaberov. Like Georgiy Kostylev, he received his LaGG-3 in August and, most unusually for a Soviet pilot, became infatuated with it. Perhaps he was favourably comparing it to the I-16, which he had previously flown. Its landing gear was raised or lowered at the touch of a button instead of by hand cranking, as with the I-16, and it was faster than the I-16. Even after he had had a chance to fly the Yak-1, which was almost universally considered a superior fighter, he continued to prefer the LaGG-3. Even in wartime, there is no accounting for taste.

Leningrad

In the latter part of 1941, the 5th IAP was assigned the role of protecting the vital 'Ice Road' over Lake Ladoga, which connected the city of Leningrad with the rest of the Soviet Union and through which supplies flowed to the besieged city. In one of his patrols over the Ice Road, Kaberov's LaGG-3 encountered two Bf 109s. A round from one of the Bf 109s fired at long range pierced the radiator, and after the engine had seized, Kaberov made a forced landing. His ordeal was not quite over yet, as he was upbraided with the admonition that he had no right to be killed as he was the only accordionist in the regiment. Every regiment had its musicians, and apparently, Russian music, at least during the Great Patriotic War, was inconceivable without an accordion. Igor Kaberov finished the war with twenty-nine total victories, of which eleven were individual and eighteen were shared. It is presumed his prized accordion survived as well.

Black Sea

Series 66 LaGG-3s were used in the Caucasus and Black Sea area, for instance by the 9th IAP of the Black Sea Fleet. This unit saw action at Novorossiysk in the spring of 1944. In May 1944, it was transferred to the Baltic Sea Fleet as part of the 11th ShAD (Shturmovik or Ground Attack Division), where it saw action against the Finnish in the Karelian Isthmus in June in the operation that knocked Finland out of the war.

Experimental Versions

LaGG-3UTI

Two trainer versions of the LaGG-3 equipped with two seats were built, of which one crashed during testing. This version did not go into production. It is not clear from the record which version or series these trainers were based upon.

The LaGG-3 of Senior Lieutenant Igor Kaberov during the winter of 1942–43 at Leningrad. This appears to be a series 35. The aircraft's topside has been painted in a temporary white winter paint. The bottom of the tail has sustained some damage. (*Viktor Kulikov's collection*)

LaGG-3 with M-107 Engine

Lavochkin decided to equip a LaGG-3 with the Klimov M-107 engine, which was more powerful at 1,400 hp than the standard Klimov M-105P (at 1,100 hp), in the hopes of improving the LaGG-3's performance. The M-107 was very underdeveloped at the time and once the swap had been made, thirty-three flights with this Klimov engine resulted in thirty-three forced landings due to the engine overheating.

Gu-82

In an attempt to improve the performance of the LaGG-3, Gudkov fitted the entire engine assembly from an M-82-equipped Su-2 light bomber to a LaGG-3 airframe. The Gu-82 was made redundant by the superior M-82-equipped LaGG-3, which led directly to the La-5. The Gu-82 is described in more detail in the La-5 Section.

LaGG-3 M-82

This was a LaGG-3 test-fitted with an M-82 engine in a purpose-built installation (unlike the Gu-82). Since this was essentially the prototype for the La-5, see the section on the La-5 further on for a full description and history of this variant.

Type '105' (I-105)

This version, developed at Z.31 in Tbilisi, was a last attempt to further refine and improve the M-105-engined LaGG-3, and the design effort was headed by Vladimir Gorbunov, one of the original designers of the LaGG-3. The first prototype was built in May 1943 and featured a take-off weight of only 6,061 lb (2,749 kg). Like early versions of the LaGG-3, it had no wing slats, perhaps to cut down on weight. It had a cut-down rear fuselage and all-around vision canopy, similar to those used on the La-5FNs and the Yak-9s.

Two prototypes were built—the '105-1' and '105-2'. The '105-2' differed externally from the '105-1' in having larger propeller blades cuffed at the bottom, a single-piece windscreen, and no scoop under the nose, resulting in an aerodynamically cleaner profile. The all-round vision canopy, coupled with the inline engine and the cleanly profiled nose, gave the '105-2' a certain resemblance to the Yak-3, its competitor (described further on). It used the M-105PF-2, which had 1,290 hp at its maximum rating, as opposed to the 1,260-hp maximum rating of the M-105PF used by other LaGG-3s at this time.

During tests with the NII VVS, the '105' was found to be inferior to the Yak-3, and all further development of the LaGG-3 was stopped. Z.31 started producing the Yak-3, which it produced from 1944 on.

The LaGG-3 Described

The following list of differences between the different series of LaGG-3s should be taken as a general guide to the evolution of the LaGG-3. Not all the factories made these changes at the same time, nor to the same series. Some may have even skipped specific series and changes. This list is based on the alterations made at the main factory, Zavod 21 in Gor'kiy and should not be taken as gospel for specific changes to specific series at specific factories. Not all series are described, only those where notable and important changes were made.

Notable LaGG-3 Series

Series 1

This first series had the Berezin UB 12.7-mm (50-calibre) machine gun installed in the spinner—instead of the intended MP-6 23-mm cannon as that cannon had been abandoned—which gave a total of three Berezin machine guns. It introduced two 7.62-mm (30-calibre) ShKAS rapid-fire machine guns, which had not been present on the I-301. The wing root intakes were oval. This version probably had a retractable tailwheel on a long strut and a small tailwheel as with the I-301. Mass balances, which were not present on the I-301, were introduced on both the top and bottom of the rudder. The outer wheel cover that was attached to the landing gear cover on the I-301 was removed from this and all subsequent production LaGG-3s, except for a few of the series 66. The series 1 also introduced a landing light on the port wing that was present on all subsequent LaGG-3s except for the 60s series. The series 1 featured a small antenna mast, and there was no stub mast on the tail.

Series 4

This version had an unsynchronised ShVAK MP-20 ('M' for *Motor* or 'Motor(-mounted)') 20-mm cannon in the nose (introduced on the series 2), while the starboard UBS 12.7-mm (50-calibre) machine gun was removed to lighten the aircraft (the lack of availability of UB machine guns may also have entered into this decision). The bottom rudder balance was removed. The shape of the metal exhaust shield on each side, which extended past the metal engine panelling to protect the finish from scorching, was also changed, with a pointed rather than rounded aft end, as on the earlier series. There was now a small intake in front of the main intake on the underside of the nose. The wing root intakes were now rectangular. Although some of this series, perhaps only the early versions, may have had a retractable tailwheel, it appears that most had a fixed tailwheel, although it is unclear whether they were built this way or this was done in the field, although it is probable that the majority were delivered from the factory with the fixed tailwheel. A longer antenna mast was now used as opposed to the relatively small mast used on the series 1, most likely to improve radio reception. The series 4 also featured the M-105PA engine, which had the same horsepower (1,100 hp at take-off) as the M-105P, but featured an improved float-less carburettor, the K-105PB, which allowed negative loads in a dive and inverted flight.

Series 29

Three exhausts per side, which probably added a small amount of thrust, replaced the single-engined exhaust collector tube on each side, present on all earlier LaGG-3s. The extended metal exhaust shield on each side, which had continued past the metal engine

A LaGG-3 from the 44th IAP at take-off at Leningrad. This is a series 1 as it has a Berezin 12.7-mm (50-calibre) machine gun firing through the spinner, and not a cannon (the cannon was introduced on the series 2). It also has the sliding canopy removed. Note how the doors covering the wheels have been removed. This was sometimes done in the field to keep them from becoming fouled with mud or debris. (*Viktor Kulikov's collection*)

An early LaGG-3, with the external rudder balances. This aircraft is armed with a ShVAK 20-mm cannon firing through the spinner. (*Viktor Kulikov's collection*)

LaGG-3s of the 267th IAP in flight during the first half of 1943. The nearest aircraft is a series 29 being flown by Soviet ace Dmitriy Tormakhov, who was shot down in this machine on 27 May 1943, but he survived his injuries and finished the war with fourteen individual kills and two shared kills. (*Viktor Kulikov's collection*)

panelling, was now deleted. The engine was also changed; instead of the M-105PA, with 1,100 hp at its maximum rating, the series 29 was equipped with the M-105PF, with 1,260 hp for its maximum rating. Although the high-altitude performance was less with this engine, this was of little account as most combat on the Eastern Front took place at low altitudes, often well below 16,404 feet (5,000 m).

The first of the new series were delivered from Zavodi 21 and 31 in June 1942. Only a few of the series 29 were produced at Z.21, as production there shifted to the new La-5 fighter. After this series, LaGG-3 production was limited to Z.31 in Tbilisi.

Some late examples of the series 29 had the larger rectangular water radiator intake associated with the series 35 and others the new VISh-105V propeller and bulbous spinner. Some were also fitted with skis that were now retractable, as opposed to the fixed skis fitted to some series 11 aircraft. The tailwheel was still non-retractable.

Series 35

This series reintroduced the retractable tailwheel into large-scale production, in an effort to better streamline the LaGG-3 (only a relatively small batch of the series 34 had been produced). Metal leading-edge slats, which helped with handling, were also present (these were also present on the LaGG-3-37/series 34). This necessitated moving the pitot tube from the leading edge of the wing to a position under the wing, a position which all subsequent wartime Lavochkin fighters featured.

The propeller spinner was of a more bulbous profile than the series 29, as a new propeller had been fitted: the VISh-105V ('VISh' stood for *Vint Izmenyayemovo Shaga*, 'Variable-Pitch Propeller'). The under-fuselage radiator scoop was larger than in the previous series and was now made of metal as this was easier to repair than a wooden scoop; on the other hand, it was more likely to be damaged in the event of a wheels-up landing because of its larger size. The wing root intakes were rectangular on series 4 aircraft onwards. From the series 35 on, the elevators were slightly enlarged, as were the elevator trim tabs.

From August 1942 until the spring of 1943, the series 35 was produced solely by Z.31, which by the time production had ended on the series 35 was the only *zavod* then manufacturing the LaGG-3.

Series 66

This was the last main production series of the LaGG-3. It incorporated the various changes that had been made to lighten and improve the airframe, including the reduced armament, the leading-edge slats, and the reintroduced retractable tailwheel. All these changes had first been incorporated together in series 35. The series 66 introduced a flat (though still unarmoured) windscreen, which prevented distortion of the pilot's forward view caused by the curved windscreen. This flat windscreen feature was copied from the La-5s that by 1943 were also in production. The sliding canopy was also changed from the series 35, with a framed clear strip behind the main rear frame (this was not present on the high-back La-5s, which had a sliding canopy like the series 35). Unlike the series 35, the series 66 featured four, not three, engine exhausts per side and incorporated a shield above the exhausts to protect the pilot from the glare of the exhaust flames.

Although none of my sources have mentioned this feature, I have seen two photographs that clearly show a series 66 LaGG-3 with small gear doors attached to the fuselage. These would have served to cover the outer part of the main wheels, as on the La-7. Whether this was an experimental installation or fitted to some production series 66 remains unclear.

A LaGG-3 series 66 in 1943. This aircraft appears to still be painted in the black/green scheme, although many series 66 aircraft were in service long enough to wear the subsequent two-grey scheme. The aircraft is still at the factory, Z.31, in Tbilisi. (*Viktor Kulikov's collection*)

The under-nose scoop was enlarged compared to the series 35, while the scoop for the under-fuselage radiator was smaller and wooden, like those used on LaGG-3s before the series 35. The landing light on the port side was now removed, leaving this series with no landing light. The wing root intakes were oval as on series 1 aircraft but larger.

The series 66 was only built at Z.31 at Tbilisi, as by 1943, production had ceased at *Zavodi* 21 and 99. Since for a time both the La-5 and LaGG-3 were produced simultaneously, some improvements, such as the flat windscreen, appeared on both the series 66 and the later high-back La-5s. However, only a few La-5s were actually built at Z.31, which concentrated its production on the LaGG-3, until it switched to producing the Yak-3 from 1944 on.

The series 66 had a top speed of 336 mph (542 kph) at sea level, an improvement on the series 29's 315 mph (507 kph) at sea level. The top speed for the series 66 was 367 mph (591 kph), which was better than the earlier series of LaGG-3s.

As the above figures indicate, the series 66 was a much better aeroplane than the earlier LaGG-3s, with more speed and good manoeuvrability (including an excellent horizontal turning capability, helped by its leading-edge slats). Yet by the time the series 66 was introduced, there were better Soviet fighters available, including the LaGG-3's development and successor, the radial-engined La-5. Due to this, its use was mainly limited to the southern part of the Soviet Union, near Z.31 at Tbilisi in Georgia, where it was produced. It was here that the very last LaGG-3s were produced into 1944, when 229 were built. This brought the total of all LaGG-3s built at all its factories to 6,528. Even with the cessation of production, the LaGG-3 continued to be used throughout 1944, winding up in Courland (Kurland) by 1945, and in the Manchurian Campaign, the final offensive of the entire Second World War.

LaGG-3 in Detail

The LaGG-3 was a mainly wooden, low-wing cantilever monoplane with a fully retractable main landing gear and a fixed or retractable tailwheel depending on the series. The pilot sat in a fully enclosed cockpit.

LaGG-3 sub-assemblies. (*1940 Technical Manual*)

FUSELAGE

The fuselage was mainly wooden, of an oval semi-monocoque structure. Only the gun- and engine-bearing structures were metal, and only the engine was metal-covered with detachable aluminium alloy plates. To give added strength to the airframe, the fuselage longerons were made of *delta drevresina*. The engine and gun mountings were made of steel alloy tubes attached to the wooden fuselage structure, with the bottom attachments being to the wooden front spar. The fin was constructed integrally with the rest of the fuselage.

The pilot was protected from the back by a seat back consisting of 0.39-inch (10-mm) steel armour. There was no armoured windscreen on any of the LaGG-3s, although the series 66 had a flat windscreen that alleviated the distortion caused by the curved windscreens characterising most LaGG-3s.

The sliding canopy was made of nitro-cellulose in the early LaGG-3s, which yellowed with age, impairing the pilot's visibility to the point where some LaGG-3s had the sliding canopy portion removed. This is seen in early LaGG-3s, such as series 4 aircraft, for example, but not in later examples such as series 35 and 66 aircraft. Since the La-5s apparently had Plexiglas mouldings from the start, this leads me to believe that at some point during the production run of the LaGG-3 the poorer quality cellulose clear parts were replaced with Plexiglas mouldings. When this change might have occurred is unclear, but my guess is around the time the La-5 was first put into production, in mid-1942.

WINGS

The wings were made mainly out of spruce and birch and covered in plywood, while the ailerons and flaps were of metal (dural) structure, with the ailerons covered in fabric and the flaps all-metal. The main structure of the wings consisted of two wooden spars, with caps made of *delta drevresina* for added strength. Only the port aileron had a trim tab.

From the series 34 on, the outer leading edge of the wings was equipped with metal slats to improve handling and especially to minimise the stalling of earlier LaGG-3s. The pitot tube now had to be attached to the lower wing, so the slats could clear it, instead of extending out from the wing's leading edge, as on previous LaGG-3s, which were not equipped with the slats. As on the La-5 and La-7, the slats were operated aerodynamically, moving in or out with the slipstream.

TAILPLANES

The fixed parts of the tailplanes, such as the horizontal stabilisers and the fin, were of wooden construction, like the wings; the moveable surfaces, such as the rudder and elevators, were of a metal structure and covered by fabric. From the series 35 on, the elevators were slightly increased in area, as were the trim tabs.

ENGINE

The engine for all production variants of the LaGG-3 was the Klimov M-105 (VK-105) V-12 inline liquid-cooled engine. Designed by Vladimir Yakovlevich Klimov

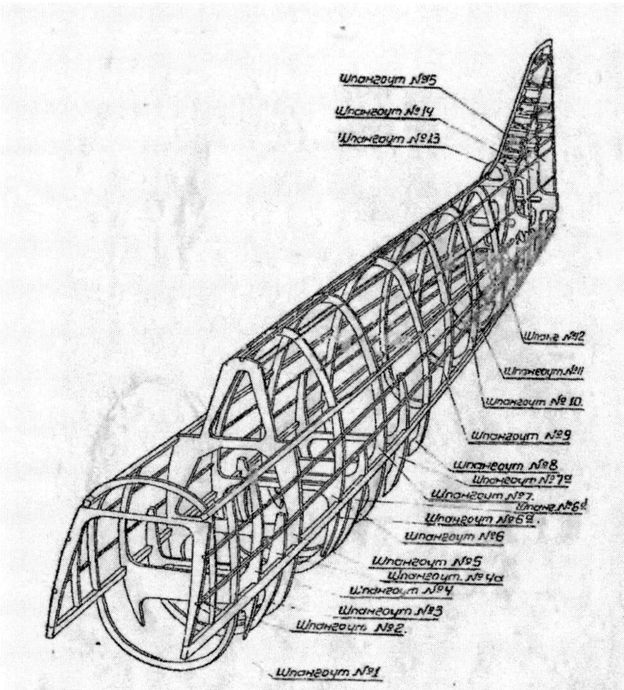

Рис. 1. Фюзеляж.

вклеены два слоя из дельта-древесины и два слоя из сосны. С обеих сторон шпангоут обшивается фанерой сорта «А» толщиной 3 мм. Толщина шпангоута 30 мм. В местах подхода к нижним лонжеронам фюзеляжа шпангоут имеет фанерную бобышку, которая доводит толщину шпангоута до 35 мм. Шпангоут устанавливается на каркасе под углом к шпангоуту № 2.

Шпангоут № 2 — состоит из 3-х частей: верхней и двух

Зак. 5429. 17

LaGG-3 rear fuselage structure. (*1940 Technical Manual*)

LaGG-3 early version instrument panel. (*1940 Technical Manual*)

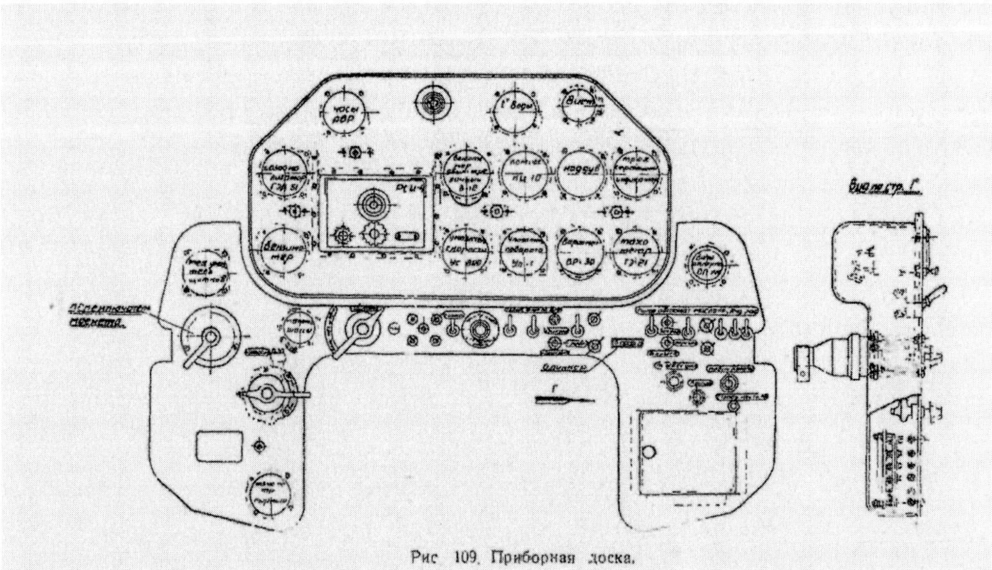

Рис 109. Приборная доска.

(1892–1962), this engine could trace its ancestry back to the French Hispano-Suiza 12Ybrs engine through the M-100, the Soviet licence-built version. Like these two engines, it was possible to mount a gun between the cylinder banks, firing through the propeller spinner. All production LaGG-3s had a gun firing through the spinner, ranging from a 12.7-mm (50-calibre) Berezin machine gun in the series 1 up to the Sh-37 37-mm cannon in the LaGG-3-37 and the NS-37 37-mm cannon in the series 34.

The engine had a centrifugal two-speed two-stage supercharger for use at low and medium altitudes. From the series 34 onwards, the three-bladed all-metal VISh-61P propeller was replaced with the three-bladed all-metal VISh-105V, which had a more bulbous spinner. An R-6 hydraulic pitch control developed especially for cannon-armed fighters was used for the variable-pitch propeller.

Fuel System

There were five fuel tanks in the LaGG-3, one in the central section of the fuselage under the cockpit and two each in the wings between the spars. These fuel tanks consisted of aluminium-magnesium alloy covered by a self-sealing layer, which was made up of four layers of phenol-formaldehyde resin-impregnated fabric. In addition to their self-sealing qualities, the fuel tanks were also fed neutral gases from the engine, which had been filtered and cooled before flowing into the fuel tanks. These gases displaced the flammable mixture of oxygen and petrol vapour as the fuel tanks emptied through use, thus greatly reducing the risk of fire.

Controls

The control column consisted of the 'spade-grip' used by the Red Air Force since at least the early 1930s, which was also used on contemporaneous aircraft such as the Il-2 and MiG-3. The control surfaces consisted of the rudder, ailerons, flaps, and elevators. The rudder was controlled by rudder pedals (yaw control). The ailerons and elevators were moved by the control column, with sideways motions changing the attitude of the ailerons (roll control) and backward and forward motions of the control column changing the position of the elevators (pitch control). The rudder had a trim tab, the elevators had trim tabs on both sides, and the port aileron had a trim tab.

Radio Equipment

Initially, only flight commanders received complete radios, with receivers and transmitters, while the rest of the flight had to make do with receivers only. This receiver was the RSI-4D *Malyutka* ('Baby') receiver from August 1942. It is unclear from the record when full radios (receivers and transmitters) were fitted to all LaGG-3s, but the practice with other VVS aircraft, such as the Il-2, would indicate it was most likely from some time in 1943 onwards.

Landing Gear

The main landing gear was fully retractable, retracting inwards with doors that were attached to the legs covering the gear and partially covering the wheels when retracted. Some LaGG-3s were equipped with skis during the winter of 1941–42. Depending

A LaGG-3 with skis instead of wheels. The ski-equipped landing gear is retractable. Note the bomb racks and rocket rails under the wings. This may be a series 29. (*Viktor Kulikov's collection*)

on the series, the tailwheel could be fixed or retractable, retracting backwards and covered by twin doors. From the series 34 onwards, the tailwheel was again made retractable as it had been with the I-301 prototype and the first three series, although as with the later La-5 versions, this was occasionally fixed in the 'down' position in the field due to reliability issues. The landing gear was hydraulically retracted.

Fixed Armament

The fixed armament varied on the LaGG-3 with the different series, although most had a cannon firing through the propeller spinner. This cannon was usually the ShVAK MP-20 20-mm cannon. For the series 2 and 3, the LaGG-3 had the rather heavy armament of a ShVAK 20-mm cannon firing through the spinner (with the series 1, it was a Berezin 12.7-mm (50-calibre) machine gun) as well as two 12.7-mm (50-calibre) UBS and two 7.62-mm (30-calibre) ShKAS machine guns mounted on the upper cowling. This armament was changed in an effort to make the underpowered LaGG-3 lighter, with one of the UBS machine guns being first removed in the series 4 LaGG-3. Later series LaGG-3s only had the cowling-mounted port UBS and the engine-mounted ShVAK 20-mm cannon. As detailed previously, a few LaGG-3s carried 37-mm cannons: first the Sh-37 cannon (in the LaGG-3-37), then the NS-37 cannon (in the series 34).

Some of the series 8 aircraft were fitted with the VYa-23 23-mm cannon. This cannon, which was the main fixed armament of the Il-2, was much more powerful than the ShVAK 20-mm cannon. Apparently, later series of the LaGG-3 could also carry this cannon in place of the normal 20-mm cannon. The way to determine if this cannon was fitted would be to see if the barrel extending from the spinner was longer than usual; if it was longer, then the VYa-23 was fitted.

Disposable Armament

Although not designed for the role, the general toughness of the LaGG-3 and the desperate situation of the Red Army during the initial stages of the Great Patriotic War forced its use as a fighter-bomber or ground attack aircraft. In this role, it carried up to six RS-82 or the larger RS-132 rockets on three RO-82 rails under each wing. In addition, its machine guns and cannon were used for strafing the enemy, and it could carry up to 441 lb of bombs (200 kg), i.e. one 220-lb (100-kg) bomb under each wing.

The guns were aimed using a PBP-1 (*Pritsel dlya Bombometaniya S Pikirovaniya*, or 'Bomb Sight for Dive Bombing') reflector-collimating gunsight. It had two settings, one for a target speed of 124 mph (200 kph) and another for 186 mph (300 kph). Later LaGG-3s used the improved PBP-1A gunsight.

Colour and Markings

The I-301 prototype was finished in a striking glossy all-red scheme, which was actually a polished varnish finish, with the metal engine panels and propeller spinner painted a similarly glossy red. The first production LaGG-3s were finished in the standard VVS camouflage scheme of 1940. This consisted of AII *3* Green (where *3* is actually the Cyrillic letter 'Z', for *Zashchitniy*, or 'Protective' in Russian) on the topside and AII Blue (Sv.gol.—*Svetlo Goluboi* or 'Light Blue' in Russian) on the underside. From the middle of 1941, the paint was changed to the new nitrocellulose paints of the AMT series, which were designed for use with wooden and mixed-construction aircraft. These paints were AMT-6 Black and AMT-4 Green over AMT-7 Blue underside. The LaGG-3s that continued flying into 1944 and 1945 were painted in the late 1943 fighter scheme of AMT-11 Grey-Blue and AMT-12 Dark Grey over AMT-7 Blue.

The main insignia was the red star, which had been in use since the Russian Civil War of 1918–22. According to a May 1940 directive (for aircraft with a single green upper surface), red stars with a black outline were specified, to be applied in six positions—the fuselage sides and lower and upper wing surfaces.

A June 1941 directive (for aircraft with the black/green camouflage scheme) did not specify any border—stars were supposed to be borderless with this scheme. Factories did generally follow this as an instruction, but in operational units, white, black, or silver borders were added to make the stars more visible against the black/green background. Stars were not painted on the upper wings. In addition, there would normally be stars on the rudder and the fuselage. Some of the LaGG-3s continued to feature the pre-war-style red star with black outline.

From September 1943 (for aircraft with the two-grey colour scheme), stars with a white border and a thin red outline were specified. This directive has been followed to the present day. These stars, known by some as 'Victory' or '1943 Stars', still appear on modern Russian aircraft. This star appeared on LaGG-3s from 1944 on. There may have been a bit of a lag time (no pun intended) between when the two-grey scheme was introduced and the new-style star was applied (this lag time also occurred with the La-5 variants). In addition to the '1943 Star', an ornamental '3-D' star also featured, sometimes referred to as the 'Kremlin Star', after its resemblance to the stars over the Kremlin.

Representations of the different types of stars can be seen in the aircraft profiles in the colour plates section, as well as representations of both the black/green and two-grey camouflages.

It was not uncommon for there to be personal markings as these were not forbidden. Most common were patriotic slogans; religious or erotic themes did not feature (there were no 'pinups' on Soviet aircraft), but animals (such as lions and eagles) were popular mascots.

A New Engine and a New Fighter: The La-5

The LaGG-3 was a disappointment for the Red Air Force. It was too sluggish to keep up with the single-engined German fighters, either in speed or manoeuvrability, especially in the vertical plane. If Lavochkin wished to continue to produce fighters for the Red Air Force, a drastic change was needed as attempts to lighten the airframe did not sufficiently improve the LaGG-3.

That change now centred on the engine—a more powerful engine than the Klimov M-105 was needed. Lavochkin was attracted to the idea of using the inline M-107 as this would be a much easier modification than trying to fit a radial engine onto the slim fuselage of the LaGG-3. However, the M-107 was a very immature powerplant at this point and not considered suitable for a production Lavochkin fighter. When experimentally fitted to the LaGG-3, the M-107 had been extremely unreliable, prone to overheating, with all thirty-three test flights resulting in emergency landings.

However, the engine designer Arkadiy Dmitriyevich Shvetsov (1892–1953) had developed a new radial engine—the fourteen-cylinder twin-row air-cooled radial called the M-82 (referred to as the ASh-82 from 1944 onwards). This engine had been developed at his OKB in Molotov (Perm), in central Russia, but the production of the aeroplane this engine was designed for—the Su-2 light bomber—ceased in early 1942. Production of the Tu-2 medium bomber did not start until 1942, for which the M-82 was also slated (only a small batch of Tu-2s was produced in 1942, and large-scale production of the Tu-2 would not start until 1944). Here was the happy coincidence of an aircraft in search of an engine, and an engine in search of an aircraft. This fortuitously led to the development of the La-5, the next in the Lavochkin series of fighters.

The M-82 itself had already passed its state tests by 15 May 1941 and been cleared for production on 17 May 1941, with production to take place at Z.19 in Molotov.

LaGG-3 M-82

As early as 3 July 1941, the NKAP had ordered the M-82 installed on the LaGG-3 with Order N 610ss. This became the Gu-82 (see further on). In addition, by NKAP Order N 438ss, the M-82A engine was to be installed on the Yakovlev fighter the

Yak-7 M-82, the MiG-3 (which eventually became the I-211 (developed from the I-210)), and the Polikarpov I-185, as well as the Tu-2 bomber. The fighters are discussed further on.

Following his meeting with Arkadiy Shvetsov at a conference, Lavochkin wanted to design a completely new fighter using the M-82 and had assembled a team for the task at Z.21. Shvetsov sent a mock-up of the M-82 and an engineer, Valendinskiy, to help Lavochkin with the construction. An engineer at the Lavochkin OKB, Semyon Mikhailovich Alekseyev (1909–93), believed the way to achieve an M-82-powered fighter was to fit the M-82 engine to the already existing LaGG-3 airframe. Some at the OKB thought this idea was impracticable as the M-82 was 18 inches (460 mm) wider at its maximum width than the LaGG-3 fuselage. In addition, the M-82 was 551 lb (250 kg) heavier than the M-105P, which altered the centre of gravity.

However, Alekseyev believed that by the time a completely new fighter had been designed and tested, it would no longer be needed since Yakovlev, Mikoyan-Gurevich, or Polikarpov would by then have provided the required M-82-powered fighter. The Lavochkin OKB would then be out of the fighter business, so an attempt had to be made to fit the M-82 to the LaGG-3. One of Alekseyev's supporters was the plant director, Gostinstev. Another was the chief of engineering, K. Slepnyov.

Fitting a bulky twin-row radial engine to a slim fuselage originally designed for a small cross-section inline engine was no easy undertaking. Designers Semyon Alekseyev and K. Slepnyov fitted the M-82 engine to the LaGG-3 by adding pine formers to the original stressed outer plywood skin. They then added plywood skinning over these formers to achieve the correct width to fair the bulky M-82 engine onto the fuselage. This was done so well that to look at the aircraft it would appear that the 'LaGG-3 M-82' (as it was first designated) had been specifically designed for the M-82 engine.

The sort of radially mounted cooling gills that characterised most radial engine installations at the time were not feasible for the LaGG-3 M-82, so a large cooling flap on each side was installed instead—this feature was designed by Valendinskiy, the designer from the Shvetsov OKB. This worked, but the top cylinders still tended to overheat; this problem persisted with all the M-82-powered Lavochkin wartime fighters.

It had been intended to fit the new fighter with four ShVAK SP-20 ('S' for *Sinkhronizovanniy* or 'Synchronised') 20-mm cannons, but the presence of the cooling flap on each side of the cowling prevented this. As a result, all La-5s were armed with just two cannons. A few early La-5s may have been equipped with only one ShVAK 20-mm cannon, the other gun being a UBS 12.7-mm (50-calibre) heavy machine gun. Whatever the case, the vast majority of the La-5s (and La-7s) were equipped with two ShVAK 20-mm cannons on top of the cowling.

The engine was mounted in a close-fitting metal cowling, with louvres at the front that could be adjusted to control the flow of air. The wing root intakes that characterised the LaGG-3 aircraft were omitted, being replaced by the intake on top of the engine cowling.

Alekseyev was able to draw upon data taken from the ill-fated Polikarpov I-185 fighter (described further on), a prototype aircraft that also employed the M-82 in one of its variants, in designing the engine bearers and the cannon mountings. Nikolaiy

Polikarpov had been directed to forward this information on to other designers working with the M-82 engine.

The LaGG-3 M-82's engine mount design was different from that chosen by one of the original designers of the LaGG-3, Mikhail L. Gudkov, who may have simply taken the entire engine installation from an M-82-powered Su-2 and fitted it to the LaGG-3 with fairly minimal modifications. His creation, called the Gu-82 (also known as the LaGG-2 or LG-2), was already flying by September 1941. The NKAP showed interest in this modified LaGG-3, and there were even plans to put this version into mass production at Z.21 in place of the inline-engined LaGG-3. These plans were never put into practice, however, because Gudkov did not aggressively pursue this design, and the LaGG-3 M-82's more purposefully designed integration of the engine performed better due to the more efficient streamlining of its faired-in installation.

However, for a time, it looked like the LaGG-3 M-82 might not be proceeded with either. Aleksandr Yakovlev was busy trying to turn Z.21 entirely over to the production of his fighters while Lavochkin surreptitiously worked on his new fighter. However, by February 1942, the LaGG-3 M-82 was ready for testing. This was effectively the first prototype of what was to become the La-5.

G. Mischenko, the first to fly the LaGG-3 M-82, reported (from *Soviet Combat Aircraft of the Second World War: Volume One: Single-Engined Fighters* by Yefim Gordon and Dmitry Khazanov, p. 40): 'The aircraft is good, pleasant to control and responsive, but the cylinder heads become hot. Measures should be taken.' State tests continued from 5 to 14 April 1942 for a total of eleven flights. The tests showed the new aircraft had a good performance, with a top speed at sea level of 320 mph (515 kph) and a maximum speed overall of 373 mph (600 kph) at its service ceiling of 21,161 feet (6,450m). These performance figures were better than any other current production Soviet fighters.

Despite the good performance, there were problems, as the test pilot observed. The engine was prone to overheating and, conversely, super-cooling (due to the initial lack of airflow-controlling gills in front of the engine), which could cause the engine to stall. The small under-cowling oil cooler was replaced with a larger, more efficient unit that was reportedly taken from an M-107 slated for installation in a Yakovlev fighter at Z.21.

Oil tended to leak out of the engine and splash the windshield, obscuring the pilot's vision. The new fighter took twenty-five seconds to make a complete turn, which was considered excessive, and it was difficult to transition from a banked turn in one direction to a banked turn in another (the LaGG-3 M-82 did not feature wing slats). The pilot had to exert an undue amount of effort during turns, yet the LaGG-3 M-82 does not appear to have ever been installed with slats. The problem with the turns was at least partly due to the LaGG-3 M-82 being overweight, with a weight of 7,451 lb (3,380 kg). On the plus side, it was found that the ShVAK 20-mm cannons worked well, particularly in terms of synchronisation.

Still, the design was considered an improvement over the inline-engined LaGG-3, with a great deal of potential for further development. After a meeting between Semyon Lavochkin and Josef Stalin at the Kremlin on 18 May 1942, Order No.

1786ss was issued by the GKO, requesting that the LaGG-3 M-82 be put into large-scale production at Z.21. On 20 May, Order No. 319ss halted the transfer of the Lavochkin OKB from Gor'kiy to Tbilisi and the planned production of Yakovlev fighters at Gor'kiy. Thus, the closure of the Lavochkin OKB was avoided.

The first eight production batches of the LaGG-3 M-82 (series 1-8) used existing LaGG-3 airframes (apparently series 35 airframes, as this series was being produced at the same time), so had the rounded windscreen, port landing light, bulged tailwheel doors, and aileron and elevator trim tabs of the original LaGG-3. From the series 9 onwards, newly manufactured fuselages and wings were used; these incorporated changes such as a flat, unarmoured windscreen, flush tailwheel doors, and no landing light in the port wing.

By 12 July 1942, only eight LaG-5s had been produced, as the fighter had been re-designated from the LaGG-3 M-82, although one source estimates that the number was, in fact, thirty-two by the end of June 1942. The first operational example was delivered on 20 June 1942. In August 1942, 145 LaG-5s were produced, along with 148 LaGG-3s, the production of which continued at Z.21 in Gor'kiy until the end of the year. It, therefore, appears that the LaG-5 and LaGG-3 were produced alongside each other at Z.21 for a short time. On 8 September 1942, NKAP Order No. 683 changed the name from 'LaG-5' to 'La-5'.

A La-5, not of the earliest series, as it has the flat, unarmoured windscreen. Serial-numbered 37210853, this aircraft was used to test improved wing and fuselage fairings. (*Viktor Kulikov's collection*)

View from the back for this La-5. (*Viktor Kulikov's collection*)

A view of this La-5 from the starboard side. (*Viktor Kulikov's collection*)

This late La-5 (note the flat windscreen) appears to have a white-painted spinner and a white rudder. (*G. F. Petrov's collection*)

Improving the La-5

In September and October 1942, a production La-5 was tested at the NII VVS. The aircraft was found to have a top speed at sea level of 332 mph (535 kph) and a maximum speed of 360 mph (580 kph) at its service ceiling of 20,505 feet (6,250 m), compared to the LaGG-3 M-82's top speed of 373 mph (600 kph). In comparison to the prototype, its vertical manoeuvrability was worse, but its horizontal manoeuvrability was better. As was so often the case with Soviet-built aircraft during the Great Patriotic War, the fit and finish were not the best. Some of the slower speed was due to the increased drag of such items as the antenna mast and the poor sealing of the cowling.

Besides the fit and finish, there were other factors that negatively affected the performance of the La-5 in service. The cockpit often became uncomfortably hot, so pilots habitually flew with the canopy open, even in combat. Due to engine overheating, the cowling flaps were often left fully opened, too, causing more drag. The retraction mechanism of the tailwheel was unreliable, so tailwheels were often fixed in the 'down' position in the field. All these factors reduced the top speed of the La-5 by as much as 25 mph (40 kph). The GKO, therefore, issued an order on 25 September 1942 for the operational procedures to be improved and for the aircraft to be lightened, all in an effort to improve the performance.

How much the operational procedures were changed in practice is unclear, but we do know that the Lavochkin OKB, the TsAGI, the LII, and the TsIAM (*Tsentralniy Institut Aviatsionnovo Motorostroyeniya*—'Central Aero Institute of Aero Engines') were all involved in efforts to improve the airframe. Three aircraft—with construction numbers '37210514', '37210850', and '37210853'—were tested. The first two were fitted with the long cowling intake fairing that appeared on the later La-5FN, while the third aircraft featured the normal intake fairing but had an improved wing/fuselage fairing. In addition, the exhaust tubes were widened, the cowling was sealed better, and the oil cooler duct was improved.

An early high-back La-5 experimentally fitted with the extended upper cowling intake seen on the La-5FN. (*Viktor Kulikov's collection*)

When a lightened La-5 was tested, it was found to be between 11 and 12.4 mph (18 and 20 kph) faster than the La-5 tested at the NII VVS in September and October 1942.

There is no official evidence to indicate when exactly the high-back La-5 was retired from front-line service, but it was apparently before the end of the war, for mention is only made of La-5Fs and La-5FNs being used in 1945. The Soviets in the Great Patriotic War very often used aircraft until they simply wore out or were otherwise inoperative, and that was probably the fate of the high-back La-5s. A few might have still been in some kind of service in 1945, but these would have been second-line 'hacks' or single-seat proficiency trainers. Some may have been converted into La-5UTI trainers after their combat careers were over. In this case, it would have been difficult to distinguish them in photographs from trainers converted from the La-5Fs.

Combat Tactics

Since the main duty of the VVS fighters was to provide escort for the bombers and Shturmoviks supporting the Red Army ground troops, the La-5 normally operated at low altitudes. This worked to the La-5's advantage as the German fighters, especially the Bf 109G-2 on, performed best at higher altitudes than aerial combat on the Eastern Front normally allowed (below 16,404 feet (5,000 m)). As the German fighters had better vertical manoeuvrability, pilots of the La-5 tried to engage them at low altitude, flying horizontally using turning combat. Conversely, they tried to stay out of vertical combat with the Germans, where their advantage lay.

Combat Use

Despite the slow initial production of the LaG-5, by 13 August 1942, combat trials had started with the 49th KIAP (Red Banner Air Regiment) of the 234th IAD of the 1st VA (Air Army) on the Western Front near Beliy, and from 20 August, the 287th IAD was in action at Stalingrad. Between 14 and 24 August 1942, the aeroplanes of this unit flew 130 combat missions, engaged the enemy twenty-seven times, and downed sixteen enemy aircraft with a loss of ten of their own. This was not as good of a kill ratio as the Soviets had hoped for with their new fighter, but it was still an improvement over that of the LaGG-3.

Stalingrad

As the Soviets executed their fighting retreat across the southern Russian steppes, they eventually fell back on Stalingrad (formerly known as Tsaritsyn), a long, narrow, industrial city of 400,000 inhabitants on the western bank of the Volga. The defence of the city fell mainly upon the 62nd Army, which was commanded by General Vasiliy Ivanovich Chuikov (1900–82) for most of the siege. The German 6th Army, under General Friedrich Paulus (1890–1957) (not 'von' Paulus, as he is often erroneously referred to), opposed him with assistance from elements of the 4th Panzer Army. It was here that the pivotal battle of the Great Patriotic War, and indeed the entire war in Europe, was fought, and it was here that the La-5 saw its first major action.

The 287th IAD, led by Hero of the Soviet Union Colonel S. Danilov, had its first aerial combat on 20 August. By this time, the division had fifty-seven LaG-5s, of which some two-thirds were serviceable. In the first three days of combat, they shot down

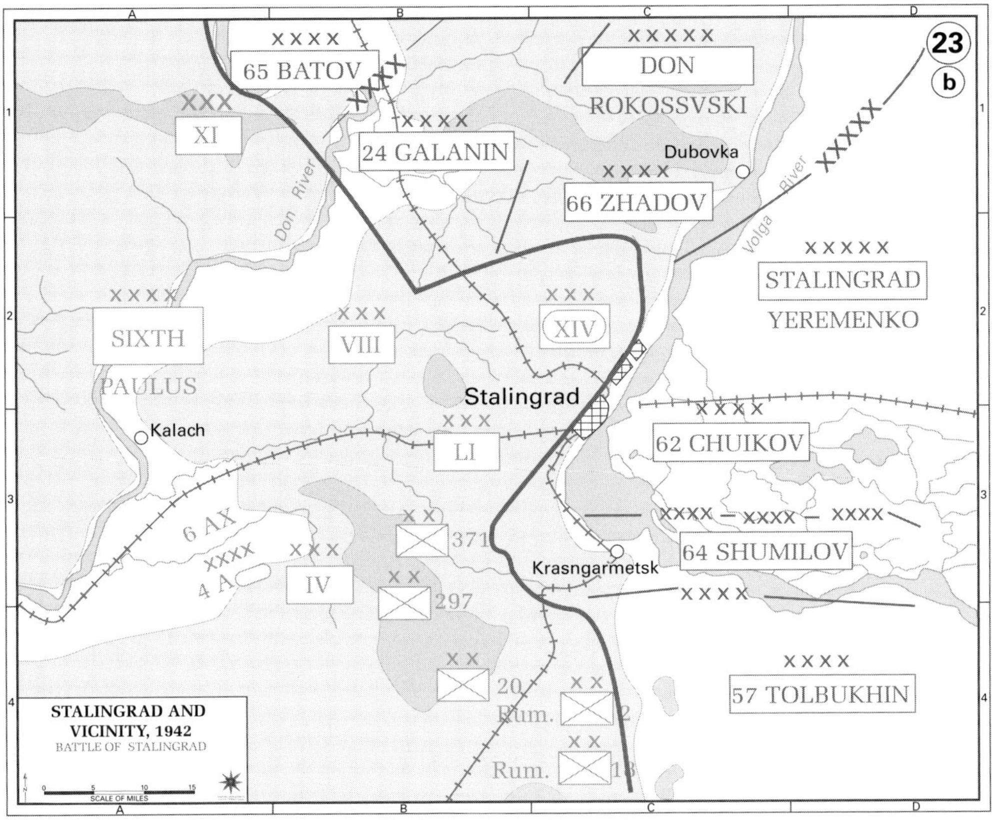

German and Soviet dispositions at Stalingrad. (*History Department of the United States Military Academy*)

eight Luftwaffe bombers and three fighters, with a loss of four of their own. From their first day of action until 13 September, the 287th IAD claimed eighty-seven Axis aircraft during 787 combat sorties.

From late 1942, the La-5s (re-designated from 'LaG-5' on 8 September 1942 by NKAP Order No. 683) were part of the reserve forces supporting the northern thrust of Operation Uranus, the operation that successfully surrounded the German 6th Army in Stalingrad. One of the units flying the La-5 at Stalingrad was the 5th GvIAP, which had started the war as the 129th IAP, flying I-16s and MiG-3s. It was re-equipped with LaGG-3s, and by November 1942, it was withdrawn to re-equip with La-5s to be used as part of the Stalingrad counteroffensive. It was then used as part of the high command reserve to be shifted from front to front as needed, until the end of the war.

One of the 5th GvIAP's most successful sorties at Stalingrad occurred on 10 March 1943. German forces in the city itself had surrendered on 2 February, although isolated resistance continued at least until March. On this day, the 5th GvIAP encountered a formation of the Fw 189 *Rama* (the Russian for 'Frame'), which was especially detested by the Soviet ground forces because wherever the Fw 189 reconnaissance aircraft went, a German attack of some sort was imminent. On this occasion, all three

Fw 189s were downed. Yet the day was not yet done for the 5th GvIAP, as their pilots received a call from some Il-2 Shturmoviks under attack. The German fighters were driven off, and then a formation of Ju 87 Stukas was seen without fighter escort. By the time the regiment had finished with them, seven Ju 87s had been shot down.

Battle for the Kuban

The La-5 participated in the Battle for the Kuban; in April and May 1943, La-5s fought against the German *Luftflotte* ('Air Fleet') 4.

Kursk (Operation Citadel)

The German retreat after the defeat at Stalingrad was stopped only by Field Marshal Erich von Manstein's (born Erich von Lewinski in 1886 and died 1973) successful counterattack when the Germans recaptured the city of Kharkov, which had just been retaken by the Soviets. It was this counterattack that established a huge Soviet-held salient in the German lines centred around the city of Kursk, with the northern German lines anchored around Oryol (often spelt 'Orel', an incorrect transliteration of the Russian) and the southern lines anchored around Belgorod. This salient was the most distinguishing feature of the Eastern Front at this time; it was an obvious target for the Germans if they wished to stop the Soviet advance and regain the upper hand, and a good starting point for future offensives, perhaps even a new push on Moscow.

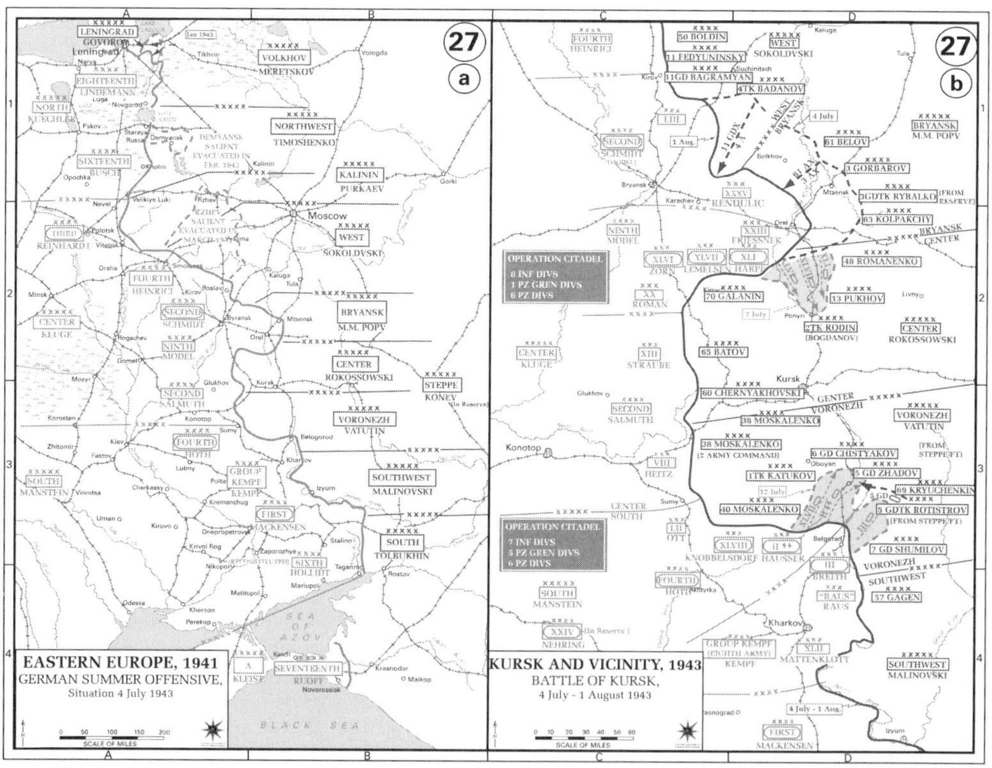

The Battle of Kursk. (*History Department of the United States Military Academy*)

It was during *Unternehmen Zitadelle* ('Operation Citadel'), the battle for the Kursk salient, that the greatest of Lavochkin pilots, and indeed the highest scoring Soviet and Allied ace of the war, Ivan Nikitovich Kozhedub (1920–91), made his combat debut.

He first flew on 6 July 1943, the second day of the operation, and it nearly proved fatal to him. Cut off from his leader and alone, he engaged some Bf 109s, two of which turned on him in hot pursuit. The Bf 109s were able to score hits on Kozhedub's aircraft, but flying at extremely low levels, he was able to evade them and return to the Soviet lines. Here, his troubles did not end as his fighter was shot at and hit by Soviet flak, the gunners evidently confusing his La-5 for the radial-engined Fw 190. Despite all this, he was able to safely land the damaged aircraft and learned the important lesson of maintaining contact with his fellow pilots. By the third day of the German offensive, he had shot down two Ju 87s and two Bf 109s, and by the end of the battle, he had earned the Order of the Red Banner.

On 23 July 1943, the La-5s of 5th GvIAP, along with some Yak-1s, were involved in a major fight with Ju 87s being escorted by Bf 109s. As the Soviets sent more aircraft into the battle, the Germans responded in kind, sending sixteen Bf 109s to assist those already involved. The flight of future Hero of the Soviet Union Vitaliy Popkov was despatched, along with more Yakovlevs. By the end of the fight, the Soviets had claimed ten German aircraft and damaged another two, although the 5th GvIAP had lost two pilots of its own.

As part of the German attack at Kursk, the Germans had made efforts to regain air superiority by flying aerial attacks between 17 and 19 August 1943, using up to fifty bombers escorted by thirty fighters. On the 17th, the 5th GvIAP flew ninety-six combat sorties, with seventeen enemy aircraft claimed during five aerial engagements. This came at a cost, for the regiment lost six pilots with two more wounded—a quarter of its strength. Nonetheless, the *polk* gained its 500th aerial victory by the end of the month.

The regiment was soon withdrawn in early September, to make good its losses in men and materiel and re-equip with the La-5FN (its subsequent combat adventures will be discussed further on in that section). It is likely that most if not all of the units equipped with the high-back La-5s were re-equipped with later versions of the La-5 by late 1943 or early 1944.

During the Battle of Kursk, the Soviets lost around 3,500 aircraft on all fronts, most of them over the Kursk battlefield. Of these, some 500 were various versions of the La-5. During this same period, the Luftwaffe losses on the whole of the Eastern Front was 2,419. The Soviets were still losing more aircraft, but the gap was closing, and while the Soviets could replace all their losses in aircraft and pilots, the Germans could not.

High-back La-5s appear to have been withdrawn from front-line units and replaced with the boosted La-5s (the La-5F and La-5FN) well before the end of the Great Patriotic War. For example, there is no mention of the early La-5s in the Battle of Berlin or in the Manchurian Offensive (which took place after the Great Patriotic War). La-5UTIs converted from the high-back La-5s may have served until the end of the Second World War, however, perhaps even longer.

This La-5 appears to have the entire cowling black, probably in 1943. (*Viktor Kulikov's collection*)

General Combat Effectiveness of the La-5

The La-5 was still not the equal of either the Bf 109 or the Fw 190 (which had been introduced to the Eastern Front in 1942). The La-5 was inferior to both the Bf 109F-4 and Bf 109G-2 in speed and vertical manoeuvrability. It had high rudder forces at around 310 mph (500 kph), and the gunsight was placed so high that it was difficult for the pilot to sight through it. Still, the La-5 was superior to the other Soviet-built fighters in use at the time (with the exception of the new Yak-9 fighter) and was considered to be full of potential. Along with the first of the production two-seater Il-2s (with the rear gunner) and the Yak-9 fighter, its appearance at Stalingrad came as an unpleasant surprise to the Luftwaffe, who found their previously insufficiently challenged air superiority slipping for the first time.

During the second half of 1942, 1,129 La-5s were produced. Many of these took part in Operation Uranus, which resulted in the encirclement of Axis forces in Stalingrad. Five fighter regiments were equipped with a lightened, improved La-5, (the 13th, 181st, 239th, 437th, and the 3rd GvIAP).

The combat effectiveness of the La-5 (and indeed, of all Soviet aircraft) was greatly improved by increased communications between aerial and ground forces. This communication was made possible by the fitting of two-way radios to more fighters as the war went on. The commanding officer of the 2nd Guards Army, General Rodion Yakovlevich Malinovskiy (1898–1967), wrote in *Soviet Combat Aircraft of the Second World War: Volume One: Single-Engined Fighters* (p. 43):

> The active warfare of the fighter units of the 2nd Mixed Air Corps [80 per cent of the aeroplanes of which were La-5s], by covering and supporting combat formations of Army troops, actually helped to protect the army from enemy air attacks. Pilots displayed courage, heroism and valour in [*sic.*] the battlefield. With [the] appearance of the Air Corps fighters the hostile aircraft avoided battle.

Naval Service

The first AVMF unit to receive the new fighter was the 4th GvIAP of the Black Sea Fleet. They re-equipped with the La-5 in February 1943 and first saw combat on 4 April. This *polk* bore the inscription *Eskadrilya Valeriy Chkalov* ('Valeriy Chkalov Squadron') after the famous pre-war test pilot, Valeriy Pavlovich Chkalov (1904–38), who had died flying the experimental Polikarpov I-180 fighter (described further on). It was one of several aircraft units bearing his name. KBF units also flew the La-5.

Above: The La-5 of Captain Yevgeniy T. Tsyganov from the 'Valeriy Chkalov' squadron of the 4th GvIAP-KBF at Leningrad in summer 1943 (he became a Hero of the Soviet Union on 22 January 1944). The aircraft is painted in the standard black/green scheme that was also used on the LaGG-3. Note the black-outlined star, which was common on Lavochkin fighters. (*Viktor Kulikov's collection*)

Below: A La-5 with the *bort* number 66 from the 'Valeriy Chkalov' squadron of the 159th IAP flown by Vladimir Georgiyevich Serov. The inscription on the fuselage reads 'Squadron Valeriy Chkalov', 1943. (*Viktor Kulikov's collection*)

A view of another La-5 from the 'Valeriy Chkalov' squadron, 1943. (*Viktor Kulikov's collection*)

Pilots officially receiving the Guards' banner for their division of La-5Fs as the 1st GvIAD-KBF (Red Banner Fleet) in September 1943. Note that the nearest La-5F has a star painted on what appears to be a white-painted spinner. (*Viktor Kulikov's collection*)

A Boost for the La-5: The La-5F

Although the La-5 had proven to be a marked improvement on the LaGG-3 and had finally given the Soviets an aircraft that could combat the Luftwaffe on something approaching equal terms, a better version was needed if true parity or even superiority was to be achieved. This became especially apparent with the appearance of German fighters such as the Bf 109G-2 and Fw 190A-3 by fall 1942, whose top speed of 390 mph (628 kph) or more made them much faster than the high-back La-5, the maximum speed of which was only 362 mph (583 kph) at 20,000 feet (6,096 m). Therefore, an order was issued by the government on 9 December 1942, authorising further development of the La-5.

One of the best ways to improve the La-5 was to fit a better version of the M-82. This was the M-82F ('F' standing for *Forsirovanniy*, or 'Boosted'), which eliminated the burnt-out spark plugs and burned-through exhaust pipes of the un-boosted M-82. The maximum horsepower of this engine was no greater than the un-boosted version (1,700 hp at take-off), but it could run at its maximum horsepower with no limitations, whereas the un-boosted version was limited in this respect to five minutes to avoid burnt-out parts. NKAP Order No. 778, dated 16 September 1942, ordered Shvetsov to begin production of the M-82F at Molotov (Perm). With this engine, the La-5F (as the La-5 with the M-82F was now designated) had a top speed of 364 mph (586 kph) at 12,000 feet (3,658 m), which was superior to the top speed of the Fw 190A-4 at this altitude.

An immaculate La-5F finished in the black/green scheme. This is an early La-5F with the cut-down rear fuselage undergoing tests at the NII VVS between 8 and 27 August 1943. Note the two small sets of numbers on the upper fin and rudder—these are the aircraft's serial numbers. A Cyrillic 'F', for 'La-5F' can also be seen on the top of the rudder. (*Viktor Kulikov's collection*)

A fine in-flight study of the La-5F. A profile of this aircraft appears in the colour plates section. (*Viktor Kulikov's collection*)

With this La-5F you can clearly make out the Cyrillic 'F' in a circle on the cowling. The spinner appears to be painted white. (*Viktor Kulikov's collection*)

La-5F apparently of the 159th IAP with the 'Valeriy Chkalov' markings and the black/green scheme, probably in 1943. The unpainted exhaust panel immediately behind the exhausts shows up very well here. (*Viktor Kulikov's collection*)

When the La-5F first entered service in large numbers in early 1943, it had a failure rate that was three times that of other service fighters. The cockpit was still too hot, and the engine still overheated, namely, when the aeroplane was being run on the ground. The aircraft also had a tendency to turn to the right upon take-off due to the strong torque (caused by the shorter fuselage and a more powerful engine compared to the LaGG-3), and there were difficulties in taxiing on soft ground. However, the La-5F was more survivable than the LaGG-3 and the Yakovlev fighters due in no small measure to its tougher radial engine, and in overall ability, it was considered to be the equal of the German fighters.

Improving the La-5F

The first La-5Fs had the raised rear fuselage decking of the La-5 (inherited from the LaGG-3), but early in production, the cut-down rear fuselage and all-around vision canopy that distinguished all later La-5s and the La-7 were introduced (and were already being used by contemporaneous Yakovlev fighters). This happened with the series 9 on, from November 1942, when the Lavochkin OKB's internal designation for the fighter changed from *tip* 37 to *tip* 39. To protect the pilot, a semi-circular piece of armour glass was placed behind the seat. An armoured windshield was apparently not added until later. This new canopy was first tested from October 1942 for two months, even as the first high-back La-5Fs were already rolling off the production line. It was quickly adopted for the production versions, however, so the vast majority of the La-5Fs had the clear-vision canopy. This increased the effectiveness of the La-5F as you cannot shoot down (or avoid) what you cannot see.

In addition to the new canopy, efforts were made to lighten the La-5F. The outer fuel tanks were removed, and the total number of fuel tanks was reduced from five to three.

Changes were made to the trim tabs, and the area of the flaps was increased in order to enhance manoeuvrability and controllability. At some point in its development, the La-5F was given small scoops below the windshield to direct cooling air into the cockpit (it appears from the photographic record that the high-back La-5Fs did not have the small air scoops).

A La-5F that had thus been modified was tested at the LII and NII VVS. Results showed that the maximum speed was now 380 mph (612 kph) at 19,029 feet (5,800 m). The manoeuvrability of the aircraft was also improved with a turn time of between eighteen and nineteen seconds for a full 360 degrees. Tests conducted at Gor'kiy confirmed these performance figures.

By the spring of 1943, Z.21 was supplying between 350 and 400 La-5Fs to the front each month, and Z.381, which had moved from Nizhniy Tagil to Moscow, and Z.99 in Ulan-Ude (near Lake Baikal in Siberia) had commenced production. At first, only every other La-5F had the RSI-4 receiver—it is not clear from the records when all aircraft started receiving full sets with both transmitters and receivers.

I have seen photographs that show La-5F airframes apparently re-fitted with ASh-82FN engines, with the long top-mounted supercharger intake, and the 'FN' logo on the cowling. These are plainly La-5Fs, as even though they have the all-around vision canopies, they do not have the triangular exhaust shields extending underneath the cockpit. As far as I can determine, all La-5FNs had these exhaust shields, and they were not removed in the field. It is unclear how these hybrid La-5s were designated.

The La-5F in Combat and Combat Tactics

The La-5F was first used in combat as early as the Soviet counterattacks at Stalingrad in the winter of 1942–43. See 'The La-5F and La-5FN in Combat' section for further information. The La-5Fs and La-5FNs were used at the same time and even in the same units, so it is often impossible to tell from combat accounts which version is being described. Sometimes, I will refer to the La-5F and La-5FN together as the boosted La-5s—that is, the La-5s with the boosted M-82 engines, the M-82F and M-82FN (ASh-82F and ASh-82FN). One source describes the La-5FN as not so much a successor to the La-5F, but a contemporaneous, different version. This is rather close to the truth.

Naval Service

The La-5F served alongside the La-5FNs with the Soviet Red Banner (Baltic Sea) Fleet in up to three regiments. As with the La-5FN, it is not clear if it served with other fleets.

The La-5FN

The La-5F, especially the versions with the clear vision canopies (which was most of them), were better fighters than the La-5, but there was always room for improvement. As with the La-5F, this improvement centred on the engine—in this case, a direct fuel-injection version of the tried and combat-tested M-82. This engine, known as the M-82FN (known initially as the M-82FNV, and later as the ASh-82FN), was fitted to the final production variant of the La-5, the La-5FN.

La-5FN in flight; here, you can clearly see how the supercharger intake goes in a continuous raised fairing almost to the edge of the engine cowling. Also, note how the pitot tube on the starboard wing is lowered from the wing leading edge to clear it of the leading-edge slats; this was characteristic of all La-5s, La-7s, and those LaGG-3s that were equipped with these slats. (*Viktor Kulikov's collection*)

This direct fuel injection M-82 now produced 1,850 hp at take-off (as opposed to the 1,700 hp of the M-82A and M-82F), 1,670 hp at 5,000 feet (1,524 m), and 1,460 hp at 15,000 feet (4,572 m). With the new engine came other improvements over the La-5F. The firewall was fitted tighter with the cowling and the oil cooler was insulated, which reduced cockpit temperature. In addition, the La-5FN inherited the small air scoops mounted under the windshields on the 'bubble-top' La-5Fs to help deal with cockpit overheating.

The first true prototype of the La-5FN, now sporting the all-around vision canopy that characterised all production La-5FNs, first flew on 15 March 1943. The factory tests did not take long and concluded two days later, when the aircraft was turned over for state tests. These took place between 24 and 28 March and were performed by the experienced pilot-engineer, A. I. Nikashin, who had piloted the I-301. The test results were good, with a speed of 370 mph (595 kph) at sea level and 403 mph (648 kph) at 20,669 feet (6,300 m), with a turn taking 18.5 seconds. The aircraft weighed 6,984 lb (3,168 kg).

Although the La-5F and La-5FN were nearly identical in external appearance, one recognition feature for the La-5FN was the supercharger inlet over the engine continuing along almost the entirety of the upper cowling. In addition to the unpainted rectangular metal plate immediately behind the exhausts that characterised all La-5 variants, there was another, roughly triangular protective metal cladding behind this plate on the La-5FN. This triangular plate was painted in the camouflage colours. The exhausts themselves were now increased to five on each side, instead of a single exhaust on each side. The La-5F's single exhaust necessitated a bulged cowling flap, whereas this was now smooth on the La-5FN, slightly reducing drag. In addition, the rectangular plate immediately aft of the exhausts was changed, in that the two small vents at the forward part of the plate were replaced by three small vents at the back. This plate remained unpainted. La-5FNs also had an area of metal cladding on the wooden wing roots to protect them from the wear and tear of the pilot's traffic going to and from the cockpit. The La-5F apparently did not have this protective metal covering on the wing roots.

The take-off weight of the production aircraft was higher than it was supposed to be—between 7,242 lb (3,285 kg) and 7,264 lb (3,295 kg), as opposed to the expected maximum weight of 7,165 lb (3,250 kg).

The antenna wiring now consisted either of two lines from the fin mast to just aft of the main antenna mast, then down to the fuselage (or the radio), or a single line from the fin mast to just aft of the main antenna (which part of the line was still attached to), then through the aft canopy to the radio, instead of bifurcated just beond the smal antenna post on the tail, then to the mast and the fuselage (as on the La-5F and early La-5FNs).

In tests conducted in May and July 1943 at the LII and NII VVS against captured Bf 109G and Fw 190 fighters, the La-5FN proved superior in manoeuvrability at heights up to 9,843 feet (3,000 m); above this height, the German fighters were superior. However, since so much of the aerial combat on the Eastern Front took place below 9,843 feet (3,000 m), this was not much of a tactical advantage.

Improving the La-5FN

Although the La-5FN was capable of engaging the German fighters on equal terms, it was not without its problems. There was a shortage of NB-3U injection pumps from Z.296, which led to a shortage of the M-82FN (ASh-82FN) engines, which in turn resulted in a shortage of La-5FNs and the continued production of the slightly inferior La-5F. The design of the sliding cockpit canopy was found to be faulty in that it was hard to move aft in an emergency; however, a redesign of the sliding canopy and rails on later La-5FNs alleviated this problem, and the sliding canopy and rails were made jettisonable. The antenna line running from the antenna mast to the fuselage now ran through an insulator on one of the aft clear canopy panels, usually on the starboard side, to attach directly to the radio.

As production proceeded, the thickness of the armour glass plate behind the pilot was increased from 2.6 to 2.68 inches (66 to 68 mm). Another change was the provision for a small hatch on the lower engine cowling.

One of the improvements that was supposed to have been incorporated into the La-5FN from the beginning were metal wing spars, which were lighter than the wooden spars all previous Lavochkin fighters had featured. These metal spars were designed by P. D. Grushin (who also designed the GR-1 fighter, described further on). Due to a surplus of wooden-sparred wings at Z.21, the La-5FNs first produced there continued to feature the wooden spars (they were still internally designated by the Lavochkin OKB as the *tip* 39, like the La-5Fs). Due to concerns over the strength of the metal spars, Z.381, which was supposed to have begun production of metal-sparred La-5FNs by May 1943, did not begin production of these aircraft (re-designated as the *tip* 41) until a year later. These metal-sparred aircraft also featured a larger, more rectangular metal sheeting under the cockpit than earlier La-5FNs.

Fabric separation was a severe issue that affected not only La-5s, but other aircraft, such as the LaGG-3. Fatal crashes were caused when the fabric covering the wooden structure came loose from this underlying structure due to a defective adhesive. Some 133 LaGG-3s and seventy-five La-5s were affected. The substitution of iron minium for lead (royal) yellow in the putty that adhered the fabric to the underlying plywood covering was ultimately found to be the cause. This putty (designated ASh-22) cracked under the heat of summer. The new ASh-22, therefore, had the lead yellow reintroduced, which solved this particular problem. An unforeseen effect was that this contributed to the need to reduce the use of lead yellow to create the camouflage colour AMT-4 Green (created by mixing it with Prussian Blue). AMT-4 was dropped from fighter camouflage altogether when the fighters went to the two-grey scheme in late 1943, and its usage on other aircraft, such as the Il-2, was cut in half with the change in camouflage schemes in 1943.

The La-5FN in Combat and Combat Tactics

The La-5FN first saw combat on 8 July 1943 at the Bryansk Front with the 32nd GvIAP commanded by Hero of the Soviet Union Col. V. Davidkov. See 'The La-5F and La-5FN in Combat' section for further information.

Naval Service

As with the earlier Lavochkin fighters, the La-5FNs served with the Soviet Red Banner (Baltic) Fleet with up to three regiments. One mission involving naval La-5s comes from *Famous Russian Aircraft, Ilyushin Il-2/Il-10* by Yefim Gordon, Sergey Komissarov, and Dmitriy Komissarov (p. 179):

> On 16th May 1944 reconnaissance aircraft detected an enemy ship convoy in the Gulf of Finland which included landing craft, minesweepers, patrol ships and patrol boats (15 vessels in all). To destroy it, 18 Pe-2 dive bombers and 20 IL-2 attack aircraft were sent under cover of 49 escort fighters. In addition, a group of 12 Lavochkin La-5 fighters started patrolling a coastal area from where enemy fighters could appear.
>
> Diving from 2,000 m (6,560 feet), the Pe-2s were the first to attack the enemy ships, using fragmentation and high-explosive bombs. In about 30 seconds they were followed by a group of 11 IL-2s which used their guns, rockets and small bombs to suppress the ships' anti-aircraft weapons. Next came the turn of eight more Il-2s using the skip-bombing technique (the ninth aircraft in this group had been shot down by enemy fighters). As a result of the strike, three minesweepers and two patrol boats were sunk and one patrol ship was damaged. Eight Fw 190s were shot down. This was considered a satisfactory result. Own losses comprised three IL-2s (shot down by enemy fighters) and three Yak-9s from the fighter cover group.

This was probably a fairly typical naval mission, involving Pe-2s and Il-2s as the bombers and attack aircraft and Yak-9s and La-5s for fighter escort.

La-5FN from a naval unit, judging by the naval uniform of the officer standing in front. The bomb rack on the starboard side can just be made out. Of interest is that the base of the propeller blades appears to be unpainted. (*Viktor Kulikov's collection*)

The La-5FN in Czechoslovakian Service

The Czechoslovakian Air Force was the only foreign user of the La-5 and had begun use of the La-5FN during the Great Patriotic War as part of the Red Air Force. The official date for the creation of the 128th Independent Czechoslovak Fighter Air Squadron in the Soviet Union was 3 May 1944. By 16 May, sixteen second-hand and six brand-new La-5FNs were handed over to the squadron. They began operations on 10 September 1944 with a combat patrol. Some of these aircraft saw action in the Slovak National Uprising.

La-5UTI

There was no dedicated trainer version of the LaGG-3, although two experimental LaGG-3UTIs had been built and tested. UTI stood for *Uchebniy Trenirovochniy Istrebitel'*, Russian for 'Training Fighter'. Pilots went from trainers such as the UTI-4 (the two-seater I-16 trainer) to soloing on the LaGG-3. With the La-5, there were problems with new pilots handling the high torque and landing speed, so it was felt that a two-seat trainer was needed to properly train pilots for the La-5. Consequently, a two-seat trainer variant was developed. A rear position for the instructor-pilot was fitted, at first open, then with a canopy. The trainee-pilot occupied the original pilot's position. In addition, the starboard cannon was removed, as was the original pilot's armour. These measures were taken to reduce the weight, with the RSI-4 radio for the early La-5UTIs removed for this same reason, along with the radio mast and the stub mast on the tail. Later La-5UTIs reintroduced the radio and the stub mast, but not the mast, with the antenna wire running directly from the stub mast to the fuselage aft of the instructor's canopy.

This La-5UTI has been converted from a La-5F, as the 'F' logo on the cowling indicates. It is being tested at the NII VVS. The hexagonal pavement slabs are characteristic of the NII VVS airfield. (*Viktor Kulikov's collection*)

The UTI version began testing at the NII VVS in July 1943. The first prototype had an open cockpit for the instructor-pilot, although all subsequent La-5UTIs had a sliding canopy for him. While the aircraft flew similarly to the single-seater, the instructor-pilot's position was too cramped, and the aircraft did not pass the state trials conducted from 3 to 30 November 1943.

One of the La-5UTIs (perhaps the reworked prototype) featured a more raised canopy in the back, giving better forward and rearward vision for the instructor-pilot. This may have been an experimental installation, as it does not appear on other La-5UTIs. The first La-5UTIs seem to have featured a squared-off rear frame for the instructor's canopy, while later La-5UTIs featured a slanted frame, giving the instructor-pilot slightly better visibility.

As it never fully passed state trials, only twenty-eight new La-5UTIs were produced with the ASh-82FN engine, although an unknown number of airframes were modified into two-seaters in the field. One of these conversions may have featured the modified canopy with better forward and rearward vision previously mentioned. These field-modified versions apparently included conversions from both the La-5F and the La-5FN (and evidently some high-back La-5s) and were primarily used by reserve polks, or ZAPS (ZAP, from *Zapasnoy Aviatsionniy Polk*: 'Reserve Air Regiment'). These ZAPs were involved in conversion training and preparing new units for the La-5 (and other fighters).

A mass-produced trainer version for the Lavochkin fighters did not appear until the development of the La-7UTI, and this after the Second World War. For the second half of the war, the main advanced trainer for all fighter pilots was the Yak-7V, a two-seater trainer version of the Yak-7 single-seater fighter.

La-5—Experimental Versions

La-5 M-71 (See La-7)

Since this aircraft was part of the performance-enhancing efforts for the La-5 that led directly to the La-7, it is discussed in that section.

La-5TK

In order to improve the high-altitude performance of the La-5, NKAP Order N. 853ss was issued on 12 November 1942 to fit two TK-3 turbo-superchargers to a La-5F. This was done to provide a high-altitude fighter for the PVO units and to improve the high-altitude characteristics of Soviet aircraft flying over 16,404 feet (5,000 m).

The first La-5TK had flown seventeen flights by 17 April 1943. The turbo-superchargers worked fine, but the engine overheated because of problems with the carburettor. The second La-5TK flew with a different carburettor. Factory trials were taking place by 9 July and went on until 2 September. These flight tests established the service ceiling as being 41,011 feet (12,500 m).

NKAP Order N 523ss, which was issued on 31 August 1943, called for an ASh-82FN (M-82FN) and TK-3-equipped La-5 with a service ceiling of 44,291 feet (13,500 m). This La-5 also had an enlarged wing and tailplane. It was flown for the first time on 17 March 1944 by LII pilot G. M. Shiyanov, but there were still problems with engine overheating. The flights were continued until the end of 1944 and helped with the development of the TK-3-equipped La-7.

Combat Tactics of the La-5F and La-5FN Versions

Captain Vasiliy Feodorovich Golubev, a Hero of the Soviet Union, observed this about combat with the Fw 190, as quoted from *La-5/7 vs Fw 190: Eastern Front 1942–45* by Dimitriy Khazanov and Aleksander Medved (p. 65):

> The Fw 190, whilst it had powerful weaponry, seeks head-to-head combat, and the rest of the tactics employed remain the same (using the sun, cloud cover *etc.*) as when fighting the Me 109 [sic]. You [the Fw 190] can only break off combat in a dive. When we first encountered the enemy, we found that we climbed more rapidly in the La-5, and when we gained an advantage in speed the Fw 190 rolled onto its back and dived away. After a few vertical attacks the Focke-Wulf fighters always ended up beneath us. When fighting in the horizontal plane, the La-5 had the better performance in a combat turn, and we were not afraid of engaging a Fw 190 at slow speeds.

He continues, with the best combat tactics to use against the Fw 190:

> If you find a Fw 190 on your tail, never attempt to break away from it by diving. You need to disengage either by climbing or side-slipping. Frontal attacks on the Fw 190 are not to be recommended either, as the aircraft has a small cross-section and is heavily armed. It is best to attack from the rear, as accurate fire from this

> direction will damage the fighter's fuel tanks. You need to direct your fire at the cockpit and along the right hand side of the fuselage, where the wiring for the fighter's electrical system is located. If this is destroyed the Fw 190 pilot will have to quickly force-land.

This last part is interesting as it suggests that the Fw 190's much-vaunted automated control system (*Kommandogerät*, or 'Command Device', which automatically controlled the boost, propeller pitch, fuel mixture, and magneto timing) could be knocked out by destroying the electrical system. If so, this is an example of how sophisticated (or complicated) is not always better in combat situations. Sometimes in warfare, simpler is better.

In April 1943, a pre-production La-5FN was tested against a captured Bf 109G-2. The La-5FN proved superior in speed at low and medium altitudes and also bested the Bf 109 in vertical and horizontal manoeuvring. Testing also showed that the La-5FN was superior in climb up to 9,843 feet (3,000 m). It must be remembered that this Bf 109G-2 was most likely a war-weary and repaired machine, whereas the La-5FN it was compared against was brand new; still, the tests were promising. In particular, the La-5FN excelled in dogfighting and turning. Even the Germans' test flights with a second-hand La-5FN at their test centre in 1944 in Rechlin, Germany, confirmed this.

A combat formation used by the La-5s from late 1943 to the end of the war consisted of four La-5s (a *Zveno* or 'Flight') in loose cooperation, with two flight leaders and their wingmen. This formation had been copied from the German *Schwarm* or 'Finger-four' and gave the formation a tactical flexibility that had hitherto been lacking. These pairs (*pari*) would either fly at the same altitude or the second pair would fly slightly above or below the lead pair (*para*) on the left.

Less frequently, Soviet fighter regiments also employed a six-aircraft formation whereby four aircraft in *zveno* configuration, known as the 'binding four', would fly ahead of the other two aircraft that flew at higher altitude, known as the 'striking pair'. These two aircraft would engage any Axis aircraft that had evaded the first four. This formation was used particularly in the later stages of the Great Patriotic War. A variation of the six-aircraft formation used when larger areas of enemy territory had to be swept consisted of the binding four being split into more widely separated pairs, with the striking pair still following behind at a higher altitude.

Combat Use of the La-5F and La-5FN

The La-5F and La-5FN were used contemporaneously, so it is often difficult to determine which of the boosted versions of the La-5 (La-5F or La-5FN) were used in a particular operation. Therefore, I have combined details of combat operations for the La-5F and La-5FN variants into this one section. Where the information is available, I will note which particular version was used.

The La-5F was first used in combat as early as the Soviet counterattacks at Stalingrad in the winter of 1942–43, where it no doubt proved an unpleasant surprise to the Germans, who were used to fighting the un-boosted La-5.

The Germans flight-tested at least two La-5s. This La-5FN was tested at Rechlin, Germany, in 1944, and has been repainted with German insignia, but still retains its Soviet *bort* and the La-5FN logo on the cowling. In addition to the insignia, it has white lines painted on the spinner, typical of Luftwaffe aircraft. (*Viktor Kulikov's collection*)

'Mongolskiy Arat' La-5FNs of the 2nd GvIAP in flight. These La-5FNs were presentation aircraft paid for by workers in Mongolia, a very close ally of the Soviet Union. (*G. F. Petrov's collection*)

Although the photograph makes the colours appear darker than usual, this La-5F has the two-grey paint pattern. It is probably relatively fresh paint because when freshly-applied, the AMT-12 Dark Grey was very dark, almost black. However, it may be that the cowling was, in fact, painted black, as appears to be the case in the next photograph. (*Viktor Kulikov's collection*)

La-5F readying to take off. The cowling on this aircraft appears especially dark as if it and the spinner had been painted black (it is definitely not red if you compare it to the stars). It served with the 21st IAP in the spring of 1944 on the Leningrad Front. (*Viktor Kulikov's collection*)

Another La-5F from the 21st IAP taking off. (*Viktor Kulikov's collection*)

La-5F finished in the two-grey camouflage scheme. You can see the two locks near the centre of the cowling that allowed the panels to open up (the upper panel) or down (the lower panel). The louvres behind the propeller spinner that controlled the flow of air to the engine can also be seen. (*Viktor Kulikov's collection*)

The 32nd GvIAP of the 1st GvIAK (Guards Fighter Air Corps) was the first combat unit to receive La-5FNs, which it received at Malino Airfield, south-east of Moscow, where it had been withdrawn to in late March and early April 1943 in order to re-equip. Here two squadrons received La-5Fs, and one other La-5FNs. In early May, the *polk* was sent back to the Bryansk Front in anticipation of the fight for the Kursk salient.

Kursk (Operation Citadel)

The La-5FN first saw combat in July and August 1943 over the Kursk battlefield with the 32nd GvIAP. What was probably the first victory by a La-5FN took place over Maloarchangelsk on 8 July, when a Fw 190 was shot down by Lieutenant Vladimir A. Drekhov.

As an example of how successful in aerial combat the La-5FN initially was, a look at the victory claims of the 1st Eskadrilya of 32nd GvIAP is sufficient—thirty-three enemy aircraft were claimed in twenty-five missions, including twenty-one Fw 190s, five Ju 88s, three Bf 109s, three He 111s, and one Ju 87. This was accomplished with the combat loss of only four La-5FNs (though one source states six). The 32nd GvIAP as a whole claimed thirty enemy aircraft on 12, 13, and 15 July 1943. It should be emphasised that this was a Guards unit, with excellent pilots, and not all La-5FN units would have experienced the same success. Nonetheless, this shows that the Soviets finally had an aircraft that, when flown by competent pilots, could challenge German fighters, even the new Bf 109G-6 and Fw 190A-6. Captain V. Garanin, Hero of the Soviet Union, had this to say about the La-5FN as reported in *Soviet Combat Aircraft of the Second World War: Volume One: Single-Engined Fighters* (p. 50):

> Combats were fought at altitudes of up to 4,000 m [13,123 feet] with obvious advantages over the Fw 190 and Bf 109, both in speed and in horizontal and vertical manoeuvres. With an open canopy [as Soviet pilots often flew it], the La-5FN overtakes hostile fighters, albeit slowly, gets on their tails during banked turns, and in a vertical air combat always turns to get above the enemy.

Another La-5 ace, Vladimir Orekhov, also had complimentary things to say about the La-5FN, at least in its combat against the Fw 190, as quoted from *La-5/7 vs Fw 190: Eastern Front 1942–45* by Dimitriy Khazanov and Aleksander Medved (pp. 65–66):

> The aircraft [Fw 190] as a whole is not bad. It's best not to make a frontal attack on the Fw 190, as it has very powerful weaponry—four cannons [four 20-mm cannons]. It is very good in a dive and breaks off combat well if the pilot is engaged at medium to high altitude. An experienced Fw 190 pilot practically never fights in the vertical plane. If you were to compare the Fw 190 to the Me 109G [*sic.*], the 'Messer' [Bf 109] would be slightly stronger overall when employed as a fighter, possessing greater speed and better manoeuvrability in a vertical fight.

These views were echoed by Pavel Boykov of the 113th GvIAP, who states in *La-5/7 vs Fw 190: Eastern Front 1942–45* by Dimitriy Khazanov and Aleksander Medved (p. 66):

> The Fw 190's powerful engine guaranteed high speed, but in combat it could be both heavy and inert. In an effort to offset these disadvantages the fascists created mixed groups. The Focke-Wulfs, as a rule, flew lower, and willingly pressed our fighters in combat head-on, but the Me 109s [*sic.*] overhead preferred to dive on us from above and behind.

Yet, even with its apparent superiority over the Fw 190 and at least parity with the Bf 109, this ultimate version of the La-5 series was still imperfect. As was usual with Lavochkin fighters equipped with the ASh-82 (M-82), the cockpit was reportedly hot, filled with engine vapours. The raised cowling intake partially obscured the forward vision of the pilot, which was especially troublesome while trying to get the gunsight on the enemy. The radio equipment was also reported to be inadequate—not an unusual complaint about Soviet-built aircraft. Whatever its shortcomings, the Germans still considered the La-5FN to be their most dangerous adversary in the summer and autumn of 1943.

On 14 December 1943, over the Dnieper, Senior Lieutenant Ivan G. Sklyarov achieved a notable victory in the La-5 when he downed two Ju 87s on his first sortie, then two Ju 88s and two Fw 190s on his second sortie. This tied for the most victories in a day by a Soviet fighter pilot—a Yakovlev pilot had achieved the same feat; P. Dymchenko of the 659th IAP on 11 September 1942 shot down six aircraft over the Kletskaya bridgehead north of Stalingrad, but he was killed in the battle.

As an example of how effective the La-5s were, at least in 1944, one can look at the combat record of the 4th Air Army (4th VA). This unit's La-5s flew 4,161 combat sorties in which they engaged the enemy in 270 combats, during which they claimed 177 Axis aeroplanes for a loss of twenty-seven of their own. The win to loss ratio was 6.55:1. Of course, the quality of the Soviet fighter pilots had improved immensely since the beginning of the Great Patriotic War, whereas that of the Luftwaffe had declined; yet even taking into account some exaggeration of enemy kills, this is still an impressive ratio.

The situation was alleviated for Soviet fighters from 1944 onwards when aircraft such as the Bf 109 and the fighter versions of the Fw 190, such as the Fw 190As, were generally withdrawn to Germany to deal with the Anglo-American strategic bombing campaign (the Combined Bomber Offensive). Eventually, all that remained were *Schlachtgruppen* (ground attack units) of Fw 190Fs. These units were typically manned, not by experienced fighter pilots, but ex-Ju 87 and Hs 129 pilots who were experienced in dive-bombing and ground attack, not aerial combat. This gave the progressively battle-hardened and experienced Soviet fighter pilots an additional edge on top of their improved aircraft.

Nonetheless, these fighter-bomber versions of the Fw 190 still posed problems for even the La-5FNs. A report from the 322nd IAD, as quoted in *La-5/7 vs Fw 190: Eastern Front 1942–45* by Dimitriy Khazanov and Aleksander Medved (p. 69), states:

> Fw 190 attack aircraft usually hit targets in groups of six to nine. They release their bombs from a dive, which allows them to accelerate to high speed and depart for their own territory at low level. They don't enter into battle with our fighters, choosing to depart like serpents when they come under attack. Enemy pilots never fight in the vertical plane, where the La-5FN is stronger, preferring to break off combat by rolling away—a tactic long employed by conventional Fw 190 fighters.

These hit-and-run raids could not effectively be countered until the faster La-7s came into service; only these proved capable of intercepting the fleeing Fw 190s. Indeed, complaints concerning the difficulty of pursuing the German fighters led to Semyon Lavochkin accelerating development of the La-7. At full boost, the Fw 190A-8 fighter was also faster at sea level than even the new Yak-3 and Yak-9U fighters, with only the La-7 being faster. However, these figures may have been obtained from a Fw 190A-8 tested at the NII VVS, with the Fw 190A-8 having only two cannons instead of the normal four. This would have lightened the aircraft, and the speeds might have been faster than with a normally armed Fw 190A-8. Whatever the case, being a dedicated fighter, unlike the Fw 190F-8 fighter-bomber, the Fw 190A-8 was not as heavily used on the Eastern Front, instead finding most of its use in the west, against the bomber streams and their escort fighters.

Vistula to Oder Operation

On 12 January 1945, the Soviets began the huge Vistula to Oder Operation, which would take them from Warsaw to the approaches to Berlin. In this operation, 6,719 aircraft were assembled—517 were La-5s, of which 479 were serviceable (a serviceability rate of nearly 93 per cent), and 227 La-7s, of which 189 were serviceable (a serviceability rate of 83 per cent). These are good serviceability numbers, especially for the boosted La-5s, which at one time had suffered from an unusually high failure rate. Even the serviceability rate for the La-7 was respectable, given that it was still a relatively new aircraft.

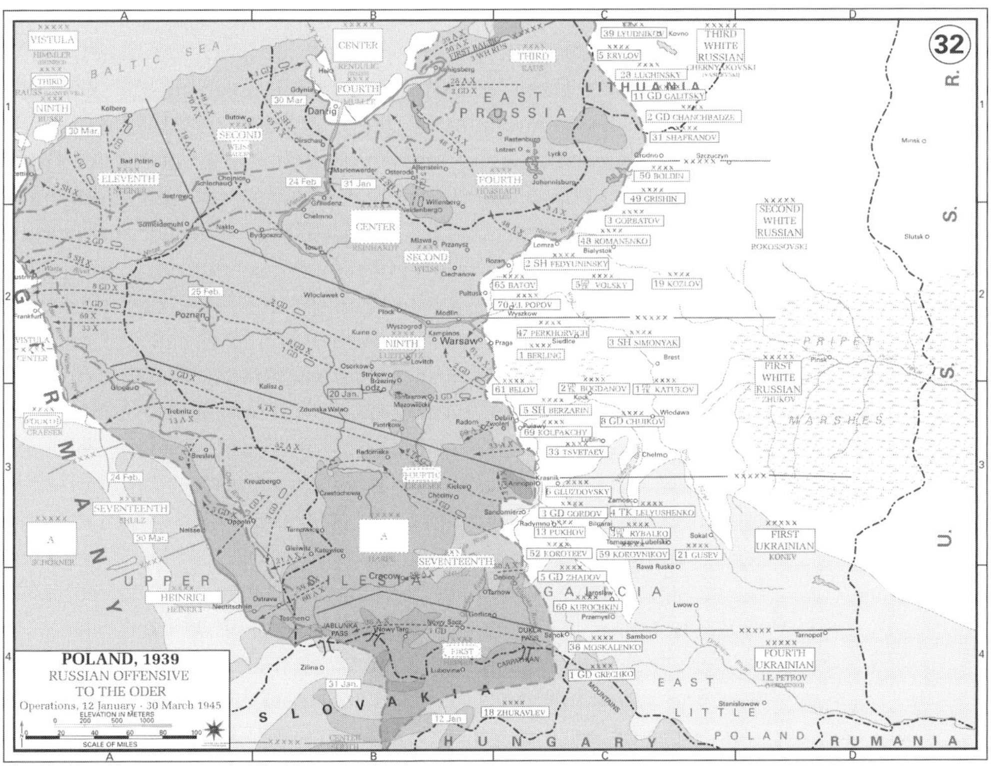

The Vistula to Oder Operation. (*History Department of the United States Military Academy*)

Their pilots held the boosted La-5s in such high esteem that some were reluctant to exchange them for the La-7 or the Yak-3. The 5th GvIAP exchanged its trusty boosted La-5s for Yak-3 VK-107As in early April 1945, but both the pilots and maintenance crew found the Yak-3 VK-107A lacking, with its unreliable VK-107A engine, and switched back to their old La-5Fs and La-5FNs (luckily, the La-5s had not yet been disposed of). Some units had commanders who continued to fly La-5s, even when the unit had re-equipped with Yakovlevs. Both the La-5F and the La-5FN remained in active duty until the end of the Great Patriotic War and beyond, in the Manchurian Strategic Offensive Operation. As with the LaGG-3, I cannot find an official retirement date, but it is very probable that the La-7 quickly replaced the La-5F and La-5FN in post-war usage.

The La-5 Described

Different Versions (Types)

There were several different versions of the La-5 series. Below is a list, with the Lavochkin OKB's internal *tip* (or 'Type') number, VVS designation, and a brief description of the aircraft. Note that some share *tip* numbers, even when the other designation, such as the Red Air Force (VVS) designation 'La-5F', was different, while others of the same variant, such as the 'La-5FN', might have different *tip* numbers. The *tip* numbers were assigned by the Lavochkin OKB, not by the VVS.

Tip 37 (early La-5): the first of the La-5s, which directly utilised surplus LaGG-3 airframes with the rounded windscreen, raised-fuselage deck, and bulged-tailwheel doors. The *tip 37* used the M-82/M-82A engine.

Tip 37(mid and late La-5 and early La-5F): still utilising the raised-fuselage deck, later La-5s and early La-5Fs utilised a flat windscreen like that used on the LaGG-3 series 66 and flush tailwheel doors. It utilised the M-82/M-82A engine in the La-5 version and the M-82F in the La-5F version. These were completely new-built machines and were designated as either 'La-5' or 'La-5F' by the VVS, depending on the engine used.

Tip 39 (mid and late La-5F): this variant had a cut-down rear fuselage with an all-around vision canopy and boosted M-82F (ASh-82F) engine; normally called by the VVS designation of 'La-5F'.

Tip 39 (early and mid La-5FN): usually called by the VVS designation 'La-5FN', this version had the ASh-82FN (M-82FN) engine along with the all-around vision canopy and retained the wooden wing spars.

Tip 41 (late La-5FN): this version of the La-5FN had the ASh-82FN (M-82FN) engine, but it featured the metal wings spars that were also used by the La-7.

Tip 43 (La-5UTI): the two-seater La-5UTI trainer, which used the La-5FN airframes as a production aircraft, but it used both La-5F and La-5FN airframes as field-modifications. It is also possible that some high-back La-5s were converted into two-seater trainer versions.

La-5 in Detail

General Description

The La-5 was a mainly wooden, low-wing cantilever monoplane with a fully retractable main landing gear and a retractable tailwheel. The pilot sat in a fully enclosed cockpit; early versions had a raised-fuselage deck behind the pilot, while later versions, including most La-5Fs and all La-5FNs, had a cut-down rear fuselage and all-around vision cockpit canopy.

Fuselage

Being based on the LaGG-3 fuselage, the construction of all the La-5 variants was likewise of a mainly wooden oval-section semi-monocoque construction, although the front portion of the fuselage, with the mounting frames for the engine and cannons and including the engine cowling, was of metal construction. The mounting frames for the engine and cannons were made out of steel alloy tubes. In addition, the area of the fuselage immediately aft of the engine exhausts was covered in a rectangular plate of zinc-covered steel sheet to prevent the possibility of the exhausts scorching the fabric-covered wooden structure. The engine cowling was covered with dural sheets that were held in place by two circular steel clamp rings that were usually unpainted.

The fuselage consisted of stressed-skin plywood shells of birch veneer composed of three to seven layers of 0.75- or 1.15-mm thickness, which were moulded under heat into halves, then attached to the bulkheads and stringers, using the VIAM B-3 phenol-formaldehyde resin glue. The *tip* 39, with the cut-down fuselage, compensated for the loss of fuselage stiffness with an additional strip of birch veneer 1.15 mm thick; this was glued to the wooden part of the fuselage along its entire length. As with the LaGG-3, the fin was constructed integrally with the rest of the fuselage.

In the high-back La-5, the fuselage had the raised rear fuselage decking of the LaGG-3, which smoothly faired into the sliding canopy. In all but the earliest La-5Fs and all of the production La-5FNs, the rear fuselage decking was cut-down to provide for a rear canopy that afforded the pilot all-around vision. For the versions with the cut-down rear fuselage, the pilot was protected by a piece of 2.6-inch (66-mm) armour glass placed behind the seat, which was increased to 2.68 inches (68-mm) on later La-5FNs. In addition, the pilot's seat back was comprised of steel armour that was 0.39 inches (10.5-mm) thick. Later La-5s had an armour plate of 0.33 inches (8.5-mm) to save weight. From the *tip* 39s (La-5FNs) on, the windscreen was armoured, although it is not clear exactly when it was first introduced (perhaps even on the *tip* 37's La-5s and early La-5Fs), with a 2.17-inch (55-mm) piece of armour glass (called 'transparent armour' by the Soviets) in the central panel. This was later thickened to 2.24 inches (57 mm). Initially, the high-back La-5s (series 1 to 8) had featured the rounded unarmoured windscreen used on most of the LaGG-3s (these La-5s were built using LaGG-3 series 35 airframes), but they had then changed to the flat unarmoured windscreen used on series 60 and onward LaGG-3s.

Evidently, the clear mouldings were now made of Plexiglas, whereas in the earliest LaGG-3s they had been made of cellulose. When this change was made is unclear, but

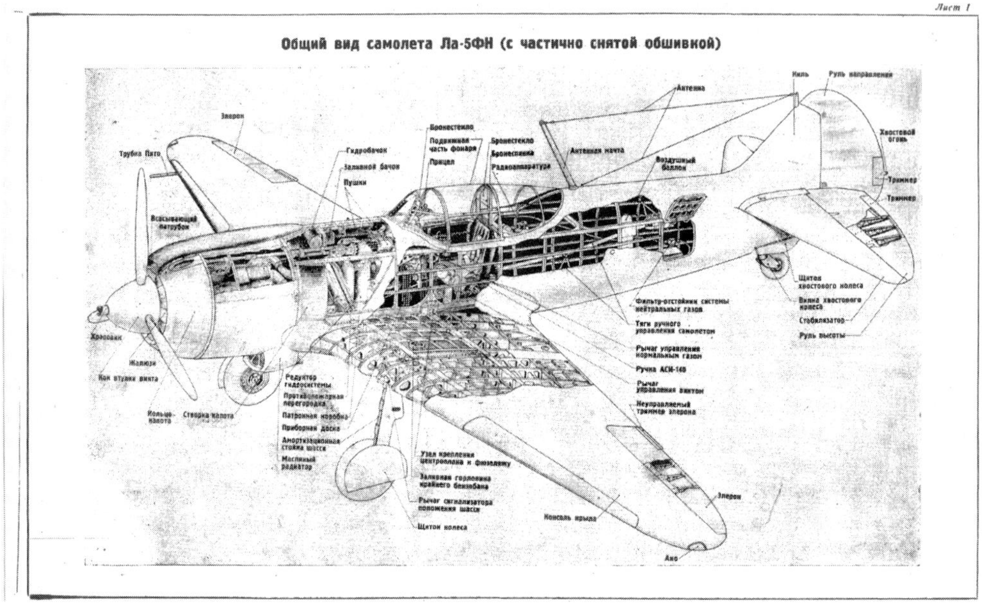

La-5FN cutaway. (*La-5FN Technical Manual*)

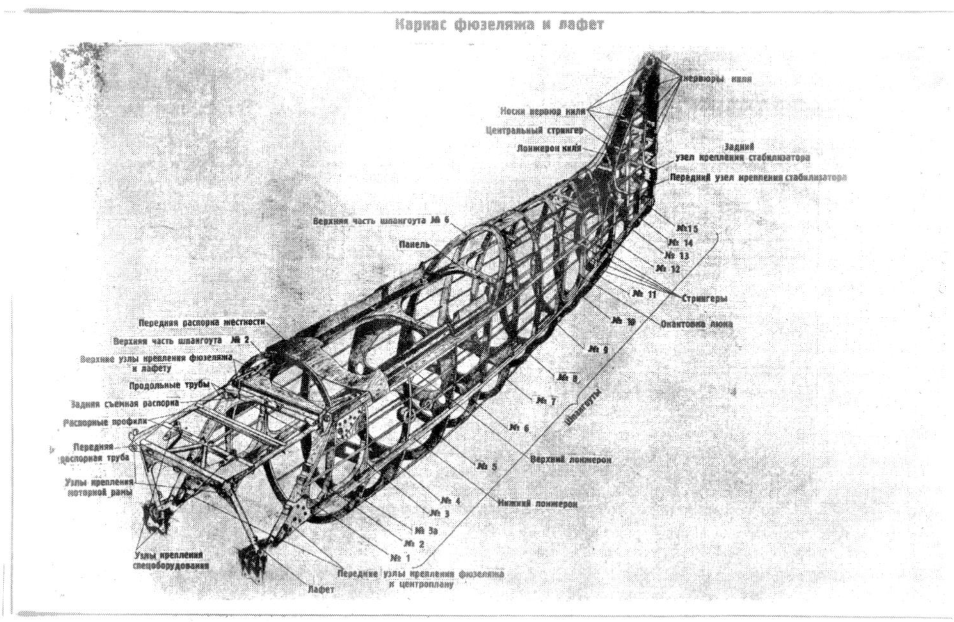

La-5FN rear fuselage structure. (*La-5FN Technical Manual*)

since the cellulose yellowed with age, the decision to replace it with the clearer Plexiglas was likely made during the production run of the LaGG-3, and so Plexiglas was probably present on the La-5 from the start of its production run. A few of the boosted La-5s (La-5Fs and La-5FNs) had an additional vertical frame in the middle of the sliding canopy; this was evidently a field-modification, probably done to strengthen the canopy.

The first all-around vision canopies (on the early *tip* 39s, the La-5F) were not jettisonable and were characterised by a slightly curved top profile on the sliding version, without a pronounced step between it and the fixed rear canopy. Upon sliding back, the canopy raised up slightly. On the La-5FNs (later *tip* 39s and all *tip* 41s), however, the sliding canopy and its guide rails could be jettisoned by pulling on a cable. This version of the sliding canopy had a straight profile on the top and there was a clear step between it and the fixed rear canopy. It did not raise up upon opening, and there was a noticeable detachable plate covering the guide rails. On previous Lavochkin fighters, the canopy had to be manually slid back for an emergency exit, which could make bailing out more difficult; this even led to the canopy's removal from some LaGG-3s.

The rear glazing on the *tip* 39s and *tip* 41s featured a movable panel on the port side that could be swung open on a piano-type hinge to allow access to the radio equipment behind the pilot's seat.

Although the pilot's seat was equipped with both lap belts and shoulder belts (as was normal with Soviet aircraft), according to the testimony of one La-5 pilot, the shoulder belts were not used. They were apparently removed on some aircraft. The reason for their non-use was that they prohibited the free movement of the pilot while looking for the enemy.

Wings

Most La-5s had wings of all-wooden construction, although the last La-5FNs had wings of composite construction, introducing the metal wing spars that were used by the La-7. The Frise-type ailerons were always of aluminium alloy structure, covered with AVLK fabric, while the flaps were of dural construction and were hydraulically operated with a maximum deflection of 60 degrees downwards (one source indicates 50 degrees downward). A Frise-type aileron is an aileron having a nose portion projecting ahead of the hinge axis and a lower surface in line with the lower surface of the wing. The wing root was subjected to heavy traffic by the comings and goings of the pilot, so on the La-5FNs it was made out of 3-mm thick *delta drevresina* and protected by metal sheeting.

The centre-section of the wing, to which both the fuselage and the outer wings were attached, had two spars made out of pine and plywood on the *tip* 39 and two metal spars made out of chrome molybdenum steel caps and dural webs on the *tip* 41. The wooden spars in the centre section were made of five pieces of pine web, reinforced on the sides with plywood then all sandwiched together. These wooden spars continued into the outer wing sections on the *tip* 39, while the *tip* 41 had metal spars in the outer wing sections. The stressed skin was made out of birch plywood glued to the inner wing structure with VIAM B-3 glue. The entire wooden wing structure was fixed together with the VIAM B-3 glue.

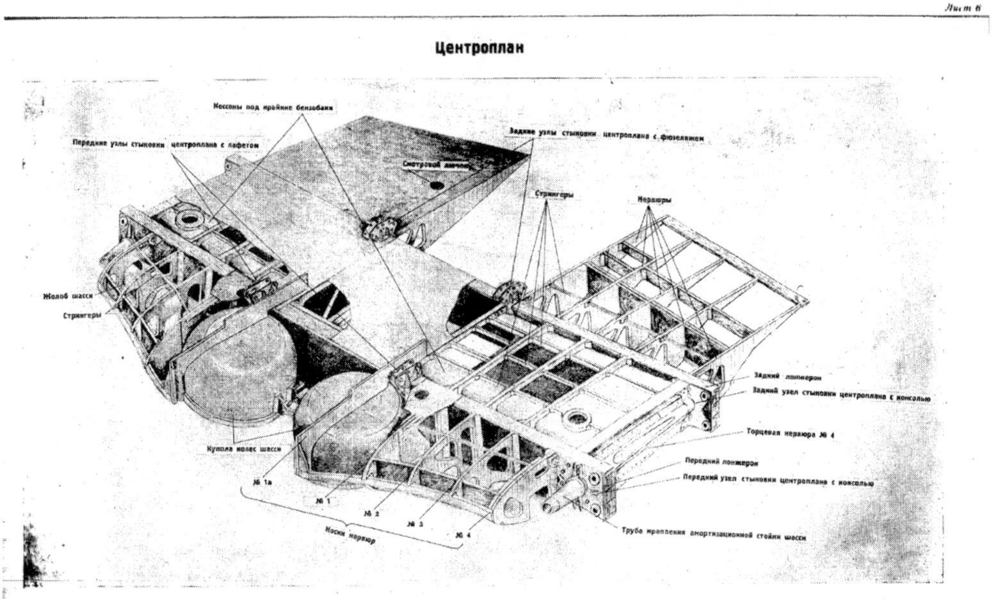

La-5FN wing centre section with wooden wing spars. (*La-5FN Technical Manual*)

The skin of the wings was made out of 2.4- to 4-mm-thick plywood covered with a nitrocellulose putty-impregnated fabric. Due to some separation problems, these fabric skins were taped to the ribs and the fabric thoroughly filled with the nitro putty and sanded.

The outer leading edges of the wings were equipped with riveted dural leading-edge slats. This necessitated having the pitot tube attached to the lower wing, so the slats could clear it, instead of extending out from the wing leading edge as on those LaGG-3s that were not equipped with the slats. These slats were opened and closed by aerodynamic forces. On the early high-back La-5s, the pitot tube was the same size as that used on the LaGG-3, but most of the La-5s (probably beginning with the new-build high-back La-5s) had an enlarged pitot tube. Also, on the early La-5s built from LaGG-3 airframes, the trim tab was probably present only on the port aileron and not extended (later La-5s had extended fixed trim tabs on both ailerons).

La-5s that were used by the PVO had a landing light in the port wing, a position it had occupied in most of the LaGG-3 series but was absent from in most versions of the La-5. This light was used to assist the PVO La-5s in night operations. The only other La-5s with this landing light were the first eight series of high-back La-5s, which had been built using LaGG-3 airframes (probably series 35 airframes).

Tailplanes

Like the LaGG-3, the fixed portions of the tail surfaces were of all-wooden construction, with the fixed horizontal tailplanes consisting of two wooden spars. The fixed portions were covered with a 2-mm-thick bakelised *delta drevresina* skin. The moveable portions, such as the rudder and the elevators, were of aluminium alloy structure, covered with AST-100 fabric. The trim tab on the port elevator was unusual in that it was of wooden structure and covered in a dural sheet. There was no trim tab on the starboard elevator, except for the first eight series of the high-back La-5s, which used the surplus LaGG-3 airframes.

The horn-balanced rudder was of a similar fabric-covered metal structure to the elevators and could move 25 degrees to either side. The rudder had a trim tab.

Engine

The engine for all the production La-5 variants was the M-82 14-cylinder twin-row air-cooled radial engine, also known as the ASh-82 (from 1944 on), after its designer, Arkadiy Shvetsov. It had a two-speed centrifugal gear-driven supercharger. This engine had been developed from the M-62 single-row engine, itself a development of the M-25, a licence-built version of the American Wright Cyclone R-1820 9-cylinder single-row radial engine. Three variants were fitted to the La-5s—the M-82 on the La-5, the M-82F on the La-5F, and the M-82FN (ASh-82FN) on the La-5FN. The engine's designation was reflected in the service designation of the last two variants of the La-5.

The M-82FN engine could be started either by compressed air from an on-board bottle or by using the Hucks starter dog on the spinner, whereby a shaft fitted to the small dog on the front of the spinner was turned around by a motor mounted on a truck. The 'dog' itself was actually part of the cannon barrel protruding from the spinner and had projections to fit onto the starter shaft of the truck.

The first engine used, the M-82 (or 'M-82A'—this term was probably used retroactively, to distinguish it from the boosted variants), had a take-off rating of 1,700 hp. With the M-82F (ASh-82F), where the 'F' stood for *Forsirovanniy*, meaning 'Boosted', the take-off rating was the same as the M-82A, but the engine was now no longer limited in how long it could be used at maximum power. The M-82A had been limited to five minutes, as the exhaust tubes tended to burn out after too much time at maximum power. The M-82FN differed from the previous two versions of the M-82 in not being carburetted and having direct fuel injection to the cylinders. It had a take-off rating of 1,850 hp and not only powered the La-5FN but also its successors—the La-7, the La-9, and the La-11.

Not only did the M-82FN feature direct fuel injection, utilising an NB-3U injection pump, but the piping was also improved over the earlier versions of the engine. With the earlier variants of the M-82 engine, the piping consisted of a mixture of steel, dural, and copper pipes. With the M-82FN these were replaced by braided, armoured pipes that leaked less than the earlier piping and were more resistant to battle damage. The air intake was enlarged, which increased the flow of air to the engine, thus enabling the engine to generate greater power at the same altitudes as the M-82A and M-82F. The exhaust tubing was also changed; instead of the exhaust from the cylinders being collected into one tube on each side, there were now five exhaust tubes on each side. These contributed to the equivalent of an additional 80 hp, mainly through a jet thrust effect.

The M-82FN drove a VISh-105V propeller of 10.17 feet (3.1 m) in diameter, as used on later series of the LaGG-3. It was covered in a dural cowling, with panels that

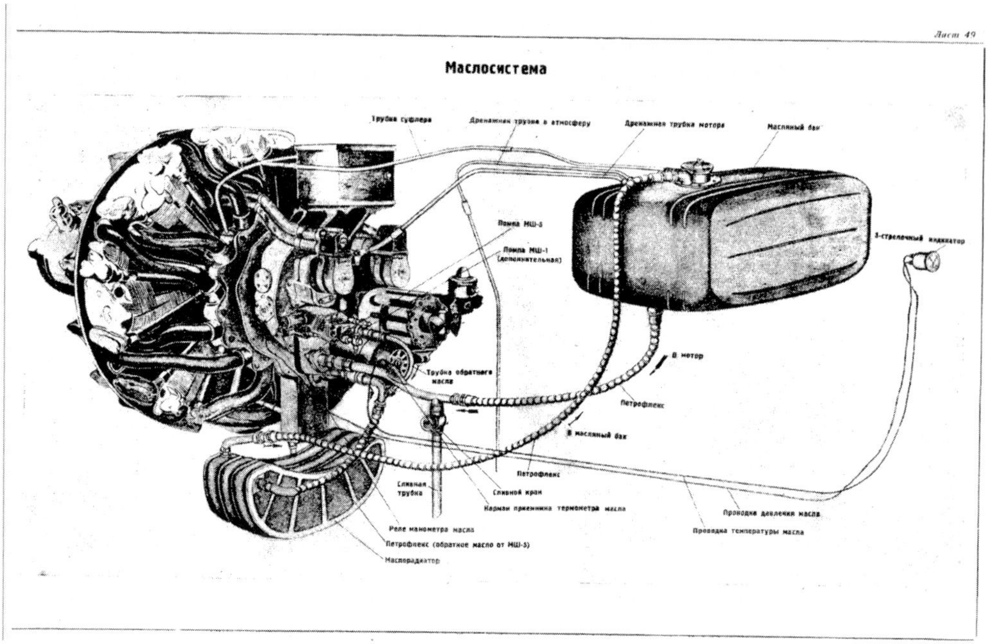

La-5FN oil cooling system. (*La-5FN Technical Manual*)

could open to allow servicing. In the La-5, the La-5Fs, and early La-5FNs, these panels were composed of two plates on each side, separated in the middle. Early La-5FNs had cowling panels like earlier La-5 versions, which opened in the middle, with the lower panel swinging down, and the upper panel swinging up, with latches on either side of where the panels opened in the middle of the cowling. In later La-5FNs, the panels on each side consisted of two hinged pieces of dural that swung upwards and folded and hinged in the middle along the top of the cowling just below the supercharger intake. This feature was similar to that used on the La-7, although the La-7's panels were a single sheet on both sides and were hinged at the top, there being no intake on the top of the cowling. The La-5 cowling's dural sheeting was 1.2 mm thick.

The fuel that the M-82 used was 4B-78 petrol, of at least 95 octanes. In the non-fuel-injected versions, this was then mixed with the air from the intake in the AK-82BP carburettor. In the M-82FN, the fuel was injected directly into the cylinders using FB-10 injection nozzles.

Whichever version of the M-82 was used, there were adjustable louvres behind the propeller (sometimes mistaken for fans) which regulated the flow of air to the cylinders. All the La-5s featured these louvres.

Fuel System

The earliest La-5s had five fuel tanks, like the LaGG-3, but these were replaced with three fuel tanks from the completely new-build series 9 La-5 on (at the same time that the original LaGG-3 airframes were used up). The removal of the two outer fuel tanks lightened the La-5, at only a relatively small cost in range, because of the saving in weight. The fuel tanks were self-sealing, consisting of aluminium alloy covered by the self-sealing layer, which was made up of five layers of rubber and fabric. In addition to their self-sealing qualities, the fuel tanks were also fed neutral gases from the engine, which had been filtered and cooled before being flowed into the fuel tanks. These gases displaced the flammable mixture of air and petrol vapour above the petrol as the fuel tanks emptied through use, thus greatly lowering the chance of fire.

Controls

For all the La-5 versions, the control column consisted of the 'spade-grip', which had been used by the LaGG-3 and was standard for many Soviet aircraft of the Great Patriotic War.

The control surfaces themselves consisted of the rudder, ailerons, elevators, and flaps. The rudder was controlled by rudder pedals (yaw control). The ailerons and elevators were controlled by the control column, with sideways movements changing the attitude of the ailerons (roll control), and back and forth motions the position of the elevators (pitch control). The ailerons and elevators themselves were connected to the control column by a system of push-pull rods and bell cranks. The trim tabs on the elevators and rudder were adjustable in flight by trim wheels located on the port side of the cockpit, the tabs being adjusted by cables. The ailerons had fixed tabs that could be adjusted on the ground by carefully bending them (they were metal). The starboard elevator did not have a trim tab from the series 9 La-5 on.

The rudder was controlled by pedals, the system being improved during the production of the La-5 to give better control (it is unclear when). The flaps were hydraulically adjusted by a ram and levers, controlled by a lever in the cockpit.

Landing Gear

Both the main landing gear and the tailwheel were hydraulically retractable on the La-5, and covered with doors upon retraction, with the main wheels being only half-covered by doors, as with the LaGG-3. The wide-track main landing gear retracted inwards, while the tailwheel retracted aft. The main landing gear doors were of dural and were attached to the landing gear legs, while the dural tailwheel doors were attached to the fuselage. Small indicators in the wings indicated whether the landing gear was in the up or down position, with up meaning the landing gear were down, and down meaning the landing gear were up (retracted).

Due to troubles with the tailwheel retraction mechanism, in service, the tailwheels were often locked in the 'down' position, with the doors closed. From the series 34 of the La-5FN on, reliability was improved by replacing the non-return valve that used oil pressure to hold the tailwheel in the retracted position, with a hydraulic jack.

Originally the *tip* 37 and *tip* 39 main landing gear had a stroke of only 180 mm, which proved insufficient and made for a dangerously bumpy ride on rough ground. This hydro-pneumatic stroke was increased to 220 mm from the series 34 of the La-5FN on, which somewhat improved the ride. The main wheels were 650 × 200 mm in size, while the tailwheel was 300 × 125 mm in size. The landing gear could be manually extended in an emergency, such as battle damage to the hydraulics.

Radio Equipment

The radio consisted of a transmitter, the RSI-3M *Oryol (Eagle)*, and a receiver, the RSI-4D *Malyutka*, introduced in August 1942 on the LaGG-3. The antenna mast was made out of plywood with a streamlined cross-section, and on the La-5 high-back version was vertical and mounted behind the cockpit—on the La-5 versions with the cut-down rear fuselage, it was still mounted behind the cockpit but was slanted forwards, with a height of 2.3 feet (700 mm). The small antenna post on the tail was also wooden, with a height of 0.49 feet (150 mm). According to one source, at first, only every other La-5F was equipped with the RSI-4 receiver; it is unclear when all the aircraft received both the receiver and the transmitter.

Fixed Armament

All versions of the La-5s had as their fixed armament two ShVAK SP-20 20-mm cannons mounted in the top part of the cowling, hydro-mechanically synchronised to fire through the propeller disc. Due to the design of the M-82 engine, it was not possible to fit a gun to fire through the propeller spinner, as had been the case with the LaGG-3. Apparently, four ShVAK cannons were originally intended to be fitted to the La-5, but space limitations with the cowling prevented this.

The muzzle velocity of the cannon was 815 m/s at a rate of 800 rpm. Two different types of rounds could be fitted—the Bz armour-piercing incendiary round and the Oz high-explosive round. The cannons were equipped with 200 rounds per gun, giving fifteen seconds of continuous firing time.

The guns were fired using a PBP-1A collimating reflector gunsight; this was replaced with the superior PBP-1B gunsight during the production of the La-5F, which was standard on the La-5FN. The gunsight had two settings—one for a target speed of 124 mph (200 kph) and another for 186 mph (300 kph). The guns could be either pneumatically or mechanically charged.

Disposable Armament

For use as a fighter-bomber, the La-5 could be fitted with two small bombs attached to two DS-40 bomb racks, one underneath each wing. The bombs were normally 110 lb (50 kg) or 220 lb (100 kg) for a maximum bomb load of 440 lb (200 kg). Either FAB high explosive, ZAB incendiary, or small (55-lb, or 25-kg) AO-25M fragmentation bombs could be carried. It is unclear from the record if the La-5 could carry RS-82 or RS-132 rockets like some of the LaGG-3s could, but I have never seen a photograph of a rocket-carrying La-5. Although the Soviets did not habitually use the La-5 versions as fighter-bombers, the Czechoslovakian-flown La-5FNs sent to Slovakia in 1944 were heavily used in ground support of the rebels in the Slovak National Uprising. When not in use, the bomb rack attachment points were covered by a small, streamlined fairing.

Colour and Markings

Since it entered service in 1942, the high-back La-5s had the 1941 camouflage scheme of AMT-6 Black and AMT-4 Green over AMT-7 Blue. This camouflage was also sometimes seen on the La-5F, but it was somewhat rare on the La-5FN, and La-5FNs that served from late 1943 onwards featured the later fighter camouflage scheme of AMT-11 Grey-Blue and AMT-12 Dark Grey over AMT-7 Blue.

As with the LaGG-3s, for some La-5 versions, there apparently was a bit of a lag time between the introduction of the two-grey scheme and the application of the '1943 Star', which replaced the earlier plain red or red with black outline star. However, the stars would normally have been the '1943 Stars' on the aircraft with the two-grey scheme. As with other Soviet aircraft, some La-5s of all versions bore personal insignia and inscriptions, and those on presentation machines often described the donor of the aircraft. Examples of La-5s with inscriptions and other personal markings can be seen as profiles in the colour plates section.

The La-5F featured a Cyrillic letter 'F' in a circle as an emblem on both sides of the engine cowling and the fin, although these were sometimes painted out (or perhaps not even applied at the factory). The La-5FN first featured the Cyrillic letters 'FN' in a circle, then in a diamond-shaped logo. Again, this emblem was sometimes missing from service aircraft.

The high-back La-5s were almost always finished in the early black/green scheme, and when stars were outlined, it was in black, white, or even silver, but usually in black. If the change was made to the two-grey scheme in late 1943 and early 1944, the stars were changed to the outlined '1943 Stars'. It would appear from the photographic record, or lack thereof, that the high-back La-5 in the two-grey scheme was something of a rarity. As with the LaGG-3, some La-5s carried the ornamental 'Kremlin Stars'.

An innovation introduced by the ace Aleksandr Semyonov was painting the cowlings of the La-5s under his command red all the way to the firewall (322nd IAD). This made it easier to distinguish the La-5s from the Fw 190s during the heat of battle; it also distinguished his La-5s from other units' La-5s, thus increasing his ability to control them. This quick recognition feature was seen later on some La-7s. Indeed, as the war went on and the Soviets sent up larger formations of aircraft, these types of identification markings became more and more common on other aircraft as well, such as the Il-2, as the need for control became more important.

The Soviets had, for the most part, stayed away from colourful unit identification markings earlier in the war as the danger of the Luftwaffe attacking aircraft on the ground had been very real. As the Luftwaffe slowly disappeared from the Eastern Front, this danger receded, and the identification markings became common. By the end of the war, some aircraft were very colourful indeed.

It is not known to this author whether any of the La-5 versions were painted in the Soviet post-war scheme of grey or green topside over blue. Given the rapidity with which they were removed from service after the war, this seems unlikely.

The Last and Best—The La-7

The La-7 can be thought of as an enhanced La-5FN, which retained and improved upon the changes made to later La-5FNs. It was not a radically different aircraft and could have easily kept the 'La-5' designation and was indeed initially known as the 'La-5 1944 Etalon'. One of the most distinguishing and visually significant changes was the move of the oil cooler from under the aft portion of the bottom of the engine cowling to under the fuselage, between the wings, which not only improved the aircraft's aerodynamics but improved the airflow through the radiator. The supercharger intake was moved from the top of the nose to the wing roots (this move was not without its problems, but more on that further on), and the La-7 had a generally more aerodynamically clean form than that of the La-5, especially since the engine cowling had a smaller diameter.

There were two aeroplanes that led from the La-5 to the La-7. The first was the La-5 M-71, and the second was the '206'.

Precursors

La-5—M-71

The M-82FN (Ash-82FN) was not the only engine that was considered for improving the La-5's performance. The Shvetsov Bureau had also been working on the M-71F (ASh-71F) engine, which was an eighteen-cylinder engine created by joining together two 9-cylinder M-63 engines and, like the M-82FN, featured boosting and direct fuel injection. The new engine was capable of 2,000 hp at take-off. The M-71F engine that was installed on the La-5 was even more powerful, with a rating of 2,200 hp at take-off, which was 350 hp more than the 1,850 hp of the M-82FN of the production La-5FN. The M-71F was still capable of 1,800 hp at an altitude of 8,530 feet (2,600 m).

The La-5 M-71F was developed in parallel with the M-82FN-equipped La-5FN. It differed externally from the La-5FN by the intake being moved from the top of the engine to the bottom, the shorter, bulkier appearance of the M-71 engine, and the radiator cooler being moved to the centre of the under-fuselage (as with the '206' and the La-7). The La-5 M-71 also featured the main wheel doors of the '206' and the La-7.

The sole La-5 M-71. Note that it is painted in the black/green scheme because it flew in 1943, before the two-grey scheme came into common usage. (*Viktor Kulikov's collection*)

In order to move the heavier engine closer to the centre of gravity, the fuselage was shortened by some 2.74 feet (0.835 m), adding even more to the bulkier appearance of the aircraft. With the heavier engine, the La-5 M-71 weighed 7,751 lb (3,516 kg) at take-off—789 lb (358 kg) more than the La-5FN.

This aircraft first flew on 28 April 1943, which was only a few weeks after the first La-5FN had flown and was tested until June. It performed well; its top speed at sea level was 380 mph (612 kph) and 425 mph (685 kph) at 18,044 feet (5,500 m), which was considerably better than the La-5FN despite the La-5 M-71's extra weight.

Despite its good performance, the La-5 M-71 did not go into serial production as the troublesome M-71 engine itself was destined never to go into mass production. However, at least two of the innovations of the La-5 M-71—the main wheel doors and the under-fuselage radiator cooler—were adopted by the '206' and the La-7.

'206'

The TsAGI tested ways to increase the performance of the La-5FN. Sealing the gaps in the airframe resulted in a 14.9-mph (24-kph) increase in speed. Another relatively simple expedient was fitting small doors to completely cover the main wheels when retracted, as with the La-5 M-71. This added another 3.7 mph (6 kph) to the aircraft's speed. The oil cooler was also relocated, as with the La-5 M-71, from under the nose to under the central portion of the fuselage, which decreased drag and increased airflow into the oil cooler intake.

The '206' was a production La-5FN that was pulled from the production line at Z.21 to test the above (and other) TsAGI recommendations on the airframe for improving the La-5's performance. The name '206' was derived from the serial number c/n 39210206. The TsAGI worked with Lavochkin in making the appropriate changes to the airframe. This aeroplane, with its improved performance, validated the changes the TsAGI had proposed and most of the improvements found their way onto the production La-7. The '206' can be thought of as the first unofficial prototype of the La-7.

Some of the changes made to the '206' were a general lightening of the airframe (for example, the metal wing spars were used), and the landing gear was now fully enclosed with small doors covering the outer part of the main wheels, which decreased aerodynamic drag. Additionally, there was an improvement in the fit of the internal components, and the oil cooler was moved from under the cowling to under the fuselage at the wing-trailing edge. This change increased the airflow into the cooling intake by 30 per cent and reduced parasitic drag by 50 per cent. The supercharger intake was also moved from the top of the cowling to the bottom (again as with the La-5 M-71). To further reduce drag, the metal sheeting under the cockpit and the radio antenna mast was removed, with the wires of the latter running directly from the small post on the tail to the fuselage behind the cockpit canopy.

With all these changes, the '206' out-performed a normal production La-5FN. The '206' was sent to the LII to undergo tests from 14 December 1943 to 10 February 1944. These tests revealed a top speed at sea level of 391 mph (630 kph), and a top speed at 20,177 feet (6,150 m) of 425 mph (684 kph). This last figure was some 31 mph (50 kph) higher than that for a production La-5FN, despite the '206' being heavier, weighing in at 7,594 lb (3,445 kg), which was some 330 lb (150 kg) more than a production La-5FN.

After the first flights, the LII decided to send a version of the '206' into production and designated it the La-5 1944 Etalon (*Etalon* translates from Russian as 'Standard').

La-5 1944 Etalon

The La-5 1944 Etalon not only incorporated the TsAGI-suggested changes, but it had additional improvements which, in effect, made it the first official prototype of the La-7.

One external difference from the '206' was the change in the placement of the supercharger intake from under the cowling to the wing roots. Although this served to further streamline the aircraft and increase its top speed, it created unforeseen problems. While the M-82 engine had performed well on all the La-5 variants, there were problems with the M-82FNs fitted to the La-7, including engine failure. These were traced to dust, grit, and other foreign objects being ingested into the wing root intakes and thereby into the engine. This had not been a problem when the intake was mounted on top of the cowling as with the La-5, but now the wing root intakes were much closer to the ground. Filters were eventually fitted to the intakes, but these were not installed until after the war. On the ground, the wing intakes were sometimes covered, which helped. However, moving the supercharger intake did improve the view of the pilot over the cowling.

Internally, the 'spade-grip' control column was replaced with a single-handle 'joystick' like those fitted to German fighters, such as the Bf 109 and the Fw 190. This improved the control response.

One change from the '206' that was not adopted was the removal of the metal sheeting under the cockpit. This was restored to the Etalon but was larger and more rectangular than the protective sheeting used on the La-5FN.

The Etalon was completed in January 1944 and first flown on 1 February by LII test pilot Captain Georgiy Mikhailovich Shiyanov. It was 121 lb (55 kg) lighter than the La-5FN. The first flights were promising and showed a very good performance—a top speed at sea level of 371 mph (597 kph), and a top speed overall of 423 mph (681 kph) at 19,686 feet (6,000 m). This made it some 50 mph faster than the Fw 190A-8 at sea level. The aircraft was submitted to the NII VVS for state trials by 16 February. A second Etalon, a *Dooblyor* ('Doubler' or 'Understudy'), was constructed and used to finish the state trials, which were completed by 27 March.

For the most part, the testing had gone well, and the La-5 1944 Etalon was obviously a fine fighter, but nonetheless, there were some problems. The escape procedure was not satisfactory, the hot oil from the oil radiator passing directly under the feet of the pilot caused discomfort and made an already uncomfortably warm cockpit even hotter, and the rudder pedals were hard to move. The placement of the oil radiator caused the cockpit's heat, always a problem with the La-5, to rise even more, with temperatures in the cockpit reportedly reaching 131 degrees F (55 degrees C). Despite these problems, the aircraft was promising enough to be recommended for full-scale production, with the intention that the problems would be addressed while in production.

The Production La-7

Accepted for production in May 1944, the 1944 La-5 Etalon now received the official designation of 'La-7', and the internal Lavochkin OKB designation of '*tip* 45'. The first production aircraft rolled off the production lines at Z.21 in Gor'kiy that same month, and by June 1944 108 La-7s had been delivered. By the end of the year, 1,782 had been produced and 1,044 had reached service units. Production had also been started at Z.99 in Ulan-Ude and Z.381 in Moscow.

A change made to the production La-7 as compared to the Etalon and the '206' was the reintroduction of the radio antenna mast. It was similar to the slanted installation on the La-5FN, and like that mast was wooden, but thinner and more streamlined, to decrease drag.

All the La-7s were intended to be armed with three of the new Berezin B-20 20-mm cannons, which had been developed from the Berezin UB 12.7-mm (50-calibre) machine gun. However, the troubled development of the cannons led to most Great Patriotic War La-7s being equipped with two of the same ShVAK SP-20 20-mm cannons the La-5s carried. Another problem was that in some flight regimes, the ejected shell cartridges from the B-20 cannons would strike the tail. Thus, most of the combat La-7s carried the same armament as the La-5s, although some three-cannon armed La-7s did see limited combat in the final stages of the Great Patriotic War. One source states that 368 of the three-cannon-armed La-7s were delivered by the end of the conflict, but it is not clear how many of these aircraft saw any action. It is possible that some of the three-cannon La-7s played a role in the Manchurian Strategic Offensive.

Production examples from Z.21 and Z.381 were tested at the NII VVS in September 1944 to determine their performance. This ranged from 355.4 to 359 mph (572 to 578 kph) at sea level, and a top speed of 407 to 409 mph (655 to 658 kph) at 19,357 to 20,013 feet (5,900 to 6,100 m). The La-7s could gain 3,280 to 4,035 feet (1,000 to 1,230 m) in a combat turn. This was impressive, considering it was achieved at a normal power rating. With augmented power, the La-7 could gain 4,593 feet (1,400 m) in a combat turn, performance that could only be matched by the Soviet Yak-3 and Yak-9U. The German fighters, such as the Bf 109G, could not match this. This in turn forced to the Germans to modify their combat tactics as they could no longer rely upon superior vertical performance.

The initial production La-7s had reached their first combat units by June 1944, and the 63rd GvIAP, commanded by Lieutenant Colonel Yevgeniy Gorbatyuk, undertook official combat trials from 15 September to 15 October 1944, even though the first La-7s had already seen combat in June. The combat trials confirmed the overall excellent performance of the La-7 but also highlighted issues with the hydraulics and engine stoppages. The supercharger air intake had been moved from the top of the cowling (where it was in the La-5s) to the wing roots, which led to increased ingestion of foreign matter and could cause the engine to seize up. Despite the seriousness of this problem, it was not truly solved until after the war, when dust filters were fitted to the intakes. Also, excessive heat in the cockpit had to be solved by field modification. Lieutenant Colonel Gorbatyuk concluded the following of the La-7, as reported in *Soviet Combat Aircraft of the Second World War: Volume One: Single-Engined Fighters* (p. 55):

A production La-7 being tested at the NII VVS. Note the absence of a cowling intake and that the antenna mast is slimmer than that of a La-5FN. (*Viktor Kulikov's collection*)

Another view of this La-7. (*Viktor Kulikov's collection*)

> The La-7 exhibited unquestionable advantages over German aircraft in multiple air combats. In addition to fighter tasks, photographic reconnaissance and bombing were undertaken with success. The aircraft surpasses the La-5FN in speed, manoeuvrability, and especially in landing characteristics. It requires changes in its armament, and urgent fixing of the engine.

Other weaknesses of the La-7 were that, compared to the La-5, its guns were less accessible for loading, and, like the La-5, its firepower was considered inadequate against the strongly-built and well-armoured Fw 190s. The La-7's cannons were often unable to bring them down even at close range.

Another problem cropped up in October 1944, when six aircraft and four pilots were lost; there was a lack of density in the metal used for the wing spars. After grounding the La-7s, this was resolved and the La-7s returned to action.

Unlike the La-5, the La-7 did not retire at the end of the Second World War, but continued in service with Soviet combat units until 1947. It was the last mainly wooden fighter in Soviet service.

Combat Tactics

One of the problems facing the La-7 was finding German aircraft to engage in combat. As the war on the Eastern Front ground on into 1945, the Luftwaffe was increasingly nowhere to be seen. Its fighter units, including the majority of its Bf 109s, had been withdrawn to Germany to counter the Anglo-American strategic bombing campaign. The remaining units, mostly ground attack Fw 190s, were frequently grounded due to a crippling lack of fuel and parts, as the German supply system began to break down under relentless Allied pressure.

A formation that was used to try to find the increasingly elusive Luftwaffe was the 'front-line formation', whereby six La-7s flew in a staggered line, searching for Fw 190 fighter-bombers that might be flying at low altitudes against Soviet ground forces. This formation was also employed when the La-7s attacked German ground units.

Although the Fw 190 fighter-bombers had been able to outrun the La-5Fs and La-5FNs by diving down and using their methanol-water boost (MW 50) system, the La-7s were just fast enough to pursue and catch the Fw 190s. Once they had caught up with the Fw 190s, they could engage them in aerial combat, where the Focke-Wulfs were at a distinct disadvantage. Large numbers of Fw 190s on the Eastern Front were lost to La-7s in this way during the last year of the war. Now it was the turn of Germany to be engaged in a hopeless struggle to stop the enemy's relentless advance and to face superior fighters and pilots. The situation had come full circle.

Combat Use

Operation Bagration (The Destruction of Army Group Centre)

The La-7 first saw combat in June 1944, during Operation Bagration. The first unit to re-equip with the La-7 was the 63rd GvIAP, which had originally received the La-5 in late 1942 (at this time it was still the 169th IAP, as it was not re-designated as the 63rd

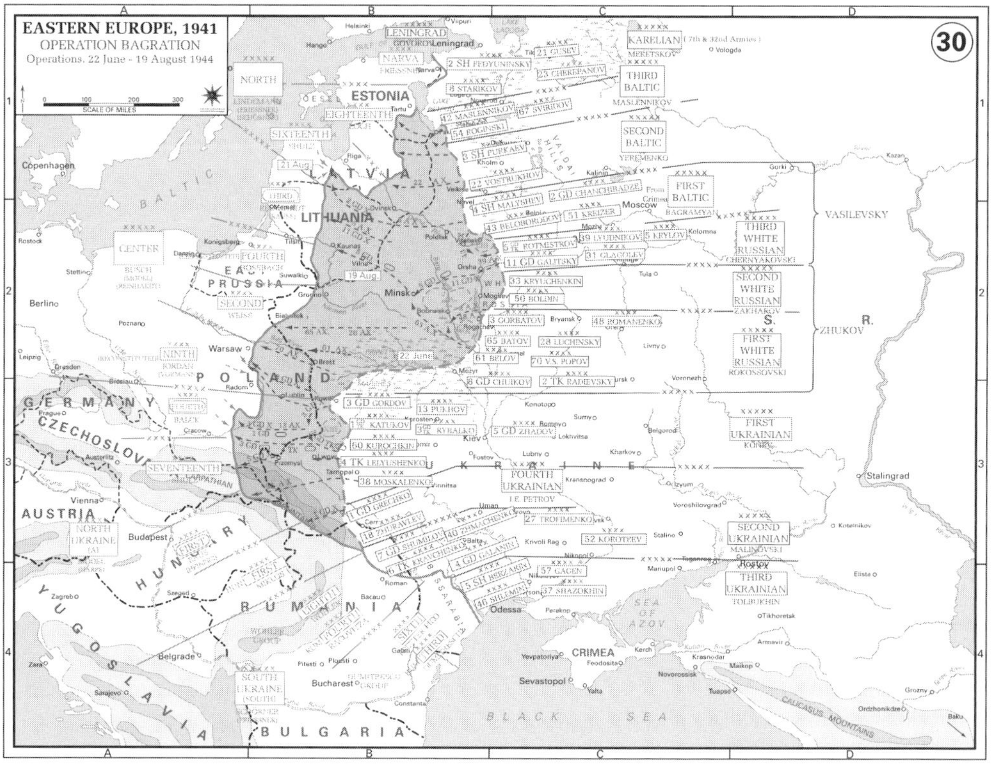

Operation Bagration. (*History Department of the United States Military Academy*)

GvIAP until 18 March 1943). The second *polk* to convert to the La-7 was the 156th IAP, which was sent back into combat in June 1944 after converting to the La-7.

The third *polk* to convert to the La-7 was the Guards unit, the 9th GvIAP, which had started the war as the 69th IAP, fighting with I-16s and MiG-3s over Odessa in the summer of 1941. It had flown Yak-1s and American Lend-Lease Bell P-39 Airacobras until converting to the La-7 in July 1944, then being held back in reserve until being recommitted to action in November 1944. From 13 January 1945, it was involved in the Soviet's huge Vistula to Oder Operation, supporting the troops of the 3rd Byelorussian Front.

This most famous of Guards units included such aces as twice Hero of the Soviet Union Sultan Ahmet Khan, a Crimean Tartar, who ended the war with thirty individual and nineteen shared victories, gained during 630 combat sorties and 150 combat engagements. Most of his victories were gained on the P-39 Airacobra, however, with only three coming on the La-7.

One of Ahmet Khan's victories on the La-7 occurred on 18 January 1945, during the Vistula to Oder Operation. Ahmet Khan's victim was a Fw 190, which he downed after the six La-7s he was leading met twenty Fw 190s. He quickly shot one down, and in total, five Fw 190s were shot down by his squadron during this engagement. During the afternoon of that same day, five La-7s under twice Hero of the Soviet Union Captain Pavel

Yakovlevich Golovachev met a force of fifteen Fw 190s, of which three were downed—two by Golovachev himself, and the other by his wingman, Chernik. By the end of the day, the 9th GvIAP had downed twenty-three aircraft in total. Golovachev would end the war with thirty individual victories and one shared victory, gained during 457 combat sorties and 125 enemy engagements. Twelve of his victories were gained on the La-7. Of the top Soviet aces, it appears that only the Soviet and Allied Ace of Aces, Ivan N. Kozhedub, with seventeen victories on the La-7, shot down more aircraft with the La-7.

One of the first units to receive the La-7 was the 176th GvIAP, which was also Kozhedub's unit. On 24 June, during Operation Bagration, the La-7s of the 176th GvIAP downed two Fw 190s over Baranovichi, Byelorussia, without loss to themselves. These may well have been the first victories gained by the La-7. On 7 July 1944, during a 'free hunt', aircraft of this same unit engaged two Bf 109s, downing one with no loss. The victorious pilot was Viktor Ilyich Aleksandryuk.

It was at about the time that VVS units were converting to the La-7 (i.e., in the middle and latter stages of 1944) that they started using the 'free hunt' technique, whereby they would specifically search out German aircraft and attack them suddenly out of clouds or the sun but not engage them in long combats. This represented a shift from earlier in the war, when the VVS fighters were primarily assigned as escorts to protect bombers and Shturmoviks supporting ground troops and was a further indication of the reduced presence of the Luftwaffe (for the bombers and Shturmoviks no longer needed such close protection). This 'free hunt' technique mirrored that which was long used by the Luftwaffe.

The 63rd GvIAP gained fifty-five victories during the period from 23 August 1944 to the middle of October 1944 flying from airfields in Lithuania, losing only four aircraft and three pilots. These victories were gained in the course of 116 combat missions, during which they engaged the enemy forty-seven times. Of these victories, fifty-two were over Fw 190s and only three over Bf 109s, demonstrating how the Fw 190 had become by far the predominant German fighter on the Eastern Front. Although these victory tallies may well have been inflated, there is no doubt that the La-7 was more than the equal of the German fighters they faced.

Berlin Strategic Offensive Operation (Battle of Berlin)

Despite the La-7's success as a free-hunting fighter, the lack of aerial targets in the last stages of the Great Patriotic War forced it into action as a fighter-bomber. During the Battle of Berlin, La-7s from just one regiment, the 2nd GvIAP, claimed 358 soldiers, 333 unarmoured vehicles, thirty-seven transport vehicles, twenty-two buildings, five railway engines, and four tanks. This was accomplished in 401 ground support sorties between 16 and 30 April 1945.

Appropriately enough, the last fighter victory of the Great Patriotic War belonged to a La-7, flown by Lieutenant A. A. Galich, on 8 May 1945.

As the La-7 was considered an elite aircraft, a disproportionate number of La-7 units were elite, Guards units. Of the twenty-six polks equipped with the La-7 during the Second World War, eighteen were Guards polks. It is also interesting to note that the fighter inspector pilots were mostly equipped with La-7s by the end of the war.

The Berlin Strategic Offensive Operation (Berlin Operation or Battle of Berlin). (*Wikimedia*)

Manchurian Strategic Offensive

La-5Fs, La-5FNs, and La-7s were used in the Manchurian Strategic Offensive, the last major operation of the Second World War, which began on 9 August 1945. Even the LaGG-3 saw service during this operation. Lavochkin fighters were flown by the regiments of the 9th VA of the 1st Far Eastern Front (remember that with the Red Army, 'Front' also referred to an Army Group, not a location), the 10th VA of the 2nd Far Eastern Front, and the 12th VA of the Trans-Baikal Front. Not a single La-5 or La-7 was lost to the enemy in aerial action; only one La-5FN and three La-7s were downed by Japanese flak.

Naval Service

The AVMF used only 198 La-7s. One of the few units to receive it was the 4th GvIAP of the Red Banner (Baltic) Fleet (KBF). It received its twenty La-7s on 25 September 1944 in a ceremony that was attended by Semyon Lavochkin himself. The *polk* was mainly used to escort ship convoys and transport aircraft and had little chance to engage the Germans in air combat. It was also used for escorting ground attack and bomber aircraft operating against the heavily defended cities of the Baltic Coast, such as Pillau and Königsberg. By the end of the Great Patriotic War, the unit had shot down only three German aircraft for no loss of their own. The paucity of their victory total is another indication of just how depleted the Luftwaffe had become on the Eastern Front.

The 17th IAP of the Pacific Ocean Fleet was also equipped with the La-7, almost certainly operating in the Manchurian Strategic Offensive Operation.

La-7TK

This version of the La-7 was created to provide a high-altitude fighter for the PVO units to combat high-flying German reconnaissance aircraft overflying Moscow. In order to improve its high-altitude performance, a La-7 was fitted with two TK-3 turbo-superchargers (designed by S. Treskin) and an M-82FNV (ASh-82FNV).

This version was fitted with the earlier propeller used on the La-5, the VISh-105V, which featured a Hucks starter dog. The performance at a height of 26,240 feet (8,000 m) was 420 mph (676 kph), and although certainly adequate, by 1944, there was no longer a need for high-altitude fighters as the danger of high-altitude German reconnaissance aircraft flying over Moscow was now over. Nonetheless, ten La-7TKs were built, equipped with one ShVAK 20-mm cannon on the port side of the engine cowling; these were used by the Moscow PVO in 1944. The service ceiling for the La-7TK was 38,713 feet (11,400 m).

La-7UTI

As with the La-5, it was felt that a two-seater trainer variant of the La-7 was needed. This led to the two-seater La-7UTI. Development started in late 1944. An extra seat and a canopy over it were added, the starboard cannon was removed, the armour behind the original pilot's seat and the armoured windscreen were removed, and the tailwheel was fixed. Flight tests started in August 1945 and showed that the aircraft's stability had been adversely affected by a change in the centre of gravity. Due to this, the aircraft was not considered suitable for production, and La-7 pilots continued to train on other aircraft, including La-5UTIs and Yak-7Vs. In April 1946, the oil cooler was moved from under the wing to under the cowling, the position in which it had been on the La-5, although the cooler was now larger. This helped to solve the centre of gravity problem.

Although the La-5UTI was produced in only very small numbers—twenty-eight in all—the La-7UTI was produced in much larger numbers, albeit after the war—some 584. Lavochkin's internal designation for this version was the *tip* 46. It is possible that single-seater La-7s were converted into the two-seater La-7UTIs, as was definitely the case with the La-5UTI.

La-7UTI, possibly the prototype. (*Viktor Kulikov's collection*)

The prototype La-7UTI at the factory airfield in 1946. Notice that the under-fuselage radiator has not been moved to under the cowling, where it was located on most production La-7UTIs. (*Viktor Kulikov's collection*)

La-7—Experimental Versions

La-7 M-71

As with the La-5, the temperamental but powerful M-71 engine was fitted to the La-7 to improve its performance, in this case with a rating of 2,017 hp (one source mentions 2,200 hp) compared to the 1,850 hp of the M-82FN (ASh-82FN). A distinguishing feature of this aircraft was that it had a thicker cowling lip than the M-82FN-equipped La-7s. The aircraft showed no significant performance gain, and as with the La-5 M-71, the M-71 powerplant proved to be an unreliable engine that never went into large-scale production, precluding its use on production La-7s.

La-7 M-83

Like the M-71, the M-83 (ASh-83) at 1,900 hp was a more powerful engine than the standard M-82FN (ASh-82FN) with its 1,850 hp at take-off. Yet unfortunately, like the M-71, it never went into production, so despite an impressive top speed of 450.5 mph (725 kph) at 24,272 feet (7,400 m), this version of the La-7 remained a one-off aircraft. It was fitted with two Nudelman-Suranov NS-23 23-mm cannons. Factory testing continued until 12 September 1945.

La-7R

In an attempt to dramatically improve the top speed of the La-7, this version had a small rocket engine fitted in its tail, under the modified tail assembly, the 'R' standing for *Reaktivonniy* ('Reaction' or 'Rocket-powered'). The engine fitted was the RD-1 engine, designed by Valentin Petrovich Glushko (1908–89). A mixture of kerosene and nitric acid powered the rocket engine, the kerosene serving as the fuel, and the nitric acid serving as the oxidant. The rocket was limited to 661 lb of thrust (330 kg) and only two to three minutes of use. With the rocket engine turned on, the La-7 was able to reach 460 mph (742 kph), but this was considered disappointing, despite its being much faster than a normal La-7.

The La-7R. Notice the outlet under the tail, and how the latter has been enlarged from a standard La-7's tail. (*Viktor Kulikov's collection*)

A revised La-7R was built with a larger fin and a revised fuel system. This aircraft was flown to a top speed of 499 mph (805 kph) and had a service ceiling of 42,640 feet (13,000 m). Even though this top speed neared and even surpassed some of the early jets, the extra weight of the rocket engine detracted from the overall performance, and the run time of two to three minutes was inadequate for combat use. No production ensued.

La-7S/La-7PPVRD

Underwing pulsejets were fitted to a La-7, which became the La-7S. Similar to those used on the German V-1 'buzz-bomb', the pulsejets were designed by the engineer Mikhail M. Bondaryukov and referred to as the PVRD-430. Pulsejets designed by M. M. Bondaryukov had earlier been unsuccessfully tested on a LaGG-3.

Another La-7 was equipped with D-12 pulsejets and referred to as the La-7PPVRD. As with the La-7R, the pulsejets increased speed for a short period of time, but otherwise degraded performance, so these variants were not pursued. Vibration while the jet engines were running was also a problem.

La-7L

In 1944, a La-7 was tested with a laminar flow wing, evidently with a single spar (the normal wing used on Lavochkin fighters featured twin spars, whether wooden or metal). This version was designated as the La-7L. Although the actual full-sized aircraft was tested in the huge T-101 wind tunnel at the TsAGI, it was never flown. The flight tests were cancelled in February 1945, probably due to developments that led to the La-9, which featured a similar wing.

'120'

This experimental variant of the La-7 was in the line of development that led to the La-9, a post-war Lavochkin fighter that lies outside the scope of this work.

La-7 in Detail

General Description

The La-7 was a mainly wooden, low-wing cantilever monoplane with a fully retractable main landing gear and a retractable tailwheel. The pilot sat in a fully enclosed cockpit, with a cut-down rear fuselage and an all-around vision cockpit canopy, very similar to that used on most of the La-5Fs and all of the La-5FNs. The wing spars were of metal construction. The La-7 was, in construction terms, very similar to a late, metal-sparred La-5FN.

Fuselage

Like the LaGG-3s and La-5s, the oval-section fuselage was of mainly wooden construction, but with the front half covered more completely with aluminium alloy plates, in addition to the dural engine cowling. The engine itself was fixed by a tubular steel alloy framework to another metal framework, the cannon platform, which was attached to the wooden fuselage just in front of the cockpit.

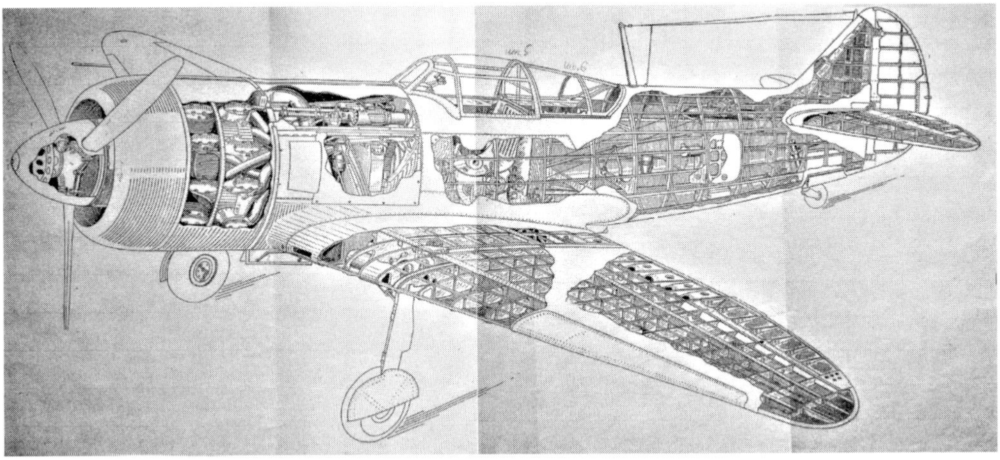

La-7 cutaway. (*La-7 Technical Manual*)

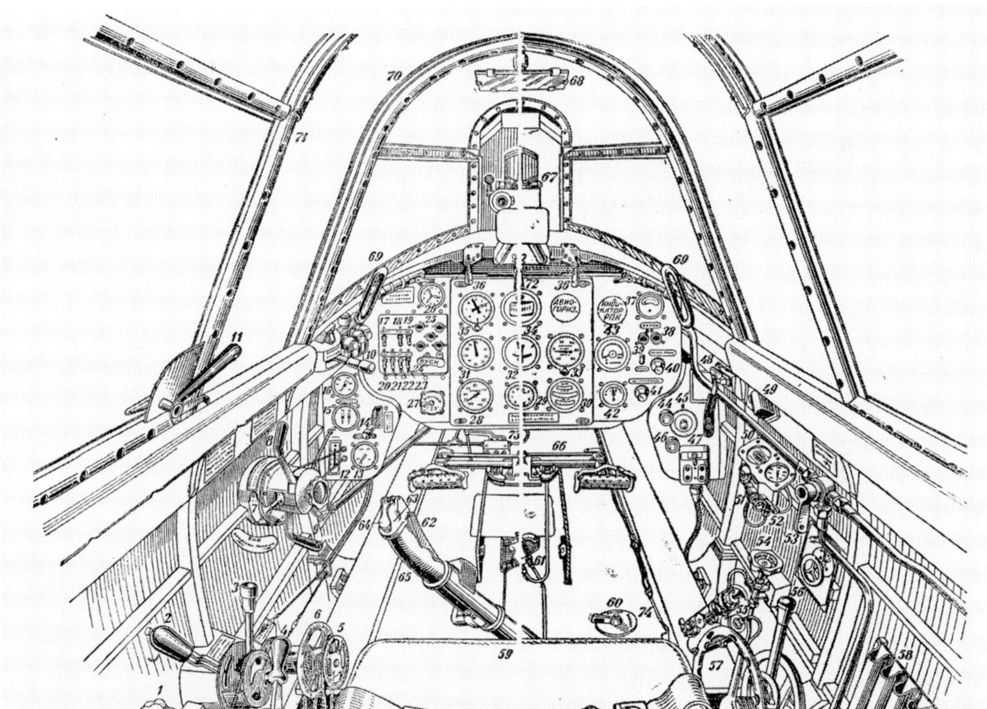

Фиг. 145. Кабина самолета Ла-7.

1—вентиль баллона сжатого воздуха; *2*—рычаг двухскоростной передачи к нагнетателю; *3*—рычаг совка маслорадиатора; *4*—рычаг механизма сбрасывания бомб; *5*—штурвал триммера руля направления; *6*—штурвал триммера руля высоты; *7*—ручка управления стопкраном; *8*—рычаг газа; *9*—рычаг управления шагом винта; *10*—кран управления закрылками; *11* — замок фонаря; *12*—указатель положения закрылков; *13*—манометр гидросистемы; *14*—кран управления шасси; *15*—манометр тормозов; *16*—манометр сжатого воздуха; *17*—тумблер включения фары; *18*—тумблер включения подогрева трубки Пито; *19*—тумблер включения сигнализации шасси; *20*—тумблер включения лампы УФО; *21*—тумблер включения радио; *22*—тумблер АНО; *23*—тумблер включения аккумулятора; *24*—пусковые кнопки; *25*—лампочки сигнализации положения шасси и хвостового колеса; *26*—часы АВР; *27*—переключатель магнето; *28*—мановакуумметр; *29*—тахометр ТЭ-22; *30*—трехстрелочный индикатор; *31*—указатель скорости УС-800; *32*—указатель поворота; *33* — вариометр ВР-30; *34* — компас КИ-11; *35*—высотомер двухстрелочный; *36*—ручка пневматической перезарядки; *37*—вольтамперметр; *38*—лампы сигнализации сброса бомб; *39*—тумблер включения бензиномера; *40*—реостат подсвета кабины; *41*—реостат прицела и компаса; *42*—термопара ТЦТ-9; *43*—бензиномер; *44*—ручка настройки; *45*—шкала настройки; *46*—ручка настройки (на волну); *47*—щиток рации; *48*—аварийный сбрасыватель фонаря; *49*—лампа УФО освещения кабины; *50*—кислородный прибор; *51*—бортовой вентиль кислородного баллона; *52* — тройник; *53* — кран нейтрального газа; *54*—кран аварийного выпуска шасси; *55*—пусковой насос ПН-1; *56*—рычаг управления передними жалюзи; *57*—штурвал управления боковыми створками капота; *58*—патронташ для ракет; *59*—сиденье пилота; *60*—ручка управления перекрывным бензокраном; *61*—клапан ПУ-6; *62*—рычаг управления тормозами; *63*—кнопка управления огнем пушек; *64*—предохранитель кнопки 63; *65*—ручка пилота; *66*—педали ножного управления; *67*—прицел ПБП-А; *68*—зеркало; *69*—ручка ручной перезарядки с предохранителем; *70*—козырек; *71*—створка фонаря; *72*—ручка постановки пушек на предохранитель; *73*—диференциал тормозов; *74*—трос аварийного выпуска шасси.

Примечание. На самолетах последних серий управление рацией *47* перенесено на левую сторону кабины на борт фюзеляжа.

La-7 instrument panel. (*La-7 Technical Manual*)

The wooden structure was similar to that used on the LaGG-3 and the La-5s, and comparisons between structural drawings of the La-5FN and the La-7 show the wooden part of the fuselages to have been almost identical. The La-7 featured the cut-down rear fuselage and all-around vision cockpit canopy introduced on the La-5F, and as with these La-5Fs and the La-5FNs, the La-7 also featured a piece of armour glass behind the seat to protect the pilot while preserving rearward visibility. The canopy was also jettisonable, as with the later La-5FNs. Like the earlier Lavochkin fighters, the wooden fin was constructed integrally with the rest of the fuselage.

Wings

The wings were of composite-construction with two metal spars—a feature that was introduced on the last La-5FNs—with steel alloy caps and dural webs. The metal spars helped to make the La-7 lighter than earlier, wooden-sparred La-5s. As with the La-5FNs, the wing roots were covered in metal to protect them from wear, with the metal covering being more extensive than that for the La-5FNs. As with earlier Lavochkin fighters, the wings were covered with plywood, which was then covered in a putty-impregnated fabric, leaving a smooth surface without panel lines.

Like the La-5, the outer leading edge of the wings was equipped with metal slats, which again necessitated that the pitot tube was mounted to the lower surface of the starboard wing. It appears that, like most of the La-5s, the La-7 was equipped with fixed trim tabs on both ailerons, and these trim tabs were bendable on the ground.

Tailplanes

As with the La-5 and LaGG-3, the fixed portions of the La-7's tail surfaces were constructed from wood. The moveable portions, such as the rudder and the elevators, were of aluminium alloy structure (dural), covered with fabric. The rudder and the port elevator had trim tabs, while the starboard elevator did not.

Engine

The La-7 utilised the same engine as the La-5FN, the M-82FN (ASh-82FN). The cowling was cleaned up aerodynamically, with the intake for the supercharger moved from the top of the cowling to the wing roots and the oil cooler moved from under the cowling to under the mid-fuselage. The propeller used was the VISh-105V-4, which was similar to the VISh-105V utilised on the La-5s, except that it did not have the Hucks starter dog on the front of the spinner, which made it more streamlined.

One difference between the La-5's engine installation and the La-7's was that the La-7 had seven exhausts per side, as opposed to the La-5's five. The cowling flaps were also smaller on the La-7 to improve streamlining.

The dural cowling panels were different on the La-7s compared to the La-5s, with the La-7's panels being a single sheet on both sides (the La-5 had two sheets on both sides), hinged at the very top, there being no intake on top of the cowling.

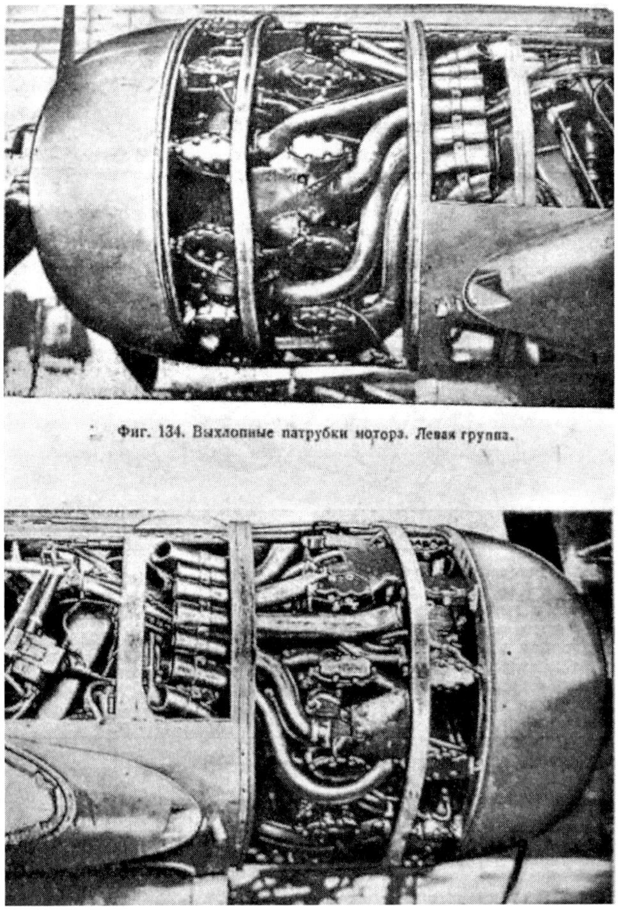

La-7 engine exhausts from both sides. (*La-7 Technical Manual*)

Fuel System

The La-7 had three fuel tanks, with one mounted in the fuselage centre section and two in the wings. These fuel tanks were self-sealing, consisting of aluminium alloy covered by a self-sealing layer, which was made up of five layers of rubber and fabric. The fuel tanks were fed neutral gases from the engine, which had been filtered and cooled before being flowed into the fuel tanks. These gases displaced the flammable mixture of air and petrol vapour as the fuel tanks emptied through use, thus greatly lowering the chance of fire.

Controls

The traditional 'spade-grip' control column that had characterised earlier Lavochkin and many other Soviet aircraft was replaced with a single handle joystick, like those fitted to German fighters, such as the Bf 109 and the Fw 190. This made it easier to transmit control changes from the stick to the control surfaces, enhancing responsiveness.

The control surfaces themselves consisted of the rudder, ailerons, flaps, and elevators. The rudder was controlled by rudder pedals. The ailerons and elevators were controlled by the control column, with sideways movements changing the attitude of the ailerons, and backward and forward motions of the control column changing the position of the elevators. The starboard elevator did not have a trim tab, although the rudder and port elevator did.

Landing Gear

The landing gears were of conventional tailwheel type, with fully retracting main landing gear and a fully retractable tailwheel. The main landing gear retracted inwards, while the tailwheel retracted backwards. Both the main landing gear and tailwheel were fully covered by doors, the main landing gear also having small doors hinged to the wings that completely covered the wheels; these were only partially covered in the LaGG-3s and La-5s. The main wheels were 650 × 200 mm in size. Unlike the La-5s, the tailwheels do not appear to have ever been locked in the 'down' position for the Soviet La-7 fighters (as opposed to the La-7UTI, which did have a fixed tailwheel), probably due to the increased reliability of the retraction mechanism.

Radio Equipment

Similarly to the all-around-vision La-5s, the wooden radio mast for the La-7 was mounted behind the cockpit at an angle, but it was smaller and thinner as part of the overall effort to make the La-7 more streamlined than the La-5. All La-7s were equipped with receiver/transmitter radios. The antenna wires on the La-7 were similar to those on the high-back La-5s, with two lines leading from the tail post to near the antenna mast where they combined, and from here, another line attached to the fuselage. The La-7 was evidently equipped with the RSI-4 radio, and by this time, all of the La-7s would have had radios with both receiving and transmitting capabilities.

Fixed Armament

All production La-7s were to be armed with three synchronised Berezin B-20 20-mm cannons (which were lighter than the ShVAKs) mounted in the top part of the cowling. However, this cannon was not considered reliable enough for installation when the La-7 first went into production, so most wartime La-7s had the same fixed armament as the La-5, i.e., two synchronised ShVAK SP-20 20-mm cannons mounted in the top part of the cowling. Some La-7s did have the three B-20 20-mm cannons fitted and did see some limited action very late in the Great Patriotic War. It was a more powerful weapon than the two ShVAK 20-mm cannons fitted to earlier La-7s, though it was not as reliable. Many of the La-7s used post-war did have the three B-20 20-mm cannons.

The guns were aimed using a PBP-1B reflector-collimating gunsight, which had been standard on the La-5FN. The gunsight had two settings, one for a target speed of 124 mph (200 kph) and another for 186 mph (300 kph).

Disposable Armament

As with the La-5, small bombs could be carried underneath the wings to enable the La-7 to operate as a fighter-bomber. The La-7 could carry up to two 220-lb (100-kg) bombs, one under each wing, for a maximum load of 441 lb (200 kg). As with the La-5 and unlike the LaGG-3, the La-7 did not carry rockets of any sort.

Although not designed as a fighter-bomber, some La-7s were used in this role late in the war due to the absence of Luftwaffe aircraft to engage, and while the air war had dissipated, there was still a great deal of heavy ground fighting, which the La-7 could support with its bombs and cannons.

Colour and Markings

Most production La-7s were equipped with the standard fighter camouflage of AMT-11 Grey-Blue and AMT-12 Dark Grey topside over AMT-7 Blue underside. As with the La-5F and La-5FN, they featured logos on the engine cowling and the fin. This logo consisted of a stylised Cyrillic 'La-7' in red on a yellow disc. Those aircraft that did not carry this logo had either not had it painted on at the factory or it had been painted out in the field. Most La-7s had white borts outlined with a thin blue line.

Conclusion

Over the course of four years, the Lavochkin fighters evolved from the mediocre LaGG-3 to the superb La-7, one of the best piston-engined fighters of any combatant in production at the end of the war. Although not a particularly good fighter, the LaGG-3 was available in quantity early in the Great Patriotic War when better aircraft such as the Yakovlev fighters were lacking. As such, it made an important contribution to the war effort. The radial-engined La-5 was one of the first Soviet fighters (along with the Yak-7 and Yak-9) that enabled the VVS pilots to fight the German fighters on something approaching equal terms, while the La-7 gave the Soviets a fighter that was superior at low altitudes to all German fighters. Although not produced in as great a number as the Yakovlev fighters, the Lavochkin fighters were a vital part of the Soviet Union's successful effort to defeat the Germans.

Lavochkin Fighter Specifications

One note about the specification tables in this book in general—the maximum horsepower of the engine is not necessarily the take-off power, although it often is. As listed in the following tables it is the maximum output of the engine at its most highly rated altitude, and usually includes any type of boosting, if applicable. This is different from what is usually listed in other books; for example, the 'maximum' power of the M-105PF is often listed as 1,180 or 1,210 hp, instead of the 1,260 hp listed in my tables. Regarding the maximum ratings for these engines, I have gone with the figures of Vladimir Kotelnikov (Kotel'nikov) as laid out in his authoritative book on Soviet-built piston engines, *Russian Piston Aero Engines* (see Bibliography).

Another note is that a 'N/A' will be used where the field is not applicable; for example, when an aircraft did not have any disposable armament, 'N/A' will be used. If the information is just not available—for example, I am unable to find the maximum weight for an aircraft—a '-' will be used.

N.B. Metric measurements are in parentheses						
Type	LaGG-3 Series 1	LaGG-3 Series 4	LaGG-3 Series 8	LaGG-3 Series 11	LaGG-3 Series 29	LaGG-3 Series 34 (LaGG-3-37)
Year	1941	1941	1942	1942	1942	1942
Engine	M-105P	M-105PA	M-105PA	M-105PA	M-105PF	M-105PF
Max. Power (Horsepower)	1,100	1,100	1,100	1,100	1,260	1,260
Fixed Armament	2 × ShKAS 7.62-mm, 3 × UBS 12.7-mm machine guns	2 × ShKAS 7.62-mm, 1 × UBS 12.7-mm machine guns, 1 × ShVAK MP-20 20-mm cannon	1 × UBS 12.7-mm machine gun, 1 × ShVAK MP-20 20-mm cannon	1 × UBS 12.7-mm machine gun, 1 × ShVAK MP-20 20-mm cannon	1 × UBS 12.7-mm machine gun, 1 × ShVAK MP-20 20-mm cannon	1 × UBS 12.7-mm machine gun, 1 × NS-37 37-mm cannon
Disposable Armament	N/A	6 × RS-82 Rockets?	6 × RS-82 Rockets?	6 × RS-82 or RS-132 Rockets, 2 × 110 lb (50 kg) bombs	6 × RS-82 or RS-132 Rockets, 2 × 110 lb (50 kg) bombs?	6 × RS-82 or RS-132 Rockets
Length—feet (m)	28.9 (8.81)	28.9 (8.81)	28.9 (8.81)	28.9 (8.81)	28.9 (8.81)	29.20 (8.9)
Wingspan—feet (m)	32.15 (9.8)	32.15 (9.8)	32.15 (9.8)	32.15 (9.8)	32.15 (9.8)	32.15 (9.8)
Weight (Empty)—lb (kg)	5,908 (2,680)	5,754 (2,610)	-	5,644 (2,560)	-	5,842 (2,650)
Weight (Loaded)—lb (kg)	7,377 (3,346)	7,231 (3,280)	-	6,790 (3,080)	-	7,414 (3,363)
Max. Speed at Sea Level—mph (kph)	309 (498)	302 (486)	295 (474)	304 (490)	315 (507)	311 (501)
Top Speed—mph (kph)	357 (575)	341 (549)	341 (549)	343 (552)	351 (566)	348 (560)
Range—miles (km)	684 (1,100)	541 (870)	-	472 (760)	-	379 (610)
Service Ceiling—feet (m)	31,168 (9,500)	31,168 (9,500)	-	30,840 (9,400)		29,500 (9,000)
Turn Time (sec)	-	-	25	25.2	22	22

LaGG-3 Series 35	LaGG-3 Series 66	LaGG-3 M-82 (La-5 prototype)	La-5	La-5F	La-5FN	La-7
1942	1943	1942	1942	1943	1943	1944
M-105PF	M-105PF	M-82	M-82	M-82F	M-82FN	M-82FN
1,260	1,260	1,700	1,700	1,700	1,850	1,850
1 × UBS 12.7-mm machine gun, 1 × ShVAK MP-20 20-mm cannon	1 × UBS 12.7-mm machine gun, 1 × ShVAK MP-20 20-mm cannon	2 × ShVAK SP-20 20-mm cannons	2 × ShVAK SP-20 20-mm cannons	2 × ShVAK SP-20 20-mm cannons	2 × ShVAK SP-20 20-mm cannons	2 × ShVAK SP-20 20-mm cannons (from 1945, 3 × Berezin B-20 20-mm cannons)
6 × RS-82 or RS-132 Rockets, 2 × 110 lb (50 kg) bombs	6 × RS-82 or RS-132 Rockets, 2 × 110 lb (50 kg) bombs	N/A	2 × 110 lb (50 kg) bombs	2 × 110 lb (50 kg) bombs	2 × 110 lb (50 kg) bombs	2 × 110 lb (50 kg) bombs
28.9 (8.81)	28.9 (8.81)	28.58 (8.71)	28.54 (8.7)	28.44 (8.67)	28.44 (8.67)	29.21 (8.9)
32.15 (9.8)	32.15 (9.8)	32.15 (9.8)	31.5 (9.6)	31.5 (9.6)	32.15 (9.8)	32.15 (9.8)
5,357 (2,430)	5,467 (2,480)	-	-	-	-	-
6,967 (3,160)	6,592 (2,990)	7,451 (3,380)	7,407 (3,360)	7,098 (3,220)	7,407 (3,360)	7,496 lb (3,400)
310 (499)	337 (542)	320 (515)	316 (509)	346 (557)	362 (583)	381 (613)
352 (566)	367 (591)	373 (600)	360 (580)	373 (600)	394 (634)	409 (658)
565 (910)	555 (893)	-	407 (665)	-	360 (580)	413 (665)
32,808 (10,000)	32,152 (9,800)	-	31,000 (9,500)	31,250 (9,550)	31,168 (9,501) (one source has 35,000 feet (10,688))	37,000 (11,278)
21.9	22.3	25	22.6	20	19	20.5

4
Mikoyan-Gurevich Fighters

This OKB, which came to fame after the war with its jet fighters, was created in the Second World War from part of the Polikarpov OKB. Its first aircraft was the I-200 fighter, which was developed into the MiG-1 and MiG-3 fighters.

I-200 (*Izdeliye* 61, 'Kh')

When in January 1939, the Defence Commissariat issued its specification for modern fighters to re-equip the VVS, it also issued a specific requirement for a high-altitude fighter. The Polikarpov OKB responded with the I-200, although development was continued by what would become the new Mikoyan-Gurevich OKB. The I-200 was the progenitor of the MiG-1 and the MiG-3. As with the OKB of Lavochkin, Gorbunov, and Gudkov (LaGG), this was the very first design of this new OKB (MiG). It would not be their last design, and the name of the OKB, 'MiG', would eventually become synonymous with Soviet fighters after the Second World War.

At the time of the initial development of the I-200 (*Izdeliye* 61 ('Object 61') or the 'Kh' (*X* in Cyrillic)), Nikolaiy Polikarpov was given responsibility for the fighter's design, with Artyom (often transliterated as 'Artem') Mikoyan and Mikhail Iosifovich Gurevich (1893–1976) being assistant aircraft designers assigned to his team. Polikarpov soon fell out of favour with Stalin (for reasons which are discussed further on in the Polikarpov section), so while Polikarpov was visiting aircraft factories in Germany, his OKB was stripped of most its personnel, to be assigned to the new OKO (OKO-1, in charge of Z.1 in Moscow, later OKB-155), headed by Mikoyan and Gurevich; they continued the development of the I-200 under their new design bureau, which would become famously known by the initials of its chief designers, 'Mikoyan-Gurevich', or 'MiG'.

There is some controversy regarding the design of the I-200, given that Polikarpov had been involved with the initial design. It is unclear how much of what became the actual aircraft Polikarpov was responsible for as opposed to the team of Mikoyan and Gurevich, who took over the design of the aircraft from Polikarpov when he fell out

Right: Artyom Ivanovich Mikoyan (after the Second World War). (*Viktor Kulikov's collection*)

Below: I-200 no. 1, the first prototype of the MiG-1, in 1940. (*Viktor Kulikov's collection*)

of official favour. Given the passage of time, it is unlikely that this controversy will ever be completely resolved.

Whoever was mainly responsible for the design, the I-200 was a streamlined, modern-looking cantilever monoplane, with all three landing gear being fully retractable. The pilot sat back rather far behind the large inline Mikulin AM-35A engine, this position giving the MiG-1 somewhat the appearance of a racing aeroplane (not inappropriate, given its fast top speed). This position did not give the pilot a good view for take-off and landing, however. The AM-35A engine was used as the intended Mikulin AM-37 engine was not available, and in the event, it never went into production. The construction of the aircraft was mixed, with a steel tube forward fuselage covered in metal panels and a metal centre-section with metal inner wing panels, connected to a semi-monocoque wooden rear fuselage and wooden outer wing panels. The landing gear, including the tailwheel, was completely enclosed by doors, with the main landing gear doors being one piece, the part covering the outer wheels hinged to the rest. The cockpit canopy swung open to the starboard side, mounted on hinges, instead of sliding back.

One innovation of the I-200 was its ease of assembly. Drawing upon his experience as a production technician, Artyom Mikoyan designed the I-200 to be of modular design, with subassemblies that could be constructed at different locations, then easily assembled to complete the aircraft. The aircraft also featured moulded and cast parts that eased production. The modular design not only aided in production but in maintenance and repair in the field. Indeed, whole MiG-3s would later be built with parts from different aircraft. This ease of repair and maintenance kept the MiG-3 in service long after production had ended in 1942, indeed almost to the end of the Second World War.

The first prototype of the I-200 (I-200 no. 1) flew for the initial time on 5 April 1940 at Khodynka in Moscow. The aircraft participated in the May Day parade on 1 May 1940, flown by *Zavod* 1's chief test pilot, Arkadiy N. Yekatov (who had flown the I-200 on its maiden flight). On 24 May 1940, the I-200 no. 1 achieved the impressive top speed of 403 mph (648.5 kph) at 22,638 feet (6,900 m). Yekatov would later die in a crash of an operational MiG-1 (as the I-200 had been redesignated) on 13 March 1941. Yekatov's aircraft crashed after the supercharger exploded due to a failure of the impeller blades. This accident led to the impeller blades being strengthened.

The second prototype (I-200 no. 2) differed from the first in having oil coolers on both sides of the cowling instead of just the port side. During its state acceptance trials, on 5 August 1940, the I-200 no. 2 reached a top speed of 405 mph (651 kph). The I-200 successfully completed its state trials in August 1940. Unlike the I-301 (LaGG-1/3) and the I-26 (Yak-1), the I-200 completed its state trials on its first attempt. The I-200 no. 3 had outer metal wings, perhaps to accommodate the cannon pods it was supposed to carry. Although the I-200 no. 1 had no armament, the no. 2 (at some point) and no. 3 prototypes were equipped with one UBS machine gun and two ShKAS machine guns in the upper cowling, as on the production MiG-1s (and MiG-3s).

Although it was very fast—faster than the best contemporaneous production fighters, such as the German Bf 109F-2 (379 mph (610 kph)) and the British Spitfire Mk Vb (370 mph (595 kph))—the I-200 was not without its issues. The AM-35A was still an immature and unreliable engine. The I-200 had stability issues, the pilot's visibility on the ground was poor (not surprising considering the pilot's aft position and the long nose), and the aircraft could enter into an irrecoverable spin from a stall, especially at high altitudes. The canopy's clear panels were not of the best quality and were hard to see through, and the side-opening canopy itself was difficult to open and could not be opened in flight (some test flights were conducted without the side-opening hood, in case the pilot had to bail out). The handling was difficult due to the stability issues.

MiG-1

Despite the number of deficiencies noted in the I-200, so anxious were the Soviets to introduce modern fighters into their inventory that the I-200, as the 'MiG-1', was ordered into production at *Zavod* 1 in Moscow on 31 May 1940 (even before the completion of its state acceptance trials), with the deficiencies to be worked out during production. This policy, born of desperation and anticipation of war sooner rather than later with Nazi Germany, was also followed with the LaGG-3 and Yak-1 fighters. Some 100 MiG-1s were produced before production changed to the improved MiG-3.

Improvements were made to the MiG-1 during its short production run. The cockpit canopy was changed from a side-opening hood to a hood that slid back on rails, rubber sheaths were added to the fuel tanks to make them self-sealing, and underwing racks were added to enable the aircraft to carry a 220-lb (100-kg) FAB-100 bomb under each wing.

The first MiG-1s were introduced into service with the 41st IAP, which was designated as the operational trials unit on 3 December 1940, and whose pilots trained on the new aircraft at Kacha, in the Crimea. By 22 February 1941, eighty-nine of the 100 MiG-1s had been issued to the 89th IAP at Kaunas (Kovno), in Lithuania, and to the 41st IAP based at Bialystok, in Soviet-occupied Poland. By 1 June 1941, seventy-seven MiG-1s were available to the VVS, with fifty-five being operational. In addition, eight were assigned to the AVMF.

As they were serving with front-line units in the western military districts, only a few MiG-1s survived the initial onslaught of the German invasion, and little or nothing remains of their combat record. The few that survived served in the same units with their development and successor, the MiG-3. One MiG-1, however, improbably survived as late as 1944, as the VVS records this particular aircraft as being withdrawn that year. How this remarkable aircraft survived this long, and in what capacity, is not recorded.

MiG-1 Variants

I-200 NO. *2* WITH *AM-37*

Although the I-200 no. 1 was never fitted with its intended AM-37, the second prototype, the I-200 no. 2, was. The I-200 no. 2 was converted by 8 December 1940 to fly with this experimental engine. It was expected that the engine would give 200 hp more than the standard AM-35A. The armament was removed, and the propeller was changed to the VISh-61AP with broader chord blades. The first flight with the AM-37 took place on 6 January 1941, piloted by A. I. Zhukov. Testing showed that the engine ran roughly above 13,123 feet (4,000 m). On 7 May 1941, the I-200 no. 2 crashed due to improper fuel transfer by the pilot, I. T. Ivashchenko, and the aircraft was not rebuilt. In the event, the AM-37 engine never went into production as the Mikulin OKB was devoting its time towards the AM-38 engine, which powered the Il-2. However, the AM-37 was also tested on the MiG-3, redesignated as the MiG-7 (described further on).

ITP-201 (I-200 NO. 3)

This aircraft was an I-200 intended to carry one MP-3 23-mm cannon apiece in underwing pods, in addition to the two ShKAS machine guns mounted in the cowling. The UBS gun was omitted. The MP-3 cannon, designed by Y. G. Taubin and M. N. Baburin of OKB-16, had a rate of fire of 300 rpm, which was considered inadequate by the NII VVS. In response, Taubin and Baburin designed the MP-6, which had a rate of fire of 600 rpm. The I-200 no. 3 was equipped with the MP-6 cannons underneath its all-metal wings and two of the Taubin and Baburin designed AP 12.7-mm (50-calibre) machine guns in the cowling. Installation of the cannons caused flexing in the wings. On 1 December 1940, test pilot V. N. Gurskiy flew the modified I-200 no. 3 (or 'ITP-201') for the first time, but the aircraft had to force-land, damaging the ITP-201. Repair of the aircraft continued into February 1941, and in March 1941, tests began again, but it was apparent by now that the guns were inadequate and testing was stopped. Taubin was executed and Baburin died in a labour camp due to the failure of these guns, especially the MP-6, on which many high hopes had been placed, as it was expected to be the main armament for several aircraft (including the Il-2).

MiG-3

To correct or alleviate at least some of the MiG-1's issues, the MiG-3 was developed. The outward-opening canopy of the early MiG-1s was replaced by an easier-to-use sliding canopy (this was actually introduced from the 9th production MiG-1 and was made standard on all MiG-3s), with the canopy sliding backwards, which facilitated entry and egress for the pilot. In response to a new requirement that Soviet aircraft have a range of at least 621 miles (1,000 km), a fuel tank was added underneath the pilot. The engine was moved forward 3.94 inches (100 mm), to maintain the centre of gravity with the new fuselage fuel tank, a larger ventral water radiator was fitted, the wing dihedral was increased by 1 degree to improve stability, and the horizontal tailplanes were slightly increased in size, among other changes to the aircraft. These modifications were fully implemented on the fourth I-200 prototype (I-200 no. 4), which first flew in on 29 October 1940. It is not clear if this was implemented on the I-200 no. 4, but the ammunition for the ShKAS machine guns on production MiG-3s was increased to 750 rounds per gun.

Early MiG-3—note the cut-out for the tailwheel in the tailwheel doors. This is a radio-equipped MiG-3, as can be seen by the antenna mast in front of the cockpit. (*Viktor Kulikov's collection*)

The first MiG-3 was completed on 20 December 1940, and twenty production examples were delivered by the end of 1940, with full-scale production commencing in 1941 at Z.1. State acceptance tests by the NII VVS of two 1940 production aircraft between 27 January 1941 and 26 February 1941 revealed the MiG-3 (as it had been renamed on 9 December 1940) to be heavier than the MiG-1, with reduced manoeuvrability and a lower service ceiling, but with higher speeds at sea level and at altitude (at least with these earlier MiG-3s). It still had a high landing speed and a wide turning radius at low and medium altitudes due to its high wing-loading. The MiG-3s were initially sent to the 41st IAP in the Crimea, which was already using the MiG-1, for operational testing.

In the first four months of 1941 alone, fifty MiG-1s and 283 MiG-3s were delivered to the western military districts and to the Moscow district. In the western military districts, 917 of the 4,426 fighters were MiG fighters (eighty were not operational, as these aircraft were undergoing maintenance work), which amounted to nearly 21 per cent of the total number of fighters available in these districts. An additional 300 MiGs were deployed with PVO air defence units in the Leningrad and Moscow areas.

Despite the difficulties of transitioning to the fast MiG-3 from slower more tractable biplanes, such as the I-15bis and I-153, and the I-16 monoplane, it was apparently easier for pilots to transition to the MiG-3 than to the LaGG-3 and the Yak-1. The MiG-3 was finished to a higher standard than these aircraft (perhaps not surprising considering the status of Z.1 as the Soviet Union's premier aircraft manufacturing facility) and it did not suffer from the manufacturing defects these other aircraft did. For example, multiple defects were uncovered in the LaGG-3, and despite the LaGG-3 being found easier to fly than the MiG-3, the head of the VVS, General Pavel Zhigarev, proposed that some of the regiments slated for the LaGG-3 and the delayed Yak-1 instead be equipped with the MiG-3.

MiG-3 Variants

Unlike the Lavochkin and Yakovlev fighters, which were developed into many different variants, there was only one main production variant of the MiG-3, and it was designated simply as the 'MiG-3'.

MiG-3: Late Variant

During its relatively short production run, the MiG-3 was progressively changed and improved. This resulted in some notable differences between the early production MiG-3s and late production examples. The exhausts, for example, were different between the early and late MiG-3s, with a fairing in front of the first exhausts in the late MiG-3s. Not only were the exhausts changed, but the reduction gear ratio for the AM-35A engine was changed from .902 to .732, and the VISh-22Ye propeller changed to the AV-5L-123, which had a greater range of pitch angles. This change was affected in the second half of 1941.

The MiG-3s featured a larger tailwheel than the MiG-1, which required a cut-out on the tailwheel doors to accommodate the larger tyres on early MiG-3s. On the later MiG-3s, this was dealt with by bulged tailwheel doors.

One major difference between the early MiG-3s and the late MiG-3s was the provision of leading-edge slats on the wings. These slats improved the rather tricky handling of the MiG-3, including its poor stall characteristics. With the installation of the slats, the pitot tube was moved from the wing's leading edge to under the wing, as with slat-equipped Lavochkin fighters. The tips of the horizontal stabilisers were increased in chord length. Some late MiG-3s featured a piece of armour glass behind the windshield. It is hard to detect this in photographs, however, and it is unclear how many MiG-3s were so equipped.

The very last MiG-3s to be produced featured two ShVAK SP-20 20-mm cannons in place of the earlier machine gun-only armament. This includes the thirty constructed from components in 1942 by OKB-155 in Moscow. These last MiG-3s brought the total production to 3,172.

MiG-3s with Enhanced Armament

In combat, it soon became clear that the MiG-3's standard armament fit of two 7.62-mm machine guns and one 12.7-mm machine gun was inadequate against the tough, strongly-built German aircraft they faced. In an effort to improve the armament, some MiG-3s were fitted with two UBK 12.7-mm machine guns mounted in pods, one under each wing. These guns were unsynchronised as they were mounted outside the arc of the propeller. Although the firepower was greatly enhanced, these installations were not popular with pilots as they decreased the speed (by at least 12.4 mph (20 kph)) and manoeuvrability of the MiG-3 due to their weight and drag. Consequently, most of these aircraft had their pods removed in the field to return to the normal armament fit of the MiG-3, while some kept the pods but flew with reduced fuel to keep the weight down. A total of 821 aircraft of this type were reportedly constructed from September 1941. Yefim Gordon has these as being refits, not newly manufactured aircraft, although given the unpopularity of the pods with

This MiG-3 has been fitted with underwing RS-82 rockets for use in a ground attack mission. Although not especially suited to this role, in the desperate first year of the war, the MiG-3 found itself used for ground attack. (*Viktor Kulikov's collection*)

Mig-3 of HSU Alekseyev. (*Viktor Kulikov's collection*)

service units, this seems somewhat unlikely; perhaps they were a combination of production aircraft and refits. Another source has the 821 aircraft being produced from 20 February 1941 through 27 July 1941.

Some late MiG-3s had their two ShKAS machine guns replaced by a single UBS 12.7-mm machine gun for an armament of two UBS machine guns. Despite having fewer guns, this version had a greater weight of fire than the standard version fitted with the two ShKAS and one UBS machine guns.

Fifty late production MiG-3s were equipped with two ShVAK SP-20 20-mm cannons. These were apparently in addition to the AM-38-powered examples which received this armament (see below). With two cannons, this version had a much greater weight of fire than the standard machine gun-only MiG-3. Thirty of these MiG-3s were constructed at the OKB-155's facility in Moscow and were the last MiG-3s produced.

MiG-3 Factory-Modified with AM-38

The AM-35A engine was designed for high-altitude work and was not optimised for use at low altitudes. The AM-38, designed for the ground attack Il-2, on the other hand, was designed for use at low altitudes. As combat in the Great Patriotic War most often took place at lower altitudes, it was decided to fit an AM-38 to the MiG-3 airframe. The engine fitted had a take-off rating of 1,600 hp and was equipped with an AV-5L-110A propeller. This re-engined MiG-3 flew for the first time on 31 July 1941 piloted by Y. K. Stankevich. The testing of this aircraft continued for the next twelve days. Overall testing showed the aircraft to have good low-altitude characteristics, but the engine had a tendency to overheat in temperatures over 61 degrees Fahrenheit (16 degrees C), and this problem would need to be eliminated.

Another MiG-3 was modified at the factory to use an AM-38 engine. This aircraft differed from the first in having the bomb racks removed, redesigned exhaust fairings, and with the inert gas fire-suppression system installed. The first aircraft displayed a top speed at 11,155 feet (3,400 m) of 362 mph (582 kph) while the second had a top speed of 368 mph (592 kph) at the same altitude. The top speed at sea level was increased by 32 mph (52 kph) as compared to that of the MiG-3s tested during state acceptance trials. The second aircraft crashed on 5 October 1941 during a test flight, apparently shot down by an Axis aircraft, killing the test pilot N. P. Baulin.

Below 13,123 feet (4,000 m), it was felt that the AM-38-equipped MiG-3 could do combat with the Axis fighters, and its turn time was reduced to twenty-one seconds. However, as the AM-38 engine was desperately needed for the Il-2, it was not practical to produce the MiG-3 with this engine, although some MiG-3s were field-modified to fly with the AM-38 (see below).

MiG-3 Field-Modified with AM-38

When their AM-35A engines had worn out, around eighty MiG-3s were equipped with the AM-38 engine normally utilised by the Il-2. This was a sensible move as the AM-38 was basically the AM-35 adapted for low-altitude use and could be fitted to the MiG-3 airframe with minimal modifications to either the airframe or the engine. These AM-38s were salvaged from damaged, worn-out, or otherwise unserviceable

Il-2s. Not surprisingly, as the AM-38 was optimised for low-altitude performance, the speed at low altitudes was improved, although the top speed at higher altitudes and the service ceiling suffered. Some of these re-engined aircraft had the machine guns replaced with two ShVAK SP-20 20-mm cannons with 100 rounds per gun. These MiG-3s were assigned to PVO units. These aircraft represent what could have been with the MiG-3, with an engine specifically designed for low-altitude work, and with a more powerful cannon armament replacing the machine guns.

In addition to these aircraft assigned to the PVO, two aircraft from the 402nd IAP of the VVS were converted to carry the AM-38 engines in November 1941, with one of the aircraft being assigned to the regiment's commander Maj. K. A. Grudzdev.

MiG-3 Reconnaissance Version with Cameras

Four aircraft were modified at Z.1 in July 1941 to carry the AFA-I camera. After service testing, a fifth aircraft was modified to carry the camera, and the five aircraft were released for service use by the VVS.

Experimental MiG-3s

MiG-3 – Lightened

Two MiG-3s were lightened by the NII VVS in 1943, after production had ended. One of these MiG-3s was lighter by 412 lb (187 kg), with a loaded weight of 6,830 lb (3,098 kg), and its ceiling was 38,550 feet (11,750 m). It is not known if any further MiG-3s were lightened.

MiG-3U (I-230, D, MiG-3D)

As the MiG-3U, despite its service designation, was a significantly different aeroplane from the production MiG-3, it is described further on in the Experimental Fighters section.

MiG-7—MiG-3 with AM-37 (Izdeliye 72)

Although the I-200 no. 1 was fated to never be fitted with its intended engine, the Mikulin AM-37 (although the I-200 no. 2 was; described previouly), one MiG-3 was equipped with this experimental engine and designated the 'MiG-7' (the in-house designation was *Izdeliye* 72 or 'Object 72'). It was fitted with this engine in spring 1941, but tests revealed poor performance, and the aircraft would have needed to be extensively modified, so tests were discontinued. The AM-37 engine was removed and installed on the DIS-200 (described further on). Just as a note, the Soviet propensity to give completely different designations to very similar aircraft (in this case a re-engined MiG-3 is given a completely new service designation) can prove to be a bit confusing, even to the aviation historian.

I-231

The I-231 was an effort to improve the I-230 (MiG-3U), itself an effort to improve the MiG-3. It is described further on in the Experimental Fighters section. The I-231 represented the last effort to improve the MiG-3.

Combat Tactics

The MiG-3 had been designed for high-altitude combat, above 20,000 feet (6,096 m). At low altitudes, its speed dramatically dropped off to where it was actually slower than the Bf 109 at sea level (314 mph (505 kph) for the MiG-3 as opposed to 332 mph (535 kph) for the Bf 109F-4). The best tactic for the MiG-3 was to engage German aircraft at high altitudes, where its excellent speed gave it an edge. Unfortunately for the MiG-3, most of the fighting on the Eastern Front took place below 16,404 feet (5,000 m). In addition, the weak armament of most MiG-3s required its pilots to fly to very close quarters with the Germans to have a good chance of shooting them down. This tactic, however, required manoeuvrability that the MiG-3, with its high wing loading, simply did not possess. It was this lack of any real advantage over German fighters that led to the cessation of MiG-3 production early in the Great Patriotic war.

One of the few pilots who took a liking to the MiG-3 (as a member of the 55th IAP) was the ace Aleksandr Ivanovich Pokryshkin (1913–1985), who scored five victories on the type. He went on to fame as the second highest-scoring Soviet ace of the war with fifty-nine individual kills, being awarded the title of Hero of the Soviet Union three times and rose to the rank of marshal with the post-war Soviet Air Force. He found that the proper tactic to use with the MiG-3 was to utilise its vertical speed and diving ability, in what were essentially 'boom and zoom' tactics. Once the MiG-3 had attempted a firing pass, it would gain altitude to repeat the process. It is not clear how many other pilots adopted this tactic or even had the skill to (besides being a fine tactician, Pokryshkin was an exceptionally good pilot, as evidenced by his multiple-ace status).

Combat Use

As the most numerous of the new modern fighters in the VVS inventory at the start of Operation Barbarossa, the MiG-3 saw very heavy action in the first six months of the war. This heavy action resulted in heavy losses, and all through 1941, production of the MiG-3 struggled to keep up with these losses.

Note: Maps regarding these actions can be referred to in the Lavochkin fighters 'Combat Use' section. This note applies to all the remaining 'Combat Use' sections in this book.

Operation Barbarossa

The MiG-3 constituted a large percentage of the fighters available to the western districts facing the German invasion. Thirteen regiments were fully equipped with them, and six regiments partially so. Sixty-four were serving with the Red Banner and Black Sea fleets. However, so heavy were the initial losses that the MiG-3 (and MiG-1) went from 917 aircraft available in the western districts on the first day of the Great Patriotic War (22 June 1941) to only 234 operational aircraft two days later. However, production continued apace so these numbers grew as new MiG-3s were produced and sent to the front to replace the lost aircraft, and by 1 January 1942, there were 686 MiG-3s in VVS service (this number excludes those MiG-3s serving with the fleets and the PVO).

The Germans were not the only ones who captured Soviet equipment as evidenced by this MiG-3, which has been captured by the Romanians and repainted in Romanian markings. It appears flyable, and a pilot appears to be sitting in the cockpit. (*Viktor Kulikov's collection*)

MiG-3s preparing to take off from a dirt field. They are painted in the green and black over blue colour scheme introduced in 1941. (*Viktor Kulikov's collection*)

A MiG-3 of the 7th IAP in October 1941. By this time, the aircraft has been painted with black bands over the green topside colour. The cut-out in the tailwheel doors shows up well here. (*Viktor Kulikov's collection*)

As mentioned previously, one of the pilots who flew the MiG-3 early in the war was the three times Hero of the Soviet Union pilot Aleksandr Pokryshkin. He had this to say about the MiG-3 (*Osprey Aircraft of the Aces 102: MiG-3 Aces of World War 2*, p. 14):

> On 22 June my regiment faced the enemy with the MiG-3, the new fighter that required many new skills and a major effort to get the best out of it. As for me, I fell for the aircraft at once. It was like a mettlesome racehorse. Handled by a forceful rider it would go like an arrow, but if you lost control it would smash you with its hooves. Designers rarely achieve a perfect balance between an aircraft's flight performance and its ability as a gun platform. In any design there are always some problems to be found.

Every qualified pilot was needed to try and slow down the German invasion. Test pilot Stepan Pavlovich Suprun (1907–1941) suggested that units comprised of test pilots be organised and sent to the front. In response, the VVS created the 401st IAP, commanded by Suprun himself, and the 402nd IAP, which was commanded by Lt-Col. Pyotr Mikhailovich Stefanovskiy (1903–1976), another experienced test pilot. These regiments were equipped with sixty-seven new MiG-3s and sent to the front on 30 June 1941. One of their duties, besides military duties, was to teach other pilots how to properly use their new MiG-3 fighters as there was a shortage of pilots trained to fly the MiG-3. Indeed, all along the front, there were more MiG-3s than there were pilots qualified to fly them.

The 401st IAP was based at Zubovo, an airfield near Smolensk, in western Russia, and besides conducting fighter sorties, they also conducted reconnaissance and ground attack duties. Unfortunately, its commander Suprun was killed in combat on 4 July 1941, but not before claiming four German aircraft. He was awarded the title of Hero of the Soviet Union for the second time, this time posthumously.

Although initially based near Leningrad, the 402nd IAP, along with the 401st IAP, was assigned to the Moscow PVO in the summer of 1941, in preparation for the expected German assault on the capital.

The Odessa Military District (which later became the Southern Front), in southern Ukraine, had 100 MiG-3s on hand at the start of Barbarossa, out of a total of 827 fighters. It claimed to have destroyed forty Axis aircraft for the loss of twenty fighters. Although undoubtedly exaggerated, this result indicates that this district enjoyed more success in the air than the other western military districts.

Battle of Moscow

Serving mostly with PVO units, Moscow-based MiG-3s initially saw use in July 1941, when the Germans first bombed the Soviet capital. On 21 July 1941, the Luftwaffe bombed Moscow with 195 bombers, consisting of Ju 88s and Do 17 twin-engined medium bombers. Some 170 Soviet fighters, including forty MiG-3s, were despatched to intercept the bombers. It is not clear from the record how many German aircraft were lost on this raid, but it may be telling that after August 1941, the Germans no longer attempted large-scale bombings of the Soviet capital. The Germans had expected to find Moscow poorly defended and were unpleasantly surprised to discover

The pilots of this MiG-3 PVO unit are lined up as their unit officially becomes the 12th GvIAP (Guards Air Regiment) in Moscow in March 1942. (*Viktor Kulikov's collection*)

Another photograph of the pilots of this MiG-3 PVO unit, this time kneeling as their unit officially becomes the 12th GvIAP (Guards Air Regiment) in Moscow in March 1942. (*Viktor Kulikov's collection*)

MiG-3s of the 12th GvIAP PVO unit lined up at their airfield in Moscow in March 1942. Note that most of the aircraft are painted in winter camouflage, but one aircraft at least retains its summer camouflage. The nearest aircraft appears to have a replacement outer starboard wing, still in its green summer camouflage. This has often been misinterpreted in colour profiles as being red, but careful comparison with the red stars shows it to be a different colour. (*Viktor Kulikov's collection*)

how heavily defended the city actually was, with barrage balloons, searchlights, large numbers of flak emplacements, and hundreds of interceptors. Not for the first nor the last time did the Germans underestimate the Soviets.

Not only PVO units, but a few regular VVS MiG-3 units also saw combat to the immediate west of and over Moscow during the fall and winter of 1941. One of these was the 41st IAP.

The MiG-3 was used both in daytime and nighttime in defence of Moscow. In addition to its use as an interceptor, the MiG-3 saw use as a fighter-bomber, equipped with rockets or bombs. Despite its limited usefulness in this role, the MiG-3 saw heavy usage in the desperate attempt by the Soviets to slow down the German advance towards Moscow. It was also used as a reconnaissance aircraft, to gather information about German positions and movements.

Leningrad

The last time the MiG-3 saw extensive combat use was as a fighter in the defence of Leningrad in 1941 and 1942. Here, it was used not just to protect the city but to protect the vital Road of Life across the frozen Lake Ladoga, which provided a tenuous link and lifeline to the rest of the unoccupied Soviet Union.

After its use at Leningrad in 1942, most of the surviving VVS MiG-3s were assigned to naval units or PVO units. By 1 May 1942, it was reported that no MiG-3s remained with VVS units, while the AVMF had 37, and the PVO had 323 in service on 10 May 1942. By the end of 1942, the VVS had written off 326 MiG-3s. With the PVO units, they served in ever-decreasing numbers through at least part of 1944. By 1 June 1944,

MiG-3s of the 7th IAK (Fighter Air Corps) flying over Leningrad. The Neva River flows beneath them. The tailwheel has been fixed on the nearest aircraft, which was commonly done with MiG-3s in service. (*Viktor Kulikov's collection*)

the PVO had only seventeen MiG-3s still in service. All of the MiG-3 fighters had apparently been withdrawn from the PVO by the beginning of 1945, although some remained in non-combat roles, such as training, after that. Yefim Gordon has some MiG-3s serving until the end of the war with PVO units, although it is possible these were no longer operational or were in secondary roles, such as trainers. By 1945, MiG-3s were still being used as ground instructional airframes for training ground crew.

Naval MiG-3s

Not only did the MiG-3 serve with regular VVS and PVO units, but it also served with the various naval fleets, as part of the AVMF (Naval Air Forces). The MiG-3 served with the Red Banner (Baltic) Fleet, the Black Sea Fleet, the Northern Fleet, and the Pacific (Far East) Fleet. The last MiG-3s in service were those serving with the Pacific Fleet, which served into 1945. Total losses of the AVMF MiG-3s amounted to 138 aircraft.

Red Banner (Baltic) Fleet

On 22 June 1941, the 5th IAP of the KBF (Red Banner Fleet) had six MiG-1s and seven MiG-3s on hand. The first sorties took place against German reconnaissance aircraft in late June. The MiG-3s were used as escorts for the SB and DB-3 medium bombers and were also used as ground attack aircraft (as was almost inevitable at this desperate time of the war, in 1941). The MiG-3s were used for ground attack, despite being considered inferior to the I-153 and I-16, which with their radial engines and manoeuvrability were more survivable than the inline-engined MiG-3, as well as the LaGG-3 and Yak-1. At least four *tarans* are recorded as being successfully attempted by KBF MiG-3 pilots during 1941, with the pilots surviving. By 19 April 1942, twenty-four MiG-3s had been lost. Many of these were lost flying ground attack sorties.

KBF MiG-3s participated in the defence of Leningrad, flying patrols over the vital 'lifeline' through Lake Ladoga. One of the units participating in these patrols was the 12th Independent Red Banner Squadron, which by early 1942 was equipped with two of the few remaining MiG-1s, eleven MiG-3s, and seven LaGG-3s. This unit apparently operated MiG-3 fighters for the KBF until May 1943 when the eight remaining MiG-3s were transferred to a training regiment of the Baltic Fleet, and the two remaining MiG-1s were transferred to target-towing duties. It may have been one of these MiG-1s that was struck off duty in 1944, being the last MiG-1 in service. The unit received Yak-7Bs as replacement aircraft. This was not the end of the MiG-3's use with the KBF, as the 12th OIAE (*Otdelnaya Istrebitelnaya Aviaeskadrilya*, 'Independent Fighter Air Squadron') is reported as using MiG-3s until spring 1944.

Black Sea Fleet

By 22 June 1941, the 32nd IAP of the CMF (Black Sea Fleet) had just received its MiG fighters. Naval MiG-3s participated in the defence of the Crimea, where besides being used as fighters, they were used in ground attack duties and to perform reconnaissance duties, where their lack of a camera limited their usefulness. Over Sevastopol, the MiG-3s patrolled the skies, as well as occasionally being used for ground attack missions.

The CMF MiG-3s were flying in defence of the port of Novorossiysk in the summer of 1942, patrolling to protect Soviet shipping without conspicuous success. The number of MiG-3s in CMF service continued to fall in 1942, until by 22 December the 7th IAP was down to only seven MiG-3s, only one of which was serviceable. However, as late as April 1943, MiG-3s were reported as being flown by 7th IAP pilots near the port of Tuapse on the Black Sea. In May 1943, 7th IAP MiG-3s flew mock combat missions against Lend-Lease American-built Curtiss P-40 Kittyhawks. Perhaps surprisingly, the MiG-3 normally was recorded as beating the American fighters, in part because of superior vertical manoeuvrability. It is not clear when the last MiG-3s were used by the Black Sea Fleet.

Northern Fleet

Only a few MiG-3s, from ten to seventeen in total, served with the Northern Fleet. These MiG-3s were flown by the 72nd SAP (Mixed Air Regiment). Although few in number, these aircraft did see action, most notably over the port of Vayenga on 9 August 1941 when the 72nd Regiment intercepted German aircraft attempting to bomb the port. The Soviets claimed six Ju 88s, although the Germans only admitted to losing three aircraft, two being written-off after landing.

By the second half of 1942, the MiG-3s were mostly idle due to a lack of spare parts. The last three MiG-3s of the Northern Fleet were transferred to the KBF in April 1943.

Pacific (Far East) Fleet

By 22 June 1941, the Pacific Fleet already had seventeen MiGs, these being used by the 6th IAP, based near Vladivostok. As at this time, and for four years after, there was peace with Japan, these and additional MiG-3s sent to the Pacific Fleet saw no combat action.

Some MiGs served with the Pacific Fleet, in ever-diminishing numbers, into 1945. It was their relatively easy maintenance and repair that allowed them to be in service this long. It appears that all had been written-off as worn out (they had undergone several overhauls by this time), and none were in service by August 1945, so they did not participate in the Manchurian Campaign. Apparently, no MiG-3s served into the post-war period in any capacity.

MiG-3 in Detail

As the production of the MiG-3 occurred almost completely in one year—1941—the aircraft did not change greatly during its relatively short production run. The aircraft described below would be a 'typical' late production example, although MiG-3s that deviated from this standard are also noted.

General Description

The MiG-3 was a low-wing single-seat cantilever monoplane, with a tailwheel-type retractable landing gear, a single liquid-cooled inline engine, and an enclosed cockpit; it was of a mixed metal and wooden construction. It was characterised by a sturdy modular construction, which made it easy to assemble, repair, and maintain.

Fuselage

The oval-section fuselage was of mixed construction, consisting of a forward half that comprised a structure of welded chromansil-type steel tube. This forward structure was covered by detachable aluminium panels with Bf 109-type quick-release fasteners (in early MiG-3s these were 'Dzus'-type fasteners) to the back edge of the cockpit, joined to an all-wooden semi-monocoque rear fuselage, with wooden frames, longerons, and stringers with a fabric-covered plywood skin. The fin was integral to the rear fuselage and was likewise of wooden construction.

The pilot was provided with an aft-sliding canopy and a 0.35-inch (9-mm) thick armoured seat; the early MiG-3s had 0.31-inch (8-mm) thick armour. The aft part of the canopy was extended as compared to the MiG-1 to give the pilot better rearward vision, and a shelf was provided underneath the canopy for a radio, although the radio was not always fitted. In service, the sliding portion of the canopy, as it could be difficult to open in flight, especially at high speeds, was in service omitted completely on some MiG-3s, despite the penalty in drag and the rather draughty cockpit that resulted. The late MiG-3s had an interior plate of armour glass behind the windshield, which was absent from earlier MiG-3s.

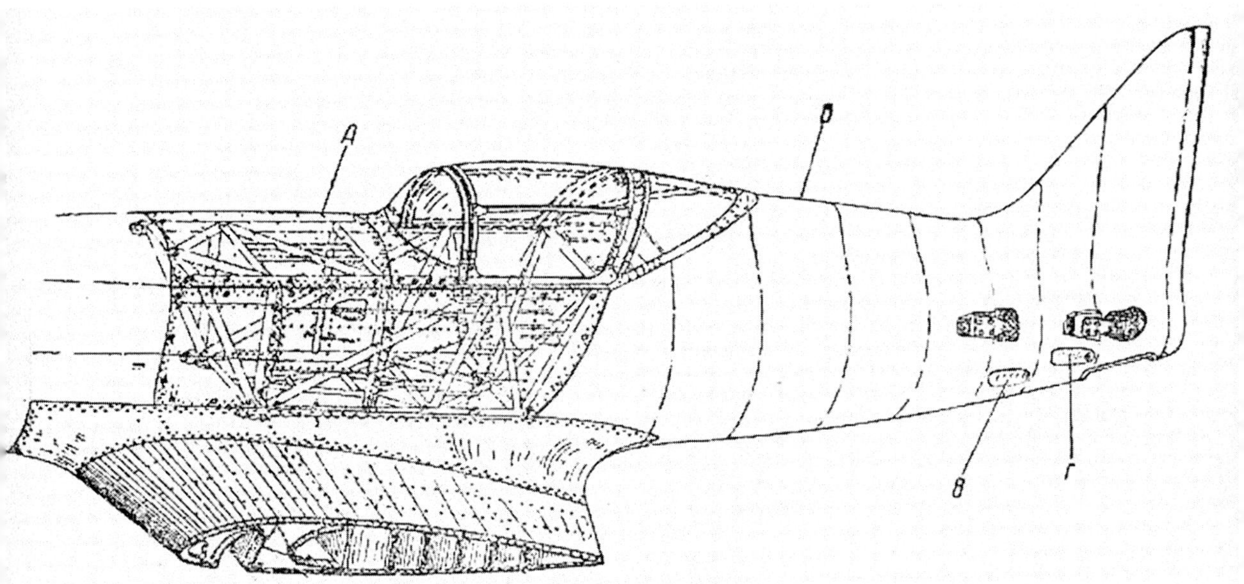

Рис. 13. Фюзеляж.

I-200 fuselage construction showing the metal tube framework of the front fuselage and the metal wing roots. (*I-200 Technical Manual*)

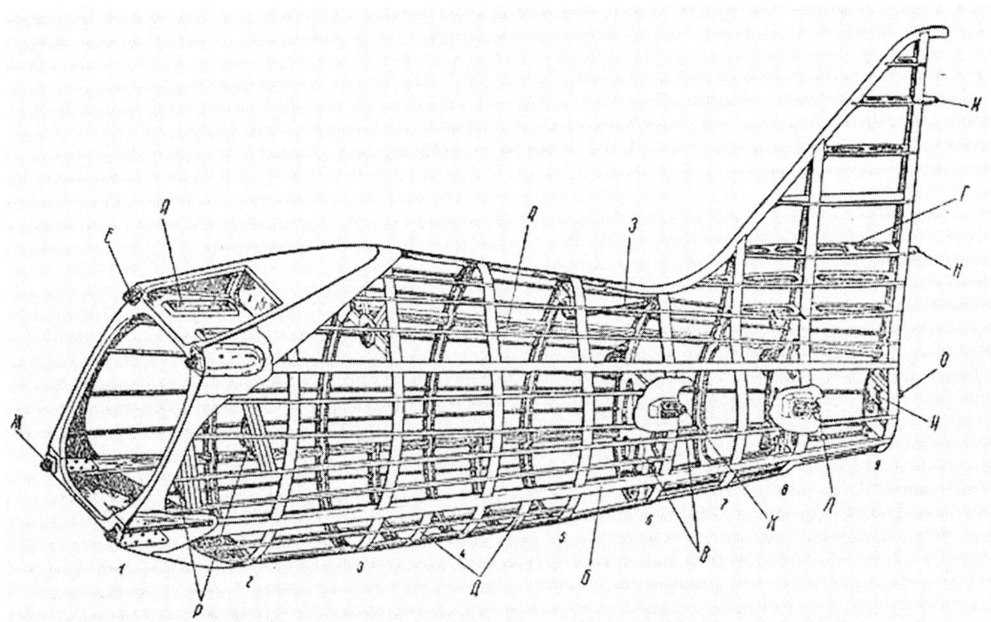

Рис. 22. Хвостовая часть фюзеляжа.

I-200 rear fuselage construction showing the wooden framework. The fixed fin is integrally constructed with the rest of the rear fuselage. (*I-200 Technical Manual*)

Рис. 111. Установка доски приборов.

I-200 instrument panel. (*I-200 Technical Manual*)

Wings

With the wings, as with the fuselage, the construction was mixed, with the inner part of the wings being of metal construction, with a metal structure, including a metal main and two auxiliary spars, with ten ribs, covered by an aluminium alloy skin. The outer wing panels were of wooden construction, with wooden wing spars of *delta drevresina* and pine along with fifteen ribs covered by a bakelite ply covering, which was then covered by fabric, the fabric being rubbed down to give a smooth finish. The inner wing panels had no dihedral, whereas the outer wing panels had a dihedral of 6 degrees (the MiG-1 had a dihedral of 5 degrees). The wings were of a Clark YH profile, with a thickness chord of from 14 per cent at the wing root to 8 per cent at the wingtip.

Tailplanes

The tailplanes were of mixed construction with a fixed wooden fin integral with the wooden rear fuselage, all-metal fixed stabilisers with a metal covering over a metal structure, and moveable control surfaces, the rudder and elevators being of dural construction with a fabric covering. The fixed stabilisers were the only part of the MiG-3 that utilised modern stressed-skin metal construction. The tips of the stabilisers on late production MiG-3s were increased in chord over earlier versions.

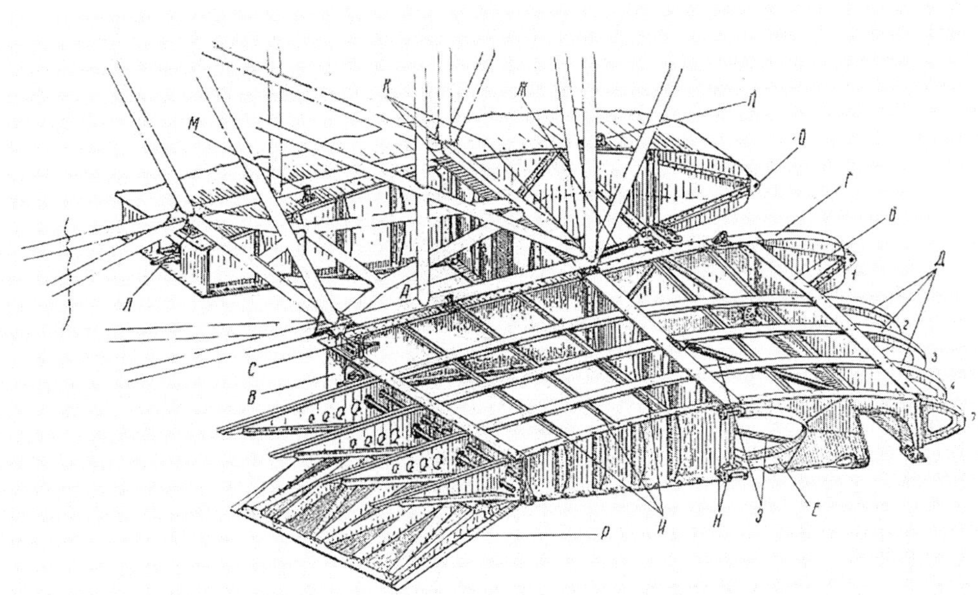

Рис. 31. Каркас центроплана (первый вариант).

Central portion of the I-200 showing the metal inner wings and the metal tubular framework of the forward fuselage. (*I-200 Technical Manual*)

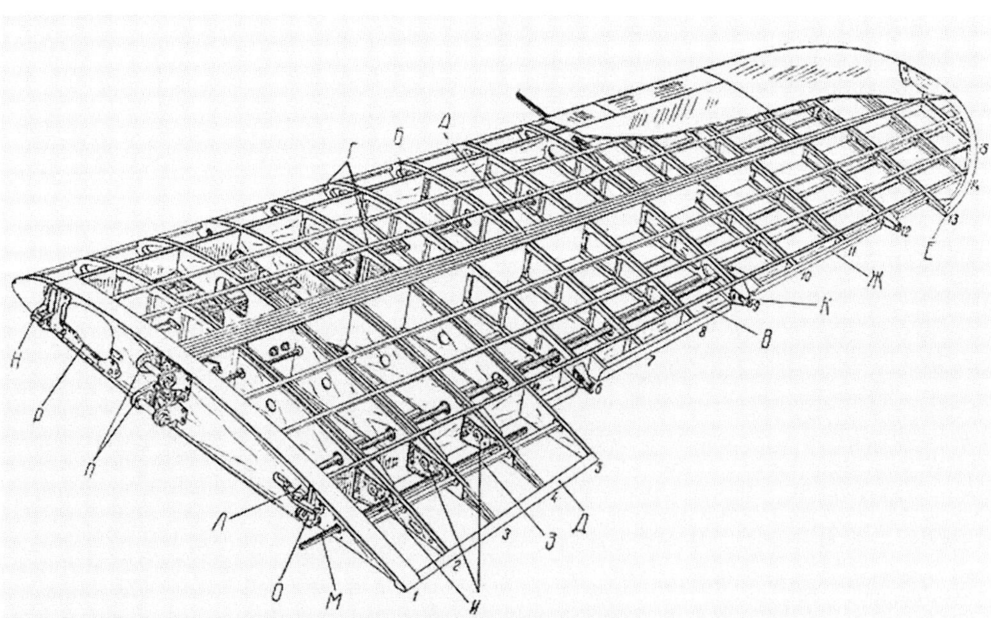

Рис. 32. Консоль крыла.

Outer portion of the starboard wing showing the wooden construction. (*I-200 Technical Manual*)

Engine

The engine on all production MiG-3s as produced was the Mikulin AM-35A V-12 supercharged liquid-cooled inline engine with 1,350 hp at its maximum rating. This large engine had been developed from the earlier AM-34 and would be developed into the low-altitude AM-38 engine for use by the Il-2. Interestingly, as mentioned previously, during the Great Patriotic War some MiG-3s (around eighty) had their worn-out AM-35As replaced by surplus AM-38s taken from salvaged Il-2s, which had a rating of 1,600 hp (Yefim Gordon has 1,500 hp; this may have been the rating at a certain altitude and not the maximum rating, or this may have been the maximum rating on these well-used engines).

An OPO-13 water radiator for the engine was fitted under the fuselage in a large, streamlined fairing on all MiG-3s. The exhausts were paired, with one exhaust pipe for two cylinders, for a total of six exhausts, three on each side, the exhausts imparting a small amount of thrust. Streamlined supercharger intakes were mounted on the engine cowling. Two oil tanks (the MiG-1 had only one) were mounted underneath the engine. The engine's power was transmitted to an AV-5L-123 three-bladed variable-pitch metal propeller with a pitch angle range of 30 degrees. Early MiG-3s had a VISh-22Ye three-bladed variable-pitch metal propeller with a pitch angle range of 20 degrees. This change in propellers was linked to an adjustment in the gear reduction ratio of the AM-35A engine, from .902 to .732, which was changed in the summer of 1941.

Fuel System

There were three fuel tanks on the MiG-3, with two self-sealing tanks installed between the main spar and an auxiliary spar in the wings. A third tank, with 37 gal (140 l) of fuel, was mounted in the fuselage, under the pilot's seat. Early MiG-3s had a fuselage tank of 66 gal (250 l). Gas from the engines, which had been cooled and filtered, was fed into the fuel tanks to lessen the chance of fire, as the filtered neutral gas replaced the explosive mixture of fuel and air that remained as the tanks were emptied. The gas was bled from the exhausts by a small pipe on the port side attached to the second and third exhausts. This feature was introduced in the second half of 1941.

Controls

The MiG-3 was equipped with large Frise-type ailerons on the wings for roll control, these ailerons being of dural structure, with a fabric covering. The Schrenk-type flaps, which were of all-metal construction, were mounted under the wings and fuselage and extended to either side of the large water radiator housing under the central fuselage. A Schrenk-type flap is a flap that is lowered from the bottom only, with the top being a fixed integral part of the wing. For pitch control, fabric-covered metal-structured elevators were used, while the fabric-covered metal rudder was used for yaw control. A spade-grip type control column (typical of many Soviet Second World War aircraft) controlled the ailerons and elevators, while floor-mounted rudder pedals controlled the rudder via wires. There were controllable trim tabs on the rudder, the starboard elevator, and a fixed but probably ground-bendable trim tab on the port aileron.

Landing Gear

The wide-track main landing gear was pneumatically operated, retracting inwards, and was completely enclosed by doors, with small outer doors attached to the underside of the fuselage. The doors were 'knuckled', with the centre-section hinged, which straightened out as the landing gear were retracted, the landing gear lengthening as the load was released on the gear legs. The main wheels were 650 × 200 mm in diameter, which was larger than those used on the MiG-1, which had main wheels of 600 × 180 mm. The shock absorbers were oleo-pneumatic. The tailwheel was also retractable (as produced) and enclosed by small twin doors. On the MiG-1 the tailwheel was a solid rubber unit; on the MiG-3, it was pneumatic. On early MiG-3s, the tailwheel partially protruded through a small opening in the doors when retracted. On later MiG-3s, the tailwheel doors were bulged to completely enclose the tailwheel when retracted. On many aircraft in service, the tailwheel was locked in the down position, probably due to problems with the pneumatic system, with the doors removed and the tailwheel opening closed by a leather or bezant boot.

Radio Equipment

Many MiG-3s were not equipped with any sort of radio equipment. Those that had radios initially had a RSI-1 radio fitted, which was upgraded to a RSI-4 receiver; these radio-equipped MiG-3s were characterised by a long antenna mast mounted on the starboard side of the fuselage in front of the cockpit, slanting outwards. A line ran from the top of the mast to the top of the tail fin. The radio equipment was mounted on a shelf behind the pilot underneath the fixed aft portion of the cockpit canopy.

Fixed Armament

The fixed armament normally consisted of two ShKAS 7.62-mm (30-calibre) machine guns and one UBS 12.7-mm (50-calibre) machine gun mounted on top of the engine cowling, all synchronised to fire through the spinning propeller. The UBS gun was mounted slightly off the cowling centreline to the port side. The guns were fired pneumatically, with a mechanical backup, and were aimed using a PBP-1A gunsight, which replaced the PBP-1 used on the MiG-1. The ShKAS guns had 750 rounds of ammunition per gun. From September 1941, some MiG-3s were equipped with two UBK 12.7-mm (50-calibre) machine guns mounted in pods under the wings to increase the firepower. These were not popular because of the effect the weight and drag of the installation had on the MiG-3's already somewhat lacklustre performance, although they did substantially increase the firepower. These pods were often removed in the field. Some MiG-3s had the two ShKAS machine guns removed, being replaced by a single UBS, giving these MiG-3s two UBS machine guns.

It is notable that the configuration of the AM-35 engine and its accessories prevented the installation of a nose-mounted gun to fire through the spinner, as was possible with the M-105 engines of the LaGG-3 and Yakovlev fighters. Some of the MiG-3 aircraft re-engined with AM-38s were re-equipped with twin ShVAK SP-20 20-mm cannons mounted on top of the engine cowling equipped with 100 rounds per gun, giving them the same armament as the contemporaneous La-5 fighters.

Some aircraft with the original AM-35A engine also received these two cannons, especially in the last production examples.

Disposable Armament

For use as a fighter-bomber, the MiG-3 could be equipped with six RS-82 or ROS-82 rockets mounted on RO-82 rocket rails under the wings, with three per wing. The rockets were initially used in the anti-aircraft role (their original purpose), but they were mainly used for ground attack. The rails and the rockets did create drag, reduce the manoeuvrability, and lower the top speed by around 9 mph (15 kph), so on 10 May 1942, the GKO issued an order making carrying them optional. In place of the rockets, the MiG-3 could carry small bombs under the wings, with two hardpoints under each wing. These hardpoints could carry up to a total of 485 lb (220 kg) of bombs, a typical load consisting of two 220 lb (100 kg) FAB-100 bombs or four 110 lb FAB-50 (50 kg) bombs. Due to its relatively weak gun armament and less than sparkling low-altitude performance, the MiG-3 left a lot to be desired in the role of fighter-bomber. Nonetheless, it saw heavy usage in the early part of the Great Patriotic War in this role, as did all the fighters in the Soviet armed forces—such was the need for ground support in the early part of the conflict (and afterwards).

MiG-3s in flight. The underwing rockets can be seen, as can the fixed tailwheels.

Camouflage and Markings

As it had entered service in early 1941, the early MiG-3s bore the 1940 camouflage scheme of A-18f Blue and A-19f Green on the metal portions of aircraft, as well as AII Blue (Sv.gol.—*Svetlo Goluboi* or 'Light Blue' in Russian) and AII *3* Green on the wooden/fabric-covered portions. The stars were red with a black outline, per 1940 practice. After the beginning of the Great Patriotic War, the new nitrocellulose lacquers such as AMT-6 Black were used and were painted in bands on the AMT-4 Green (also a new lacquer) upper surfaces. MiG-3s which served from late 1943 onwards do not appear to have been repainted in the later fighter camouflage scheme of AMT-11 Grey-Blue and AMT-12 Dark Grey over AMT-7 Blue, but instead retained the earlier black/green over blue scheme. As with other Soviet aircraft, some MiG-3s bore personal insignia and inscriptions, and those on presentation machines would have described the donor of the aircraft.

The MiG-3s that were finished in the early black/green scheme had stars that, when outlined (some were not), were outlined in black, white, or even silver (but usually in black). If any MiG-3s were painted in the two-grey scheme introduced in late 1943 and early 1944, the stars would have probably been the outlined '1943' stars.

Winter schemes, with white topsides, were common on the MiG-3 and appeared in some cases to have been carefully applied at the factory.

Conclusion

Of the three new Soviet fighters that went into production and service just before the Great Patriotic War (the LaGG-3, the MiG-3, and the Yak-1), the MiG-3 was the least important in terms of the Soviet war effort. This was partially due to inadequacies of the aircraft itself, such as relatively poor handling and manoeuvrability, but it was also due to changing requirements. The MiG-3 was designed as a fast, high-altitude fighter, as high altitude is where combat had been expected to take place in the upcoming war. Therefore, it was equipped with a large, heavy engine equipped with a powerful supercharger for maximum output and speed at high altitudes.

However, it was found that what was actually required in the war was a fighter capable of successfully engaging Axis aircraft at low to medium altitudes, with most of the combat taking place below 16,404 feet (5,000 m). The MiG-3's speed advantage disappeared at these low altitudes (it was actually slower than the Bf 109F at sea level), and it was not manoeuvrable enough to make up for this lack of low-altitude speed. It was also weakly armed, with only a few being equipped with cannons (both the LaGG-3 and Yak-1 were equipped with cannons). However, not all of the limitations of the MiG-3 were due to innate faults. Some were due to poor pilot training, poor tactics, and poor manufacturing. Due to all these factors, the MiG-3 was the wrong aircraft for the wrong war and did not have the major impact that the Lavochkin and Yakovlev fighters did, despite being heavily used out of necessity in the first year of the Great Patriotic War. However, it should be remembered that it was used heavily in the critical Battle of Moscow, where it gave useful service. Even so, as a result of the LaGG-3 and Yakovlev fighters' clear superiority at lower altitudes, only some 3,172 MiG-3 fighters were built (this number does not include the 100 MiG-1s that were produced), compared to over 22,000 Lavochkin fighters, and nearly 37,000 Yakovlev fighters that were produced.

Air superiority would be wrested from the Axis by Lavochkin and Yakovlev fighters, not Mikoyan-Gurevich fighters. Nonetheless, the MiG-1/MiG-3 is notable in that it was the first large-scale production fighter (or indeed any aircraft) of the OKB that would go on to great post-war fame for its fighters. Just as the name 'Tupolev' would become synonymous with post-war Soviet bombers, the name 'MiG' would become synonymous with post-war Soviet fighters.

Mikoyan-Gurevich Fighter Specifications

N.B. Metric measurements are in parentheses					
Model	I-200 no. 1	MiG-1	MiG-3	MiG-3 (enhanced armament)	MiG-3 AM-38
Year	1940	1941	1941	1941	1942
Engine	AM-35A	AM-35A	AM-35A	AM-35A	AM-38
Max. Power (Horsepower)	1,350	1,350	1,350	1,350	1,600 (YG has 1,500)
Fixed Armament	N/A	2 × ShKAS 7.62-mm, 1 × UBS 12.7-mm machine guns	2 × ShKAS 7.62-mm, 1 × UBS 12.7-mm machine guns	2 × ShKAS 7.62-mm, 3 × UBS 12.7-mm machine guns	2 × ShKAS 7.62-mm, 1 × UBS 12.7-mm machine guns (some had 2 × ShVAK SP-20 20-mm cannons in place of the machine guns)
Disposable Armament	N/A	6 × RS-82 Rockets, or 485 lb (220 kg) of bombs?	6 × RS-82 Rockets, or 485 lb (220 kg) of bombs	6 × RS-82 Rockets, or 485 lb (220 kg) of bombs	6 × RS-82 Rockets, or 485 lb (220 kg) of bombs
Length—feet (m)	26.76 (8.155)	26.76 (8.155)	27.07 (8.25)	27.07 (8.25)	27.07 (8.25)
Wingspan—feet (m)	33.46 (10.2)	33.46 (10.2)	33.46 (10.2)	33.46 (10.2)	33.46 (10.2)
Weight (Empty)—lb (kg)	5,456 (2,475)	5,736 (2,602)	5,950 (2,699)	-	5,692 (2,582)
Weight (Loaded)—lb (kg)	6,543 (2,968)	6,832 (3,099)	7,385 (3,350)	-	7,397 (3,355)
Max. Speed at Sea Level—mph (kph)	316 (508)	302 (486)	314 (505)	-	340 (547)
Top Speed—mph (kph)	403 (648.5)	395 (636)	398 (640)	-	368 (592)
Range—miles (km)	454 (730)	360 (580)	777 (1,250)	-	746 (1,200)
Service Ceiling—feet (m)	39,370 (12,000)	39,370 (12,000)	39,370 (12,000)	-	31,168 (9,500)
Turn Time (sec)	22	20-22.3	25.5	-	21 (on the 2 MiG-3s factory-fitted with the AM-38)

5

Polikarpov Fighters

The main Soviet fighter designer of the 1930s, sometimes referred to as the 'King of the Fighters', Nikolaiy Nikolaiyevich Polikarpov designed and produced a series of small and manoeuvrable biplanes and monoplanes, starting with the I-5 of 1930. His last successful design was the I-153 biplane, after which he designed several biplane and monoplane fighters, none of which entered large-scale production. He died in 1944 of natural causes, after which his OKB was eventually closed.

I-5 (ANT-12)

The first in the series of fighter biplanes that along with their monoplane stablemate, the I-16, dominated the Red Air Force in the 1930s, the I-5 was a small unequal-span biplane that first flew on 29 April 1930. Interestingly, it was designed in a *sharashka*, a special prison where Polikarpov was a 'guest' of the NKVD at the time (the Pe-2, the Tu-2, and the Tomashevich '110' fighter would later be designed in a different *sharashka*). It was powered by an imported British Bristol Jupiter VII radial engine of 450 hp. It was armed with two PV-1 7.62-mm (30-calibre) machine guns, with 600 rounds per gun. As with later Polikarpov biplanes, it had a mainly fabric-covered metal structure fuselage, with wooden fabric-covered wings.

The first I-5s were delivered to the VVS in 1931, and by the end of 1933, they accounted for 40 per cent of all VVS fighters. In all, 803 I-5s were produced from 1931–34, a substantial number for a between-the-wars aircraft. The I-5s were removed from front-line units in 1937, being replaced by aircraft such as the I-15bis. They were used as advanced trainers to train pilots for front-line fighters such as the I-15 and I-16, sometimes by way of the UTI-4, the two-seat trainer version of the I-16.

Nikolaiy Nikolaiyevich Polikarpov in 1940. (*Viktor Kulikov's collection*)

Combat Use

Great Patriotic War

At the beginning of the Great Patriotic War, the I-5 was still in use as an advanced trainer. Until then, it had seen no combat. However, so desperate was the need for combat aircraft after the terrible losses of summer 1941 that I-5s were taken from training units, even from aircraft dumps, and equipped as attack aircraft and night bombers. Amazingly, during the Battle of Moscow, so precarious was the military situation that it saw action as a night bomber. For example, the 604th and 605th air regiments used them as light bombers. The I-5 was out of front-line service in the Moscow region by February 1942. It is not clear from the record how much action it saw during the defence of Moscow, and the remaining aircraft may have returned to their training duties when they were retired from combat service. Similar units were raised in the Crimea and by the Black Sea Fleet in September 1941, with a total of thirty-two I-5s being available by October 1941, during the siege of Sevastopol; these saw service until February 1942. Sometimes, the aircraft had their PV-1 machine guns replaced with the rapid-fire ShKAS machine guns, and some had rockets installed. Again, their eventual fate is unclear. The I-5 was even used as a night fighter, without success.

One interesting type of mission the I-5 is recorded as flying is that of a sort of flying 'target'. This happened with a Black Sea Fleet regiment in August 1942. During night missions, an I-5 would fly over German positions, drawing fire, which would expose the exact position of anti-aircraft guns, for example. Light night bombers, such as UTI-1Bs (a modified trainer) would then attack the now-exposed enemy positions. One wonders how the pilot of the I-5 was chosen. It is possible that pilots who were being punished for some infraction would be given this rather dangerous assignment instead of being sent to a penal battalion. Apparently, the I-5s were painted in an all-black scheme to reduce at least somewhat their visibility, the noise of their engines being enough to draw enemy ground fire. It is very doubtful if any I-5s made it to the end of the Second World War in any capacity, and it is not clear when the last one was withdrawn from service, but the combat I-5s were withdrawn before the end of 1943.

I-15 (TsKB-3)

The basic I-5 design was further developed into the I-15, with a more powerful engine (the Shvetsov M-25 in later I-15s), heavier armament, and a gull-winged upper wing, among other changes. This gull-wing arrangement gave rise to its popular nickname of *Chaika*, or 'Seagull'; this nickname was later used on the similarly gull-winged I-153 (described further on). It proved to be extremely manoeuvrable, with the prototype executing a 360-degree horizontal turn in a little over eight seconds. Some 671 were built in total, with 284 produced in the Soviet Union and a further 287 built under licence in Spain. The relatively small number produced in the Soviet Union is indicative of the very mixed feelings the VVS had about this aircraft.

Despite the heavy use it saw during the Spanish Civil War (1936–39), surprisingly, the I-15 does not appear to have been used during the Great Patriotic War, even as a trainer. By the time of the Great Patriotic War, it had been replaced by further developments of the basic design, the I-15bis ('I-152') and the I-153 (I-15ter). In Spanish service, where it was known as the *Chato*, or 'Flat-nose' in Spanish due to its blunt profile, the I-15 continued in use during and after the Second World War. Its rapid disappearance from Soviet service may have been partly due to the purportedly disliked gull-wing, which restricted the pilot's view downwards. The heads of the VVS had even been prepared to remove it from Soviet service as early as 1936.

I-15bis ('I-152')

The I-15bis dispensed with the gull-wing of the I-15 (reportedly disliked by some pilots, and apparently harder to produce) in place of a conventional upper wing braced to the fuselage by struts. The I-15bis (often erroneously referred to as the 'I-152', especially in older literature) also featured a more streamlined, fully cowled (NACA cowling) M-25V boosted radial engine, dispensing with the narrower chord Townend ring of the I-15 (the first example of what became the I-15bis, the TsKB-3 No. 7, still featured the Townend Ring). The I-15bis had the same mixed construction as the I-15, with a metal structure fuselage and tail and wooden wings.

State trials on the I-15bis were passed during tests from 2 August to 3 October 1937. Full-scale production started in the middle of 1937 at Z.1, with the first military series (trial versions) actually being ready in spring 1937. The production I-15bis differed from the prototype in having a smaller windscreen, a tailskid in place of the

I-15bis in flight. The aircraft bears the green over blue camouflage introduced in 1940. (*Viktor Kulikov's collection*)

small tailwheel (reintroduced on the I-153), and an OP-1 telescopic sight in place of the PAK-1 reflector gun sight (which was also reintroduced on the I-153). The I-15bis was equipped with four PV-1 7.62-mm machine guns in the nose.

In all, a total of 2,408 I-15bis were built by the time production ended in 1940, which was nearly ten times the 284 I-15s that were produced in the Soviet Union, indicating its much greater acceptance by the Red Air Force (and perhaps the realisation that war was approaching). Despite the much greater numbers, the I-15bis had few advantages over the I-15, except perhaps for its better vision on take-off and landing. It was less manoeuvrable, and the top speed was similar. The I-15 could climb better because it was lighter, but conversely, the I-15bis could dive better because it was heavier. The I-15bis was also found to be a good, stable gun platform.

As with the I-15, the I-15bis was produced with spatted main wheels, but these spats were often removed in the field as mud and debris would fill the interior of the spats, fouling the wheels. The tail skid on the I-15bis consisted of a small ski on the bottom of a strut, capable of moving up or down. The tail skid/ski was not steerable. During the Great Patriotic War, some I-15bis were retro-fitted with tailwheels from salvaged I-153s.

Experimental Versions

DIT

A prototype for an advanced trainer, the DIT featured two cockpits, one for the trainee-pilot and one for the instructor-pilot, the 'DIT' standing for *Dvukhmestniy*

Istrebitel' Trenirovochniy, or 'Double (or 'Two-seat') Training Fighter'. The first prototype flew in the spring of 1939, and the flight characteristics were found to be similar to the single-seat I-15bis. The aircraft was equipped with two ShKAS machine guns firing through the cowling and the propeller arc, aimed with a PAK-1 reflector gunsight. Three were built, and although this I-15bis development did not go into production, two were used during the Great Patriotic war as observation and artillery-spotter aircraft in the Novorossiysk region on the Black Sea in 1942–1943 in the Kuban, after having been sent to Sevastopol in 1940.

I-15bis GK

One aircraft was built with the A. Shchyerbakov-designed pressure cabin in 1939. It was apparently the first successful sealed pressurised cabin used in the Soviet Union. The 'GK' in its name stood for *s Ghermeticheskoy Kabinoy*, meaning 'Hermetic Cabin', indicating the sealed nature of the cockpit cabin.

The aircraft was tested at the NII VVS from 29 August to 4 October 1939, flown by the test pilot P. Yu. Fedorov. Unfortunately, on 4 October 1939, while taxiing on the runway at the NII VVS, the I-15bis GK collided with a captured Polish bomber (PZL P.37) that was being tested, and the I-15bis was destroyed, with the pilot, who was not Fedorov, being killed. Development was stopped after this.

I-15bis TK

This was an experimental high-altitude version of the I-15bis that featured a TK-3 turbo-supercharger for the M-25V engine. A supercharger was mounted on both sides of the engine cowling. The empty weight was increased by 309 lb (140 kg). A speed of 270 mph (435 kph) at 19,685 feet (6,000 m) was recorded. Only one aircraft was built in 1939.

Combat Tactics

The only realistic chance for the slow I-15bis against the much faster German Bf 109s was to engage them in a turning contest, where the outstanding manoeuvrability of the I-15bis gave it a fighting chance. However, because of the Bf 109s' much greater speed, if it encountered trouble in a manoeuvring contest, it could simply break off combat at will. The most the I-15bis could normally hope for was a stalemate.

Combat Use

Spanish Civil War

At least partially incorporating lessons learned during this war, the I-15bis was introduced in 1938, when twenty were sent to the Republican forces. Since the I-15 was the *Chato*, the improved I-15bis became known as the *Super Chato*. As it arrived late during the war, and in small numbers, it had little influence upon the air war.

Khalkhin-Gol

Although the I-15bis' use during the Spanish Civil War was limited, it saw much more use in Mongolia during the Khalkhin-Gol conflict, where it faced Japanese monoplane fighters such as the Nakajima Ki-27 fixed-landing gear cantilever monoplane. It was inferior to these aircraft in speed, but was more manoeuvrable, with an impressive 360-degree horizontal turn time of only eleven seconds. It also had more firepower, with four machine guns to the Japanese fighters' two guns. It fought throughout the five-month-long conflict, which ended with a decisive victory for the Soviets and their Mongolian allies. Approximately 100 I-15bis were used during the conflict, in which combat losses were a considerable fifty-six aircraft. By the end of the conflict, only fifteen were still in service and were used mainly for training flights. The Khalkhin-Gol conflict revealed the obsolescence of the I-15bis when facing monoplane fighters.

Winter War

As it was still in front-line service, the I-15bis, despite its obsolescence, saw service against the Finnish forces in 1939–40. In the first part of the war, it was used for reconnaissance and ground attack missions. It appears that its opportunities for aerial combat were limited, with only a few Finnish aircraft being shot down. It was even used to carry supplies to units surrounded by the Finnish. It served with the Red Banner (Baltic) Fleet primarily as a ground attack aircraft. It is unclear from the record how many I-15bis were lost, but it was not evidently a large number of aircraft. The Finns acquired five I-15bis that landed on their territory, which they used in the Great Patriotic War (the 'Continuation War' for the Finnish).

Great Patriotic War

On 22 June 1941, over 1,000 I-15bis were still in use as fighter aircraft in the Soviet Union, although only 268 were operational in the Western Military Districts. Despite the heavy losses it suffered in the first week of the war, the I-15bis continued to see action. The I-15bis saw the most usage during the Great Patriotic War as a fighter-bomber, utilising small bombs (it had a bomb load of 331 lb (150 kg)) and RS-82 rockets installed under the lower wings. One place where the I-15bis saw use as a fighter-bomber was in the Crimea. It was used by the 653rd IAP in the Crimea, where somewhat amazingly in early 1942 Vasiliy Nikolayevich Kubarev managed to down a Bf 109. In the western part of the Soviet Union, it was used until 1943 as a fighter-bomber. As of 1 June 1943, there were still thirty-two I-15bis active in the VVS. After this, it continued to be used in training units, and as a fighter in the far north and far east.

Not only was the I-15bis used as a daylight fighter-bomber, but it was used to supplement the U-2 (Po-2LNB) in the night-bomber role. Several aircraft were modified with a second seat for an observer and were used as artillery spotter aircraft by the 5th Air Army in the summer of 1943 in the Kuban. It was in use in the far north on the Soviet Arctic islands of Novaya Zemlya until the end of the Great Patriotic War (the last I-15bis was not written off until 1 October 1945). Although it saw no action in the Manchurian Campaign, it was still in front-line service in the Soviet Far East until just before that offensive began, when it was finally retired from front-line Soviet use. As there was no combat in the Far East until the Manchurian Campaign (the Soviet Union being at peace with Japan for most of the Second World War), the Soviet Far East had become something of a military backwater. In Spanish service, the I-15bis served into the mid-1940s in the ground attack role.

Although still retaining its bomb armament, this I-15bis appears to be derelict or captured as seen in the fabric partially torn away around the underwing star (the red stars were a prized souvenir of German soldiers). The braces that keep the bomb-arming vanes from rotating on the ground are still attached to the front of the bombs in 1941. (*Viktor Kulikov's collection*)

I-15bis near Leningrad having its engine warmed up by a portable heater in winter 1941–42. This aircraft is painted in winter camouflage, and has ski undercarriage, with the propeller spinner removed. A colour profile of this aircraft appears in the colour plates section. (*Viktor Kulikov's collection*)

I-152

This designation causes some confusion as it has often been used for all the I-15bis aircraft. In fact, the 'I-152' was to have been the I-15bis standard for the second half of 1938. It was named the 'I-152' to distinguish it from the new I-153 aircraft, which was being worked on at the time (1938). One I-152 was actually built, which incorporated improvements such as a new way of fastening the fabric covering and a PAK-1 gunsight. It was test flown at the NII VVS from 3 June to 29 July 1938 by P. M. Stefanovskiy. Since it had been decided to start producing the I-153 from the beginning of 1939, the I-152 did not go into production, but the designation has endured, to confuse and bedevil Soviet air historians, both amateur and professional.

I-153

The last in the series of production Polikarpov biplane fighters, the I-153 (or rarely, the 'I-15ter') was notable in featuring a fully retractable (although manually operated) main landing gear as a concession to modernity. Unlike the I-15bis with its conventional upper wing, it returned to the upper gull-wing of the I-15, which earned it the semi-official nickname of *Chaika*, or 'Seagull', which had been used as the unofficial nickname of the I-15. This reversion to the gull-wing configuration was an interesting development as the pilots had supposedly disliked the gull-wing of the original I-15. However, speed considerations (dispensing with the wing-to-fuselage struts of the I-15bis made the I-153 more streamlined) may well have overcome any objections pilots might have had, at least as far as head designer Nikolaiy Polikarpov was concerned. The success of the I-15 in the Spanish Civil War may have also influenced the decision to revert back to the gull-wing.

The accomplishments of biplanes such as the Polikarpov I-15 and the Fiat CR.32 in the Spanish Civil War had convinced the Soviets (and Italians) that there was still a place for the biplane, with its manoeuvrability, in an aerial environment increasingly dominated by faster monoplanes. The idea was to combine fast monoplanes (the I-16) with manoeuvrable biplanes (the I-153).

The I-153, with the contemporary Italian Fiat Cr.42 Falco (influenced by the success of the earlier Fiat CR.32 in the Spanish Civil War), was the best biplane fighter ever produced, but it came too late and was already obsolete by the time production ended in 1941, with 3,437 being built.

The I-16 monoplane and the I-153 were numerically the most important VVS fighters at the start of Operation Barbarossa. Like the I-16 (see further on), the I-153 suffered huge losses in the first week of the Great Patriotic War, with most of these losses occurring on the ground.

I-153 Prototypes (I-15ter)

As the VVS had still not lost interest in biplane fighters, especially with the surprisingly strong showing of the I-15 in the Spanish Civil War, Polikarpov sought to improve the

An abandoned but otherwise intact I-153, probably from summer 1941. This aircraft appears to be painted in an overall aluminium finish. (*Public Domain*)

basic I-15 design, with the first attempt being the I-15bis. The second attempt was the 'I-15ter', more commonly known as the 'I-153', its service designation. Notably, the I-153 reverted to the gull-wing configuration of the I-15 (for reasons explained previously) as opposed to the conventional upper wing of the I-15bis and had a manually retractable main landing gear installed in place of the I-15 and I-15bis' fixed main landing gear.

The first I-153 flew in August 1938 with Aleksandr I. Zhukov as the pilot. Factory tests were conducted from 27 September to 5 October 1938. State tests took place with the second prototype from 25 February to 20 March 1939, flown by test pilot P. Ya. Fedrovi. Another prototype was used for further state tests, which lasted from 16 June to 16 August 1939 (by which time the I-153 had already seen combat service in Mongolia).

I-153 Production Examples

The first production I-153s were produced with the M-25 engine of 775 hp. On later production I-153s, the more powerful 1,000 hp M-62 engine replaced the M-25. Most I-153s were produced with the M-62. Some 345 I-153s were produced with the still more powerful M-63 engine, which had a maximum output of 1,100 hp. Although the I-153s with the M-63 engines were not faster in terms of top speed, they climbed faster than the earlier versions.

I-153P

This version of the I-153, of which only eight were produced, featured two ShVAK SP-20 20-mm cannons mounted to fire through the propeller arc. The cannons replaced the four ShKAS 7.62-mm machine guns. One of their problems was that when fired, the smoke from the cannons obscured the pilot's vision.

I-153TK

In an effort to improve the high-altitude performance of the I-153, the TK-1 turbo-compressor was fitted to four I-153s, with both M-25V and M-62 engines. The I-153 with the M-25V and the TK-1 fitted achieved a top speed of 283 mph (455 kph) at 28,707 feet (8,750 m). An I-153 with the M-62 equipped with the TK-1 had a top speed of 300 mph (482 kph) at 33,793 feet (10,300 m). In total, twenty-six I-153TKs were built or converted and were intended to be used by PVO units. It is not clear if these aircraft saw any combat.

Experimental Versions

I-153DM

An I-153 was modified to accommodate two DM-2 (*Depolnityelniy Motor*, 'Supplementary Motor') 400-mm ramjets. In September 1940, the ramjets were tested on the I-153. On 27 October 1940, the I-153 achieved a speed of 273 mph (440 kph) at 6,562 feet (2,000 m) with both ramjets running.

I-153UD

This was a mainly wooden version of the I-153, with the metal tubular fuselage replaced with a wooden monocoque rear fuselage. It was built in an effort to save on the use of metals on aircraft. It was successfully tested from 30 September to 5 October 1940. It was equipped with a M-62 engine. Only one was built as the decision had been made to end production of the I-153.

I-153V (I-153GK)

This aircraft, with the 'V' standing for *Vysotniy*, or 'High-Altitude', was a high-altitude adaptation of the I-153. As with the I-15bis GK, the 'GK' stood for *s Ghermeticheskoy Kabinoy* or 'Hermetic Cabin', indicating the sealed nature of the cockpit cabin. The pressurised cabin was designed by A. Shchyerbakov. The aircraft had a service ceiling of 36,089 feet (11,000 m). The aircraft was tested from 20 to 30 July 1940, logging eleven flights. Only one I-153V (I-153GK) was built, despite the recommendation for production.

Combat Tactics

As with the I-15bis, the best chance for the relatively slow I-153 against the much faster German Bf 109s was to engage them in a turning dogfight, where the excellent manoeuvrability of the I-153 gave it a fighting chance. In addition, if an I-153 executed a surprise attack against a Bf 109, it might score a kill. Due to the Bf 109's much greater speed, if it got into trouble in a manoeuvring contest, it could simply break off combat at will. Nonetheless, some kills were recorded by I-153s against Bf 109s.

Combat Use

Unlike the I-15bis and the I-16, the I-153 did not see use in the Spanish Civil War as it went into service too late for that conflict, being used for the initial time in Mongolia in 1939.

Khalkhin-Gol

The I-153 *Chaika* first saw use during the Khalkhin-Gol (Nomonhan) Incident, seeing action on 25 July 1939 with the 30th IAP, not long after the state tests had taken place on the I-153. These aircraft flew in combat until 6 September. Mongolia also received some I-153s. It was able to hold its own against the Japanese Army fighters, even the Nakajima Ki-27 'Nate' monoplane, which was only marginally faster than the I-153 and not as manoeuvrable, and was more weakly armed, with only two rifle-calibre machine guns to the I-153s' four. The I-153 was faster than the Kawasaki Ki-10 'Perry' biplane fighter with its fixed landing gear, which had a top speed of 249 mph (400 kph), while the I-153s used at the Khalkhin-Gol had a top speed of 265 mph (427 kph).

There is an oft-repeated story that the I-153s would enter into aerial combat with their landing gear down to lull approaching Japanese fighter pilots into thinking they were attacking the slower, inferior I-15bis, and when the Ki-27s neared, the I-153 pilots 'suddenly' retracted their landing gear and were able to shoot down some of the unsuspecting Japanese fighters. Frankly, I find this story rather hard to believe. The I-153 had manually retracted landing gear, which required several dozen turns of a handle to winch the landing gear up. With enemy fighters approaching head-on at full speed, it would not be a good time to be busily cranking up your landing gear.

Winter War

In the war against Finland in the winter of 1939–40, the I-153 was one of the main Soviet fighters used. The record is not clear on its losses or kills, or indeed on when or where it saw action. Perhaps the Soviet record is silent because the I-153 suffered heavier than expected losses, but this is speculation. It is recorded that eight I-153s were captured by the Finnish when they made forced landings. Regarding losses, the VVS as a whole suffered heavier losses than anticipated, at least partly due to poor military leadership, at least in the first part of the Winter War.

Early Second World War

As the I-153, along with the I-16, was the main Soviet fighter numerically in 1939 and 1940, it participated in the actions against the Baltic States and Poland, and very likely Romania. As with the Winter War, there appears to be very little in the record about the specific actions, other than that the I-153 was used (a similar situation with the I-15bis). Red Air Force records do not indicate any air combat occurred over Poland.

Great Patriotic War

The I-153 saw substantial use in the early part of the Great Patriotic War, both as a fighter and fighter-bomber. On 22 June 1941, there were nearly 1,500 I-153s in service with the Western Military Districts, which was over one-third of the 4,226 fighters that were available. Many of these I-153s were destroyed on the ground in the first few days of the war.

The Chaika's excellent horizontal manoeuvrability was no match for the superior speed and vertical manoeuvrability of the Luftwaffe fighters, however, as the German fighters' superior speed allowed them to break off combat at will. The I-153 was

I-153 in flight over Leningrad. The sleek appearance of the aircraft in flight with its main undercarriage retracted is notable. (*Viktor Kulikov's collection*)

soon being operated mainly as a fighter-bomber. Equipped with small bombs such as the 110-lb (50-kg) FAB-50, and with RS-82 rockets fitted underwing, the I-153 saw heavy use as a fighter-bomber. In addition, it was used to protect light night bombers, such as the U-2, serving in mixed air regiments. The I-153 achieved some success as a fighter-bomber, as its manoeuvrability and tough radial engine made it more survivable than the LaGG-3 and Yak-1 when they were used as fighter-bombers. At one point, it was even suggested by the commander of the 1st VA, S. A. Khydyakov, that the I-153 (along with the I-16) be reinstated into production, but Stalin stopped this. This occurred in September 1942.

The I-153 proved especially valuable in the Caucasus region, such as the Kuban, where its manoeuvrability allowed it to operate with ease in the tortuous valleys of that mountainous area. It was used as a fighter-bomber by the VVS until as late as February 1944, if not later, apparently outlasting its stablemate the I-16 monoplane in front-line Soviet service (see further on). Indeed, it continued to serve into 1945 in such areas as the northern Soviet Union and the Soviet Far East. Until the end of the Great Patriotic War, it was used by the Northern Fleet for protection of ship convoys in the White Sea (the port of Arkhangelsk' is located on the White Sea). It appears that along with the I-15bis, it continued to serve on Novaya Zemlya until the end of the Great Patriotic War. It was not replaced in the Far East until just before the Manchurian Campaign.

Two I-153s of the 71st IAP of the Red Banner (Baltic) Fleet taxiing out on a mission carrying eight RS-82 rockets apiece in spring 1942. The large size of the aircraft numbers is interesting, as is the three-digit number—'102'—of the furthest aircraft, three-digit codes being uncommon on Soviet fighters. 'White 24' is an I-153 M-62 flown by Capt. Konstantin V. Solov'yov. (*Viktor Kulikov's collection*)

I-153 in Detail

General Description

The I-153 was an unequal-span single-seat biplane, with retractable landing gear, a radial engine, an open cockpit, metal-structured fabric-covered fuselage and tail, and fabric-covered wooden wings.

Fuselage

The fuselage consisted of a chromansil steel tube structure, covered by detachable aluminium panels to the back edge of the cockpit, and fabric aft of the cockpit, except for the top of the fuselage, which was covered with metal panels. The rear fuselage fabric was laid over metal stringers that gave the fuselage a streamlined oval shape. The fin was attached to the rear fuselage frame and was likewise of fabric-covered metal construction. The pilot was accommodated in an open cockpit, on a seat provided with an armoured back, and with a fixed windscreen giving some protection from the slipstream. A raised aft fuselage deck incorporated a headrest for the pilot.

Wings

The wings were of a sesquiplane configuration, that is, one set of wings (in this case the lower) was less than 50 per cent the area of the other set of wings (the upper in this case). With the upper wings, the construction was mixed, with the inner part of the

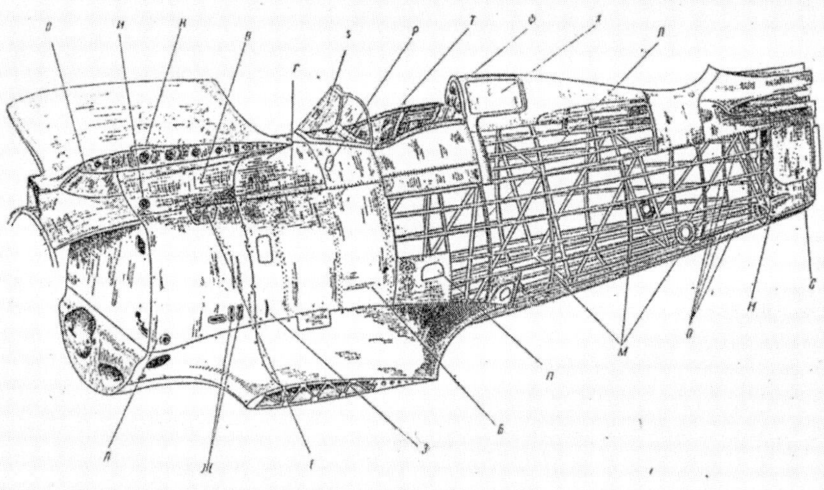

Рис. 34. Каркас обшивки фюзеляжа

All-metal fuselage structure of the I-153. Even the formers on the rear fuselage are metal. Note how the inner portions of both the upper and lower wings are integral metal structures with the fuselage. (*I-153 Technical Manual*)

upper wings being of metal construction (the 'gulled' portion), with a metal structure, including metal spars, covered by metal. The outer wing panels on the upper wings were of wooden construction, with wooden wing spars and ribs covered by fabric. From early in the production run, the wings had the leading edges covered in plywood. The large ailerons, which were only on the upper wings, were metal structured with a fabric covering. The upper wings were larger in area than the lower wings, which were of all-wooden construction with a fabric covering, except for the wing roots, which were of metal structure with metal covering. There were no struts connecting the upper wing to the fuselage (as there were on the I-15bis), as the gull-shaped inner portions turned downwards to attach directly to the upper fuselage. The upper and lower wings were attached to each other by 'I'-shaped interplane struts, which consisted of a streamlined aerofoil metal covering over an internal metal framework. In addition, there was wire bracing between the upper and lower wings and with the fuselage.

On those I-153s that were equipped to carry RS-82 rockets on the underside of the lower wing, the area around the rockets was skinned in metal to prevent scorching of the wing's fabric skin.

Tailplanes

The tailplanes consisted of a fabric-covered metal fin attached to the metal framework of the fuselage, fixed stabilisers with a fabric covering over a metal structure, and moveable control surfaces, a rudder, and elevators, of metal construction with a fabric covering. The horizontal tailplanes were braced to the lower fuselage by two streamlined metal struts on either side, the struts joining together at the base where they were attached to the lower portion of the rear fuselage ('V' struts).

Engine

The engine on early production I-153s was the Shvetsov M-25V boosted radial engine, with later versions having the Shvetsov M-62 or M-63 radial engines. The M-25V was based upon the American Wright Cyclone R-1820 9-cylinder radial engine, and had a rating of 750 hp. The M-62 and the M-63 were more powerful developments of the M-25, with the M-62 rated at a maximum of 1,000 hp, and the M-63 having a maximum output of 1,100 hp. This power was transmitted to a fixed-pitch metal two-bladed propeller on those aircraft with the M-25V. This propeller had a diameter of 9.19 feet (2.8 m). Those aircraft with the M-62 and M-63 engines had an AV-1 two-bladed variable-pitch metal propeller of 8.86 feet (2.7 m) or 9.19 feet (2.8 m) in diameter, which was sometimes equipped with a small spinner covering the hub for AV-1s fitted to the M-63, although this spinner was at times removed in the field. The I-153s with the M-63 engine had an enlarged oil radiator.

Fuel System

The I-153 had one welded dural fuel tank, located behind the engine, with a capacity of 83.48 gal (316 l). There was a firewall between the fuel tank and the engine, but not between the fuel tank and the pilot.

Controls

For roll control, the I-153 had long-span ailerons on the top wings, the bottom wings having no ailerons. There were no flaps as the large ailerons operated like modern ‘flaperons’, providing lift for take-off and landing, as well as roll control. The rear control surfaces consisted of a rudder, for yaw control, and two elevators, for pitch control, the elevators being attached to a common tube passing through an opening in front of the rudder. There was, therefore, no differential movement of the two elevators. There were no moveable trim tabs, although there were fixed trim tabs on the ailerons and rudder, the tabs being possibly ground-adjustable. The control column was of a typical Soviet spade grip-type, controlling both the ailerons and the elevators via connecting rods. Rudder pedals controlled the rudder via cables and pulleys.

Landing Gear

The main landing gear was manually operated, retracting backwards to lay fully in wells in the underside of the fuselage, and enclosed by doors, with hinged doors attached to the fuselage underside to cover the gear struts, and partial doors attached to the wheels. Sometimes, these wheel doors were removed in the field, to keep the doors from becoming fouled with mud or soil. The main wheels were 700 × 150 mm in size. The tailwheel was non-retractable, with a small solid rubber tyre of 150 mm diameter and moved in conjunction with the rudder. The wheeled landing gear could be replaced by retractable ski landing gear in winter, with the skis pressed up against the fuselage when retracted, and with a small ski replacing the tailwheel. Apparently, this small ski was sometimes used instead of the tailwheel even in non-winter as it worked better on muddy fields, the tailwheel becoming fouled with mud.

Radio Equipment

The I-153 was not normally equipped with any radio, neither a receiver nor a transmitter. It is possible that some may have been equipped with these in the field during the Great Patriotic War.

Fixed Armament

The fixed armament consisted of four ShKAS 7.62-mm (30-calibre) rapid-fire machine guns mounted around the engine cowling, synchronised to fire through the spinning propeller. The four ShKAS machine guns were equipped with 2,600 rounds of ammunition. The guns were aimed using a PAK-1 reflector-type gunsight. A few I-153s were fitted with two UBS 12.7-mm (50-calibre) machine guns or even two ShVAK SP-20 20-mm cannons (only a handful of the cannon-equipped I-153s were produced). These heavier-calibre guns were synchronised to fire through the propeller disc.

Disposable Armament

For use as a fighter-bomber, the I-153 could be equipped with up to eight RS-82 rockets mounted on RO-82 rails under the lower wings, with four per wing. In addition, it could carry small bombs under the lower wings, with two hardpoints under each wing. These hardpoints could carry up to a total of 485 lb (220 kg), a typical load consisting of two 220-lb (100-kg) FAB-100 bombs or four 110-lb (50-kg) FAB-50 bombs. In order to keep the rockets from scorching the fabric covering of the wings, the RO-82 rails were attached to a rectangular section of metal skinning on the lower wings.

An armourer installing bombs on a wartime I-153 in July 1941. Note the branches partially camouflaging the aircraft and the pre-war style underwing red star, with the circle in the middle. (*Viktor Kulikov's collection*)

I-16

As the TsKB-12bis, the I-16 first flew in prototype form on 30 December 1933. The I-16 was the first single-seat cantilever monoplane fighter with fully retractable landing gear to go into service anywhere in the world when it entered service in late 1934. This was before the prototypes of the Supermarine Spitfire, Hawker Hurricane, Messerschmitt Bf 109, and Curtiss P-36 had even flown. Serving throughout the rest of the 1930s, the I-16 was still in widespread use as a fighter at the start of the Great Patriotic War, by which time it was obsolescent. As with its biplane cousins, the I-15bis and the I-153, hundreds of I-16s were destroyed mainly on the ground in the first week of the Great Patriotic War, but enough survived to be heavily used in the first two years of the war. In all, 10,292 I-16s were produced (excluding six produced as replicas post-war), as determined by the expert on the Polikarpov fighters, the Russian air historian Mikhail Maslov. It was the most heavily produced fighter of the between the wars era (1919–1939).

TsKB-12bis

This first prototype of what became the I-16 first flew on 30 December 1933. As it was winter, it was equipped with a fixed ski landing gear instead of the retractable landing gear that was to be normally fitted and was painted in a striking overall red primer. It was fitted with an M-22 radial engine, a licence-built version of the French Gnome-Rhône Jupiter engine (which was itself a licence-built copy of the British Bristol Jupiter) of 480 hp. Unlike production I-16s, it was equipped with a three-bladed metal propeller (production I-16s had two-bladed propellers).

TsKB-12bis, the prototype of the I-16 in winter 1933–34. The aircraft is fitted with fixed skis for its initial flights instead of the normal retractable landing gear as these flights took place in winter. (*Viktor Kulikov's collection*)

I-16 Versions (Tip)

Below I shall describe some of the most important production versions of the I-16. The Russian for 'variant' or 'version' is *tip* ('type').

I-16 TIP 4

The first version, or type of the I-16 to go into service, the *tip* 4 was powered by the M-22 engine as was the case with the TsKB-12 bis. It first went into service in late 1934 and was not produced in as large of numbers as subsequent I-16s as it was something of a service trial aircraft. Nonetheless, 400 of the I-16s were produced with the M-22 engine. It was the first single-seat fighter with retractable landing gear to go into service anywhere in the world. Somewhat remarkably, a few may have still been in service at the time of the German invasion in summer 1941 and seen action.

I-16 TIP 5

The *tip* 5 was the first truly mass-produced version of the I-16, which continued in use into the Great Patriotic War. It had a M-25 engine of 700 hp (a licence-built Wright Cyclone R-1820) replacing the M-22 of the prototype and the previous *tip* 4, and the engine was enclosed in a longer, more streamlined cowling. It retained the enclosed cockpit of the TsKB-12bis and the *tip* 4 in its early production versions. The PV-1 machine guns of the *tip* 4 were replaced by rapid-fire ShKAS machine guns of the same calibre, 7.62 mm (30 calibre). The gunsight remained the telescopic OP-1 gunsight. Production of the *tip* 5 started in early 1936 at *zavodi* 21 and 153. Later production versions featured the open cockpit introduced on the *tip* 10.

I-16 TIP 10

On the *tip* 10, the armament from the *tip* 5 was doubled with the addition of a pair of synchronised ShKAS machine guns, mounted on top of the engine cowling supplementing the machine guns retained in the wings. The OP-1 'telescopic' gunsight was replaced by the PAK-1 reflector gunsight. Another major way the *tip* 10 differed from the *tip* 5 was the replacement of the forward-sliding canopy with a fixed windscreen, the cockpit now being open (some of the later *tip* 5s were also produced with the open cockpit). The pilots had disliked the restricted vision of the enclosed cockpit of the earlier I-16s, a prejudice that was shared with the pilots of other early monoplane fighters such as those used by Italy and Japan. The *tip* 10 was generally strengthened and was equipped with a boosted M-25V engine of 750 hp. Flaps were introduced on the I-16 for the first time with the *tip* 10. With the inclusion of the flaps, the ailerons were now decreased in span. Production of the *tip* 10 took place in 1938.

I-16 TIP 17

This version of the I-16 was typified by a much more powerful armament than earlier versions, featuring an unsynchronised ShVAK KP-20 ('K' for *Krylo* or 'Wing') 20-mm cannon in each wing, in addition to the two ShKAS machine guns mounted in the upper cowling. It retained the open cockpit and tail skid of the *tip* 10 and was likewise

I-16 *tip* 17 undergoing official tests in 1939. The long barrels of the ShVAK 20-mm cannons are well-evident. (*Viktor Kulikov's collection*)

equipped with the boosted M-25V engine. It could be equipped with retractable skis (the *tip* 10, which was produced at the same time, could also be so equipped). Combat tests of the *tip* 17 took place in Spain in 1938.

I-16 tip 18

The I-16 reverted to an all-machine gun armament with this *tip* with four ShKAS machine guns, as with the *tip* 10, two being mounted on top of the cowling, and two in the wings replacing the ShVAK cannons. The M-62 engine was now standard, along with a variable-pitch propeller on most of the *tip* 18s. In addition, a tailwheel was fitted as standard to later *tip* 18s for the first time on the I-16, consisting of a small solid rubber tyre (similar to that used on the I-153). This version was built in 1939.

I-16 tip 24

Introduced in 1939, the most-produced *tip* of the I-16, the *tip* 24 saw heavy use in the first few years of the Great Patriotic War as both a fighter and fighter-bomber. Equipped with the M-63 engine with an R-2 constant speed regulator to control the engine revolutions, the *tip* 24 was the fastest of all I-16 production variants, with a top speed of 304 mph (489 kph). It differed from most of the *tip* 18s in having the VISh AV-1 variable-pitch propeller. It was equipped with four ShKAS machine guns in the manner of the *tip* 18, and as a fighter-bomber could carry six RS-82 rockets under the wings.

I-16 tip 27

This was basically the *tip* 17 re-engined with the M-62 replacing the M-25V engine.

I-16 *TIP* 28

Very similar to the *tip* 24, with that variant's M-63 engine, this *tip* reverted to the machine gun (two ShKAS) and cannon (two ShVAK in the wings) armament of the *tip* 17. The heavier armament made the aircraft heavier and slower than the *tip* 24, although the firepower was considerably increased.

I-16 *TIP* 29

The main difference between the *tip* 29 and the preceding *tip* was the provision for a UBS heavy machine gun of 12.7-mm (50-calibre) in the bottom of the cowling, in place of the two ShVAK cannons in the wings. This gave it more concentrated firepower in the nose, in keeping with the then-current VVS philosophy on gun armament, which stressed having guns in the nose, including heavy machine guns. This left the wings free of fixed armament, which made the wings lighter and simpler, allowing rockets and bombs to be more easily carried (there were no guns to get in the way of the wiring).

The *tip* 29 was the last fighter version of the I-16 to be produced, with production ending in 1941, with eighty being built at Z.21 that year, before the *zavod* switched to producing LaGG-3s. Some *tip* 29s were equipped with radios and had large antenna masts on the starboard side of the front fuselage, slanting outwards. From 1941, the *tip* 29 was equipped to carry RS-82 rockets, bombs, or fuel tanks under the wings.

UTI-4 (I-16 *TIP* 15)

This dedicated trainer version of the I-16 had an additional seat added so both a trainee-pilot and an instructor-pilot could be accommodated, with the instructor-pilot normally sitting in the aft seat. For blind (instrument) flying, a hood or cover could be fitted over the aft cockpit, which was then to be occupied by the trainee-pilot. Production of the I-16 ended in 1942, when eighty-three UTI-4s were built at Z.458 at Rostov-on-Don (Rostov-na-Donu). Even after the fighter versions had been retired from service, this version saw use until at least the end of the Great Patriotic War, and a little beyond. Retired single-seat fighter versions of the I-16 also saw use as advanced trainers.

Combat Tactics

Since the German fighters were considerably faster than the I-16, the only effective tactic for the I-16 was to entice the Bf 109s into a manoeuvring contest, where the superior turning ability of the I-16 gave it an edge. Nonetheless, the I-16 was still outclassed by German fighters, such as the Bf 109E and Bf 109F, with their much superior speed, which allowed them to break off combat at will. Unless it surprised the German aircraft, the best the I-16 could normally hope for was stalemate. Interestingly, the speed at sea level for both the I-16 *tip* 24 and the Bf 109E was the same, at about 273 mph (440 kph), but above this, the speed of the Bf 109E rapidly became greater than that of the I-16 and at no altitude was the I-16 faster.

I-16s, apparently *tip* 24s, in flight. The nearest aircraft is equipped with an antenna mast, indicating it has a radio. (*Viktor Kulikov's collection*)

Combat Use

Spain

The first combat use of the I-16 was during the Spanish Civil War, when it was used by the Spanish Republican forces, sometimes with Soviet pilots and sometimes with Spanish pilots. The appearance of these very advanced fighters (for the time—1936) over Madrid has been attributed by some as saving the capital from the advancing Nationalist forces. The first I-16s, *tip* 5s, were received by the Spanish Republic in late October 1936, and the first I-16s appeared over Madrid on 9 November 1936.

For the next three years, it saw very heavy use and was not matched on the Nationalist side until the introduction of the early Bf 109s in 1937 (Bf 109As and Bf 109Bs). The I-16 and the Bf 109 were relatively equal in terms of combat ability, with neither having a clear advantage, except at higher altitudes (above 9,843 feet (3,000 m)), where the Bf 109 was superior to the I-16. In an effort to improve the I-16, the I-16 *tip* 10 was developed and deployed to Spain in March 1938, where its increased armament of four ShKAS machine guns (the *tip* 5 had only two) was greatly appreciated. The high-altitude performance was also improved with the boosted M-25V engine.

Throughout the Spanish Civil War, from its introduction, the I-16 was the best fighter the Spanish Republicans possessed in any quantity, and it was even licence-built in the Republic. Despite its abilities and contribution to the war effort, it was not able to prevent the eventual defeat of the Republic in April 1939. Captured I-16s were used during the war by the Nationalists, and I-16s that were present at the fall of the Republic continued to be used by the new Spanish government until at least 1952 as trainers. These were the last I-16s in service anywhere.

During the Spanish Civil War, the I-16 received two nicknames: *Rata*, or 'Rat', in Spanish, bestowed by the Nationalists, and *Mosca*, or 'Fly', bestowed by the Spanish Republicans (the I-16 *tip* 10 was sometimes known as the *Super-Mosca*). The nickname *Rata* continued to be used into the Great Patriotic War by the Germans, some of whose pilots had flown in the Spanish Civil War (as had some of the Soviet pilots).

Khalkhin-Gol

By May 1939, there were seventy-six I-16s in theatre, most of them *tip* 5s. *Tip* 10s and the cannon-equipped *tip* 17s arrived during the conflict, and by August, there were a total of 200 I-16s. Some *tip* 10s were re-engined with M-62 engines, thereby converting them into what were basically *tip* 18s, with the increased performance of the *tip* 18. These aircraft were then sent to the front. By the end of the conflict, 311 I-16s had taken part.

The I-16 acquitted itself well at the Khalkhin-Gol, having an advantage in armament, four guns to two guns, over the main Japanese fighter—the Nakajima Ki-27. The I-16 used RS-82 rockets for the first time, although it used them in an air-to-air role where it was reported that on 20 August 1939, two Ki-27s were downed by the rockets, with the rest of the Japanese fighters promptly leaving the area. In total, thirteen Japanese aircraft were claimed to have been downed by I-16s firing the RS-82s.

Winter War

Unfortunately for the Soviet Union and the I-16, the Winter War was an altogether different affair than the Khalkhin-Gol conflict. Here the Soviets were fighting a determined enemy on their own ground. The open cockpit, which I-16 pilots had successfully lobbied for, was not surprisingly uncomfortable in the intense cold of wintertime Finland. Skis helped with take-off and landing, but they were difficult to retract, and sometimes did not retract at all. Fuel tanks were used in quantity to help extend the I-16's rather short range.

Early Second World War

The Soviet invasion of Poland in September 1939, although the I-16 took part, apparently did not involve any air combat for the I-16s. It does not appear that the I-16 was involved in any combat in the incorporation of the Baltic States and Bessarabia in 1940.

Great Patriotic War

By June 1941, the I-16 was still in large-scale usage in the Soviet Union as a front-line fighter. As it was one of the main fighter aircraft of the VVS, along with the Polikarpov I-15bis and I-153, and as it was situated in the western military districts, the I-16 suffered huge losses on the initial day of the German invasion (22 June 1941) and in the weeks that followed.

Probably the most unusual use of the I-16 came during the early stages of the Great Patriotic War, when the I-16s were used as 'parasite' fighter-bombers. On 1 August 1941, two Tupolev TB-3 heavy bomber 'mother ships' each transported under their wings two bomb-carrying and piloted I-16 SPB (*Skorostnoiy Pikiruyushchiy*

Bombardirovshchik, 'Fast Dive-Bomber') fighters. The I-16s were successfully released and bombed oil tanks in Romania, continuing on to land at Soviet airbases. The *Zveno* operations were stopped in 1942 because of the vulnerability of the carriers, the TB-3.

Especially in the first six months of the Great Patriotic War, the I-16 saw heavy use as a dedicated fighter aircraft, despite its obsolescence and the heavy losses it suffered in the first few weeks of Operation Barbarossa. Due to its obsolescence, after the first year or so of the Great Patriotic War, the I-16 found itself mainly relegated to lesser fronts or for use as a fighter-bomber, often equipped with underwing rockets such as the RS-82, or small bombs. In this guise, it continued in use with the VVS' western units until late 1943 (or perhaps early 1944), after which it continued in use as an advanced trainer, sometimes with two seats (the UTI-4), until the end of the Great Patriotic War. Remarkably, one unit, the 888th IAP based in the Soviet Far East, was equipped with I-16 fighters until August 1945, at which time the unit received American Bell P-63 Kingcobras, with no I-16s taking part in the Manchurian Campaign.

A *tip* 29 equipped with RS-82 rockets under the wing, preparing to take off. The wartime green and black camouflage is very evident on this I-16, probably 1942.

Ace Boris Safonov beside his *tip* 24 of the 72nd IAP of the Northern Fleet in summer 1941. The inscription reads *Za Stalina* ('For Stalin!'). (*Viktor Kulikov's collection*)

An I-16 *tip* 29 of the 71st IAP armed with two RS-82 rockets under each wing. The aircraft is undergoing maintenance, as shown by the opened engine compartment. The horizontal attitude of the aircraft indicates it may be testing its guns. Note that all the landing gear covers have been removed on this I-16, probably 1942. (*Viktor Kulikov's collection*)

This line-up of I-16s contains both machine gun-armed I-16 *tip* 24s and cannon-armed I-16 *tip* 27s, probably 1942.

A *tip* 17 of the 4th GvIAP, Red Banner (Baltic) Fleet in spring 1942. The hinged outer portion of the main landing gear covers has been removed. (*Viktor Kulikov's collection*)

I-16 in Detail

General Description

The I-16 was a single-seat single-engined low-wing cantilever monoplane of mixed metal and wooden construction, with retractable main landing gear, a radial engine, and an open cockpit in most versions. The description below is in general applicable for a *tip* 24, which was the variant most commonly used during the Great Patriotic War, with differences of earlier versions being noted.

Fuselage

The circular-section fuselage was of wooden construction, consisting of a semi-monocoque structure, with wooden frames, longerons, and stringers overlaid with a fabric-covered plywood skin. The plywood layers were layered cross-grain to each other in thin sheets of veneer which the Soviets called *shpon*. The fin was of metal construction with fabric covering and was attached to the wooden fuselage. The engine cowling was covered in aluminium panels, as was the area around the guns on those I-16s with cowling-mounted guns (which included most I-16s, including the *tip* 24). From the TsKB-12 bis prototype to the *tip* 5, the pilot was equipped with a small canopy, which enclosed the cockpit and slid forward on rails. From the *tip* 10 onwards, this was replaced by a fixed windscreen. Later *tip* 5s were also characterised by this open cockpit. The *tip* 24 introduced an entry hatch on the starboard side, in addition to the hatch on the port side.

Wings

The structure of the fully cantilevered wings was metal, with metal spars and ribs, and with metal skin on the front part of the wing, and fabric covering aft of this. There was one panel on the lower wing which was metal covered to the aileron hinge. There was a narrower panel like this on the upper wing. The long-span ailerons were of metal construction with a fabric covering. The outer wing panels were fixed to a metal central structure, or 'centroplane', which was attached to the wooden fuselage. This centroplane was covered in wood, out to where the outer wing panels attached.

Tailplanes

The fully cantilevered tailplanes were of metal construction, with a metal-structured fabric-covered fin fixed to the wooden rear fuselage and all-metal fixed stabilisers with a fabric covering over a metal structure. The moveable control surfaces, the rudder, and elevators, were of metal construction with a fabric covering.

Engine

The engine on most early production I-16s was the M-25 radial engine (the *tip* 4 had featured the M-22), with later versions having the M-62 or M-63 radial engine. The M-25 was a licence-built version of the American Wright Cyclone R-1820 nine-cylinder 700-hp radial engine. The M-62 and the M-63 were more powerful developments of this engine, with the M-62 having a maximum rating of 1,000 hp, and the M-63 having a maximum

Top of the starboard wing of the I-16 showing the metal structure and the metal skinning on the forward part of the wing. (*I-16 Technical Manual*)

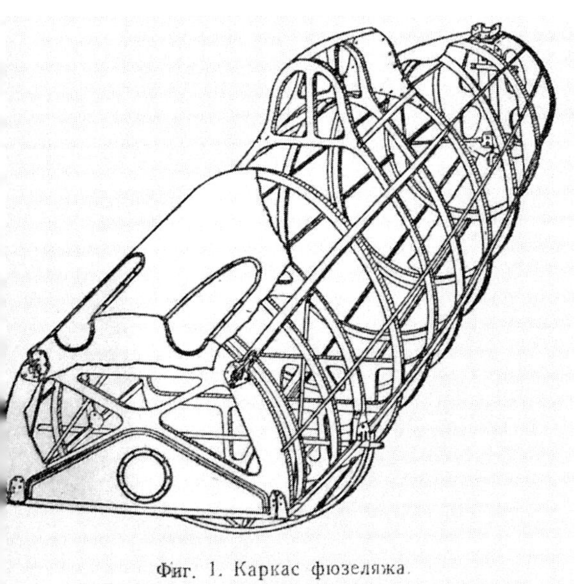

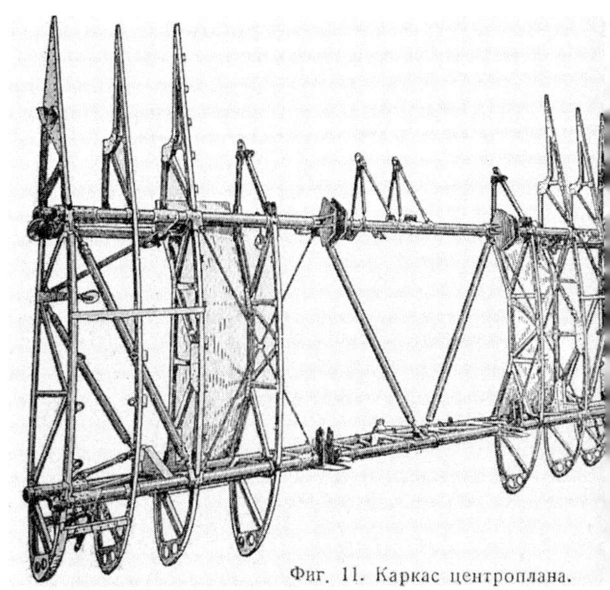

Above left: The wooden framework of the I-16 fuselage. (*I-16 Technical Manual*)

Above right: Central carry-through structure of the wings ('centroplane'). This is of all-metal construction. (*I-16 Technical Manual*) output of 1,100 hp. The propeller on all production I-16s was an adjustable-pitch metal two-bladed propeller (on the *tip* 24, this was the VISh-AV1), usually covered by a spinner. The spinner was shallow and conical in earlier versions of the I-16, such as the *tip* 5 and *tip* 10, but it was deeper and more rounded in later versions, such as the *tip* 24. A Hucks starter dog was fitted to the end of the propeller, at least from the *tip* 5 on.

Fuel System

The later I-16s (from the *tip* 18 on) had a single protected fuel tank in the fuselage. In the earlier I-16s, it was not protected. In addition, some I-16s were able to carry 'conformal'-type fuel tanks under the wings. These fuel tanks were used from the Winter War on to increase the I-16's limited range.

Controls

The I-16 until the *tip* 10 featured nearly full-span ailerons and no flaps. As with the I-153, the long ailerons on the early I-16s also functioned as flaperons. From the *tip* 10 onwards, the ailerons were shortened in span, and two all-metal flaps added, which met on the centreline of the lower fuselage.

The elevators were attached to a common tube passing through the wooden cone at the end of the fuselage. There was, therefore, no differential movement of the elevators. There were no moveable trim tabs or fixed tabs on the control surfaces, with the exception of fixed trim tabs on the ailerons of the later I-16 variants, such as the *tip* 17 and *tip* 24. These fixed tabs may have been ground-adjustable by bending them up or down. The control column was of a spade grip-type, typical for Soviet fighters of the 1930s and early 1940s and controlled both the ailerons and the elevators via connecting rods. Floor-mounted rudder pedals controlled the rudder via cables and pulleys.

Landing Gear

The main landing gear was manually operated by wires, worked by a hand crank in the cockpit, and retracted inwards, being enclosed by doors that were attached to the landing gear legs. The wheels were completely enclosed, with the outer portions of the wheels enclosed by doors that were hinged to the main wheel doors (these outer portions were sometimes removed in service). Early to mid-I-16s had a tail skid, but from the later *tip* 18 onwards, a solid rubber tailwheel was used (like that used on the I-153). Both the tail skid and the tailwheel were fixed and non-steerable.

Radio Equipment

Most I-16s were not equipped with any radio equipment, with neither a receiver nor a transmitter, though some later I-16s had at least a receiver. These were characterised by a radio mast mounted on the starboard side of the forward fuselage, canting outwards. The *tip* 24 had a hatch on the starboard side that opened up onto a compartment where the radio, when installed, was located. Although most radio-equipped I-16s had a mast, I have seen at least one photograph where there was no mast, but there was a single line from the fin that was bifurcated and attached to the fuselage, aft of the cockpit, in two places, on either side of the top of the fuselage spine. This may have been a field modification.

Fixed Armament

The fixed armament consisted of two unsynchronised ShKAS 7.62-mm (30-calibre) machine guns mounted in the wings on early I-16s, firing outside of the propeller arc, these being supplemented on later I-16s (beginning with the *tip* 10) with an additional pair of ShKAS machine guns mounted on top of the engine cowling, synchronised to fire through the spinning propeller. The *tip* 24 had four ShKAS machine guns. On the *tip* 17, *tip* 27, and *tip* 28, the wing machine guns were replaced by ShVAK KP-20 20-mm cannons, which were unsynchronised and fired outside of the propeller arc. The *tip* 29 was unique in featuring three machine guns, two ShKAS mounted on top of the cowling, and a UBS 12.7-mm (50-calibre) machine gun mounted on the bottom of the cowling, all the guns being synchronised to fire through the propeller disc. This gave it the same armament as the standard MiG-3. The *tip* 24 had a reflector gunsight, the PAK-1, which replaced the earlier OP-1 telescopic sight used on early I-16s such as the *tip* 5. The PAK-1 had been introduced on the *tip* 10 and was the same gunsight as used on the I-153.

ShVAK 20-mm cannon installation in the starboard wing of an I-16 *tip* 17. (*Viktor Kulikov's collection*)

Disposable Armament

For use as a fighter-bomber during the Great Patriotic War, the I-16 could be equipped with six RS-82 rockets mounted on RO-82 rails under the wings, with three per wing. In addition, on some versions, it could carry small bombs, such as a 220-lb (100-kg) FAB-100 under the fuselage.

Colour and Markings for the Polikarpov Fighters

Since they entered service before 1941, most of the I-15bis, I-153s, and I-16s were originally painted with the pre-Second World War scheme of AE-9 light grey and/or AII Aluminium. Some aircraft continued to wear this scheme into the Great Patriotic War. Some were repainted with the 1940 camouflage scheme of A-18f Blue and A-19f Green on the metal portions of aircraft, as well as AII Blue and AII 3 Green on the wooden portions. After the beginning of the Great Patriotic War, new nitrocellulose lacquers were used, such as AMT-6 Black, painted in bands on the AMT-4 Green upper surfaces. The red star insignia at the start of the war would have been outlined in black. With the black/green scheme, the stars could have been plain with no outline, or outlined in black, white, or silver. Since these fighters continued into use into at least late 1943 or early 1944, it is possible (though not likely) that they may have been repainted in the later two-grey fighter scheme of AMT-11 Grey-Blue and AMT-12 Dark Grey over AMT-6 Blue. If this happened, they would have had the later '1943'-style red stars.

Conclusion

The Polikarpov fighters, both the I-15bis and I-153 biplanes, and the I-16 monoplane were already at least obsolescent by the beginning of the Second World War. By the Great Patriotic War, against the best fighter in the world at the time (mid-1941), the German Bf 109F, or even against the older Bf 109E, they were obsolete, especially the biplanes. Nonetheless, as numerically the most important fighters in the Soviet inventory at the beginning of the Great Patriotic War, of necessity, they bore the brunt of the fighting in the early stages of the war, as more of the modern monoplane fighters, such as the LaGG-3, MiG-3, and the Yak-1 reached operational status.

After being transferred to lesser fronts or used as fighter-bombers, the Polikarpov fighters continued to contribute directly to the Soviet war effort until late 1943/early 1944, continuing to be used as trainers until the end of the war; they still continued in use as fighters until the end of the war in a few backwaters. That they were still the main VVS fighters at the start of the Great Patriotic War was a failure of Soviet leadership in terms of fighter development and a failure to keep up their edge in aviation technology; it was no fault of the Polikarpov OKB as the I-16 had been a true aeronautical trendsetter when it had first entered service in 1934.

Polikarpov Fighter Specifications

N.B. Metric measurements are in parentheses			
Type (tip)	I-5	I-15bis	I-153
Year	1933	1938	1940
Engine	M-22	M-25V	M-62
Max. Power (Horsepower)	480	750	1,000
Fixed Armament	2 × PV-1 7.62-mm machine guns	4 × PV-1 7.62-mm machine guns	4 × ShKAS 7.62-mm machine guns
Disposable Armament	During the GPW could be equipped with RS-82 rockets and small bombs	6 × RS-82 Rockets, 331 lb (150 kg) of bombs	6 × RS-82 Rockets, 441 lb (20 kg) of bombs
Length—feet (m)	22.24 (6.78)	20.34 (6.2)	20.24 (6.17)
Wingspan—feet (m)	33.6 (10.24)	33.46 (10.2)	32.81 (10)
Weight (Empty)—lb (kg)	2,059 (934)	2,740 (1,243)	3,031 (1,375)
Weight (Loaded)—lb (kg)	2,987 (1,355)	3,748 (1,700)	4,193 (1,902)
Max. Speed at Sea Level—mph (kph)	173 (278)	203 (327)	227 (365)
Top Speed—mph (kph)	173 (278)	236 (379)	276 (444)
Range—miles (km)	410 (660)	478 (770)	460 (740)
Service Ceiling—feet (m)	24,606 (7,500)	29,856 (9,100)	35,105 (10,700)
Turn Time (sec)	10	11	12-13

-16 *tip* 5 (early)	I-16 *tip* 24	I-16 *tip* 28
936	1939	1939
Л-25A	M-63	M-63
'30	1,100	1,100
? × ShKAS 7.62-mm machine guns	4 × ShKAS 7.62-mm machine guns	2 × ShKAS 7.62-mm machine guns, 2 × ShVAK KP-20 20-mm cannons
?20 lb (100 kg) of bombs (some may ıave been fitted with rockets during he war)	6 × RS-82 Rockets, 441 lb (200 kg) of bombs	6 × RS-82 Rockets, 441 lb (200 kg) of bombs
9.69 (6)	20.01 (6.1)	20.01 (6.1)
?9.53 (9)	29.53 (9)	29.53 (9)
?,467 (1,119)	3,049 (1,383)	3,093 (1,403)
,325 (1,508)	4,149 (1,882)	4,383 (1,988)
?42 (390)	255 (410)	265 (427)
?77 (445)	304 (489)	288 (463)
36 (540)	273 (440)	280 (450)
0,184 (9,200)	31,824 (9,700)	32,644 (9,950)
4-15	17-18	18

6
Yakovlev Fighters

The Yakovlev series of fighters—starting with the Yak-1 and ending with the Yak-3 and late-model Yak-9s—were the most heavily-produced Soviet fighters during the Second World War (indeed of all time), with over 32,000 being produced during the war, and with over 4,000 being produced post-war for a total of more than 36,000. More than 16,000 of the Yak-9 alone were produced, with production continuing until 1948. By contrast, fewer than 23,000 Lavochkin fighters were produced, and under 5,000 of the most popular Lend-Lease fighter, the American-built Bell P-39 Airacobra, saw service with the Soviet Union.

The total production run of the Yakovlev piston-engined fighters was 36,683 (one source has 36,732), which was more than the number of Bf 109s produced, which was around 35,000. This makes the Yakovlev fighters the most heavily produced fighter series of all time. Some might argue that the Yakovlev fighters were not all the same aircraft, but a Yak-1 had more in common with a late war Yak-9U or Yak-3 VK-105PF-2 than a Spitfire Mk I had with a Spitfire F.24. Even if one excludes the substantially redesigned all-metal Yak-9P and Yak-3 VK-107A, the total number of Yakovlev piston-engined fighters is still greater than the number of Bf 109s produced.

Please note that despite its being numbered before the Yak-7 and the Yak-9 in its service designation, the Yak-3 is here described after these fighters as it was introduced into service much later in the Great Patriotic War (1944 as opposed to 1941 for the Yak-7 and 1942 for the Yak-9).

Yak-1

This first of the Yakovlev fighters was the best of the three new fighters that were entering service in 1940 and 1941, the others being the LaGG-3 and the MiG-3. Although at first a rather immature design beset by various defects (especially concerning the engine) and clearly inferior to the German Bf 109F and Bf 109G, as well as the Fw 190 fighters, the Yak-1 was continuously improved and modified on the

Aleksandr Sergeyevich Yakovlev (on the left) talking to a Yakovlev fighter pilot. The fighter appears to be a late-model Yak-9. (*Viktor Kulikov's collection*)

production lines until it was at least nearly the equal of these aircraft at low altitudes. The Yak-1 remained in production until mid-1944, even after the introduction of the later Yak-7 and Yak-9 fighters, with a total of 8,667 Yak-1s being produced by the time production ended. The Yak-1 gave rise to the Yak-7 and Yak-9. The Yak-7 was a trainer that was turned into a good fighter, and the Yak-9, developed from the Yak-7, was the most produced and versatile Soviet fighter of the war. The Yak-1 also gave rise to the Yak-3, its replacement on the production lines, which proved to be one of the outstanding dogfighters of the Second World War.

I-26 (Yak-1 Prototype)

Even before Stalin had requested new fighters in 1939 for the VVS, by November 1938, A. S. Yakovlev had already completed a design drawing for a new, modern single-engined fighter, which became the I-26, with the 'I' signifying *Istrebitel'*, or 'Fighter'.

This design was submitted to the NKAP in spring 1939, and a prototype was approved for construction by a government decree dated 29 June (or July) 1939. The design was approved by October 1939 by the NKAP, and on 1 October 1939, construction began on the I-26 prototype at Z.115 in Moscow (the Yakovlev OKB's facility, the Yakovlev OKB being OKB-115). Construction of the first prototype was completed on 27 December 1939.

I-26-1 (I-26-I)

The first prototype was named the I-26-1, as a second prototype, the I-26-2, was planned to be built. On 5 January 1940, the I-26-1 commenced taxiing trials. It flew for the first time on 13 January 1940, the first of the 'new' generation of Soviet fighters to fly. The test pilot was Yu. I. Piontkovskiy, who, although pleased with the handling of the I-26-1, had to cut this first flight short because of the rising oil temperature. In all, fifteen flights had to be curtailed because of the issue with the oil temperature. Various fixes were attempted, such as redoing the oil piping and installing different oil radiators, but still, the engine had to be changed three times due to damage caused by overheating. On 27 April 1940, disaster struck when the I-26-1 prototype crashed, killing the pilot, Piontkovskiy.

The aircraft crashed after performing two barrel rolls at a relatively low altitude, 3,281 feet (1,000 m). A commission looking into the accident determined that the probable cause was that the landing gear came loose during the barrel rolls, and part of the gear broke through the wing surface, causing the aircraft to enter into a spin or lose too much speed. The wings on later aircraft were consequently strengthened.

I-26-2 (I-26-II)

The *Dooblyor*—'Doubler' or 'Understudy' (second prototype) of the I-26—differed from the first prototype in several ways, starting with the inclusion of an under nose oil cooler, which altered the smooth under-cowling of the I-26-1. All production Yakovlev fighters until the Yak-3 and the Yak-9U would feature this under-cowling-mounted oil cooler, which became a distinguishing feature for most wartime Yakovlev fighters. This new oil cooler was fitted in order to cope with the high oil temperatures that had plagued the I-26-1. That the solution was a good one can be surmised by

I-26-1, the first prototype of the Yak-1, in 1940. (*Viktor Kulikov's collection*)

its subsequent use on almost all wartime Yakovlev fighters. Another change from the I-26-1 was that armament was eventually fitted to the I-26-2; the I-26-1 was apparently never armed. The twin 'clam-shell' tailwheel doors were also removed, not to reappear until the late Yak-1Bs.

After the loss of the first prototype, the I-26-2 was the only remaining I-26 prototype, and it flew for the first time on 23 March 1940, before the first prototype had crashed. The I-26-2 was submitted for state tests on 26 May 1940. Still lacking its armament, it was initially denied acceptance for undergoing state tests by the NII VVS, at least partially because the factory tests had not been adequately completed. Nevertheless, by order of the Chief of the Aviation Supply Department Alekseyev on 29 May 1940, the I-26-2 was accepted for state trials. The state tests took place from 1 June to 15 June 1940. The tests showed the I-26-2 to have good performance as compared to other experimental fighters of the time, such as the Mikoyan-Gurevich I-200 (MiG-1/MiG-3), the Polikarpov I-180, and the Lavochkin-Gorbunov-Gudkov I-301 (LaGG-3), but it was still an immature aircraft. Interestingly, the NKAP requirement for fighter aircraft to have a minimum range of 621 miles (1,000 km) was not applied to the Yakovlev fighter, although it was applied to the new Mikoyan-Gurevich and Lavochkin fighters. Perhaps this apparent 'exemption' was due to Aleksandr Yakovlev's supposedly strong influence with Stalin.

One issue was that the aircraft was under-strength due to its being overweight. Its strength tolerances had been based upon a flying weight of 5,071 lb (2,300 kg), but the actual weight was 5,952 lb (2,700 kg). This reduced the safety factor, which limited the flying capabilities of the I-26. Another problem that appeared once the armament was fitted and fired was the issue of the spent cartridges and links hitting the horizontal stabiliser, causing damage. This was a serious enough problem that firing the weapons was halted during the state tests.

Even with its restricted flight regime, the I-26-2 did show some promise; the aircraft achieved a maximum speed of 364 mph (585.5 kph) at 16,404 feet (5,000 m). In the opinion of the pilots involved with the testing, the aircraft could be mastered by a pilot of medium capability. There were still problems, however, such as the cockpit being too hot (an all-too-common complaint for the various new fighters), a lack of longitudinal stability, the problems with the weapons noted previously, and continuing issues with the oil system. It was also felt that the wing and overall structure was too weak. Due to these issues, the NII VVS concluded that the I-26 had not properly completed its state trials (in contrast, the I-200 was considered to have passed its state trials successfully on the first try). However, the I-301 had also not properly completed its state trials. Yakovlev was instructed to fix these issues with his third prototype, the I-26-3.

I-26-3 (I-26-III)

The third prototype of the I-26 series, the I-26-3, was constructed at the OKB's Z.115; it began its state trials on 7 October 1940. Testing the weapons and handling took place from 13 October through 12 November 1940. This improved I-26 had strengthened wings, better landing gear, and better weapons; the cockpit also was cooler with improved ventilation. It was concluded on 3 December 1940 that the

I-26-3 had passed the state tests. Even before the I-26 had completed its state tests, production had already begun on the Yak-1, as the I-26 had been renamed on 1 December 1940. Mass production of the I-26 (Yak-1) had by now been organised at *Zavodi* 126, 292, and 301 by a resolution passed in May 1940.

Yak-1

The I-26 was put into production as the 'Yak-1', following the new Soviet convention of naming designs after their chief designer, in this case, Aleksandr Yakovlev. The '1' signified that this was Yakovlev's first fighter design (fighters featured odd numbers in the Soviet numbering system). Full-scale production was started at *Zavod* 292 in Saratov and at *Zavod* 301 in Moscow in fall 1940. Z.301 quit producing the Yak-1 in 1941 after only 117 had been built, but Z.292 produced the Yak-1 until June 1944, producing a total of 8,550 Yak-1s at this factory. In all, 8,667 Yak-1s were produced.

Yak-1 Military Series (Pre-production Series)

Before the Yak-1 entered large-scale production, a small batch of aircraft were built at Z.301 in Moscow for military trials. These aircraft were armed with two ShKAS machine guns in the upper cowling, and a ShVAK MP-20 20-mm cannon firing through the propeller spinner. The 20-mm cannon had 110 rounds. The engine was the M-105P, equipped with a VISh-61P propeller, with a diameter of 9.84 feet (3 m). It appears that all later Yak-1s also used this propeller. The aircraft did not have radios nor landing lights.

The first aircraft was completed on 22 March 1940, and the remaining ten aircraft were completed before the beginning of June 1940, more than a year before the launch of the German invasion.

Yak-1 (Early Production Series)

Despite some unresolved problems, so urgent was the need for modern fighters by the VVS that the Yak-1 was put into production, with the intention that the teething troubles would be resolved during production (this would not be the last time the Soviets would adopt this somewhat desperate expedient). The first production Yak-1s had a maximum speed of 348 mph (560 kph) at 15,570 feet (4,746 m), with a service ceiling of 32,500 feet (9,906 m). The aircraft was armed with one unsynchronised ShVAK MP-20 20-mm cannon mounted between the engine cylinders of the M-105P, firing through the propeller spinner, and two synchronised ShKAS 7.62-mm (30-calibre) machine guns mounted on top of the engine cowling firing through the propeller disc.

The Yak-1 could execute a 360-degree horizontal turn in a very respectable nineteen–twenty seconds, giving it good horizontal manoeuvrability, although it could not match the Bf 109F in vertical manoeuvrability. Until the series 36, the Yak-1 was equipped with the M-105P engine; from the series 36 in 1941 the engine was the improved M-105PA. The M-105PA differed from the M-105P fitted to the earlier Yak-1s in having float-less carburettors which permitted inverted flight and negative loads in a dive, and in having a longer service life. It had the same power rating as the M-105P. The tailwheel was

Early Yak-1, but not of the earliest type as it has the LaGG-3 style rear windows and a fixed tailwheel. The *tip* of the ShVAK 20-mm cannon can be seen protruding from the propeller spinner. The two-piece doors of the main landing gear show up well here. (*Viktor Kulikov's collection*)

made non-retractable due to problems with the retraction mechanism. Although the Yak-1 did not improve its performance during 1941, changes made it more reliable, and it required less time to prepare the aircraft for a sortie.

Some early Yak-1s were equipped with six RS-82 rockets mounted on RO-82 rails under the wings. The rocket rails were removed in May 1942 as these degraded the aircraft's performance too much; this was at the same time the fitting of these rockets was made optional on MiG-3s because of similar performance concerns.

The early Yak-1s were initially lacking any radio equipment, having neither receivers nor transmitters. Later, some were equipped with receivers (the RSI-4 from the series 20), but it was not until 1943 that large numbers of the Yakovlev fighters began to be equipped with both receivers and transmitters. This lack of complete or even any radio equipment early in the Great Patriotic War was common with VVS aircraft such as fighters and the Il-2 Shturmovik attack aircraft and limited their combat cohesion and effectiveness in flight.

Yak-1 with RS-82 Rockets and Bombs

Some Yak-1s were equipped to carry RS-82 rockets on RO-82 rails. This stemmed from a GKO order dated 23 September 1941, which directed Z.292 to produce Yak-1s with RO-82 rocket rails. The Yak-1s were otherwise only slightly modified, having reinforcing plates of plywood layers where the rails were installed.

These Yak-1s were first used near Moscow, where the RS-82 rockets were used in an anti-aircraft role, being fired at enemy aircraft. The firing range was from 1,640 to 2,625 feet (500 to 800 m). Although the spread of the unguided rockets made a hit rather unlikely, they were able to break up bomber formations, which made the bombers more vulnerable to individual attack as their mutual defensive fire was lessened. In the event an aircraft was hit by one of the rockets, the aircraft was destroyed. The RS-82s were also used to attack ground targets, which is where they proved most successful.

Despite some success, the rockets and rails were removed as described previously per a GKO order dated 10 May 1942. The rails and the rockets had degraded the Yak-1's performance too much, with the top speed being up to 18.64 mph (30 kph) less with the rockets mounted. Apparently, not all pilots were happy with the decision to remove the rockets. The RS-82s themselves and other rockets continued to be used against ground targets by such dedicated bombers as the Il-2 and the Pe-2. In all, a total of 1,148 Yak-1s were produced with the rocket rails and provision for the RS-82 rockets. These rocket-armed Yak-1s were produced from October 1941 to May 1942 (series 43 to 65).

Rockets were not the only underwing stores that some Yak-1s were equipped to carry. Strangely, at about the same time that the GKO was ordering the removal of the rocket rails as they degraded the Yak-1's performance, they decreed on 26 April 1942 that Yak-1s were to be provided with bomb racks. The aircraft was able to carry small bombs—two 220-lb (100-kg) bombs on two underwing racks, for a total load of 441 lb (200 kg). BI-42 bomb racks were installed on Yak-1s from the series 80 to the series 126 (February 1943). The racks were not installed for a while, then they were installed again from the series 148 until the end of production for the Yak-1. The racks were attached to dural ribs, the same ribs the landing gear were attached to.

The Yak-1 did not have a true bombsight, so it was only able to bomb large area targets. This and the fact that fighters were needed desperately just as fighters, not fighter-bombers in 1941–42 and even through the Battle of Kursk in 1943, led to the bomb racks being deleted from the Yak-1s from the series 127 on. However, from fall 1943, when the Yak-1s were being replaced as front-line fighters, they started being used again as fighter-bombers, and the bomb racks were re-installed on some aircraft. On the production line, the bomb racks were re-installed from the series 148 until the last series of Yak-1s, the series 192.

Yak-1 with Retractable Skis

In order to operate from snow-covered airfields during the winter, some Yak-1s were produced with retractable skis in the winter of 1941–42. An aircraft with skis underwent joint factory and state tests (these joint tests were sometimes done to expedite testing) at Z.292 in November 1941. In addition to the skis, the MK-7 winter finish was applied over the black/green camouflage at the factory.

The skis themselves were wooden and were fitted to the retractable landing gear struts, the skis lying flush against the underside of the wings when retracted, with the nose of the skis projecting forward of the wing leading edge. The tail skis were fixed. As the drag of the skis, even when retracted, and the extra weight lowered the performance too much, the skis were only used in the winter of 1941–42. After this, the skis were removed, and the modified aircraft were presumably re-fitted with normal, wheeled landing gear. Apparently, some aircraft in the northern sectors were still used with skis. In all, around 830 Yak-1s were equipped with skis from September 1941 to 25 February 1942.

Yak-1 equipped with retractable skis and underwing RS-82 rockets in winter 1941–42. It is finished in winter camouflage. Note the cloudy appearance of the sliding portion of the canopy. This could be due to condensation, the poor quality of the clear material, or both. (*Viktor Kulikov's collection*)

Yak-1 (Late Production Series)

As the Yak-1 continued in production, efforts were made to improve it and correct its most glaring deficiencies. One of its faults, first noted during early testing, was its propensity to nose over if the wheel brakes were applied too much or too harshly. This inability to effectively use the wheel brakes led to a relatively long landing run for the Yak-1, which thereby required a long landing strip—something that was not always readily available on the primitive forward airfields the Yak-1 often operated from. This problem was at least partially solved with the shift in the centre of gravity backwards of the Yak-7, described further on. From 1941, the Yak-1s were equipped with the improved M-105PA engine.

Due to a shortage of Plexiglas, the rear glazing on the later Yak-1s was reduced to two small semi-circular windows, similar to those used on the LaGG-3. This reduced the rearward vision of the pilot, but it was considered a necessary expedient. Including the earlier Yak-1s with the M-105P, the total number of Yak-1s produced from September 1940 to May 1942 was 2,947 aeroplanes.

Yak-1B (Yak-1 M-105PF, Yak-1b)

The appearance of improved versions of the Bf 109, such as the Bf 109F-4 with the DB-601E, which was more powerful than the DB-601N of the Bf 109F-1, led the VVS to seek ways to improve the engines and performance of their own fighter aircraft. With the DB-601N engine, the Bf 109F-1s had a speed advantage over the Yak-1 M-105P of 12 to 17 mph (19 to 27 kph). By comparison, a Bf 109F equipped with the DB-601E had a speed advantage of more than 25 mph (40 kph) over the Yak-1. This was a significant advantage that needed to be addressed. From June 1942, work began on improving the Yak-1 to match this new German threat.

This last version of the Yak-1 was characterised by its cut-down rear fuselage, which enabled an all-around vision bubble-type (or 'bubble-top') canopy to be fitted. Similar canopies were fitted to later Yakovlev fighters, such as the Yak-9 and Yak-3. Even before the appearance of the Yak-1B, this style of canopy had been applied to Yak-1s by a Maj. Shinkarenko as a field-modification to the aircraft in his regiment, the 42nd IAP. Evidently, this regiment served as a sort of field test unit for Yakovlev fighter modifications and innovations. These field-modified canopies were not exactly the same as the factory-built canopies of the Yak-1B, but similar. This canopy markedly increased the vision of the pilot and was greatly appreciated when it was introduced on production Yak-1s. The armoured seat back was lowered, and protection for the pilot's head was now provided by a slab of armour glass behind the pilot.

The pilot was also now provided with a single-grip or 'joystick'-type control column, replacing the spade-grip control columns of earlier Yak-1s. The pilot was

Above: Yak-1B Etalon for 1942 production. (*Viktor Kulikov's collection*)

Below: Side view of the Yak-1B Etalon for 1942 production. The bubble-top canopy is notable. Also note the small door attached to the front of the now-retractable tailwheel. (*Viktor Kulikov's collection*)

Above: Yak-1B fighters of the 3rd GvIAP, Red Banner (Baltic) Fleet, summer 1943. (*Viktor Kulikov's collection*)

Below: Presentation Yak-1B for fighter ace Boris N. Yeryomin of the 31st GvIAP. December 1942. The inscription refers to his being a pilot at Stalingrad and refers to the collective farmer, Ferapont Petrovich Golovatiy, who donated this aircraft. (*Viktor Kulikov's collection*)

provided with an armoured left armrest. The armament consisted of one ShVAK 20-mm cannon firing through the propeller, and one UBS 12.7-mm machine gun mounted on the upper cowling on the port side, as with the contemporaneous Yak-9 (see further on). In addition, the Yak-1B featured the boosted M-105PF (the 'F' was for *Forsirovanniy*, or 'Boosted'), which had a maximum horsepower of 1,260 at its maximum rated altitude. It was fitted with a VISh-105 propeller (the initial Yak-1s had used the VISh-61P propeller), along with a Yak-7-type OP-352 oil cooler with a larger surface. The new oil cooler required a reshaped intake. The engine's boost was increased from 17.6 psi (910 mm Hg) to 20.3 psi (1,050 mm Hg). The engine was less powerful at high altitudes than the earlier M-105s but was more powerful at lower altitudes, which is where Soviet fighters normally engaged the enemy.

The Yak-1B had a maximum speed of 366 mph (589 kph). To reduce drag, the tailwheel was made retractable. The Yak-1B version is referred to in some references as the 'Yak-1M'; this is incorrect as this properly referred to the lightened Yak-1 (described further on) that led to the Yak-3. As an interesting note, the 'Yak-1B' (or sometimes 'Yak-1b') was never officially designated as such, but by analogy with the Yak-7B, it was called the 'Yak-1B' in combat units and is commonly referred to by this name in post-war literature, as in the present book. Although not 'officially' designated as the Yak-1B, the name did make its way into official documents, such as unit histories.

The Yak-1B flew its state tests from 4 to 14 July 1942 at the NII VVS, which the aircraft passed. Tests showed that the Yak-1B was superior to the Yak-1s then in production, and full-scale production of the Yak-1B was authorised by a resolution of the GKO dated 11 August 1942. One source has production starting at Z.292 on 4 June 1942 because of a GKO order dated 29 May 1942, with full transition to the M-105PF engine taking place in July 1942 starting with the tenth aircraft of the series 79. At any rate, production of the Yak-1B was ongoing in September 1942, and from October 1942, it was the only version of the Yak-1 that was produced.

From 1942–1943, Yak-1Bs with improved streamlining were tested at Z.292, the LII, and the NII VVS. The aircraft featured better sealing, the outer finish was improved, and fairings were installed above and below the exhausts. These aircraft with the improved streamlining were produced from the series 111 to the series 192 (the last Yak-1B series), from December 1942 to July 1944.

In July 1943, a more streamlined oil radiator was introduced for the production aircraft. At some point in the production of the Yak-1B, the retractable tailwheel was changed from having a single door attached to the front of the tailwheel strut to twin 'clam-shell' doors hinged on either side of the tailwheel well that closed inward to completely enclose it, as with the Yak-9, which began production in October 1942.

Production did not end until June 1944, when it was replaced on the production lines by its development and replacement, the Yak-3, by which time 4,188 Yak-1Bs had been produced, out of a total of 8,667 Yak-1s of all types. Yak-1Bs were flown by Polish pilots operating with the Red Air Force from 23 August 1944, when the 'Warsaw' regiment flew its first mission. The Polish continued to fly the Yak-1B for a short time after the end of the Second World War. Yugoslavian pilots also flew the

Yak-1B during the Great Patriotic War and continued to fly them for several years after the war, making the Yugoslavian Air Force the last user of the Yak-1.

Some aces actually preferred the Yak-1B over the Yak-9 because it was lighter and more manoeuvrable, with the same armament of one 20-mm cannon and one 12.7-mm machine gun, and some Yak-1Bs remained in use with the VVS until the end of the Great Patriotic War.

Yak-1: Lightweight Version

In an effort to match the performance of the German fighters such as the Bf 109F, the Soviets sought ways to improve the Yak-1. One way was to lighten the aircraft. The machine guns were removed, leaving only the 20-mm cannon, and the lighter metal tail from the Yak-7 was installed. In May 1942, a lightweight Yak-1 was tested, with impressive results, such that plans were made to put the aircraft into mass production. From 12 to 17 October 1942, another lightened Yak-1 underwent state tests; this aircraft was probably one of the twenty lightened Yak-1 aircraft that were produced for combat trials.

In September 1942, twenty lightened Yak-1 aircraft were produced without the two ShKAS machine guns, no RSI-4 radio, and the metal tail of the Yak-7 installed. These changes resulted in a weight saving of 353 lb (160 kg). The top speed was now 368 mph (592 kph) at 12,467 feet (3,800 m). Flight tests against a Yak-7B showed the Yak-1 to have superior climb capabilities and vertical manoeuvrability. This improved vertical manoeuvrability enabled the lightened Yak-1 to better fight against improved Bf 109s, such as the Bf 109F-4 and Bf 109G-2.

The 512th IAP of the 220th IAD of the 16th VA was the first regiment to receive the new lightweight Yak-1s. These aircraft were flown in mixed formations with unmodified fighters, and the number of sorties before downing a German aircraft fell from twenty-six to eighteen sorties. The 520th IAP of the 220th IAD also received some of the new aircraft.

However, at about the same time as the lightweight Yak-1 was developed, various methods and modifications, including the adoption of the M-105PF engine, allowed normal weight Yak-1s to achieve similar performance, without the reduction in gun armament. Due to this, the lightened Yak-1 did not go into large-scale production. The ten aircraft that were produced (in addition to the twenty that had been produced for combat trials) went to the 12th GvIAP of the 6th IAK of the Moscow PVO.

Yak-1 M-105PF MPVO (Yak-1 MPVO)

This Yak-1 type was a modified version for use by air defence (PVO) units. The 'MPVO' stood for *Mesnaya Protivovozdushnaya Oborona* or 'Local (Point) Air Defence'. It was fitted with various equipment to make it suitable to fly the aircraft in all kinds of weather and at night. The new equipment included a RPK-10 radio-compass, a FS-155 landing light in the port wing leading edge, and an AG-5 artificial horizon. It was produced in 1943 and 1944 by Z.292, where 385 were produced. Given when it was produced, it would have had the all-around vision cockpit canopy of the contemporaneous Yak-1B and was probably almost identical in outward appearance.

Yak-1 M-106P

In an effort to increase the performance of the Yak-1, it was fitted with the new Klimov M-106P engine to create a high-altitude fighter. The M-106 engine was fitted with a VISh-61P propeller and was a development of the M-105 engine with a single-speed centrifugal Dollezhal supercharger (designed by V. A. Dollezhal of the TsIAM). The boost pressure was increased to 22.72 psi (1,175 mm Hg). It developed a maximum rating of 1,350 hp.

In addition to the new engine, the Yak-1 M-106P featured metal wing spars and the all-metal tail of the Yak-7. The water radiator was reshaped, and the armament was comprised of a ShVAK 20-mm cannon with 120 rounds and an UBS machine gun with 210 rounds (the same armament carried by the Yak-1B). The Yak-1 M-106 featured the all-around vision canopy of the Yak-1B, with which it was outwardly nearly identical.

Z.153 built the prototype Yak-1 M-106P at the end of 1942. The aircraft underwent factory tests ending on 10 January 1943, then underwent tests at the LII ending 31 January 1943. The factory tests revealed a top speed at sea level of 334 mph (537 kph) and 377 mph (606 kph) at 11,155 feet (3,400 m).

Although the M-106P was an immature engine, small-scale production started on the Yak-1 M-106P, with forty-seven being built by Z.292 by February 1943. Due to problems with the M-106P engine, none of the production aircraft entered service, and some were later re-engined with the M-105PF.

Experimental Versions

UTI-26 (I-27)

In addition to introducing the idea for the I-26 frontal fighter, Yakovlev also put forward a design for a new fighter trainer, to train pilots on how to operate the new monoplane fighters of the VVS. This design was given the OKB designation of 'I-27' and was essentially a two-seater trainer version of the I-26 (Yak-1). Two prototypes were built, the UTI-26-I, and the UTI-26-II. The UTI-26-II was equipped with two ShKAS machine guns with 500 rounds each. The UTI-26-II introduced a modified landing gear, with main wheels of 650 mm and a tailwheel of 300 mm. The landing gear was changed, with the main wheel axles now pointing inward instead of pointing outward and trapping the wheels against the gear doors. The gear doors were changed also, with a single-piece door replacing the two-piece doors of the Yak-1. The tailplanes were increased in size on the second prototype for better stability. Due to the centre of gravity being moved aft (which helped with the nose-overs during landing), the water radiator was moved forward compared to the Yak-1.

State tests were conducted from 1 January to 14 February 1941. It was this aircraft that became the Yak-7 (see further on), which was used as both a trainer and a fighter. Its development as the Yak-7 is described in that section.

Yak-1 with Two UBS Machine Guns

A Yak-1 had its two ShKAS 7.62-mm machine guns replaced by two UBS 12.7-mm machine guns, which increased the weight of firepower by 1.5 times. This was done at Z.292 in May 1941. Six experimental aircraft built to this standard were produced in January and February 1942. It passed both factory and state tests, but due to the lesser performance caused by the greater weight, it was not produced in quantity.

Yak-1M

As this lightened version of the Yak-1 led directly to the Yak-3, it is described in detail in that section.

Combat Tactics

American aircraft used so-called 'boom and zoom' techniques, whereby they made diving attacks against enemy aircraft, using the speed and diving abilities of their powerful and heavy fighters, then climbing back to make their attack again. The American aircraft were generally optimised for higher altitudes, with powerful superchargers. In contrast, with small, light, and manoeuvrable aircraft such as the Yak-1, Soviet tactics consisted of manoeuvring with the enemy, trying to turn inside the enemy aircraft to get into close contact, then using their nose guns, including their cannon, to down the opposing aircraft with a few bursts. The German fighters were between the American fighters and the Soviet fighters in terms of size and used both 'boom and zoom' tactics and manoeuvring tactics. The Yak-1s tried to engage the German fighters in horizontal turning battles, where they had the edge, as opposed to vertical manoeuvring, where the Germans had the edge. The German aircraft could also dive better than the Yak-1, due to their greater weight, the Fw 190 especially finding it a useful tactic in breaking off combat.

The improved Yak-1B, with a more powerful, boosted M-105PF, was able to keep up with the Bf 109 in terms of its speed at medium and low altitudes, and even better them in manoeuvrability.

Combat Use

The Yak-1 in its various versions was used as a fighter from the first day of the Great Patriotic War to the last. It shares that distinction with only one other major Soviet fighter, the LaGG-3. Not only was it used by the VVS until the end of the Great Patriotic War, but it was also still in use with AVMF and PVO units. Due to the location of the plant that produced the great majority of Yak-1s—Z.292 at Saratov—on the middle to lower Volga, more Yak-1s were used in the southern areas of the front, such as Stalingrad, as opposed to the northern areas, such as Leningrad.

An interesting note about the Soviets is that different versions of the Yakovlev fighters were sometimes used in the same unit. It was not just that earlier and later versions of a specific type such as the Yak-1 were used in the same unit, but different fighters, such as Yak-1s and Yak-7s were used in the same unit. This complicated maintenance and operations, but it was sometimes necessary to keep units up to strength. At times, even units that were primarily using non-Yakovlev fighters, such as Lavochkin fighters, might have a few Yakovlev fighters. These practices lessened from 1944 on, with the influx of the new Yak-9U and Yak-3 fighters, but still continued until the end of the war.

Another interesting note about the Yak-1 is that an all-female fighter regiment was created in 1941 to fly this aircraft: the 586th IAP. This was part of Hero of the Soviet Union pilot Marina Mikhailovna Raskova's (1912–43) successful effort to create all-female regiments for the VVS, which also included the 587th BAP (bomber air regiment) with Pe-2 dive-bombers, and the 588th NBAP (night bomber air regiment)—the famous 'Night Witches' with their U-2 (Po-2) light night nuisance bombers.

After training at Engels, many of the female pilots joined formerly all-male fighter regiments, while the 586th itself was considered ready for combat by spring 1942, under the command of Maj. T. A. Kazarinova, at Saratov. Here on the night of 24–25 September, Lt Valeria Khomyakova shot down the first aircraft for the new regiment, a German Ju 88A-4 bomber. After this, the regiment was sent to Stalingrad, where it joined the fierce air combat over that besieged city. Here, Ekaterina Budanova, and the famous 'White Rose of Stalingrad', Lidia (Lilya) Vladimirovna Litvyak (1921–43), now flying with the 'male' regiments, the 437th IAP, then the 9th Guards IAP, destroyed five Axis aircraft. Litvyak claimed up to sixteen victories (sources vary, but she may have shot down between five and twelve aircraft), and both pilots were awarded the title of Hero of the Soviet Union, posthumously. Litvyak died of combat wounds on 1 August 1943 after being shot down near Oryol, but the 586th IAP continued on, converting from Yak-1s to Yak-9s in 1943. In total, the regiment, which fought to the end of the GPW, flew 4,419 sorties, engaged in 125 aerial combats, and was credited with thirty-eight aircraft. It ended the GPW in Vienna.

Operation Barbarossa

As one of the three modern fighters introduced into Soviet service in 1940–41 (the others being the LaGG-3 and the MiG-3), the Yak-1 saw action in the opening stages of the Great Patriotic War. Although production had started in late 1940, few Yak-1s were in front-line units by the beginning of the Great Patriotic War. A total of 425 Yak-1s had been produced by the beginning of the war, but of these, only 105 were located in the five western Military Districts of the Soviet Union which bore the brunt of the opening phases of Operation Barbarossa, the German invasion of the Soviet Union. Of these 105, ninety-two were considered combat-ready. The AVMF also had some Yak-1s on strength, forty-one, of which only eighteen were combat-ready.

As the MiG-3 was heavily deployed by the beginning day of Operation Barbarossa, on 22 June 1941, it suffered heavy losses. The Yak-1, despite being the first of the new generation of Soviet fighters to take flight (it first flew on 13 January 1940, as compared to 30 March 1940 for the LaGG-3 prototype, and 5 April 1940 for the MiG-1/MiG-3 prototype), was just beginning to be introduced into service. This proved to be a stroke of luck for the Yak-1 as it was mostly spared the catastrophic losses of the MiG-3 and other heavily deployed fighters, such as the Polikarpov biplanes and the I-16 in the first days of the invasion. It was rapidly thrown into action as quickly as production would allow, to try and stem the German advance and replace the terrible losses Soviet aviation had suffered in the first weeks of the conflict. Once it started seeing combat, the Yak-1 also suffered heavy losses, and by September 1941, there were only 176 Yak-1s being used by VVS frontal units. Nonetheless, the Yak-1 did have its successes. During the fighting on the Southwestern Front (the Kiev Special District), from 10 to 12 July 1941, the 20th IAP claimed twenty-six Axis aircraft. Their own losses are not recorded, although, given this stage of the war, they were rather likely to have been substantial.

Despite its heavy losses, the Germans realised that the Yak-1 was the best fighter that the Soviets then possessed, better than the equally new LaGG-3 and MiG-3 fighters.

Battle of Moscow

In July, Yak-1s, of which up to 117 were being used in the defence of Moscow, were part of the Soviet force sent to attack 195 German bombers that were conducting a night raid on Moscow. Two of the He 111s were shot down by Yak-1 pilots. By 10 July 1941, 133 Yak-1s were in the 6th IAK (Fighter Air Corps) defending Moscow.

The rocket-equipped Yak-1s were first used near Moscow, where the RS-82 rockets were used in an anti-aircraft role, being fired at enemy aircraft. The firing range was from 1,640 to 2,625 feet (500 to 800 m). Although the inaccuracy of the unguided rockets made a hit rather unlikely, they were still able to break up bomber formations, making the bombers more vulnerable to be individually attacked as their mutual defensive fire was now weakened. If an aircraft was hit by one of the rockets, the aircraft was destroyed. The RS-82s were additionally used to attack ground targets, which is where they were most successful. With only 1 per cent of the launches resulting in failure, the rockets were quite reliable, despite their inaccuracy.

The Yak-1 proved its worth in the aerial defence of the capital. By the start of Operation Typhoon (*Unternehmen Taifun*, the German offensive against Moscow) on 2 October 1941, the Yak-1s were in service. For example, the mixed regiment of the 43rd SAD (Mixed Air Division) had thirteen Yak-1s on its roll by the time of Operation Typhoon.

By the time of the start of the Soviet counter-offensive on 5 December 1941, only eighty-three Yak-1s were on the VVS' roll, with only forty-seven of these being serviceable. Combat losses during the desperate struggle to keep the Germans out of Moscow had been very heavy, and production had not been able to keep up with the losses, due at least partly to the large-scale evacuation of the industry to the more eastern portions of the Soviet Union due to the German advance. Due to this lack of replacement Yak-1s, some Yak-1 units were re-equipped with the inferior MiG-3. However, during December, nine regiments of Yak-1s (and two of Yak-7s) were able to fly from snow-covered airfields using skis. Some PVO Yak-1s were even used in the ground attack role.

By 1 February 1942, 637 pilots were now qualified to fly the Yak-1. Despite the losses, some units were still able to continue flying the Yak-1. On 10 February 1942, Spanish Civil War veteran and ace (thirteen kills) Vladimir Bobrov hit a Bf 109 with a RS-82, destroying it. He ended the war having shot down thirty aircraft in addition to his thirteen kills during the Spanish Civil War.

Leningrad

The KBF began receiving the Yak-1 and the LaGG-3 by late 1941 to replace their obsolescent I-16s. Eventual twenty-eight victory ace Igor Kaberov switched from the LaGG-3 to the Yak-1 in early 1942 as a pilot with the 5th IAP of the KBF. His first flight on the Yak-1 flying over the Road of Life nearly ended in disaster when his aircraft was badly shot up by Bf 109s while he was escorting attack aircraft, as Kaberov related in *Bf 109E/F vs Yak-1/7* by Dmitriy Khazanov and Aleksander Medved (p. 62):

> 'Let's go down', said Lvov and he rolled away. I intended to follow him, but on looking round noticed shadows in the blinding rays of the sun. I turned my head sharply to the side and now saw more clearly four Me 109s [*sic.*] diving on me. Lvov had gone. He was already beside the group. I couldn't summon him for help. Of course, the enemy pilots would immediately discover the attack aircraft and pursue them. No, I must delay this group of Messerschmitts and, meanwhile, our aircraft would carry out the mission before them.
>
> The sun prevented me from observing and aiming, and the enemy fighters were coming at me. There could be no doubt that they were about to open fire. It was impossible to get away; I couldn't dodge all four. Without thinking—when was there time to think?—I performed a barrel-roll. The Yak easily turned over. Surprised by the unexpected move, the Fascists swept over me.
>
> Now this was what I had to do. With the sun clearly behind me, I now occupied an advantageous position and could see clearly. The enemy fighters divided into two groups. One pair came straight at me and the other circled to the side in order to attack from behind. Knowing that our group, having hit the target, would return this way, I tried to draw the Fascists away. This unequal battle lasted 20 minutes. At a suitable moment I attacked. One Messerschmitt started to smoke and fell away to one side. The three remaining were bedevilled by their lack of success. I had heard a little about the manoeuvrability of the Yak and I tried to conduct the fight flying vertically, as my friends had usually done. What a light machine this Yak was! My CO [Maj. Aleksander Myasnikov] was right: it's not an aircraft—it's a dream!
>
> From vertical flight (in which the Yak is an invincible machine), the Messerschmitts caught me on the turn. I pulled the stick towards me and the aircraft shuddered and shook all over as if in mortal danger of pulling out of the spin. Never fear, my friend, if that's the case, we'll die together! But there was a Fascist on my tail. Closer and closer he came. Crash! I felt as if a mallet had smashed into the rudder. The control column was torn from my hands. The aircraft turned over and went into a spin. From a height of 3,000m [9,800 feet] it was swept earthwards and turned at such a speed that is seemed that my head would be torn from my shoulders.
>
> Having failed to bring the aircraft out of its spin, I unbuttoned my harness and tried to throw myself out of the cockpit, but some kind of devilish power pressed me to the armoured seat. I was half out of the cockpit but I hadn't the strength to tear myself free. It seemed that my end had come, but at this moment, quite unexpectedly, the aircraft stopped spinning and changed to a gentle spiral.

Perhaps amazingly, Kaberov was able to land the aircraft he came so close to bailing out of. The rudder was gone, half of the port elevator was also gone, and 20 per cent of the starboard elevator was damaged. Despite the damage, the tail unit was replaced, and the aircraft was returned to combat use.

Crimea/Sevastopol (1942)

The last reinforcement for the aerial forces in Sevastopol came when the 45th IAP was sent from the Caucasus region to the Crimea. In one combat on 11 July 1942, eight Bf 109s were claimed for the loss of one Yak-1, which the pilot was able to bail out from. The results for the Soviets were not always so good. During the third assault against Sevastopol, aerial combat took place on 13 June between the 45th IAP and the Luftwaffe. The Soviets destroyed two Bf 109s for the loss of five Yak-1s, an Il-2, and a Pe-2.

During the defence of Sevastopol from 25 May to 1 July 1942, it was recorded in VVS documents that the 3rd IAD suffered fifty-three losses in aerial combat, with twenty-eight of these being Yak-1s. The losses were due both to the presence of many aces in the Luftwaffe units facing them and the superiority of their equipment, the Bf 109F enjoying a clear advantage over the Yak-1. This report is from the 62nd IAB (Fighter Air Brigade) of the Black Sea Naval Air Force, as reported in *Bf 109E/F vs Yak-1/7* by Khazanov and Medved (p. 71):

> At medium altitudes our fighters fall behind the Bf 109 in terms of speed, especially in the vertical plane, making it rather hard to wage a dogfight, and this results in extra losses. Combat, almost in every case, takes place in the horizontal plane, and looks more like a defensive circle [as used by the Il-2 assault aircraft]. The Yak-1 possesses much better flying characteristics, but it also lags behind the Me 109F [*sic.*].

Before Stalingrad

In the battles that preceded the battle for Stalingrad, as the Germans rolled over the steppes towards Stalingrad as part of *Fall Blau* ('Case Blue', the German 1942 summer offensive), the Yak-1 saw substantial action. As an example, the 434th IAP, after extensive training on the Yak-1 for a month, was thrown into the fight near Stalingrad on 13 June 1942. The fighting was intense, and individual aircraft flew four to five sorties a day. After three weeks of heavy fighting, the regiment had gone from twenty-one Yak-1s to none, and it was withdrawn for re-equipping. During these three weeks, it had flown 800 sorties and claimed thirty-five kills.

The 434th IAP was, of course, not the only Soviet fighter unit to see heavy action in these spring battles. The 273rd IAP flew 129 combat sorties from 11 to 15 May 1942 and destroyed ten Axis aircraft in the air and claimed nineteen more on the ground. The 273rd IAP paid a price for this, losing seven of its Yak-1s.

After re-equipping with new aircraft (including some Yak-7Bs), the 434th IAP found itself in action again. It was now based at Gumrak, an airfield near Stalingrad, from 13 July 1942. From here it flew 827 sorties, claiming fifty-five Axis aircraft before once again using up all of its aircraft, and being withdrawn for refitting.

Stalingrad

Once more re-equipped, the 434th IAP began operations again on 16 September, with the Germans having commenced their main assault on Stalingrad some three days earlier. As before, the regiment saw very heavy fighting, with some pilots flying five to six sorties a day. At this pace, the aircraft and pilots were used up quickly, and by the end of the month only a third of its aircraft remained, and it was down to fifteen pilots, and the regiment on 3 October was again withdrawn for re-equipping. Although this was a good unit that eventually gained Guards status as the 32nd GvIAP in November 1942, the history of this regiment during the fighting before and over Stalingrad is typical of the heavy aerial fighting that accompanied the vicious fighting on the ground.

At Stalingrad, the new version of the Yak-1, the Yak-1B saw service trials with the 32nd GvIAP (as the 434th IAP had been redesignated), from 10 December 1942 to 28 January 1943 (production had started at Z.292 in September). Older versions of the Yak-1 continued to be used, and with other Soviet fighters, including the Yak-7, the Yak-1 saw extensive use during the struggle for Stalingrad.

It was at Stalingrad that a Yak-1 pilot equalled a record for a Soviet fighter pilot by downing six enemy aircraft. P. Dymchenko, the flight commander of the 659th IAP on 11 September 1942 shot down six aircraft, two Ju 87s and four Bf 109s over the Kletskaya bridgehead but was killed in the battle.

Battle of the Kuban and the Crimea (1943)

The 3rd IAK (Fighter Air Corp) was commanded by famed Yakovlev fighter ace, Yevgeniy Yakovlevich Savitskiy, who eventually was twice awarded the title of Hero of the Soviet Union, and who became commander of the 3rd IAK (Fighter Air Corps) in late 1943, as a major general. Besides being a fine pilot, Savitskiy was also an excellent tactician, and he promoted the idea of two pairs of aircraft flying together in a fairly loose formation (like the German *Schwarm*), instead of the tight three-aircraft vee that had been the norm. He also pushed the idea of a looser fighter coverage of the Shturmoviks, as the looser formation gave the escorts greater flexibility. In addition, he was a firm advocate for the Yakovlev fighters and flew only them throughout the war.

Under his command, the 3rd IAK, which was not a part of an Air Army (VA), became a sort of reserve group for the Stavka, to be shifted to wherever it was felt it was needed, like a fire brigade. As such, it saw combat over the Kuban River, Ukraine, the Crimea, Byelorussia, the Baltic States, and finally over Berlin. Aircraft of the 3rd IAK were characterised by a flying sword emblem on their nose.

In 1943, the 3rd IAK was attached to the 4th VA, which was operating over the Kuban River. On 20 April 1943, the first mission was flown, in support of ground forces at Mount Myskhako, near the Black Sea port city of Novorossiysk. The Corps claimed forty-seven German aircraft that day, including one by Savitskiy.

Kursk (Operation Citadel)

On 23 July 1943, some Yak-1s, along with La-5s of 5th GvIAP, were involved in a major fight with Ju 87s being escorted by Bf 109s. As the Soviets sent more aircraft

Yak-1B at Kursk in summer 1943, with a T-34 tank passing by. The Yak-1B is evidently undergoing maintenance as the engine panels are removed. (*Viktor Kulikov's collection*)

into the battle, the Germans responded in kind, sending sixteen Bf 109s to assist those already involved. The La-5 flight of future Hero of the Soviet Union Vitaliy Popkov was despatched, along with more Yakovlevs. By the end of the fight, the Soviets had claimed ten German aircraft and damaged another two, although the 5th GvIAP had lost two pilots of its own.

Ukrainian Operations in 1943–44

On 25 October 1943, under the command of Lt Matynenko of the 821st IAP, six Yak-1s (these were probably Yak-1Bs given the date, although it is not clear from the record) destroyed one Bf 109 and one Ju 88.

Crimean Offensive (Battle of the Crimea, 1944)

During the Battle for the Crimea in 1944 (8 April–12 May), the Yak-1 saw combat. On 10 April, eight Yak-9s and two Yak-1s under the command of Maj. Popov of the 812th IAP attacked Reidendorf airfield. They were met on their approach by six Ju 87s covered by Fw 190s. In the ensuing battle, one Ju 87 was downed, along with three of the escorting Fw 190s. The surviving Ju 87s dropped their bombs before reaching their target. There were no Soviet losses reported.

During the Crimean Offensive, some of the first Soviet field radar units were used to help maintain air superiority. This was at least partly at the initiative of General Savitskiy, commander of the 3rd IAK.

Operation Bagration (The Destruction of Army Group Centre)

Yak-1s of the 1st Red Banner GvIAP saw action during Operation Bagration. The aircraft provided cover for Il-2s, and according to the regimental records, not a single attack aircraft was lost to enemy fighters during these missions. One squadron of this *polk* was assigned reconnaissance missions, alongside Yak-9Ds equipped with cameras. From 22 June (the beginning of the offensive) until 14 September 1944, the *polk* undertook 1,041 combat sorties in which it downed twenty German aircraft for the loss of six Yak-1s (another five were lost to flak). This *polk* replaced its Yak-1s with Yak-3s in September 1944.

Vistula to Oder Operation

By 1 January 1945 (the Vistula to Oder Operation commenced on 12 January 1945), 735 Yak-1s were still in service with active air armies. In comparison, only sixty-five Yak-7s were in service with frontal units at this time, despite the Yak-7's production ending at about the same time as the Yak-1, in the middle of 1944. However, in 1944, 1,128 Yak-1s were produced compared to 465 Yak-7s, which may partly explain the disparity in numbers.

Berlin Strategic Offensive Operation (Battle of Berlin)

By the time of the Battle of Berlin in April 1945, the only Yak-1s still in front-line service were Yak-1Bs. In addition to participating in the Battle of Berlin, some Yak-1Bs were used in the Balkans at the same time, sometimes piloted by Yugoslavian pilots under Soviet colours (the Yak-1B continued to serve in Yugoslavia after the Second World War for several years with the Yugoslavian Air Force).

Manchurian Strategic Offensive Operation

It is not clear from the record if any Yak-1Bs saw any action during this last campaign of the Second World War, although it is not unlikely.

Yak-1 in Detail

The following description is for a generalised Yak-1, with the differences between the different variants noted.

General Description

The Yak-1 was a single-engined single-seat cantilever monoplane fighter with an enclosed cockpit and retractable main landing gear and a fixed or retractable tailwheel. The aircraft was of mixed construction, with a steel tube fuselage, covered in metal, plywood, and fabric, wooden fixed tailplanes, metal structure moveable tailplanes, and one-piece wooden wings covered in plywood.

Fuselage

The fuselage structure featured a chromansil steel alloy tubular framework covered in metal panels on the forward fuselage, with some of the panels mounted on hinges to ease maintenance. The succeeding wartime Yakovlev fighters featured these hinged panels. The engine mounting was integral with the rest of the metal framework. The welded steel tubes were from 20 to 50 mm in diameter. The top of the rear fuselage was covered in bakelised-plywood, while the side and bottom were covered in AST-100 fabric over wooden stringers. The fuselage was rounded on top, with a flat underside, giving a cross-section something like a 'D' on its side.

From the series 49 on, the Yak-1s had the fixed canopy portion replaced with two small windows aft of the sliding canopy, as with the LaGG-3. It would appear that the Yak-1 had a Plexiglas sliding canopy from the beginning, unlike the LaGG-3, and

Cockpit of a rebuilt I-15bis. (*Viktor Kulikov's Collection*)

Rebuilt I-15bis. The paint scheme is appropriate for a Great Patriotic War aircraft. The yellow tips to the propellers are not appropriate for Soviet Great Patriotic War aircraft. This is done for safety purposes on this particular flyable rebuild/replica. (*Photograph by Kogo, from Wikimedia*)

Derelict I-153s in summer 1941. The aircraft are painted in light grey and aluminium paint. On the upper wing, note the pre-war style star with the circle in the middle. On the nearest aircraft, the fuselage star has been cut away by souvenir hunters, probably German soldiers. Original wartime colour photograph. (*Viktor Kulikov's Collection*)

Preserved I-153 at the museum at Le Bourget airport in France. This is the only intact I-153 still existing from the Great Patriotic War, although including parts from more than one I-153. Other extant examples are more in the way of extensive rebuilds/replicas. (*Photograph by Pline, from Wikimedia*)

Rebuilt I-153 at the Military Air Museum in Virginia, USA. This aircraft has been painted in the colours that it would have worn at the Battle of the Khalkhin-Gol and into the early part of the Great Patriotic War. The yellow propeller tips would not have been used at the time. (*Photograph by Michael Rehbaum, from Wikimedia*)

Rebuilt I-153 being worked on in Russia. Note the Wright Cyclone engine, which is used in place of the original M-25 or M-62/63 engines, themselves licenced copies of the Cyclone. This aircraft is in an overall aluminium finish. The yellow propeller tips are a modern addition not found on service I-153s. (*Photograph by Aleksandr Markin, from Wikimedia*)

Rebuilt I-16 *tip* 24. These are the colours it would have worn at the start of the Great Patriotic War. As with other recent Polikarpov aircraft rebuilds, the yellow propellor tips have been added for safety reasons, these aircraft being flyable, and would not have been present on Soviet wartime aircraft. (*Public Domain*)

LaGG-3 mock-up from Pobeda (Victory) Park, on Poklonnaya Gora (Hill), Moscow. This gives a good indication of the appearance of a late-series example with the two-grey camouflage (here rather faded), which was seen on LaGG-3s that were used after 1943. (*Photograph by Mike1979 Russia, from Wikimedia*)

La-5 mock-up from Pobeda Park, Moscow. This represents a late high-back version, in this case, the La-5 associated with the ace Georgiy Kostylev. The LaGG-3 mock-up can be seen in the background. (*Photograph by Mike1979 Russia, from Wikimedia*)

Preserved La-7 at the Kbely Aviation museum in the Czech Republic (Czechia). Note the incorrect black/green camouflage. For a Great Patriotic War example, this should be in dark grey (AMT-12) and grey-blue (AMT-11) over blue (AMT-7). Nonetheless, the aircraft appears to be original and in good condition. Hopefully, someday it will be repainted in a more authentic camouflage scheme. (*Photograph by Alan Wilson, from Wikimedia*)

Ivan Kozhedub's preserved La-7 at Monino, Russia, at the Central Air Force Museum outside of Moscow. The engine in front is the Shvetsov ASh-82FN engine that powered this type. This aircraft is depicted as a colour profile in the colour plates section, as it appeared during the Great Patriotic War (it is painted in this photograph at the museum as it appeared shortly after the war, when Kozhedub had received his third Hero of the Soviet Union title; it has since been repainted). Although not flyable, yellow propeller tips have been added, which would have not been on the aircraft as originally painted. (*Photograph by Alan Wilson, from Wikimedia*)

Another view of Ivan Kozhedub's preserved La-7, this time after repainting in a colour scheme closer to what it would have worn during the Great Patriotic War (although still with the post-war additions of the Hero of the Soviet Union medals and victory stars). Despite the repainting, they decided to keep the inauthentic yellow propeller tips. (*Photograph by Alan Wilson, from Wikimedia*)

Rebuilt MiG-3 flying in Russia at Mochishche. (*Photograph by Alex Polezhaev, from Wikimedia*)

Preserved Yak-1 at the Vadim Zadorozhniy Museum in Moscow. This Yak-1 was recovered from a lake in Northern Russia. Remarkably, the original wooden wing structure was preserved, as can be seen here. Some of the original paint is still on the hinged access panels under the cockpit. The tubular steel framework of the fuselage can also be seen. (*Photograph by Alexander Fluhmann, from Wikimedia*)

Yak-7 replica on a plinth in Naryan-Mar in Russia. Although a replica, it gives a good idea of the appearance of a wartime Yak-7 fighter, seen from below. (*Photograph by AAT, from Russian Wikipedia*)

Preserved Yak-9U at the Central Air Force Museum at Monino. (*Photograph by Mike1979 Russia, from Wikimedia*)

Preserved Yak-3 at the Vadim Zadorozhniy Museum in Moscow. The aircraft is painted in the two-grey scheme typical of most wartime Yak-3s. In the background is a Yak-11 'Moose', the radial-engined trainer developed from the Yak-3. (*Photograph by Alan Wilson, from Wikimedia*)

Leonid Galchenko's LaGG-3 series 4 in partial winter camouflage. The cat on the tail became a feature of all the aircraft that eventual Hero of the Soviet Union Galchenko flew.

A view of the port side of LaGG-3 series 66 in 1944 flown by Lt Yuriy Shchipov of the 9th IAP-CMF (Black Sea Fleet). Note the two-grey camouflage and the personal emblem of the lion in a heart.

High-back La-5 series 9 or later finished in a typical black/green camouflage.

A La-5F finished in the two-grey paint scheme used on fighters from late 1943. This aircraft has quick recognition markings in the form of a white top to the vertical tail, a white rudder trim tab, and a thin white stripe. Note that it still has the early red stars with the black outline, as opposed to the '1943 Stars' painted on most fighters with the two-grey camouflage.

La-5FN has interesting features—note the painted-out area on the aft fuselage, the silver aircraft number, silver-outlined fuselage star, partially red cowling, and the spinner and inner portions of the propeller blades, which are white. The arrow is reminiscent of that used by the Normandie-Niemen regiment, which never flew Lavochkin fighters (they flew Yakovlev fighters).

Ivan Kozhedub's La-7 in early 1945. Although usually rendered with all sixty-two kill markings and three Hero of the Soviet Union medals on the fuselage, this is how the aircraft would have appeared during most of the Great Patriotic War. This actual aircraft still exists in a museum outside of Moscow and is one of only two La-7s to have been preserved (the other is in a museum in Prague). Photographs of these aircraft appear in the colour plates section.

A particularly colourful La-7, this aircraft was flown by Hero of the Soviet Union (HSU) Alexei Dolgushin (the medal that went with this title is represented on the cowling, next to the 'La-7' logo). Apparently, red stars represent personal kills, while white stars represent shared kills (kills that were apportioned to the regiment as a whole).

MiG-3 later version in winter camouflage (winter 1941–42). Part of the canopy framing is still in the original green, while the propeller blades are white. The slanted fuselage star is noteworthy.

MiG-3 later version in summer camouflage with a fixed tailwheel. This gives the typical appearance of a MiG-3 in 1942.

I-5 fighter-bomber in 1941–42. The aircraft is in the standard 1940 camouflage of green over blue with black-outlined red stars.

I-15bis in the green/black topside camouflage introduced in 1941. The underside is still painted in light grey, instead of the normal blue that was used with this camouflage scheme. Unusually, there is neither an aircraft number nor a star on the fuselage side.

I-15bis in somewhat worn winter camouflage in Leningrad, winter 1941–42. A photograph of this aircraft appears in the text.

I-153 in pre-war paint scheme of grey and aluminium paint. The pre-war red star with the circle in the middle is noteworthy. This aircraft does not have the small propeller spinner.

I-153 in the black/green camouflage introduced in 1941. The red stars are simple, with no outline. Note how the black paint around the cockpit continues up into the wing root, covering a portion of the underside blue. This aircraft features the small spinner that was often removed from the I-153 during the war.

This same I-153 from the starboard side. Again, the black paint has crept up to cover some of the blue paint of the wing root.

From the top. Note the absence of any stars on top of the wings.

From the bottom. Note the eight RS-82 rockets. The stars are painted on the lower wings only.

I-16 (possibly a *tip* 10) in pre-war/early war camouflage of green over blue. The fuselage star is of the early war type, with no outline, as specified in 1941.

I-16 *tip* 24 in the green over blue camouflage with the simple red star.

I-16 *tip* 24 in the green over blue camouflage. In this case, the fuselage's red star has a thin white outline. Note that the tail star does not have this outline. This pilot is an ace, with five victory stars painted on the fuselage's spine.

I-16 in black/green camouflage. The insignia now consists of wing stars (almost always underside only) and one star on the fuselage side (per side) and one tail star (per side), both of the simple, not outlined type. The bort (aircraft number) is finished in the same red as the stars.

This I-16 from the starboard side. The cowling is almost entirely painted in black, a feature which was carried over from many pre-war I-16s, which also featured the black cowling.

From the top. As per usual Soviet practice during the Great Patriotic War, there are no stars on the upper side of the wings.

From the bottom. The only insignia is the plain red stars.

I-26 (Yak-1 prototype). The red finish and red and white stripes were something of a trademark look for Yakovlev aircraft.

Early Yak-1 in winter camouflage. Note that the rudder trim tab is finished in red, and this pilot has been credited with nine kills, as seen in winter 1941–42.

Later Yak-1 with LaGG-3-style rear windows. Aircraft of HSU Mikhail Dmitriyevich Baranov (twenty-four victories), 183rd IAP, Southwestern Front, summer 1942.

Baranov's Yak-1 from the starboard side.

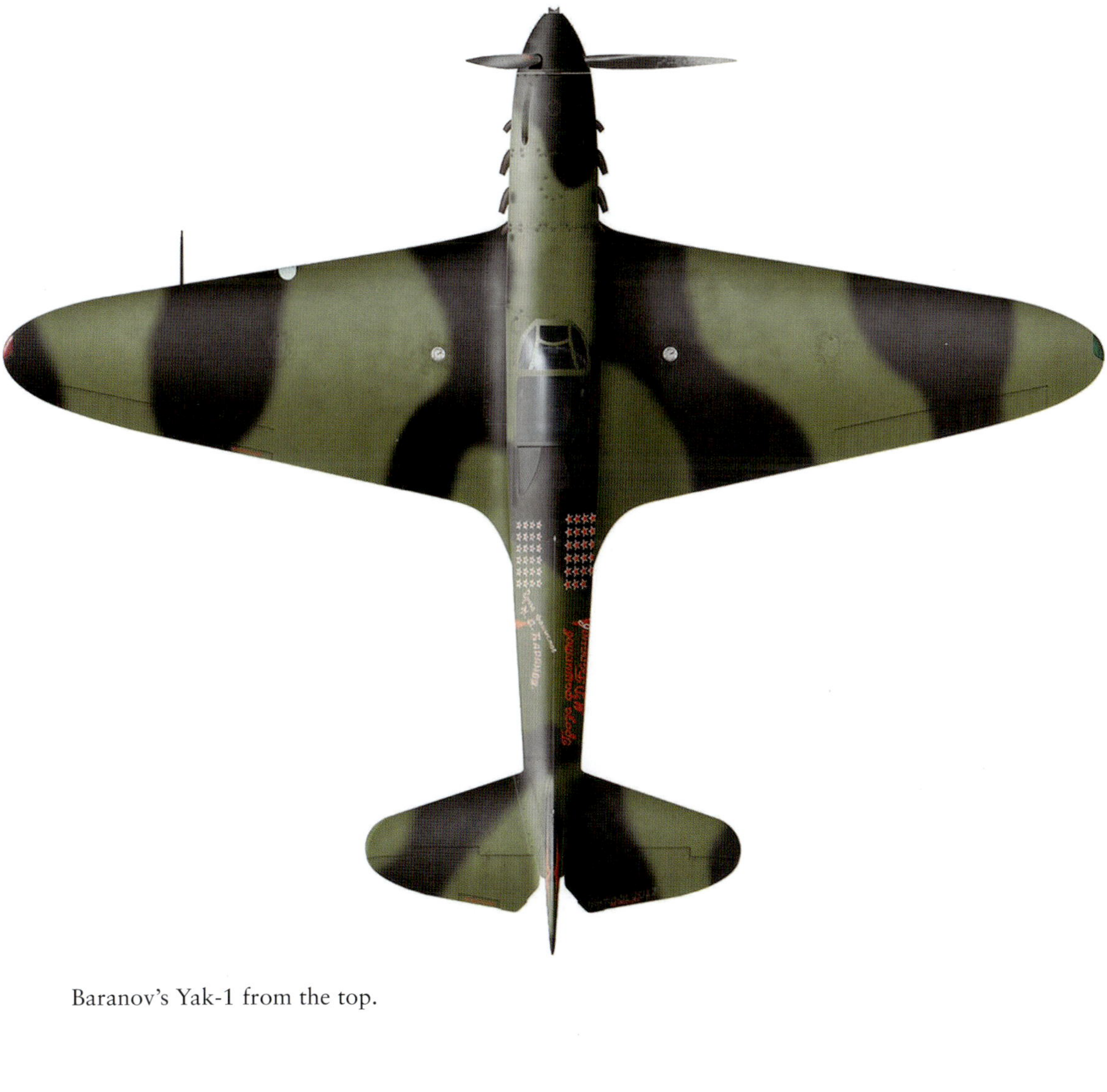

Baranov's Yak-1 from the top.

Baranov's Yak-1 from the bottom. Note the four metal covers for the two fuel tanks.

Yak-1B, characterised by its bubble canopy. The aircraft was flown by Capt. Pavel Maksimovich Chuvilev of the 427th IAP, at the Kalinin Front in August 1943. The red nose and white bands are recognition markings of the sort that became more common as the war went on.

Above: A presentation Yak-7 of the 12th GvIAP-PVO, Moscow, donated by the Communist Youth Organisation (Komsomol), from June 1942. Having a marking in the red star itself is unusual.

Below: This same Yak-7B from the starboard side.

Above: Yak-7B with red stars outlined in a thin white line (these stars were usually outlined in thin black lines). The victory stars have been painted onto a red background.

Below: Late Yak-7B with the bubble canopy. The white stripes on the tail are recognition markings. This aircraft features red stars with a black outline. There appears to have been some repainting around the horizontal tail surfaces, indicating this is a replacement tail.

Early Yak-9 with the forward-mounted cockpit. This aircraft was flown by Sr Lt Ivan Nikiforovich Stepanenko of the 4th IAP at Bryansk in July 1943. On the fuselage, a lion is chasing a caricature of Joseph Goebbels, the Nazi Minister of Propaganda.

Yak-9D in 1943. In this case, the stars are outlined with fairly wide white lines, and the top of the tail is painted a light blue.

HSU Mikhail Ivanovich Grib's Yak-9D of the 6th GvIAP-CMF (Black Sea Fleet) in the two-grey camouflage scheme from summer 1944. On the nose are first the Guards emblem, followed by the Red Banner emblem. The large size of the aircraft number is worthy of note. A photograph of this aircraft appears in the text.

Grib's Yak-9D from the starboard side. The emblems are painted on both sides of the nose.

Grib's Yak-9D from the top. The four fuel tank caps can be seen, as well as the fuel gauges (the white circles) near the wing roots.

Yak-9K of the 3rd IAK (Fighter Air Corp) with its characteristic corps symbol of the winged sword, taken in Poland in late 1944. The cockpit is now aft-mounted as compared to earlier Yak-9s. The large muzzle brake of the 45-mm cannon can be seen clearly. The lighter greys on the tail seem to indicate some repainting, not uncommon on the often battle-damaged Soviet aircraft.

Yak-9T of Snr Lt Aleksandr Ivanovich Vybornov of the 728th IAP, 2nd Ukrainian Front, in autumn 1944. This aircraft has the so-called 'Kremlin' stars painted on the fuselage and the tail. This aircraft shows lighter grey paint on the tail, although in this case, it appears to just be the paint showing up lighter on the fabric-covered control surfaces.

Above: This Yak-9T from the starboard side. Only the port side has the victory stars.

Opposite above: From the top. The grey paints are lighter on the ailerons and the elevators. There are only two fuel caps on top, as the Yak-9T had only two fuel tanks, not four as with the Yak-9D.

Opposite below: From the bottom. The stars are outlined in white, followed by thin outer red lines. This was the standard style red star used with the two-grey camouflage. It is interesting that the Kremlin stars are not painted on the wings, although they appear on the fuselage and tail.

Yak-9U. Note the aft-mounted cockpit as with the Yak-9K and Yak-9T, and the longer rear portion of the canopy. A reindeer has been painted on the nose, and a white-outlined red stripe, probably a regimental marking, has been painted on the tail.

Yak-9U with multiple emblems on the fuselage, including the Guards emblem on the nose.

Yak-3. Note the white recognition stripes on the tail.

This Yak-3 from the starboard side.

From the top.

A Yak-3 of the Normandie-Niemen regiment. The white arrow on the star and the blue-white-red painted spinner are typical markings of this regiment. Unusually, for a Soviet aircraft, the kill markings are represented as the German 'Black Cross' per the Western style of kill markings (the Soviets used red or white stars to represent their aerial kills).

Yak-3 in 1945. This aircraft is notable in being painted not just red overall on the nose, but AMT-11 Blue-Grey elsewhere on the topside. Some late Great Patriotic War fighters wore this AMT-11 only topside.

Nikitin-Shevchenko IS-2 in 1941.

Pashinin I-21, third prototype in 1941. Note the prominent bulge on the lower aft fuselage, which accommodated the retractable tailwheel.

Production I-180 with an overall red scheme and aluminium-painted stars in 1940.

I-185 with M-71 engine in 1941.

Su-1 in 1940. This aircraft bears no insignia or markings, as was sometimes the case with prototype Soviet aircraft.

Yatsenko I-28 in 1939. The reverse gull-wing can be seen, as well as the glossy appearance of the green paint.

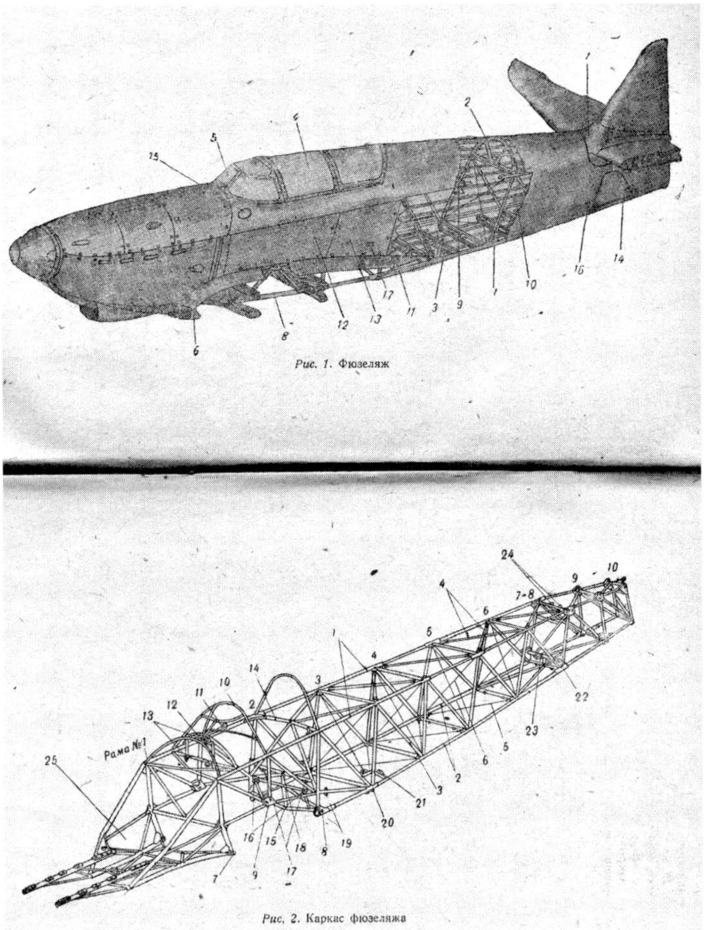

Details of the Yak-1's fuselage construction. (*Yak-1 Technical Manual*)

therefore did not suffer from the same problems with visibility resulting from the early LaGG-3's cellulose canopy, which tended to yellow with age. Nonetheless, the Plexiglas was not of the best quality and the early Yak-1s were often flown with the canopy open (slid back). The canopy slid back on runners that were sunk into the sides of the fuselage, although the canopy was not jettisonable until the series 163 on. The pilot sat on an adjustable seat that had a 0.35-inch (9-mm) thick armoured steel back.

The Yak-1Bs had a cut-down rear fuselage to accommodate the all-around vision bubble-top cockpit canopy which was also used on the last Yak-7Bs and all the Yak-3s and Yak-9s. The armoured seat top was cut-down on the Yak-1B and featured a semi-circular piece of 2.52-inch (64-mm) thick armour glass to protect the pilot from behind.

Wings

The Yak-1 had all-wooden wings, with a wooden structure covered in plywood. The wings had two wooden box spars, made of pine and plywood, with no less than forty-six wooden ribs, and the plywood surface of the wings was covered by a doped fabric that was sanded or rubbed down to give a smooth, join-less finish. The plywood layers were laid cross-grain to each other in thin sheets of veneer, or *shpon*, which had a thickness of from 5 to 2.5-mm. The wings were constructed as a one-piece unit which was attached to the fuselage during construction. This simplified production, and breakdown for transportation, but also meant that if one of the wings was damaged, the entire wing structure had to be removed if the damaged wing part could not be repaired.

The wings were of a Clark YH aerofoil, with 15 per cent thickness at the root and 7 per cent thickness at the wingtip (Yefim Gordon has 8 per cent, the same as with the Yak-7 and Yak-9). The plywood wing skin was attached to the spars by glue and screws. The wing leading edge was covered in 8-mm-thick plywood.

Tailplanes

The tailplanes were of mixed construction, with wooden-structured and covered fixed surfaces (the fin and horizontal stabilisers) and metal-structured and fabric-covered moveable surfaces (the rudder and elevators). The fin was of a wooden structure as was the horizontal stabilisers, which had two box spars with ribs and stringers, covered with bakelised-plywood of 2–2.3 mm thickness. Metal flashing faired in the fin and horizontal stabilisers to the fuselage.

Engine

The engine on all production Yak-1s was the Klimov M-105 twelve-cylinder vee-type liquid-cooled inline engine, originally of 1,100 hp for its maximum rating. The more powerful M-105PF was introduced on the Yak-1B, and developed 1,260 hp at its maximum rating, with the VISh-105 propeller replacing the VISh-61P propeller. All the M-105s could accommodate a cannon mounted between the cylinder banks firing through the propeller shaft. The engine was equipped with a VISh-61P propeller of 9.84 feet (3 m) diameter on Yak-1s before the Yak-1B (the Yak-1B had a VISh-105 propeller, as mentioned above). Both propellers were constant-speed, three-bladed metal propellers. As the M-105 was a 'left-handed' engine, all the propellers swung to the left, as seen from the back. An OP-203 water radiator was installed in a streamlined fairing under the middle of the fuselage. The neutral gas fire prevention system, using CO_2, was installed on the Yak-1 from September 1942 at Z.292.

Fuel System

There were two main fuel tanks, with one in each inner portion of the wings, with a small service tank in the middle of the under fuselage. Four detachable metal panels covered the tanks on the bottom of the wings. These four detachable underwing metal panels would remain a feature of most of the Yakovlev fighters that had either two or four main fuel tanks. A feature of all the Yakovlev fighters, which made its first appearance with the Yak-1, was the presence of external fuel gauges on top of the inner part of the wings, which indicated how much fuel was left in the tanks. The fuel tank caps were also located on top of the wings.

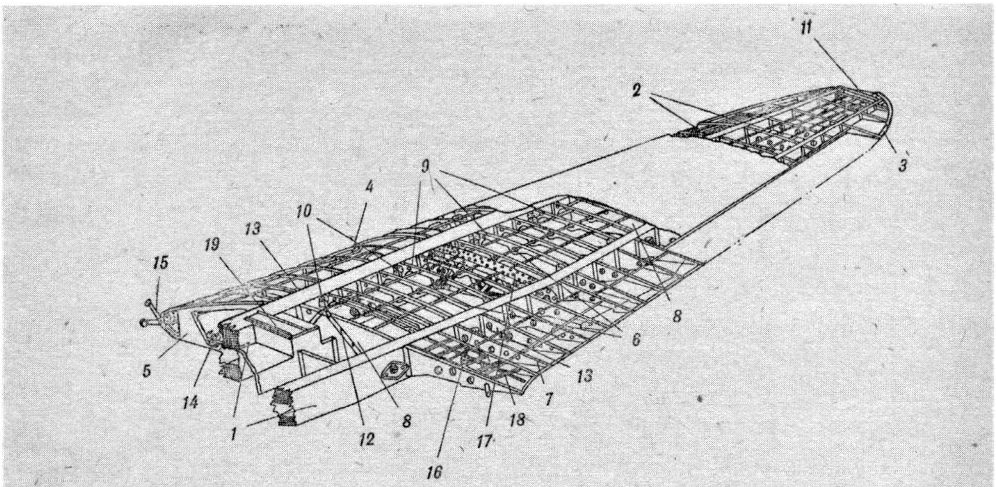

Рис. 11. Каркас консоли крыла

Above: Details of the starboard wing of the Yak-1. (*Yak-1 Technical Manual*)

Right: M-105 engine installation on the Yak-1. (*Yak-1 Technical Manual*)

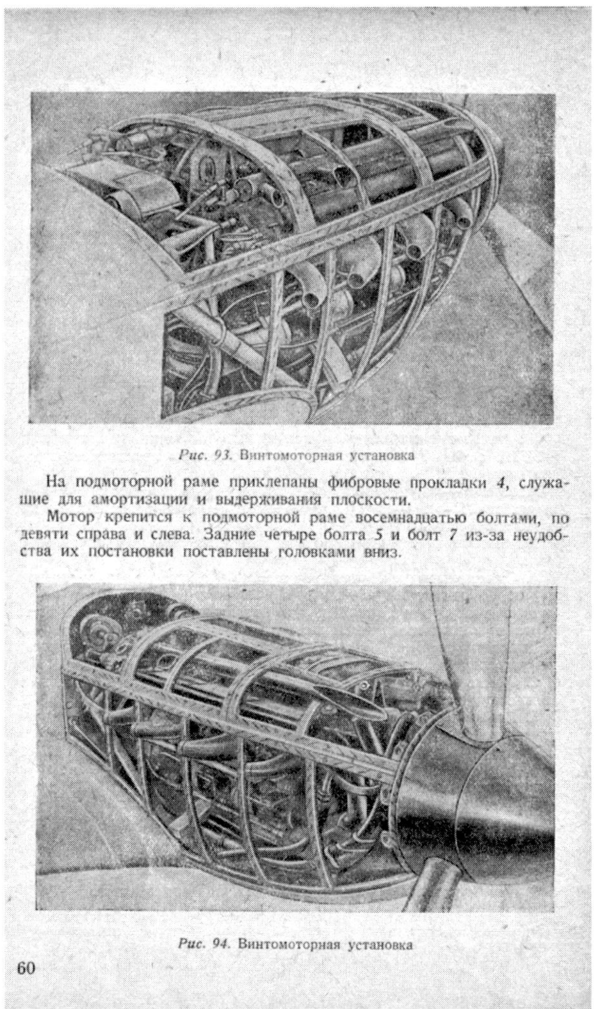
Рис. 93. Винтомоторная установка

На подмоторной раме приклепаны фибровые прокладки *4*, служащие для амортизации и выдерживания плоскости.

Мотор крепится к подмоторной раме восемнадцатью болтами, по девяти справа и слева. Задние четыре болта *5* и болт *7* из-за неудобства их постановки поставлены головками вниз.

Рис. 94. Винтомоторная установка

60

Controls

Most of the moveable control surfaces of the Yak-1 were of dural structure, with fabric covering, the exception being the underwing Schrenk-type flaps, which were of all-metal dural construction. The port aileron had a trim tab that was adjustable on the ground, while the starboard aileron had no trim tab.

The control surfaces were activated by push-pull rods for the Frise-type ailerons and elevators, and by wires for the rudder. Dispensing with the spade-grip control column found on contemporaneous Soviet fighters such as the MiG-3 and LaGG-3 (and earlier Yak-1s), from the series 158, the Yak-1 featured a single-grip column (or 'joystick') like that found on German and American fighters (it was apparently based upon that of the Bf 109). This replaced the spade-grip column found on earlier Yak-1s. All subsequent Yakovlev wartime fighters featured the single-grip type of control column. This column was more responsive to the pilot's input than the spade-grip column. The column controlled the ailerons and elevators, and twin rudder pedals controlled the rudder. The flaps were hydraulically operated.

Landing Gear

The main landing gear of the Yak-1 had the main wheels 'trapped' against the doors by the wheel axles, which were pointing outwards towards the gear doors. The upper part of the main gear doors was attached to the wing, while the separate lower doors were attached to the landing gear struts. The outer part of the wheels was uncovered when retracted. The main landing gear was retracted pneumatically. The main wheels were 600 × 180 mm in size on the Yak-1B. Depending on the Yak-1 series, the tailwheel was sometimes fixed, and sometimes retractable, the retractable examples withdrawing backwards, with the early examples enclosed by a small door attached to the front of the tailwheel strut. The tailwheel on the Yak-1B was 255 × 110 mm in size. Some of the later Yak-1Bs featured a retractable tailwheel with twin 'clam-shell' doors enclosing it, as appeared on the contemporaneous Yak-9 (the Yak-1B remained in production until mid-1944).

Radio Equipment

Some early Yak-1s did not have any kind of radio equipment, lacking both a receiver and a transmitter. Some were fitted with a receiver (from 20 August 1942, all Yak-1s had the RSI-4 receiver), but no transmitter, and it was not until 1943 that the Yak-1s (they would have been Yak-1Bs by 1943) were regularly fitted with full radio sets, comprising both receivers and transmitters. The Yak-1B had an antenna mast behind the cockpit canopy with a line running from the mast to two points on the leading edge of the fin.

Fixed Armament

Early Yak-1s were fitted with an unsynchronised ShVAK MP-20 20-mm cannon firing through the spinner, with two synchronised 7.62-mm (30-calibre) ShKAS rapid-fire machine guns (1,350 rpm for the synchronised ShKAS guns) mounted on top of the engine cowling to fire through the spinning propeller. Some later Yak-1s replaced the two ShKAS machine guns with one of the heavier 12.7-mm (50-calibre) UBS machine guns, also synchronised to fire through the propeller disc, while retaining the 20-mm cannon firing through the spinner. Since it did not have to fire through the propeller disc, the 20-mm cannon was not synchronised. The Yak-1B, the last production version of the Yak-1, featured one UBS machine gun mounted on the port side of the nose (as with most Yak-9s). On the Yak-1B, the controls on the control column for firing the guns were changed, based upon those of the Bf 109, such that only the right hand was now needed, freeing the left hand for working the engine controls. The guns were aimed using a PBP-1 reflector-type gunsight. Certain sources have some of the Yak-1s being equipped with the simple mechanical VV-1 gunsight (most Il-2s used this), which consisted of lines on the windscreen and a post on the upper cowling.

Disposable Armament

Some Yak-1s were able to carry up to six RS-82 rockets mounted on underwing RO-82 rocket rails. These rockets were used in both air-to-air attacks (their original role) and more commonly in ground attack missions, where, when used in number against large targets, they proved to be quite effective. Despite their effectiveness in ground attacks, they were removed from the Yak-1 in May 1942 because of their negative effect upon its performance. Some Yak-1s were able to carry two bombs of up to 220 lb (100 kg) for a total load of 441 lb (200 kg).

Colour and Markings

Since it entered service in 1941, the early Yak-1s had the 1940 camouflage scheme of A-18f Blue and A-19f Green on the metal portions of aircraft, as well as AII Blue and AII 3 Green for the wooden portions. After the beginning of the Great Patriotic War, new nitrocellulose lacquers were used, such as AMT-6 Black painted in bands on the AMT-4 Green upper surfaces, over AMT-7 Blue under surfaces. The Yak-1Bs that served from late 1943 onwards featured the later fighter camouflage scheme of AMT-11 Grey-Blue and AMT-12 Dark Grey over AMT-7 Blue. As with other Soviet aircraft, some Yak-1s bore personal insignia and inscriptions, and those on presentation machines often described the donor of the aircraft. Examples of Yak-1s with inscriptions and other personal markings can be seen as profiles in the colour plates section.

The high-back Yak-1s were almost always finished in the early black/green scheme and, when stars were outlined, it was in black, white, or even silver (but usually in black). If the aircraft, such as some later Yak-1Bs, were painted in the two-grey scheme introduced in late 1943 and early 1944, the stars were changed to the outlined '1943' stars. Early Yak-1s were often finished in the winter scheme of MK-7 White painted over the black/green scheme, with AMT-7 Blue underside.

Yak-7

The need for a two-place trainer to teach pilots how to fly the new high-speed monoplane fighters entering Red Air Force service soon became apparent to the VVS. Yakovlev had foreseen this need and developed the UTI-26 trainer (I-27). After the start of the war, the Yak-7UTI (I-27) trainer was modified into a fighter. Fortuitously, the changes made to the Yak-1 to make it into the Yak-7UTI trainer actually made it an excellent fighter. Although it was slightly less manoeuvrable than the Yak-1, its handling was superior due to the changed centre of gravity and larger elevators, it had better longitudinal stability, and its redesigned landing gear, designed to withstand the hard landings of trainee-pilots, were better able to stand up to the rough airfields used by frontal aviation. The landing gear was angled to make better use of the braking without nosing over, decreasing the landing run. Even the former pilot-instructor's position was put to use as it could accommodate a passenger, equipment, or an extra fuel tank. The presence of more weight towards the back made it harder to make the aircraft nose over—a problem with the Yak-1, especially when applying the wheel brakes too vigorously.

During testing of the Yak-7 at Z.153, the aircraft was found to be easy to get out of a spin; it was easier to recover from a spin than a LaGG-3 in the opinion of the TsAGI. With the start of the Great Patriotic War, there was obviously a great need for fighters, so the Yakovlev OKB at Z.301 set about converting the two-seater Yak-7UTI trainer into the Yak-7 single-seater fighter. Resolutions of the GKO and orders of the NKAP resulted in the Yak-7 being put into production at Z.153 and Z.301.

Not only was the Yak-7 a fine fighter in its own right, but it was developed into the extremely successful Yak-9, the most heavily produced Soviet fighter of the Great Patriotic War. The Yak-7 itself was produced in some numbers, with 6,399 being produced by the time production ended in July 1944, being replaced on the production lines by its development, the Yak-9.

Yak-7

The first Yak-7s produced did not have any kind of suffix, but were simply referred to as the 'Yak-7'. These were minimal modifications of the Yak-7UTI trainer, even retaining the clear canopy over the now unoccupied pilot-instructor position. The tailwheel remained fixed. The engine was the M-105PA with the VISh-61P propeller. The pilot received rear armour protection, the fuel tanks were self-sealing with the neutral gas system installed in the form of a cylinder of CO_2 filling up the gas tanks as they were used up, the armament was now one ShVAK 20-mm cannon firing through the nose, with two ShKAS 7.62-mm machine guns mounted on the upper cowling synchronised to fire through the propeller disc. The cannon was equipped with 120 rounds while the machine guns were equipped with 750 rounds per gun. The aircraft could also carry six RS-82 rockets mounted on underwing RO-82 rocket rails. Only sixty-two were produced, with fifty-one at Z.301 during September and October 1941 until it was evacuated to Novosibirsk, where it was absorbed into Z.153. Z.153 produced eleven Yak-7s in December 1941. The Yak-7 entered service with the 172nd IAP in September 1941.

Yak-7-37

Although the Yak-7 had already been fitted with a 37-mm cannon on the one-off Yak-7S, a Yak-7B M-105PA was also tested with a 37-mm cannon, and in this case, it was the Shpital'niy-designed MPSh-37 37-mm cannon. Due to the length of the weapon and the need to maintain the centre of gravity, the cockpit was moved aft 1.31 feet (400 mm) (as with the later Yak-9T) with the rear compartment being eliminated. Despite the heavier weight of the Yak-7-37, which lowered the top speed to 351 mph (565 kph), the handling was good, helped by the addition of leading-edge slats. As with the later Yak-9, the wingtips were squared-off, not rounded. The tailwheel was increased in size, probably to handle the higher weight, from the standard 255 × 110 mm to 300 × 125 mm. In addition to the 37-mm cannon with twenty rounds, two UBS machine guns were mounted on top of the engine cowling with 190 rounds for the starboard gun and 260 rounds for the port gun. The aircraft could also carry six RS-82 rockets, making it an especially heavily armed fighter.

Twenty-two trial versions of the Yak-7-37 were produced at Z.153 and tested in combat with the 42nd IAP of the 240th IAD on the North-Western Front from August 1942. In these aircraft, the MPSh-37 cannon was apparently replaced by the more reliable NS-37 37-mm cannon (although some sources have the aircraft still with the MPSh-37), and the leading-edge slats of the prototype were deleted. The Yak-7-37s claimed ten Axis aircraft for the loss of four of their own, in addition to three Yak-7-37s being damaged. In December 1942, the surviving Yak-7-37s were sent back to the Yakovlev OKB and modified with the cut-down aft fuselage and bubble-top canopy; also, the starboard UBS machine gun was deleted. These changes made them quite similar to the Yak-9T, the main difference being that the Yak-9T had metal wing spars. Perhaps not coincidentally, these modifications to the Yak-7-37 were being made at about the same time (January 1943) that the Yak-9T prototype was undergoing armament trials. It is not clear from the record how much longer the Yak-7-37s served in this modified configuration, but it is likely as valuable combat aircraft they were used until they were lost or worn out.

In addition to its success against aerial targets, the 37-mm cannon also proved effective against ground targets. The cannon could penetrate up to 50-mm of armour from 656 feet (200 m). Despite its success, there was no large-scale production of the Yak-7-37 because the decision had been made to fit the Nudelman-Suranov NS-37 to the Yak-9 in what became the successful Yak-9T variant.

Yak-7-37, April–May 1942. Notice the unusually strong contrast between the green and black bands. This high contrast is sometimes seen on Yakovlev fighters, but it could also be an artefact of the film used for this photograph. (*Viktor Kulikov's collection*)

Yak-7A

The Yak-7A was tested in joint tests (factory and state) from 16 January to 22 February at Z.153. Thirty flights were conducted to determine its flight characteristics and to test the armament.

Initially, the Yak-7 had retained the cockpit canopy over the instructor's position; beginning with the Yak-7A, this was now covered with a plywood panel, although the compartment was kept so a passenger could be carried or the space used to carry equipment or an extra fuel tank. This panel was added to the Yak-7As from the series 17 on. Most Yak-7 fighters were equipped with this plywood panel. Small doors were added to the underside of the fuselage to cover the outer part of the wheels when the main landing gear was retracted, which improved the streamlining. A retractable tailwheel was introduced from the series 19, which also improved the streamlining of the aircraft. The inert gas fire suppression system was installed from the series 14 on (it is unclear if this was the system normally installed on Soviet aircraft, which used exhaust gas from the engine as opposed to utilising gas from the CO_2 tank used in the Yak-7). The ShVAK 20-mm cannon was provided with 120 rounds, and the two ShKAS machine guns were provided with 500 rounds per gun.

A total of 277 Yak-7As were produced at Z.153 in Novosibirsk from January to May 1942.

Yak-7B M-105PA

In a successful effort to create more firepower for the Yak-7, the Yak-7B replaced the ShKAS 7.62-mm machine guns of the Yak-7 and Yak-7A with two UBS 12.7-mm machine guns. This increased the firepower by 1.5 times. The 20-mm cannon was retained, and as before was equipped with 120 rounds. The weight-of-fire was now 6 lb/sec (2.72 kg/sec), which was 3.5 times that of the Bf 109F-2, 1.35 times that of the LaGG-3, and 1.5 times that of the Yak-1 and the Yak-7A with the cannon and two ShKAS machine guns. The starboard gun had 140 rounds, while the port gun had 260

Yak-7B. The glass hood of the original Yak-7 over the rear compartment was replaced by a plywood cover by the time the Yak-7B was produced. (*Viktor Kulikov's collection*)

rounds. This asymmetry probably helped balance out the weight distribution of the aircraft or counteract the propeller torque. The Yak-7B M-105PA also featured the M-105PA engine, which replaced the M-105P of the Yak-7A. The intakes for the water and oil radiators were more streamlined. The tailwheel was made fully retractable on the Yak-7B, with a small door attached to the front of the backwards-retracting strut.

The Yak-7B M-105PA was tested in joint tests at Z.153 from 28 January to 5 February 1942 and was found to have good handling and stability.

Z.153 produced 261 Yak-7B M-105PA aeroplanes from April to July 1942, when it was replaced by the improved Yak-7B M-105PF. The Yak-7B entered service in May 1942 with the 434th IAP.

Yak-7B M-105PF

The M-105PF boosted engine was tested on a Yak-7B in state tests at the NII VVS from 30 May to 9 June 1942. There was a total of thirty-six flights, and the testing was considered successful. The Yak-7B M-105PF was mainly distinguished from the Yak-7B M-105PA by the substitution of this more powerful, boosted version of the M-105 engine from the series 22 of the Yak-7B. The engine power of the M-105PF was increased from a maximum of 1,100 hp for the M-105PA to 1,260 hp. At sea level, the Yak-7B M-105PF was faster than a three-gun Bf 109G-2 and was still faster at 3,281 feet (1,000 m) although by 16,404 feet (5,000 m) the German aircraft was faster.

The last of the Yak-7B M-105PFs featured the cut-down rear fuselage and bubble-top canopy of the Yak-1B, and as a result, they were very similar in appearance to the Yak-1B and the early Yak-9s. Some late Yak-7Bs had the tailwheel enclosed by two doors, one on each side, like the installation on the Yak-9, which by 1943 was also being produced.

Z.153 produced the Yak-7B M-105PF from August 1942 to December 1943, and Z.82 produced the aircraft from May 1942 to July 1944. In total, 5,120 Yak-7B M-105PFs were produced, making it by far the most-produced version of the Yak-7.

A Yak-7B presentation aircraft in well-weathered winter camouflage. The inscription refers to the donor, a collective farmer from Tambov, or the Tambov Oblast (Province), which is south of Moscow. (*Viktor Kulikov's collection*)

Another Yak-7B presentation aircraft in winter camouflage, this time with the donors presenting the aircraft in person. The donors were supposedly from Moldavia, which had been incorporated into the Soviet Union in 1940, and the aircraft was donated in the name of Marina Raskova, a famous female navigator. However, Moldavia was captured by the Axis in the very early part of the Great Patriotic War, so the real source of the donation funds for this aircraft is a bit of a mystery. (*Viktor Kulikov's collection*)

New Yak-7Bs awaiting their delivery flights. Again, there is a strong contrast between the green and black bands of the camouflage. (*Viktor Kulikov's collection*)

Right: Yak-7B of the ace Lt Pyotr Lukianovich Gryshchenko (twenty-seven kills). Although Soviet aircraft were not noted for the high quality of their fit and finish during the Great Patriotic War, this aircraft at least appears to be well-constructed, with the panels seeming to be well-fitting. (*Viktor Kulikov's collection*)

Below: Yak-7B in flight in a still taken from a newsreel. (*Viktor Kulikov's collection*)

Yak-7B (PVO Version)

Some Yak-7Bs were modified on the production line for use by the PVO. These modified Yak-7Bs were equipped with the RPK-10 radio-compass and the FS-155 landing light in the port wing. Around twenty modified Yak-7Bs were delivered to the PVO every month.

Yak-7B (U)

After production of the Yak-7V ended (described further on), there was still a need for an advanced two-seat fighter trainer. In 1944, Yak-7Bs that had been withdrawn from combat duty were converted by Z.87 at Rostov-on-Don (Rostov-na-Donu) into two-seat trainers with dual controls. Some aircraft were also converted into trainers in the field. It is unclear from the record how many Yak-7Bs were so modified. The (U) in the name stood for *Uchebniy* or 'Trainer'.

Yak-7R (Yak-7B with AFA-IM)

The Yak-7R was a reconnaissance version of the Yak-7B fitted with an AFA-IM camera (the 'M' stood for *Modernizirovaniy*, or 'Modernised'). The first Yak-7s modified to carry cameras were two Yak-7UTIs in August 1941, which were equipped with the AFA-IM and the RSI-4 radio. This version was not put into production as Yakovlev needed to concentrate on the production of the single-seat fighters.

Later, Yak-7Rs based upon the Yak-7B were produced. The 'R' in the name stood for *Razvedchik*, or 'Reconnaissance'. The aircraft was meant to operate at altitudes of from 984 feet (300 m) to 9,843 feet (3,000 m). The AFA-IM camera was installed in the aircraft between the third and fourth fuselage frames. The camera opening could be closed off by a door to protect the lens. Some 300 Yak-7Rs were produced at Z.82, while around fifty were produced at Z.153, which brought the total to 350 purpose-built Yak-7Rs. In addition to the production examples, the AFA-IM could also be fitted to Yak-7s in the field to create field-modified Yak-7Rs.

Yak-7UTI

The Yak-7 had originally been designed as a trainer, and it was produced as such, under the designation 'Yak-7UTI', with the 'UTI' standing for *Uchebniy Trenirovochniy Istrebitel'* or 'Fighter Trainer'. The aircraft was a two-seater and was based upon the experimental UTI-26-2. It had an instructor-pilot and a trainee-pilot. The aircraft retained one ShKAS machine gun on the port side with 500 rounds. Unlike the UTI-26-2, the tailwheel was non-retractable. The first Yak-7UTI was flown by P. Ya. Fedrovi on 18 May 1941.

The Yak-7UTI was produced at Z.301 from April to September 1941, and then after evacuation to Novosibirsk, production continued at Z.153 until a total of 186 had been produced. Besides its use as a high-speed trainer, the Yak-7UTI was used at the front as a reconnaissance and spotter aircraft. The Yak-7UTI was replaced on the production lines by the simplified Yak-7V.

Although the Yak-7A fighter and the Yak-7UTI trainer were almost identical in outward appearance, the presence of a pilot in the rear compartment of this aircraft identifies it as a Yak-7UTI. Unlike the later Yak-7V trainer, the main landing gear was retractable. (*Viktor Kulikov's collection*)

Yak-7V

Although the Yak-7UTI had retained the retractable main landing gear of the Yak-7 fighter, the Yak-7V trainer dispensed with the retractable landing gear as being unnecessary for a training aircraft. The landing gear was fixed, and the wheel wells were faired over. This change made the Yak-7V cheaper to produce and easier to maintain, although at the cost of speed when compared to Yak-7s with the retractable landing gear. However, this loss in speed was not considered an impediment for a trainer. The single machine gun of the Yak-7UTI was deleted. The M-105PA was initially used, but this was later changed to the more powerful M-105PF. The fixed tailwheel was increased in size to 300 × 125 mm. The instructor-pilot was equipped to disable the trainee-pilot's ability to use the wheel brakes, and the instrument panel in the front cockpit was simplified. The fuel tanks were not self-sealing.

In addition to being used as a trainer, the Yak-7V was used as a high-speed liaison or courier aircraft as even with the fixed landing gear, it had a top speed of nearly 300 mph (483 kph), making it several times faster than the U-2 (Po-2) biplane. The Yak-7V was sometimes fitted with skis on all the landing gears. A total of 597 Yak-7Vs were built, with 510 being new builds, and eighty-seven being conversions from Yak-7B fighters. It was produced from May 1942 to December 1943 and became one of the main advanced conversion trainers for the Soviets.

Experimental Versions

Yak-7 M-82A

Just as the M-82A radial engine was fitted to the MiG-3, resulting in the I-221 M-82A (MiG-3 M-82A, MiG-9), and was fitted to the LaGG-3, ultimately resulting in the production La-5 fighter, the M-82A was fitted to the Yak-7. The engine was installed in early August 1941. The new engine was not the only change as the Yak-7-37/Yak-9-type wings were fitted, with the span reduced from 32.81 feet (10 m) to 31.96 feet (9.74 m),

Yak-7V trainer. The fixed undercarriage has been equipped with skis, with even the tailwheel being replaced by a ski. The aircraft still appears in its summer camouflage, with black-outlined stars. (*Viktor Kulikov's collection*)

A row of Yak-7s lined up at an airfield. Most of the Yak-7s appear to be Yak-7Bs, but the nearest aircraft appears to be a Yak-7V or Yak-7UTI, with the clear hood over the rear pilot. Strangely, the second aircraft in this line-up appears to have unpainted propeller blades, when by this time (probably 1942), they should have been painted black. (*Viktor Kulikov's collection*)

and angular wingtips with leading-edge slats fitted. Two ShVAK KP-20 20-mm cannons were now fitted to the wings, and the wings were strengthened where the cannons were located. The cannons had 100 rounds apiece, while a single UBS machine gun, mounted on the upper cowling, was equipped with 260 rounds. RS-82 rockets could also be carried, mounted under the wings. The retractable tailwheel was enlarged to 300 × 127 mm in size. The M-82A engine was equipped with an AV-5L-127 propeller of 9.19 feet (2.8 m) in diameter. The aircraft was equipped with the all-round vision canopy, with the position raised by 3.94 inches (100 mm) to provide better forward vision.

The first prototype was constructed from August 1941 to January 1942. The re-engined aircraft was first flown by P. Ya. Fedrovi on 28 February 1942. The speed at sea level was 311 mph (501 kph). This was considered to be inadequate. The reason was the too-small propeller, which was only 9.19 feet (2.8 m) in diameter, instead of the 10.5 feet (3.2 m) that was actually needed. The propeller had to be small in diameter because of the low ground clearance caused by the relatively short landing gear of the Yak-7. A second prototype (a *Dooblyor*) was constructed from September to December 1942. It differed from the first prototype in having a metal wing, a larger propeller, and a modified engine cowling. There were no flights made on the *Dooblyor*, as by this time the La-5 was already in production, and the performance of the first Yak-7 M-82 had been disappointing. No Yak-7 M-82As were serially produced.

Yak-7D

This variant of the Yak-7 arose out of the need for a fairly long-ranged high-speed reconnaissance aircraft. Instead of the two main fuel tanks featured by other Yak-7s, this version featured four wing tanks. A major change from this aircraft and earlier Yakovlev fighters was the substitution of metal wing spars for wooden wing spars, the dural spars being both stronger and lighter than their wooden counterparts. In addition, the six inboard wing ribs were also dural, with only the outermost wing ribs being wooden. This change was made possible by the increasing availability of aluminium due to a large extent by Lend-Lease shipments of aluminium from the United States. This version served as the basis for the long-ranged Yak-7DI fighter.

As with the Yak-7M, the wingspan was reduced from 32.81 feet (10 m) to 31.96 feet (9.74 m) and the wingtips made more angular to fit leading-edge slats, which in the event were not fitted to the Yak-7D. These type wings were first fitted to the experimental I-28 (Yak-5) high-altitude fighter (described further on in the Experimental Fighters section). Either a camera or an observer could be fitted in the rear compartment.

The fuselage of the Yak-7V with a M-105PF engine was mated to an experimental wing produced by Z.153. The retractable landing gear and other elements were taken from a Yak-7B. The aircraft featured eleven fuel tanks with a total load of 244.36 gal (925 l). The aircraft was built by June 1942, and factory tests were conducted from 3 to 16 June 1942. One major problem was the time it took to fill all four tanks; since the tanks were filled from one point, it took one hour to fill all of the tanks. The additional weight of the fuel also made the Yak-7D 18.64 mph (30 kph) slower than the Yak-7B. No production ensued, with the Yak-7D remaining a one-off prototype, but it did serve as a basis for the Yak-7DI fighter, which became the Yak-9.

Yak-7DI

As this long-range fighter development of the Yak-7 was produced as the Yak-9, it is described in that section.

Yak-7GK (Yak-7 with Pressurised Cabin)

One high-back Yak-7B was fitted with an experimental Shchyerbakov-designed ventilating-type pressurised cabin. The aircraft was delivered for testing on 16 May 1943. The tests were unsuccessful, continuing in August 1943. The aircraft was modified, and the revised aircraft underwent state tests from 1 May 1944. The tests were again unsuccessful, and the aircraft was not produced. Another Yak-7, fitted with a compressor-type pressurised cabin, was just as unsuccessful in tests.

Yak-7L

This Yak-7 was used to test laminar section wings. It was converted from a Yak-7B in the summer of 1944. Although the wing was similar in shape to the normal wing, it was composed of laminar profiles developed at the TsAGI, in order to take advantage of laminar flow properties, which reduced drag. The aircraft was tested from 14 July to 9 September 1944. The tests showed that the speed for the laminar wing-equipped Yak-7 increased by 8.7 mph (14 kph) at sea level and 20.51 mph (33 kph) at the second supercharger altitude, over the speeds for equivalent aircraft with the normal profile wing. One aircraft was built, but it did not go into production, despite the increase in speed.

Yak-7M

The Yak-7M represented an attempt by the Yakovlev OKB to increase the armament of the Yak-7. In September 1941, a Yak-7 was fitted with a ShVAK 20-mm cannon in each wing, which along with the nose-mounted 20-mm gave the fighter a total of three 20-mm cannons. The 'M' in the designation stood for *Modifitsirovanniy*, or 'Modified'. The nose cannon was equipped with 120 rounds, while the wing cannons were equipped with 110 rounds per gun. A fuel tank was added behind the pilot, in what had been the second seat on the Yak-7UTI, and the pilot was provided with an armoured seatback. In addition to the cannons, the Yak-7M could carry six RS-82 rockets under the wing. One notable modification was to the wings; these were now equipped with leading-edge slats. This necessitated that the wingtips be more angular to accommodate the ends of the slats, and the wings were reduced in span from 32.81 feet (10 m) to 31.96 feet (9.74m). This same type wing, without slats, would appear on the Yak-7's development, the Yak-9.

The Yak-7M was built at Z.292 in September 1941 and flew its test flights at Chkalovskaya near Moscow from 5 to 16 October 1941. Due to the approach of German forces to Moscow (Operation Typhoon started on 2 October 1941), the NII VVS were evacuated to the Urals. Testing continued from 31 October 1941 to 27 December 1941. Flight tests showed that the Yak-7M handled much like other Yak-7s, but the slats improved its stall characteristics, and its lateral stability was improved. The critical minimum speed was decreased by 18.64–24.85 mph (30-40 kph). The firing of the wing cannons, due to unbalanced firing, could only be in short bursts or the aiming was negatively affected.

The testing was considered successful and the Yak-7M was recommended for production. Production did not occur, however, perhaps because of the aiming problems with the wing cannons. Of the innovations introduced by the Yak-7M, the armour was introduced into the Yak-7 fighters, with the fitting of the additional fuel tank behind the pilot. The wing shape reappeared again on the Yak-7D, the Yak-7DI, and on production Yak-9s, although these aircraft lacked the leading-edge slats of the Yak-7M.

Yak-7P

In a further attempt to increase the Yak-7's armament, the Yak-7P was modified from a production Yak-7B (produced in June 1943) to fit it with a heavier, all-cannon armament. The two machine guns were replaced by two Berezin B-20S synchronised 20-mm cannons. The ShVAK 20-mm cannon in the nose was retained, giving the aircraft three 20-mm cannons.

The aircraft was sent to the NII VVS on 4 November 1943 for testing, with the testing occurring from 4 to 13 November 1943 (another source has 13 December 1943). The test pilots included V. A. Modestov, V. I. Khomyakov, and Yu. A. Antipov, among others. While the installation of the heavier armament did not affect the handling, the ejection of the cannon casings and links damaged the leading edge of the horizontal stabilisers. There were also problems with synchronisation.

Although the all-cannon Yak-7P was apparently sent to the 1st VA for combat testing, the results of that testing are unclear, and the Yak-7P did not enter into production, although efforts to install all-cannon armament on Yakovlev fighters continued.

Yak-7PD

The I-28 (Yak-5) was Yakovlev's first attempt at a high-altitude fighter. The Yak-7PD continued this line of development for the OKB. The Yak-7PD was, in essence, a Yak-7B high-back airframe fitted with the high-altitude M-105PD engine equipped with the E-100 supercharger designed by V. A. Dollezhal of the TsIAM. In addition to the experimental M-105PD engine, the Yak-7PD was modified with the cut-down rear fuselage and bubble canopy found on the later Yak-7Bs. In order to decrease the weight to enable the aircraft to reach higher altitudes, the armament was restricted to one nose-mounted ShVAK 20-mm cannon with 120 rounds. Although a radio mast was fitted, no radio was installed.

The Yak-7PD underwent state tests at the NII VVS from 17 September to 23 September. The test pilot was A. G. Proshakov. There were eleven flights in total. Compared to the Yak-7B, the service ceiling was improved by 4,593 feet (1,400 m), although the handling was the same.

State tests were suspended, and no mass production of the Yak-7PD was undertaken, probably because of continuing problems with the M-105PD engine. The Yak-7PD remained a one-off prototype, although the development of high-altitude fighters by Yakovlev continued, with the Yak-9PD. As part of continuing tests with the M-105PD, after the completion of state tests, the Yak-7PD remained at the NII VVS.

Yak-7PRVD (Yak-7RVD, Yak-7B with DM-4S Ramjets)

The DM-4S ramjets were some of the first jet engines developed in the Soviet Union, and a Yak-7B M-105PF was chosen to test them. The engines were designed by I. A. Merkulov. One was mounted in a pod under each wing. The ramjets used fuel from the aircraft's fuel tanks. The presence of the compartment behind the pilot on the high-back Yak-7Bs let a flight engineer observe the aircraft while in flight. The aircraft was known as the 'Yak-7PRVD', for *Pryamotochniye Vozdooshnoreaktivniye Dvigateli,* or 'Ramjets'.

The tests took place at the LII from 24 March to 12 December 1944. The test pilot was S. N. Anokhin. The first flight where the DM-4S ramjets were used was on 15 May 1944. The drag with the DM-4S engines not operating slowed down the aircraft, and even with the engines running the increase in speed over a standard Yak-7B was only 11.81 mph (19 kph). This was considered insufficient to justify the increased drag during normal flight and the increased fuel usage when the engines were engaged. The appearance of turbojet engines made ramjets as boosters unnecessary, and work on the Yak-7PRVD with the DM-4S ramjets was discontinued.

Yak-7S

This Yak-7 was used to test the Nudelman-Suranov NS-37 37-mm cannon, mounted in the nose in place of the ShVAK 20-mm cannon. The NS-37 cannon weighed 335 lb (152 kg) compared to the 99 lb (45 kg) of the ShVAK cannon. As with the later Yak-7-37, the cockpit was moved aft due to the size of the large cannon. It appears that the 'S' in the designation did not signify anything and was just the internal OKB designation. Although the tests of the Yak-7S proved successful, passing its state tests, no production ensued, perhaps because the decision had already been made to fit the MPSh-37 to a Yak-7B airframe (the Yak-7-37).

Combat Tactics

Soviet tactics consisted of manoeuvring their small, lightweight fighters with the enemy, trying to turn inside the enemy aircraft to get into close contact, then using their nose guns, including their cannon, to down the opposing aircraft with a few short bursts. The German fighters used both 'boom and zoom' and manoeuvring tactics. As with the Yak-1, the Yak-7s tried to engage the German fighters in horizontal turning battles, where they had the edge, as opposed to vertical manoeuvring, where the Germans had the edge. Although it handled better than the Yak-1, the Yak-7 was slightly less manoeuvrable in both horizontal and vertical manoeuvring due to its heavier weight.

Combat Use

Unlike the Yak-1, the Yak-7 did not see action at the start of the Great Patriotic War as it was not introduced into service until September 1941. From this point on, it was in service until the end of the Second World War.

Leningrad

The first combat use of the Yak-7 was during the siege of Leningrad, its use starting in autumn 1941, with production having begun in August 1941 at Z.301 in Moscow.

While attacking enemy positions in the Gruzin area on the Leningrad Front, four Yak-7Bs of the 283rd IAP encountered two He 111s and shot them down. This combat took place on 30 December 1942.

Moscow

Yak-7s were introduced into combat at Moscow in late 1941. For example, they served with the 172nd IAP and were used, like so many other fighters at this time, in ground attack missions in support of the Soviet Winter Counteroffensive.

Before Stalingrad

Even before the battle for Stalingrad had begun, the Yak-7 was already seeing heavy action in the southern Soviet Union. On 23 July 1942, five Yak-7s from the 296th IAP attacked six Ju 88s, shooting down one, although one of the Yak-7s flown by a Lt M. I. Memdin was damaged enough by defensive fire to make an emergency landing. Yak-7Bs, which served alongside the Yak-1s in the 434th IAP (described previously in the Yak-1 combat section), were part of that regiment's success, which on 26 July 1942 claimed thirty-four Axis aircraft downed in eleven air combats.

Stalingrad

The Yak-7 saw heavy use at Stalingrad, alongside its Yakovlev stablemates the Yak-1 and towards the end of the battle, the Yak-7's development, the Yak-9. The 16th VA had ten fighter regiments that were equipped with the Yak-7B.

On 5 September 1942, after the battle for Stalingrad had started, Yak-7Bs from the 288th IAD claimed three Bf 109s and two Ju 88s without any loss of their own. On 18 September 1942, twelve Yak-7Bs from the 434th IAP were flying over the railroad station at Kotluban, slightly north-west of Stalingrad, when they were attacked by nine Bf 109s; one of the Bf 109s was shot down, and the others were forced to withdraw without loss to the Soviets. The Soviets were not always so fortunate. On this same day, Vladimir Mikoyan, the son of Politburo member Anastas Ivanovich Mikoyan (1895–1978) and nephew of aircraft designer Artyom Mikoyan (of Mikoyan-Gurevich or 'MiG' fame), was shot down near Stalingrad and killed. The next day, Ivan Kleshchyov, commander of the 434th IAP, was shot down; although burned, Kleshchyov was able to bail out of his aircraft and take to his parachute. Although he survived and recovered from his burns, he died on 31 December 1942 when his fighter crashed in an accident. He had flown 380 sorties and had anywhere from sixteen individual kills to twenty-four, and from eighteen shared kills to thirty-two. After his death, Vasiliy Stalin, Josef Stalin's son, became commander of the 32nd GvIAP until May 1943, when he was replaced due to his unreliability as a commander (Vasiliy Stalin suffered from drinking problems).

On 20 August 1942, the Yak-7Bs of the 288th IAD were introduced into the Stalingrad battle. The 4th IAP, which was the most effective regiment in this division, claimed twenty-nine Axis aircraft from 7 to 12 September, while losing nine of their own aircraft.

Rzhev (Operation Mars)

While the fighting raged in Stalingrad, the Red Army was also staging attacks in the north, near Moscow, against the Rzhev Salient. The Rzhev Salient was a prominent feature of the Eastern Front, which the Soviets felt pointed like a dagger at Moscow. In an attempt to reduce the salient, Marshal Georgiy Konstantinovich Zhukov (1896–1974) launched a huge offensive on 25 November 1942 called Operation Mars (the Second Rzhev-Sychyovka Offensive Operation). The Soviet Western and Kalinin Fronts were involved in the offensive. Most historians consider the Rzhev offensive to have been a costly failure as the Soviets suffered massive casualties with very little effect upon the position of the German lines. Nevertheless, the attack did have the effect of preventing the Germans from shifting resources to the Stalingrad front, where they were sorely needed. However, the value of the Rzhev offensive(s) does not concern us here; the use of modified Yakovlev fighters in the north at the time of Operation Mars does.

One area of improvement for the Yak-7 was in the pilot's vision. Although the view over the front and sides was adequate, the view to the back was not, as the raised fuselage fairing blocked the pilot's view. The Yakovlev OKB worked to improve this by lowering the rear fuselage fairing and adding an all-round vision canopy. The 42nd IAP, commanded by F. Shinkarenko, which had been used before as a sort of test regiment for changes and improvements to the Yakovlev fighters, was chosen once again to test this revised Yak-7B. The 42nd IAP conducted combat trials of the new bubble-canopy Yak-7B on the North-Western Front from 17 November to 13 December 1942, at the same time Operation Mars was being conducted to the south. These attacks by the North-Western Front may well have been designed to support the Rzhev operation by drawing the Germans' attention elsewhere.

The results were encouraging. In six air combats, four enemy aircraft were downed, including two Bf 109Fs, one Fw 189, and one Hs 126 for the loss of one Yak-7B. The pilots were pleased with the better visibility of the new canopy, and the canopy was recommended for use on all fighters.

Northern Russia

At Velikiye Luki, northwest of Moscow, on 15 January 1943, seven Yak-7s of the 653rd IAP under the command of Major G. Prokofiev faced off against six Bf 109s. In the ensuing air battle, two Bf 109s were downed by Lt Yakub, one by Capt. Kapashtin, one by Lt Vetrov, and the fifth was claimed as a shared victory. The Soviet losses, if any, were not recorded.

Over the German-held Demyansk Salient, which had been formed in the aftermath of the Soviet Winter Counteroffensive of 1941–42, Yak-7s of the 42nd IAP, under the command of N. Tikhonov, fought the Germans. On 23 February 1943, after being attacked by fifteen Bf 109s and several Fw 190s, two Yak-7s were shot down, but the regiment claimed two Fw 190s in return.

On 15 March 1943, over the Lovat River (which passes by Velikiye Luki), there was an air battle over the river crossings involving Yak-7s. Eight Yak-7Bs of the

875th IAP, commanded by Capt. M. S. Gordeyev fought against four Fw 190s and four Bf 109s that were escorting seventeen Ju 87s. In the ensuing battle, some of the Yak-7Bs attacked the fighters while other Yaks attacked the bombers. The Soviets claimed three fighters and one Ju 87 shot down. The following day was even better for the regiment, when eight Yak-7Bs attacked twelve Ju 87s that were striking the crossings and were credited with shooting down seven of the German dive-bombers.

Battle of the Kuban

Six Yak-7Bs from the 43rd IAP destroyed or damaged nine aircraft after attacking the airfield at Anapa, in the Taman Peninsula, on 26 May 1943. They were led by the unit commander, Maj. A. A. Doroshenko.

Yak-7s of the 788th IAP PVO also took part in the Kuban aerial fighting. Usually, PVO units were involved in defending high-value targets such as cities, but this unit was involved in frontal combat.

Kursk (Operation Citadel)

Yak-7s were in operation from the opening day of the battle, 5 July 1943. On this date, Jr Lt V. K. Polyakov of the 54th GvIAP, destroyed two He 111 bombers, one of which he rammed. His Yak-7 was damaged in the ramming attack, but he was able to bail out of his aircraft and parachute to safety. On 12 July 1943, eight Yak-7Bs commanded by Capt A. Krivushin of the 3rd GvIAP shot down five German aircraft out of a formation of eighteen Bf 110s being escorted by eight Bf 109s. On this same day, six Yak-7s of the 64th GvIAP attacked eight Bf 110s escorted by six Bf 109s and were able to down five of the enemy aircraft.

A *taran* took place on 23 July, when Jr Lt I. Ya. Gorovets of the 64th GvIAP rammed a Ju 87 bomber. Even though the wing of his own aircraft was torn off in the attack, he survived as he was able to parachute to safety. Two days later, N. Shutt from the 265th IAP, flying with another Yak-7B, was covering some Il-2s when they were attacked by Bf 109s. Shutt was able to shoot down one of the attackers.

On 4 August 1943, commanded by Capt Arseniy Vasilyevich Vorozheykin (1912–2001), six Yak-7Bs of the 728th IAP while on air cover for Soviet troops attacked twelve Ju 87s escorted by eight Bf 109s. Eight enemy aircraft were claimed as shot down, including four by Vorozheykin alone, who eventually went on to be credited with forty-six individual victories and fourteen shared victories. He received the title of Hero of the Soviet Union twice during the war. In addition, he shot down six aircraft during the Battle of the Khalkhin-Gol.

Ukrainian Operations in 1943–44

A rather unusual occurrence happened with a Yak-7 on 3 November 1943. While transporting a mechanic in his Yak-7A's rear compartment, Sr Lt V. A. Bashirov managed to shoot down a Ju 88. There is no record of the mechanic's reaction to this odd victory of which he was a somewhat unwilling participant, although he was no doubt happy about the outcome.

Operation Bagration (The Destruction of Army Group Centre)

During Operation Bagration, not only did the 3rd IAK use the Yak-9, but Yak-1s and Yak-7s were also used. On one occasion in July, Gen. Yevgeniy Savitskiy with his wingman were engaged by twelve enemy aircraft while flying a reconnaissance mission. During the ensuing fight, Savitskiy downed one enemy fighter, and his wingman damaged two others; both pilots were able to escape.

Vistula to Oder Operation

By the end of 1944 and the beginning of 1945, only sixty-five Yak-7s remained in frontal units, although 262 Yak-7Bs still remained in use with the PVO. The few existing frontal unit Yak-7s presumably saw service in the Vistula to Oder Operation in January.

Berlin Strategic Offensive Operation (Battle of Berlin)

It is not clear from the record if any Yak-7s remained in frontal units in the West by April 1945 or participated in the Battle of Berlin.

Manchurian Strategic Offensive Operation

By the start of the Manchurian Campaign in August 1945, some Yak-7Bs were still on the strength of the Pacific Fleet. The record is unclear on how much action they saw in this offensive, although given the sharp combat in this short campaign, they almost certainly saw some action if they were still serviceable.

Yak-7 in Detail

General Description

The Yak-7 was a single-engined single-seat cantilever monoplane fighter with an enclosed cockpit and retractable main landing gear. The tailwheel was retractable on some Yak-7 versions. The aircraft was of mixed construction, with a steel tube fuselage structure, covered in metal, plywood, and fabric, metal tailplanes with fabric-covered moveable metal control surfaces, and wooden wings covered in a plywood skin.

Fuselage

As with the Yak-1, the fuselage structure featured a steel tube framework, this framework being covered in metal panels on the forward fuselage. With the Yak-7, the engine mount was no longer integral with the steel tube framework, but was a separate structure that was now bolted to the aft framework. The top of the rear fuselage was covered in plywood, while the side and bottom were covered in fabric, and most Yak-7s had a raised rear fuselage decking (or 'high-back'). The late Yak-7Bs had a cut-down rear fuselage to accommodate the all-around vision bubble-top cockpit canopy first introduced on the Yak-1B, which was subsequently utilised on all the Yak-3s and Yak-9s. The fuselage cross-section for the high-back Yak-7s was the same as that of the Yak-1.

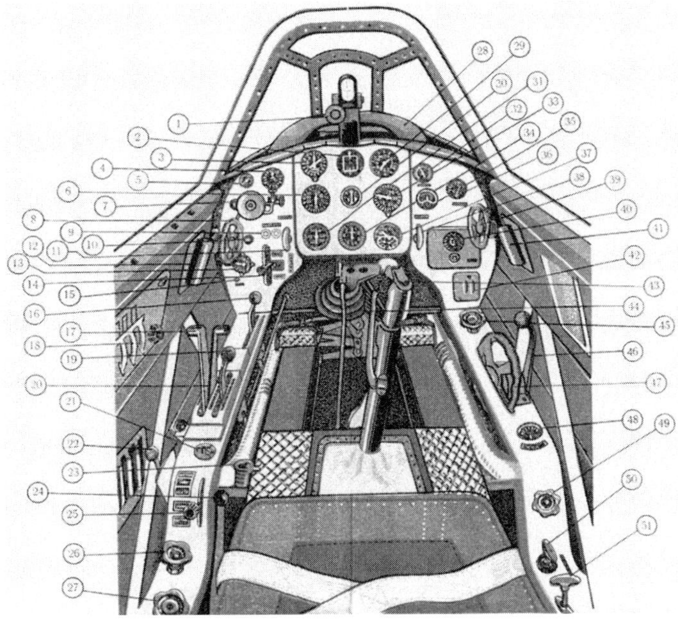

Yak-7 M-105PF cockpit. Note the simple instrument panel and the joystick-type control column. (*Yak-7 (B) M-105PF Technical Manual*)

Wings

The Yak-7 had all-wooden wings, with a wooden structure covered in plywood. The wing had two wooden spars and wooden ribs, with the bakelised plywood surface of the wings being covered by a doped fabric to give a smooth, join-less finish to the wings. This plywood surface was between 2.5 to 5 mm in thickness. The wing was constructed as a single-piece structure that was joined to the fuselage during the production process. As with the Yak-1, this simplified construction, and disassembly for transport, but meant that if the starboard or port wing was damaged, the entire wing structure had to be removed and repaired or replaced.

The wings were of a Clark YH aerofoil, with 15 per cent thickness at the root and 8 per cent thickness at the wingtip.

Tailplanes

As with the later Yak-9, the Yak-7 featured metal tail surfaces, with the fixed surfaces being covered in dural aluminium alloy over a metal structure and the moveable control surfaces being covered in fabric over a dural structure. This was in contrast to the all-wooden fixed tail surfaces of the Yak-1 and helped to make the aircraft lighter. The fixed fin and horizontal stabilisers were of a two-spar structure.

Engine

The engine on all production Yak-7s was the Klimov M-105 twelve-cylinder vee-type liquid-cooled inline engine. Initially, the Yak-7 had been equipped with the M-105PA with a maximum rating of 1,100, but this was replaced in later Yak-7s by the boosted M-105PF with a maximum rating of 1,260 hp. The propeller was the VISh-61P constant-speed propeller.

Fuel System

There were two main fuel tanks, with one in each inner part of the wings, as with the Yak-1, with a small service tank in the middle of the under-fuselage. Four detachable metal panels, despite there being only two main fuel tanks, covered the tanks on the bottom of the wings. As with the Yak-1, external fuel gauges were located on top of the inner part of the wings, which indicated how much fuel was left in the tanks. Fuel tank caps were also located on top of the wings.

Controls

Most of the moveable control surfaces of the Yak-7 were of dural structure with a fabric covering, the exception being the underwing flaps, which were all-metal on all the Yakovlev fighters. The control surfaces were activated mechanically by push-pull rods for the ailerons and elevators, and by wires for the rudder. The joystick-type control column controlled the ailerons and elevators, while the rudder was controlled by rudder pedals. The Schrenk-type flaps were hydraulically operated.

Landing Gear

The main landing gear on the Yak-7 was fully retractable, retracting inwards, giving the aircraft a wide stance (as with all Yakovlev production fighters), useful for rough field operation. The landing gear legs were covered by a single cover, with small doors attached to the wing under surface (from the Yak-7A on), which retracted mechanically and covered the outer portion of the wheels when the landing gear was retracted. These small wheel doors, absent on the Yak-1, were used on subsequent Yakovlev fighters, the Yak-9 and Yak-3. The main wheels were larger than on the Yak-1.

Brand-new Yak-7Bs rolling off the production line at Z.153 in Novosibirsk, Siberia. The screen of the under-nose radiator shows up well here on the first aircraft. (*Viktor Kulikov's collection*)

On some versions of the Yak-7, such as the Yak-7B, the tailwheel was also retractable, with a small door attached to the front of the strut of the backwards-retracting tailwheel, as was seen on Yak-1s with retracting tailwheels. Some late Yak-7Bs had the 'clamshell'-type doors as found on the Yak-9. The tailwheel was 255 × 110 mm in size. Sometimes, the tailwheel was fixed on the Yak-7, as for example on the early Yak-7As, and the training versions of the Yak-7 (the Yak-7UTI and Yak-7V, the Yak-7V also having the main landing gear fixed, with the main gear wells faired in).

Radio Equipment

The Yak-7A had a RSI-3 transmitter and a RSI-4 receiver. Only some of the Yak-7Bs had the RSI-3 transmitter. Yak-7s equipped with radio equipment featured an antenna mast behind the cockpit canopy.

Fixed Armament

The standard armament for nearly all Yak-7s was a ShVAK MP-20 20-mm cannon firing through the spinner and two synchronised UBS 12.7-mm machine guns mounted on top of the engine cowling to fire through the propeller disc. The Yak-7As featured the 20-mm cannon with 120 rounds and two synchronised ShKAS 7.62-mm machine guns with 500 rounds each. A small service trial batch of Yak-7-37s was built, which were equipped with a Shpital'niy MPSh-37 37-mm cannon firing through the spinner. At first, the Yak-7-37s featured two UBS guns, but later, one of the UBS guns was deleted for weight reasons.

Disposable Armament

The Yak-7A could carry six RS-82 rockets, and it was noted that the spread of the rockets was less than that for the MiG-3 or the LaGG-3 because of the Yak-7's superior stability. It was also capable of carrying small bombs for use as a fighter-bomber, with up to 220 lb (100 kg) under each wing, for a total bomb load of 441 lb (200 kg). From the Yak-7B on, the Yak-7 did not carry the RS-82 rockets due to the performance concerns that limited their use on the MiG-3 and Yak-1.

Colour and Markings

The Yak-7 first saw service in late 1941, and these aircraft would have been painted in the black/green scheme of AMT-6 Black and AMT-4 Green over AMT-7 Blue specified at that time. Some Yak-7Bs would have been painted in the two-grey fighter scheme of AMT-11 Grey-Blue and AMT-12 Dark Grey over AMT-7 Blue, which was officially adopted in fall 1943. If painted in the black/green scheme, it is probable that the 1940-style black-outlined red star would have normally been carried. A plain red star may also have been carried in place of the black-outlined stars. If painted in the two-grey scheme, the 1943-style red star would have been used. Examples of the Yak-7 with the black/green scheme can be seen in the colour plates section. The white winter camouflage was sometimes applied to the Yak-7.

Yak-9

Developed from the Yak-7, the Yak-9 was numerically the single most important fighter used by the Soviet Union during the Second World War, with 16,769 being produced (including those produced post-war). It was also the most versatile of the wartime Yakovlev fighters, finding use as a short-range frontal fighter, a long-range escort, a reconnaissance aircraft, a high-altitude interceptor, a tank-killer, a trainer, and a fighter-bomber, complete with an internal bomb bay.

By the middle of 1944, there were more Yak-9 versions in service with the Soviets than all other fighter types combined. First produced in 1942, it was constantly updated and improved, and continued in production post-war, with production not ending until 1948. At one point, Z.153 in Novosibirsk was producing twenty Yak-9s every day. It continued to serve with the Soviet Union until the mid-1950s, when it was given the ASCC or Allied Self-Coordinating Committee (NATO) nickname of 'Frank'. In addition to the Soviet Air Force, the Yak-9 was used post-war by several other air forces, seeing service in the Korean War with the North Korean Air Force.

Yak-7DI (Prototype of the Yak-9)

Although the Yak-7 was considered a good fighter, one area where it was felt it could be improved was in the area of range, it being somewhat limited in this capacity by the small internal fuel load it carried. It accommodated two fuel tanks in the wings, one on each side. For longer range, a fuel tank could be fitted behind the pilot in the rear compartment. This was disliked by the pilots because of the additional fire risk, most pilots not being overly fond of flying with an unprotected reservoir of flammable liquid located immediately behind them.

The Yak-7D long-range reconnaissance aircraft served as the basis for a longer-ranged fighter version of the Yak-7, designated the 'Yak-7DI', where the 'DI' stood for *Dalniy Istrebitel*', or 'Long-range Fighter'. The tailplanes and metal-sparred angular-tipped wings designed for the Yak-7D were combined with a late Yak-7B fuselage, with the cut-down rear fuselage and bubble-top canopy. The fuselage retained the rear compartment of the Yak-7, with a curved plywood cover that opened to the starboard side. The M-105PF engine was fitted. Four dural self-sealing fuel tanks were added to the wings. The fuel tanks had a total capacity of 177.79 gal (673 l) and were all interconnected, going through a 1.59-gal (6-l) auxiliary tank that ensured the fuel distribution was equal in the different tanks. The starboard UBS machine gun was removed. The port gun was retained, with 200 rounds, as was the ShVAK 20-mm cannon, with 120 rounds. Two bombs of up to 220 lb (100 kg) apiece could be carried for a total of 441 lb (200 kg). The aircraft could be used as a long-range fighter with a full fuel load or as a frontal fighter with a reduced fuel load.

The Yak-7DI was completed on 25 June 1942, with factory (OKB) tests beginning 26 June and ending on 16 July 1942, with the test pilot being Pavel Ya. Fedrovi. Thirteen flights were conducted. State tests went from 18 July 1942 to 5 August 1942, being flown by test pilot K. A. Gruzdev. Sixty flights were conducted. The aircraft passed its tests and was recommended for production. The *Dooblyor*, constructed

Yak-7DI, the prototype of the Yak-9, seen during manufacturer's tests, June–July 1942. The tail inscription reads '7-DI' in Cyrillic. Once again, the very high contrast between the green and black bands can be seen on this Yakovlev aircraft. (*Viktor Kulikov's collection*)

in July 1942, served as the Etalon for production. During tests, it was determined that overly aggressive use of the wheel brakes could cause the aircraft to nose over, which limited the short take-off and landing of the Yak-7DI, resulting in the need to use longer airstrips. This problem was to be addressed, along with any other defects, during production (as so often happened with Soviet aircraft). The aft-mounted cockpit that was fitted to later Yak-9 versions, such as the Yak-9T, Yak-9M, and Yak-9U, helped to address this issue by moving the centre of gravity aft.

When the Yak-7DI was put into production, the designation was changed to 'Yak-9'.

Yak-9

The original production version of the Yak-9 differed little outwardly from the late Yak-7B with the bubble-top canopy, differing externally mainly in its more angular wingtips. The Yak-9 also had only one UBS machine gun with 200 rounds, mounted on the port side of the cowling (the Yak-7B had two UBS guns), there being a small bulge on the cowling to signal its presence. The ShVAK MP-20 20-mm cannon, with 120 rounds firing through the spinner, was retained. The compartment behind the pilot was retained, covered by a plywood cover that swung to the starboard side. This compartment could house spare parts, a passenger (in somewhat uncomfortable and claustrophobic conditions), or a fuel tank. It was later used to carry cameras on reconnaissance versions and a bomb bay on the Yak-9B.

There were some substantial internal differences with the Yak-7B, however, with the Yak-9's metal (dural) wing spars in place of the Yak-7's wooden wing spars. This saved weight and increased the strength of the wing. One change that did not carry over from the Yak-7DI was the presence of four fuel tanks; the Yak-9 had only two fuel tanks. The Yak-9 was equipped with a M-105PF engine driving a VISh-61P propeller.

Yak-9 of the first series in 1942. The high dividing line between the topside camouflage and underside camouflage on the rear fuselage is noteworthy. (*Viktor Kulikov's collection*).

Another view of this same aircraft. (*Viktor Kulikov's collection*)

A side view of this aircraft. (*Viktor Kulikov's collection*)

An early Yak-9 of the 85th GvIAP, characterised by its large shark mouth marking on the nose. (*Viktor Kulikov's collection*)

Above left: Yak-9 of the 976th IAP in flight in March 1944. (*Viktor Kulikov's collection*)

Above right: Yak-9 of the 976th IAP on take-off (perhaps the same aircraft in the previous photograph) in March 1944. (*Viktor Kulikov's collection*)

Z.153 at Novosibirsk produced a total of 195 Yak-9s from October 1942 to February 1943. Z.166 at Omsk produced a total of 264 Yak-9s from January 1943 to August 1943. In all, 459 examples of this first version of the Yak-9 were produced, before production shifted to developments such as the Yak-9D and the Yak-9T. Note that the original version of the Yak-9 had no suffix and was known simply as the 'Yak-9'.

Yak-9B (Yak-9L)

Remarkably, given the small size of the Yak-9, a dedicated bomber version, complete with an internal bomb bay, was developed, the Yak-9B (with the 'B' standing for *Bombardirovshchik*, or 'Bomber'). The Yak-9B was modified from the Yak-9D. The internal OKB designation was 'Yak-9L', although it is not clear what the 'L' stood for, or if it stood for anything. The bombs were located in a compartment behind the cockpit, in what had originally been the rear pilot's compartment in the Yak-7, of which the Yak-9 was a development. In this compartment were located four cylindrical bomb bays, which could each accommodate one 220-lb (100-kg) bomb.

The first Yak-9B was completed by 20 March 1944, with state tests going from March to August 1944.

In place of the 4 FAB-100s, the Yak-9B could also carry up to 128 PTAB anti-tank bomblets in four cartridges, with each PTAB bomblet weighing 3.31 lb (1.5 kg). After a couple of fatal premature explosions of the PTABs, these bomblets were no longer carried by the Yak-9B. The bombs were loaded in from the top, with the FAB-100s being loaded tail first. The FAB-100s were centred using stops. The bomb tubes were slanted back at an angle of 75 degrees to the horizontal axis. Twin doors opened up on the underside of the aircraft to allow the bombs to fall, the bombs being placed directly against the doors with gravity causing them to fall when the doors were opened. The bombs could be dropped in pairs, or all four at once. Apparently, the Yak-9B was equipped with the four fuel tanks of the Yak-9D (described further on).

Although only a small batch of Yak-9Bs was built, they did see operational use as fighter-bombers in Poland in 1944, and they could carry up to 882 lb (400 kg) of bombs internally—a surprisingly large internal bombload for such a diminutive fighter.

Only 109 Yak-9Bs were built because of centre of gravity problems with the bombload and the difficulty in bombing accurately due to the absence of a proper bombsight. There were also handling problems when the aircraft was fully loaded with bombs, and loading the bombs was not easy.

Yak-9D

As the Red Army went on the offensive in 1943, penetrating deeply into the Axis defences, the VVS felt the need for a longer-ranged fighter to keep up with the ground forces, and to escort the bombers and Shturmoviks supporting the ground forces. The Yak-9, which had started out as a longer-ranged version of the Yak-7 (as the Yak-7DI), was modified to carry even more fuel. The Yak-9D returned to the four fuel tanks of the Yak-7DI, whereas the first production version of the Yak-9 had only two tanks. The Yak-9D's four fuel tanks had 171.71 gal (650 l) of fuel in place of two tanks with

Yak-9B in the process of dropping its bombs. The bomb bay doors are open and the bombs are just appearing. (*Viktor Kulikov's collection*)

Yak-9Bs in the field in 1944. These aircraft have been donated by the 'Little Theatre' (as opposed to the 'Bolshoiy', or 'Great (or Big) Theatre'), which is denoted by the inscriptions on the fuselage. (*Viktor Kulikov's collection*)

Yak-9Ds of the 6th GvIAP of the Black Sea Fleet in flight in summer 1944, including the aircraft of HSU Mikhail Ivanovich Grib, aircraft '22'. Grib's aircraft has both the Guards (furthest forward) and Red Banner emblems on the nose of his aircraft. Note that at least one of the tailwheel doors on this aircraft has not retracted. Profiles of this aircraft appear in the colour plates section. (*Viktor Kulikov's collection*)

a capacity of 116.24 gal (440 l) for earlier Yak-9s. The Yak-9D was equipped with the standard Yak-9 armament of one 20-mm cannon and one UBS machine gun. The Yak-9D was equipped with the M-105PF engine driving a VISh-61P propeller.

The prototype Yak-9D was constructed by the Yakovlev OKB in January 1943 and successfully completed its state tests at the NII VVS from 14 January to 26 February 1943, being flown by test pilot V. Ye. Golofastov.

In its production version, the Yak-9D had a maximum range of 845 miles (1,360 km) and a top speed of 371 mph (597 kph). Due to better streamlining, the Yak-9D was actually faster at sea level than the original variant, 332 mph (535 kph) to 323 mph (520 kph). It could complete a 360-degree turn in nineteen–twenty seconds, which although slower than some versions of the Yak-9, such as the original Yak-9 variant, was still quite good and comparable to or better than the horizontal turn rate of the Bf 109 and Fw 190.

Up to 11,483 feet (3,500 m), the Yak-9D had an advantage over the Bf 109G-2 and Fw 190A-8 in turns. With half a fuel load, it had comparable vertical manoeuvrability with these German fighters. On a full fuel load. the Yak-9D was inferior to other Yak-9s in terms of its performance, but with half the load, it performed similarly as the weight was lessened. The Yak-9D was, however, more vulnerable than the earlier Yak-9s, due to its increased fuel load.

At first, the Yak-9Ds operated alongside shorter-ranged versions of the Yak-9 in mixed formations, which did not allow the Yak-9D's superior range to be fully exploited as its range was limited to that of the shorter-range Yak-9s with their lesser fuel load. The heavier Yak-9D's slower speed also meant the other Yak-9s in the formation were slowed down to let the Yak-9Ds keep pace. When the Yak-9D was flown in Yak-9D-only formations, this allowed the aircraft to fully use its extra range.

It was used for special missions such as a long-range escort for bombers or breaking through deep into the rear of the enemy.

A total of 3,058 Yak-9Ds were produced from March 1943 to June 1946.

Yak-9DD

Although the Yak-9D had given the VVS a longer-ranged version of the Yak-9, the Red Army desired a still longer-range version. This resulted in the Yak-9DD, with the 'DD' standing for *Dalniy Deistvya*, or 'Long-range'. This longest-ranged version of the Yak-9 carried no less than eight main fuel tanks, and it was reputedly referred to by some pilots rather disparagingly as a 'flying cistern'. These eight fuel tanks contrasted with the four main tanks carried by the Yak-9D, or the two carried by the Yak-9T. The Yak-9DD was provided with eight fuel tanks with 223.23 gal (845 l) compared to the Yak-9D with four fuel tanks of 171.71 gal (650 l). Three large tanks were accommodated in each wing, with a smaller tank installed in the wing leading edge. The wing ribs were strengthened to accommodate the extra weight. The Yak-9DD could be distinguished from the Yak-9D by the extra fuel tank metal covers on the underside of the wing, and the extra fuel tank caps on top of the wing. It also had the aft-mounted cockpit of the Yak-9T but retained the 20-mm cannon and port UBS machine gun armament of the Yak-9D. It most resembled a Yak-9M (described further on) with four additional fuel tanks.

Per a decree from the GKO dated 20 February 1944, a Yak-9 was modified into the Yak-9DD configuration in April 1944. This aircraft underwent state trials at the NII VVS from 24 July to 2 August 1944 being piloted by the famous test pilot Pyotr M. Stefanovskiy (who by now had recovered from his injuries sustained in the crash of the Yak-9 M-107A, see further on) and test pilot Yu. A. Antipov.

Due to the weight of the extra fuel, the Yak-9DD suffered in performance and manoeuvrability, having a slower climb rate when compared to other Yak-9 models, including the Yak-9D. The longitudinal stability was also slightly worsened by the movement of the centre of gravity aft. The two outer fuel tanks were unprotected, making the Yak-9DD more vulnerable to enemy fire. However, the added fuel did provide it with very good range, and in tests against captured Bf 109s and Fw 190s, it surpassed them in horizontal manoeuvrability, although it was slower at all altitudes.

In addition to the lower performance, the Yak-9DD also suffered from maintenance problems associated with its greater weight, due to the large fuel load it carried. There were problems with the landing gear, for example, including the tyres and the tailwheel fork. However, the range was the longest of all the production Yakovlev fighters. At its ultimate range, it reached 1,420 miles (2,285 km) in range, no small feat for such a small aeroplane.

The Yak-9DD featured extra or improved navigational aids as befitted its role as a long-range fighter. This equipment included improved radio equipment (an SCR-274N with two receivers and two transmitters), an RPK-10M radio-compass, and an AG-2 artificial horizon. The antenna mast was made longer for better reception. These devices not only aided the Yak-9DD in flying long distances but also enabled it to fly in bad weather and at night.

Above: Yak-9DD undergoing testing at the NII VVS (note the characteristic hexagonal pavement of this airfield) in 1944. Note the tall antenna mast, characteristic of the Yak-9DD. (*Viktor Kulikov's collection*)

Left: The underside of Yak-9DD wing, showing the cut-outs for the eight fuel tanks. There are even tanks in the leading edges of the wing. (*Viktor Kulikov's collection*)

Despite its inferior manoeuvrability (its 360-degree turn time was twenty-six seconds compared to sixteen–seventeen seconds for the original Yak-9 variant) and maintenance issues when compared to other Yak-9 versions, the Yak-9DD did find some good use because of its long range. In one notable instance, Yak-9DDs flew non-stop from Beltsiy, a base in the Soviet Union (Moldavia), to Bari, in Italy. Some 399 Yak-9DDs were produced from March 1944 to September 1945.

Yak-9K

Despite the small size of the Yak-9, large cannons were fitted to the aircraft operationally, first 37-mm cannons on the Yak-9T, then a 45-mm cannon on the Yak-9K. Evidently not content with the very powerful NS-37 of the Yak-9T, the VVS and the Yakovlev OKB decided to up-gun the Yak-9T airframe with the even more powerful NS-45 45-mm cannon to create the Yak-9K. The engine was the VK-105PF (M-105PF) with a VISh-61P propeller 9.84 feet (3 m) in diameter.

The 37-mm cannon used by the Yak-9T had caused problems due to its powerful recoil (the problems were mostly rectified in the production aircraft), but these recoil problems were magnified with the even more powerful NS-45, which caused the aircraft to buffet when fired, ruptured lines and hoses, and damaged the radiators and even the engine itself. The recoil of the NS-45 was 15,377 lb (6,975 kg), which was 3,252 lb (1,475 kg) more than the NS-37 of the Yak-9T, at 12,125 lb (5,500 kg). The pilot could also be bounced around in the cockpit when this large weapon was fired—obviously not an optimal situation. The cockpit was mounted aft some 1.31 feet (400 mm), like the Yak-9T, to accommodate the large cannon; this had also been done with the Yak-7-37, which had a 37-mm cannon mounted like the Yak-9T. The aft-mounted cockpit helped maintain the centre of gravity and handling characteristics. It also helped to improve one of the Yak-9's deficiencies—its tendency to nose over if the wheel brakes were applied too vigorously. The weight of the aft-mounted cockpit made the Yak-9K (and Yak-9T, and Yak-9M) less nose-heavy, which had led to the nose-overs.

As with the Yak-9T, the NS-45 worked best when fired at high speed as the inertia of the aircraft helped to balance out the powerful recoil of the weapon. To help deal with this recoil, a large muzzle brake was fitted to the end of the cannon, which projected some way in front of the spinner and was an identifying feature for this Yak-9 version. The muzzle brake helped as it dissipated 75–85 per cent of the recoil, but it did not completely ameliorate the effects of the powerful recoil. The barrel and muzzle brake of the Yak-9K, which protruded from the spinner by 14.57 inches (370 mm), increased the fuselage length from 28.41 feet (8.66 m) on the Yak-9T to 29.1 feet (8.87 m) on the Yak-9K. Other than the muzzle brake, the Yak-9K was almost identical in appearance to the Yak-9T, featuring a single UBS gun on the port side of the nose, and the aft-mounted cockpit. The guns were aimed by a PBP-1A gunsight, and the windscreen was armoured.

Not surprisingly because of the large and heavy cannon, the Yak-9K had a lower performance than the Yak-9D, being 9.32 mph (15 kph) slower at sea level, 322 mph (518 kph), and 16.78 mph (25 kph) slower at 16,404 feet (5,000 m), 356 mph (573 kph), than the Yak-9. Although the Yak-9K handled much like the other Yak-9s, the manoeuvrability and landing characteristics suffered with the greater weight.

The first Yak-9K ('K' for *Krupnokaliberniy* or 'Large-Calibre (Cannon)') was built in December 1943 and was submitted for state trials at the NII VVS on 12 January 1944, the tests ending on 8 April 1944. A trial batch of fifty-three Yak-9Ks was recommended and built, and these aircraft saw service from 13 August 1944 to 18 September 1944 with the 3rd Byelorussian Front. From 15 January 1945 to 15 February 1945, they were used with the 1st Byelorussian Front. Some 304 sorties took place, with fifty-one air combats. In these air combats, the Yak-9Ks claimed twelve German fighters, with eight of them being Fw 190s and four being Bf 109Gs. Only one Yak-9K was reported as lost. No German bombers were shot down.

As the twin-engined and other bombers that were supposed to be the Yak-9K's main aerial quarry had nearly disappeared from the Eastern Front by this time, it was primarily used as a ground attack aeroplane, where its large cannon proved very effective, even being capable of knocking out armoured vehicles. It fought in battles in the Donbas, Melitopol, Nikolayev (Mikolaiv), all in Ukraine, and the Crimea (including Sevastopol). In addition, it saw combat at Vitebsk-Minsk in Byelorussia.

Despite its success, the Yak-9K did not go into large-scale production, as the war was winding down, and the later Yak-9s and the Yak-3 were superior fighters, and the new Il-10 Shturmovik was a superior ground attack aircraft. In addition, there were some reliability problems with the NS-45 cannon.

Yak-9M

In an effort to rationalise production on the Yak-9, the Yak-9M, although it did not feature the heavy cannon of the Yak-9T, featured that aircraft's aft-mounted cockpit. The 'M' in the designation stood for *Modernizirovanniy*, or 'Updated (Modernised)'. It was essentially a Yak-9D with the aft-mounted cockpit of the Yak-9T. By utilising the same cockpit position on the Yak-9M, this enabled Yakovlev to use one basic fuselage design, instead of having to produce two different fuselages—one for the 37-mm-armed Yak-9T and one for the 20-mm-armed Yak-9D. The Yak-9M featured the standard Yak-9 armament of one ShVAK 20-mm cannon firing through the spinner and one UBS machine gun mounted on the port side of the upper cowling. In addition, the Yak-9M featured the increased fuel tankage of the Yak-9D, with four fuel tanks, and a strengthened wing structure, with thicker skins and bakelised plywood to solve problems with the strength of the skin. An automatic water temperature control system, the ART-41 (apparently copied from German regulators), was installed. The radio now used a push-button system on the control column, and the antenna was shortened, and slanted forward, as with the Yak-9K and Yak-9T. The gun reloading system was changed from a mechanical to a pneumo-mechanical system. The cockpit canopy was jettisonable in an emergency.

Early in production, the engine had been the VK-105PF, but from October 1944, the engine was the VK-105PF-2 (as the M-105PF-2 had been renamed in 1944). The VK-105PF-2 had a maximum rating of 1,290 hp compared to the 1,260 hp of the VK-105PF. The propeller was a VISh-105.

State tests were conducted on a production example from 17 December to 27 December 1944 with V. G. Ivanov as the test pilot. The aircraft had a speed at sea

Yak-9Ms in March 1944. Of interest is how much darker '935' is than '930', the nearest aircraft. No. '935' may have been freshly painted, while '930' has a faded camouflage. (*Viktor Kulikov's collection*)

level of 328 mph (528 kph) and a top speed of 356 mph (573 kph) at 12,303 feet (3,750 m). The aircraft's handling and manoeuvrability were similar to those for other Yak-9s. From May 1944 to June 1945, 4,429 (some sources have 4,239) Yak-9Ms were built at Z.153, making it one of the most produced Yakovlev fighter versions.

Yak-9M PVO (Yak-9 PVO)

As with the Yak-7B, some Yak-9Ms were modified on the production line for use by the PVO air defence units as night fighters. These aircraft were equipped with extra instrumentation such as an artificial horizon, a RPK-10M radio-compass, and a RSI-4M radio, which consisted of a RSI-6MU receiver and a RSI-3M-1 transmitter. A FS-155 landing light was also fitted, armour was removed, and the fuel and oil supply lessened to lighten the aircraft. It is not clear from the record how many were produced.

Yak-9P VK-107A

With the end of the war, aluminium supplies had increased to the point where an all-metal version of the Yak-9 could be built. Although initially of mixed construction, with a mixed-construction fuselage combined with metal wings, most Yak-9Ps were of all-metal construction, with both the fuselage and wings featuring aluminium covering, only the metal-framed control surfaces being fabric-covered. The wings differed from other Yak-9s not only in their all-metal construction, but in the elliptical shape of the wingtips, instead of the angular wingtips of other Yak-9s. The aircraft was fitted with the VK-107A of the Yak-9U.

The state tests were conducted post-war from 28 June to 23 July 1946. The Yak-9P was produced from July 1946 until December 1948, seeing only post-war service as the last of the Yak-9 variants, when production was ended in favour of jet-powered fighters. Some 801 aircraft were produced post-war, including twenty-nine with a plywood-covered rear fuselage and metal wings. This aircraft is not to be confused with the experimental early Yak-9, which was fitted with two 20-mm cannons, that was also designated the 'Yak-9P'. Reusing designations was not uncommon with the Soviets.

Yak-9PD

Early in the Great Patriotic War, the Germans had been able to overfly Soviet cities, such as Moscow and Leningrad, with impunity at high altitude using such aircraft as the Ju 88 and dedicated high-altitude aircraft such as the Junkers Ju 86P bomber and Ju 86R reconnaissance aircraft. In particular, the specialised high-altitude reconnaissance Ju 86R had proven to be a particular irritant to the Soviets as it was able to overfly Moscow with total impunity, resisting all attempts to intercept it. This aircraft overflew Moscow in 1942–1943 at altitudes of 39,379 to 42,651 feet (12,000 to 13,000 m). From July 1942 to August 1943, the Ju 86R-1 made six appearances over Moscow. The Soviets had already developed a high-altitude version of the Yak-7, the Yak-7PD, to deal with these aircraft, unsuccessfully. Now it was the Yak-9's turn. This high-altitude version of the Yak-9 was essentially a Yak-9D fitted with the M-105PD engine, which was designed for high-altitude use. This engine was equipped with the Dollezhal-designed E-100 two-stage supercharger and had already been tested in the Yak-7PD (and would later be used on the Yak-3PD, described further on). The Yak-9PD was to be equipped with one ShVAK 20-mm cannon in the nose, as with the Yak-7PD, equipped with 120 rounds.

Five examples were produced by 20 April 1943 for use by the PVO. These aircraft were tested by the 12th GvIAD of the 6th IAK, the regiment being under the command of Major K. V. Marenkov. The five Yak-9PDs were tested from 16 April to 25 June 1943, performing sixty-nine flights. Flights were made at altitudes of up to 39,379 feet (12,000 m). However, it took a great deal of time to reach such heights, as due to engine over-heating the aircraft had to level off during its climb to allow the engine to return to a normal operating temperature. These levelling-off episodes took up a great deal

Yak-9PD in 1943. Although it looks like the spinner is cropped, and has sometimes been drawn as such, closer examination shows the tip to have been painted white, which tends to washout in some reproductions of this photograph. (*Viktor Kulikov's collection*)

of time for what was meant to be an interceptor. For example, to reach an altitude of 38,222 feet (11,650 m), it took the Yak-9PD twenty-five minutes. This greatly limited the utility of the Yak-9PD as it gave time for the intended target to fly away. By the time the Yak-9PD had reached the target's altitude, it would have been long gone.

One attempted interception illustrates the difficulties the Yak-9PD faced as a high-altitude interceptor against the high-flying German intruders. On 2 June 1943, PVO pilot Lt-Col. L. A. Sholokhov, a very experienced pilot, attempted to intercept a high-flying enemy aircraft, a Ju 86R-1. The pilot made it to 27,887 feet (8,500 m) without incident then received a message that the enemy had passed Vnukovo, a town to the south-west of Moscow. At this time, Sholokhov noticed contrails from the high-flying German aircraft as it was flying towards Moscow. He pursued the aircraft and caught up to it at an altitude of about 37,894 feet (11,550 m), which was still some 3,281 to 4,291 feet (1,000 to 1,500 m) below the enemy. He was close enough to see the yellow-tipped wings and black crosses of a German aircraft. The fuel pressure then dropped to zero on the Yak-9PD, but it recovered when the aircraft dropped down to 35,433 feet (10,800 m). The Yak-9PD began to gain altitude again, but the windshield became covered with ice, preventing Sholokhov from visually following the enemy aircraft. At this point, Sholokhov was forced to break off the pursuit and land, without ever getting off a shot at the Ju 86R-1. The entire flight lasted fifty-nine minutes.

Attempts were made to improve the Yak-9PD. A Yak-9PD with a modified M-105PD engine was produced on 31 July 1943. The aircraft had an extended wing, with the span increased by 3.28 feet (1 m), and the area increased by 7 sq. feet (0.65 m2). The ammunition was decreased from 120 to 110 rounds, and the fuel tank protection was removed, in an attempt to save weight. The aircraft underwent tests at the LII from 3 August to 18 October 1943. The tests were unsuccessful, and the engine was replaced by the M-106PV. This installation also proved unsuccessful.

The inability of the Soviets, even in a specialised high-altitude interceptor such as the Yak-9PD, to intercept high-flying German aircraft became a rather moot point as after 1943, the Germans had ceased most high-altitude operations over Soviet cities.

Yak-9R

Due to its high speed, the Yak-9 was considered suitable for use as a reconnaissance aircraft over heavily defended high-value targets. Once again, the compartment behind the pilot (inherited from the Yak-7) proved useful, in this case accommodating a single camera, mounted to photograph downwards through a glass aperture in the lower fuselage. There were two versions of the reconnaissance Yak-9: a short-range version with two fuel tanks, and a long-range version with four fuel tanks. The long-range version was based upon the Yak-9D. The short-range version had the standard armament of one 20-mm cannon in the nose, with one UBS machine gun on top of the cowling, while the long-range version had only the 20-mm cannon fitted.

The short-range version, based upon the original Yak-9 variant, carried the AFA-IM camera, which was the same camera used by the Yak-7R. The long-range version, based upon the Yak-9D, carried the AFA-35/50. From 21 September to 10 October 1943, a short-range version with the AFA-IM camera was tested at the NII VVS.

Five AFA-35/50-equipped Yak-9Rs were tested on the Steppe Front under service conditions. The service trials proved successful and Z.166 produced thirty-five Yak-9Rs by 13 August 1943. Although the Yak-9R was faster and more manoeuvrable than the twin-engined Pe-2R, the Pe-2R had better visibility, and the single pilot of the Yak-9R was unable to observe as much as the multi-person crew on the Pe-2R. Due to this, the Yak-9R did not supplant the Pe-2R but was rather used to supplement it, flying high-risk missions where the high speed and manoeuvrability of the Yak-9R made it more survivable.

In addition to the new-build Yak-9Rs, there were field-modifications made to Yak-9s to convert them into high-speed reconnaissance aircraft. It is not clear from the record how many Yak-9s were modified in this way.

Yak-9T (Yak-9-37)

Both the Yak-1 and the Yak-7 had featured versions with 37-mm cannons, which were suitable for both ground attack and use against aerial targets. In the Yak-9T variant of the Yak-9, an NS-37 (Nudelman-Suranov, originally OKB-16 IIP-37) 37-mm cannon was fitted between the cylinder banks of the M-105PF engine to fire through the propeller shaft and spinner (the propeller was the VISh-105SV). The cannon itself was 11.15 feet (3.4 m) long and weighed 331 lb (150 kg). The NS-37 had a recoil of 12,125 lb (5,500 kg). The airframe in the front of the aircraft had to be strengthened for such a large weapon with such a heavy recoil. Other parts of the aircraft, such as the pipes, had to be strengthened to prevent them from being damaged from the heavy recoil.

A UBS 12.7-mm (50-calibre) machine gun was retained on the port side of the cowling for sighting purposes and was equipped with 220 rounds. As with the Yak-9K, the cockpit was mounted aft to accommodate the large cannon fitted in the nose and to maintain the centre of gravity, which helped with the Yak-9Ts manoeuvrability, at a relatively small cost in visibility on the ground. The rearward visibility was improved, however, and moving the weight of the cockpit towards the back helped to keep the Yak-9 from nosing over during landing. With the added length of the cannon, which protruded from the spinner by 6.3 inches (160 mm), the fuselage length was increased to 28.41 feet (8.66 m), compared to the 27.89 feet (8.5 m) of the original Yak-9 variant. The Yak-9T prototype retained the two main fuel tanks of the original Yak-9 variant, while the production versions had the four tanks of the Yak-9D.

The 'T' in the name stood for *Tankoviy* or 'Tank-(buster)'. The prototype was built in January 1943. The aircraft underwent armament testing at the NIPAV from 10 January to 12 February 1943. State trials began on 15 February 1943 and ended on 4 March 1943, and thirty-four Yak-9Ts was tested operationally at Kursk with various regiments of the 273rd IAD from 5 July to 6 August 1943 with the 16th VA. Here it proved to be a potent air-to-air weapon. In seventy-eight air battles, flying alongside Yak-1s, Yak-7Bs, and normally armed Yak-9s (one 20-mm cannon and one UBS machine gun), the Yak-9Ts were credited with forty-nine enemy aircraft for a loss of twelve Yak-9Ts.

Despite some common misconceptions, the Yak-9T actually found more use as a fighter than as a tank-busting aircraft as in the aerial role, its hard-hitting cannon

A Yak-9T captured by the Germans. Judging by the undamaged under-nose radiator, this aircraft may have landed normally, but behind enemy lines. With the spinner missing, the barrel of the NS-37 37-mm cannon is readily apparent. The slightly canted forward radio antenna of later Yak-9s is also visible. (*Viktor Kulikov's collection*)

Yak-9T in flight. 1943. (*Viktor Kulikov's collection*)

Yak-9Ts of the Northern Fleet in February 1944. (*Viktor Kulikov's collection*)

could destroy or severely damage any enemy aircraft with just one hit. On average, one enemy aircraft was destroyed for every thirty-one rounds fired, and the Yak-9T carried from thirty to thirty-two rounds for the 37-mm cannon. By comparison, it was estimated that it took 147 20-mm rounds for every destroyed enemy aircraft. Compared to other fighters, the weight of fire was as follows: 2.24 times that of a Bf 109G-2 with three guns (including one cannon); 1.16 times that of a Bf 109G-2 with five guns (including three cannons); 1.31 times that of a Bf 110; and 1.09 times that of the heavily armed Fw 190A-8 *Sturmbock*, which had four 20-mm cannons and two 13-mm machine guns.

The best firing technique for the Yak-9T was to use its UBS machine gun for aiming purposes, limiting its 37-mm cannon to only two or three shells per pass to conserve ammunition and prevent the recoil from affecting the aim. The Yak-9T prototype had the aiming device as a VV-1 sight (as used on the Il-2), which was a simple mechanical sight consisting of a circle on the armoured windscreen and a post on the cowling. Later Yak-9Ts, perhaps all of the production versions, had a PBP-1 reflector gunsight for aiming. The cannon was reloaded pneumatically and was fired electro-pneumatically from a button on the control column.

The faster the Yak-9T went, the less intense the effect of the recoil was, so the 37-mm cannon was more effective at speeds above 217 mph (350 kph). The optimum firing distances were judged to be from 328 to 1,312 feet (100 to 400 m) against fighters and from 1,640 to 1,969 feet (500 to 600 m) against bombers. The Yak-9Ts flew in mixed units, with 30 to 50 per cent of the aircraft being Yak-9s with the normal armament of one 20-mm cannon and one UBS machine gun, and 50 to 70 per cent being Yak-9Ts. The Yak-9Ts were assigned to pilots who had superior shooting skills as the 37-mm cannon was limited in the number of shells it could carry.

One positive operational effect of the Yak-9T was its influence upon Fw 190 tactics. Against Soviet aircraft, such as the Yak-1, the sturdy and heavily armed Fw 190s had often undertaken head-on attacks. The appearance of the 37-mm-armed Yak-9T seemed to cure them of this unpleasant habit or at least make them think twice about trying it.

Although not primarily used as a ground attack aircraft, Yak-9Ts were employed in this role during Operation Kutuzov, the attack on Oryol which was a follow-up to the Battle of Kursk in 1943. This was necessitated by the lack of Il-2s. With armour-piercing shells, the 37-mm cannon could penetrate up to 30-mm-thick armour at a distance of 1,640 feet (500 m) and angles up to 45 degrees. At 90-degree angles, the armour penetration must have been still more. The Yak-9T proved successful in whichever role it was used in, and 2,748 were produced at Z.153 from March 1943 to June 1945, as compared to the small production run of fifty-three 45-mm armed Yak-9Ks. The Yak-9T was the first truly mass-produced version of the Yak-9.

Yak-9TD

A long-range version of the 37-mm cannon-equipped Yak-9 was developed under the designation of 'Yak-9TD', where the 'D' stood for *Dalniy*, or 'Long-range'. It had the same fuel tankage of the Yak-9D and could carry four 110 lb (50 kg) bombs. The increased fuel load slowed down the aircraft compared to the Yak-9T (371 mph top speed for the Yak-9T to 365 mph for the Yak-9TD (587 kph to 597 kph)), and only two dozen aircraft were modified.

Yak-9U M-106PV

A Yak-9U was re-engined from the VK-107A to the M-106PV. The aircraft was finished on 20 April 1944. The aircraft underwent factory tests from 27 April to 30 April 1944. The maximum speed of the aircraft at 34,449 feet (10,500 m) was 385 mph (620 kph), with a service ceiling of up to 44,291 feet (13,500 m). Eventually, thirty production aircraft were also re-equipped with the M-106PV engine, although

Yak-9TD in 1944. (*Viktor Kulikov's collection*)

some sources have only twelve being re-equipped. However many were re-equipped, they did not have a chance to prove themselves against high-flying German aircraft as by 1944, high-altitude overflights of the Soviet Union by Germany had ceased.

Yak-9U VK-107A

This definitive version of the Yak-9U was fitted with the VK-107A engine. It was not the first time a Yakovlev fighter had been fitted with the VK-107A engine, as one (still referred to as the M-107A) was fitted to a Yak-7 as early as December 1942. This Yak-7 was re-sparred with metal spars (as with the Yak-9) and was designated as the Yak-9 M-107A. OKB testing ensued. Besides the new engine and spars, the water radiator was mounted under the fuselage aft as compared to production Yak-9s, similar to the position it would take on the Yak-3, and the oil radiators were moved from the chin to the wing roots (as they would be on production Yak-9Us and the Yak-3). The chin radiator was eliminated, resulting in a smooth nose profile as on the Yak-9U and the Yak-3. The aircraft still retained the forward-mounted cockpit of early Yak-9s, however.

Testing showed the aircraft to have a top speed of 423 mph (680 kph) at 19,029 feet (5,800m). However, later the very day this speed was reached, on 25 February 1943, the aircraft crashed, destroying it and severely injuring the test pilot, P. M. Stefanovskiy (who did recover and continued to test fly aircraft). Despite this setback, the aircraft was highly regarded by the project head, Pavel Ya. Fedrovi, the head test pilot at Yakovlev, who recommended to Aleksandr Shakhurin, the head of the NKAP, that ten to fifteen Yak-9s be equipped with the M-107A. In the event, eight Yak-9s were equipped with the M-107A in April 1943.

Testing indicated that there were still issues with the immature engine, with ignition problems being pinpointed as the source of most of the difficulties. Despite these problems, production of the M-107A-powered Yak-9 was slated to begin at Z.155 in June 1943. As it was, production of the M-107A (VK-107A)-engined Yak-9 did not begin until May (Yefim Gordon has February) 1944, due to various problems with the engine. The VK-107A engine was mated with the VISh-107LO propeller.

The aircraft which led to the mass-production Yak-9U VK-107A was built in December 1943. Factory tests were conducted from 28 December 1943 to 12 January 1944. The state tests at the NII VVS were conducted from 18 January to 20 April 1944, with A. G. Proshakov as the test pilot. During testing, the aircraft displayed a top speed at ground level of 373 mph (600 kph) and 435 mph (700 kph) at an altitude of 18,373 feet (5,600 m). Besides the VK-107A engine, the production aircraft were fitted with new water (OP-554) and oil (OP-555) radiators. The wing was moved forward 3.94 inches (100 mm) and the elevator surface area was reduced by 12.16 square feet (1.13 m^2). In addition to the ShVAK 20-mm cannon in the nose, the armament was increased to two UBS machine guns, where the earlier Yak-9s had only one UBS machine gun. The cannon had 170 rounds, and the machine guns had 170 rounds each.

In tests against a Bf 109G-4, the Yak-9U VK-107A displayed superior manoeuvrability, outperforming the German aircraft in both the horizontal and vertical planes. In actual combat, the Yak-9U also proved its superiority to German aircraft, especially at low

Yak-9U M-107. (*Viktor Kulikov's collection*)

Yak-9Us in flight in 1944. (*Viktor Kulikov's collection*)

altitudes, where German pilots were apparently warned not to engage in combat with smooth-nosed (i.e., aircraft without an under-nose oil cooler) inline-engined Soviet fighters. Another warning advised German pilots not to attack Yakovlev fighters without an antenna mast. These warnings applied to both the Yak-9U and the equally deadly Yak-3 (see further on). On average, forty-five 20-mm shells and eighty-two 12.7-mm shells were consumed for each aircraft shot down. Running out of ammunition during combat was not considered a problem. Despite continuing problems with the temperamental VK-107A engine, generally, the Yak-9U was found to be easy to operate and reliable, its aerial handling was excellent, and its landing characteristics were good (landing was not always a strong suit for Yakovlev fighters due to their generally nose-heavy airframes).

Luftwaffe Bf 109G pilot and ace with JG 52 (137 confirmed kills) *Leutnant* Walter Wolfrum had this to say about the Yak-9U, as quoted in *Yakovlev Fighters of World War Two* by Yefim Gordon, Sergey Komissarov, and Dmitriy Komissarov (p. 194):

> The best fighters that I have encountered in combat were the American P-51 Mustang and the Russian [*sic.*] Yak-9U. Both types were clearly superior in their performance to all versions of the Bf 109, including the Bf 109K. The Mustangs had unrivalled altitude performance, while the Yak-9U was a record-holder in rate of climb and manoeuvrability.

From April 1944 until August 1945, 3,921 Yak-9Us were produced. By the end of the Great Patriotic War, 750 Yak-9Us were in service on the Eastern Front, out of a total of 6,267 fighters of all types, representing some 12 per cent of the total.

Since it continued to be used by several countries into the 1950s, the Yak-9U was given the NATO nickname of 'Frank' (not to be confused with the Japanese Nakajima Ki-84 fighter of the Second World War, which was also given the nickname of 'Frank', by the United States military).

As something of a sidebar, given the constant and seemingly insoluble problems with the Klimov M-107A/VK-107A engine, I am somewhat perplexed that the VVS persisted in the development of this apparent cripple of an engine. Although first fitted to a Yak-9 airframe as early as December 1942 (it was also fitted to the experimental Tomashevich '110' fighter, described further on, at about the same time), the VK-107A continued to have problems until after the war. It is unclear if its various problems were ever completely resolved. It may well have been the case that the VVS simply had no better Soviet-built alternative, and the VK-107A was the best small and powerful piston engine that was available for installation in the diminutive airframes of the Yakovlev fighters. However, continuing problems with the VK-107A did lead to efforts to lighten the airframe to take better advantage of the power offered by the M-105 (VK-105), efforts that led to the very successful and mostly VK-105 (M-105)-powered Yak-3.

Yak-9UT

One of the complaints regarding the standard armament fit of the Yak-9 of one 20-mm cannon and one 12.7-mm (50-calibre) machine gun was that this was too light against the well-built and armoured German aircraft. The Yak-9UT was an attempt to rectify this problem. This formidable development of the Yak-9U featured for the production variants the heavy standard armament of a Nudelman-Suranov NS-23 23-mm cannon firing through the spinner, and two Berezin B-20S 20-mm cannons mounted on top of the forward fuselage, with 120 rounds each; a similar armament fit had been used on the earlier experimental Yak-9TK (described further on). However, the cannons used on the Yak-9UT were lighter, and the engine more powerful. In most respects, the Yak-9UT was similar to the base Yak-9U variant, using the same unreliable but powerful VK-107A engine. A GKO order of 29 December 1944 requested this aircraft to be built.

The Yak-9UT prototype was equipped with the lightweight Nudelman N-37 cannon with thirty rounds firing through the spinner and the two B-20S 20-mm cannons with 120 rounds each. It was built in February 1945, and underwent state tests from 8 March to 29 March 1945, with the test pilot A. A. Manucharov flying the aircraft. The Yak-9UT 1945 Etalon was tested from 17 March to 9 July 1945 (after the end of the Great Patriotic War).

In place of the NS-23 23-mm cannon (used on the production aircraft), the Yak-9UT could also accommodate a N-37 37-mm cannon (as with the prototype), or even a Nudelman N-45 45-mm cannon (in this configuration, one of the B-20S 20-mm cannons—the starboard one—was removed because of weight considerations). These different configurations had to be applied at the factory, not in the field, field-modification being possible with the similarly armed Yak-9TK. The aircraft had a top speed at sea level of 359 mph (578 kph) and 417 mph (671 kph) at 16,076 feet (4,900 m). One problem with the Yak-9UT was that the aileron and especially the elevator forces were too high.

The aircraft with the N-37 fitted was found to be very powerful, with a weight of fire of 13.23 lb/sec (6 kg/sec), which was less than only the Yak-9UT with the NS-45 at 20.50 lb/sec (9.3 kg/sec) and an La-9 (the original source has 'La-7', although this is probably a typo as the La-7 did not carry this armament) with four NS-23 23-mm cannons, with a weight of 16.09 lb/sec (7.3 kg/sec). The N-37 did not have as much recoil as the cannons on the Yak-9T (NS-37) and Yak-9K (NS-45), which allowed the Yak-9UT to fire 4-5 rounds with little effect upon the aiming.

The Great Patriotic War ended before this extremely potent fighter could show its full potential, although even in limited use, it showed its prowess. In the last part of the Great Patriotic War, one unit that had re-equipped with the Yak-9UT claimed twenty-eight enemy aircraft (twenty-seven were the powerfully armed Fw 190A-8 *Sturmbock*) for a loss of only two of its own. Some 282 Yak-9UTs were produced in total from February to May 1945. The production aircraft had the NS-23 23-mm cannon, not the N-37 37-mm cannon in the nose, along with the two B-20S 20-mm cannons in the upper cowling.

Yak-9V ('Yak-9UTI')

This aircraft was a two-seater trainer version based upon the Yak-9 with the aft-mounted cockpit (Yak-9T and Yak-9M) and the M-105PF-2 engine. It was armed with a 20-mm cannon in the nose with ninety rounds, and there was a PAU-22 gun camera mounted in the starboard wing. It had a two-way RSI-6MU radio and included

Yak-9V. (*Viktor Kulikov's collection*)

an intercom (SPU) between the crew. There were adjusters for the seat height for both pilots and there was a partition between the two cockpits, which were connected by a continuous canopy. The instructor-pilot occupied the rear cockpit, and with the flip of a switch could keep the trainee-pilot from braking the aircraft (overuse of the brakes tended to cause all the Yakovlev wartime fighters to nose over). Overall, it was a more sophisticated aircraft than the somewhat simplified Yak-7V, and the Yak-9V was equipped with retractable landing gear, including a retractable tailwheel. Note that in some Western publications, the Yak-9V has been misnamed as the 'Yak-9UTI'.

The prototype was tested at the NII VVS from 10 April to 17 April 1945, being flown by the test pilot V. G. Ivanov. The handling and other flight characteristics of the Yak-9V were similar to those of the Yak-9T.

The Yak-9V entered production at the very end of the Second World War, from August 1945 to August 1947, with 456 built new and another 337 converted from Yak-9Ms, for a total of 793 aircraft.

Yak-9: Experimental Versions

Yak-9 'Courier'

In an attempt to produce a high-speed, long-range liaison aircraft that could operate in a high-risk environment, Yakovlev built the two-seat Yak-9 'Courier'. This aircraft was based upon the Yak-9 fighter, but with a long, continuous canopy that enclosed two seats, the front seat being for the pilot, and the back seat being for a high-value passenger, such as a general. Both seats were equipped for comfort on long-range flights and included urinals, the back position also having a false floor and upholstery.

The wings were based upon that of the Yak-9DD. The fuselage was that of the two-seat Yak-9V with a VK-105PF engine. The rear fuselage was not of the 'high-back' type, and the passenger was provided with a rear canopy like that on the normal bubble-top Yak-9s, affording all-around vision. Despite the extra seat, this aircraft was the same length as a standard Yak-9 at 27.89 feet (8.5 m). The aircraft was unarmed, relying solely upon its speed (it had a top speed of 350 mph (564 kph) at 11,811 feet (3,600 m)) and manoeuvrability (its 360-degree turn time was nineteen seconds) to evade enemy aircraft. The range was an impressive 1,118 miles (1,800 km). Only one was built at Z.153 in July 1944. Factory tests occurred from August to September 1944. The aircraft did not undergo state tests.

Yak-9 M-106

Although the Yak-9 was an improvement over the Yak-7, its use at Stalingrad indicated that there was room for improving its abilities (there is always room for improvement in aircraft). As a way of increasing the performance of the Yak-9, it was fitted with the experimental Klimov M-106 engine. The M-106 engine was similar to the M-105PF that normally powered the Yak-9, but it was capable of 1,350 hp compared to the 1,260 hp of the M-105PF.

The aircraft used for the tests with the M-106 was the Yak-7DI *Dooblyor*, and as the M-106 was interchangeable with the M-105PF, no changes were needed to mount the engine. There were other changes to the airframe, other than the new engine. The tailwheel was made fully retractable to reduce drag, and the aircraft was fitted with the all-round vision canopy. These revisions were made in October 1942.

Factory (OKB) tests took place from 17 November 1942 to 20 January 1943, with P. Ya. Fedrovi as the test pilot. The state (NII VVS) tests took place 27 January 1943 to 11 February 1943 with V. I. Khomyakov as the test pilot. Testing showed that the Yak-9 M-106 flew very much like the M-105-powered Yak-1, Yak-7, and Yak-9. It was flown in tests against a captured Bf 109G-2 equipped with three cannons and two machine guns. From 6,562 to 14,764 feet (2,000 to 4,500 m), the Yak-9 M-106 had the advantage in horizontal manoeuvring. Up to 9,843 feet (3,000 m), the Yak-9 M-106 also had an advantage in vertical manoeuvring. From 9,843–14,764 feet (3,000–4,500 m), the Yak-9 M-106 had almost the same vertical manoeuvrability as the Bf 109G-2, while above 16,404 feet (5,000 m), the advantage lay with the German aircraft.

No production of the Yak-9 M-106 was undertaken as the M-106 proved to be an unreliable engine, leaking oil and shaking, among other issues (rather like the M-107, only worse, apparently), and the M-106 was not produced in quantity.

Yak-9P M-105PF (First Use of the 'Yak-9P' Designation)

The Yak-9P was an experimental version of the Yak-9 equipped with two 20-mm cannons, with one firing through the spinner and one mounted on the cowling. A standard early Yak-9 with a M-105PF engine and the forward-mounted cockpit was used. The cannon in the cowling replaced the UBS machine gun (installed on the port side) and was equipped with 175 rounds. The addition of the 20-mm cannon increased the firepower by 1.25 over that of the Yak-9 with the one 20-mm cannon and one UBS machine gun.

The aircraft was modified by Yakovlev in March 1943, and it went through state tests at the NII VVS from 17 April to 28 April 1943, which it passed. It was flown by test pilot A. G. Proshakov.

The aircraft flew like the standard early Yak-9, and for relatively short bursts, the aim stayed true. For long bursts, the recoil affected the aim, especially at lower speeds, and the aiming needed to be corrected.

Although the aircraft passed its tests, production did not ensue as the decision had been made to equip the Yak-9 with larger weapons such as 23-mm, 37-mm, and 45-mm cannons. Therefore, the Yak-9 with the two 20-mm cannons remained a one-off prototype.

Yak-9S

This was the last attempt by Yakovlev to improve the armament of the M-105 (VK-105)-powered Yak-9, whose single 20-mm ShVAK cannon and single UBS 12.7-mm machine gun were felt by many Soviet pilots to be insufficiently heavy, especially when compared to the Yak-7, which had carried an additional UBS (the Yak-3 also had an additional UBS machine gun). Indeed, some pilots preferred the late Yak-7B over the Yak-9 because of its greater firepower, and the Yak-1B as it had the same firepower as the Yak-9 but was more manoeuvrable. The Yak-9S was based upon the Yak-9M airframe, with a different armament fit. The aircraft was fitted with a NS-23 23-mm nose cannon equipped with 60 shells and two synchronised B-20S 20-mm cannons equipped with 120 shells per gun in the upper cowling.

Two Yak-9S were built in May 1945, and they passed the factory (OKB) tests from 10 May to 28 May 1945, piloted by test pilot P. Ya. Fedrovi. The state tests took place from 28 August 1945 to 14 September 1945, with the test pilots being V. G. Ivanov and A. A. Manucharov. It was found that the 23-mm shell could penetrate 20 mm of armour at an angle of 45 degrees from a distance of 1,640 feet (500 m).

Although the armament of the Yak-9S was found to be satisfactory, the performance as compared to the Yak-3 VK-105PF-2 and the Yak-9U VK-107A was found to be inferior. The speed at sea level was 37–39 mph (59–62 kph) slower and at altitude was 42–55 mph (67–89 kph) slower. Due to this lack of performance, and the fitting of the same armament to a Yak-9U VK-107A (the Yak-9UT), there was no production of the Yak-9S.

Yak-9TK

The Yak-9TK was modified from a Yak-9T; it was equipped to carry a VYa-23 23-mm cannon firing through the propeller hub and two B-20S 20-mm cannons on top of the cowling, firing through the propeller disc.

The Yak-9TK was designed to have the ability to carry different nose cannons—the standard ShVAK MP-20 20-mm, the VYa-23 23-mm, the NS-37 37-mm, and the NS-45 45-mm cannon. These cannons could be switched out in the field with the proper equipment (unlike the Yak-9UT, which required that the different nose cannon fits had to be made at the factory). This meant that the aircraft's armament could be changed in the field for undertaking different missions, i.e., the 20-mm cannon could be fitted for normal escort missions, while the 45-mm cannon could be fitted for ground attack/tank-busting missions.

The Yak-9TK was tested at the NII VVS in October 1943 with the test pilot V. I. Khomyakov. It was noted that firing the 20-mm or 23-mm nose cannons did not affect the aim even at low speeds (155–162 mph (250–260 kph)), although a slight recoil was felt. At 249 mph (400 kph), there was no recoil at all, even with long bursts. With the larger 37- and 45-mm cannons, the situation was different. Firing the 37-mm cannon at speeds of 186–217 mph (300–350 kph), accurate aiming was only possible with the first shot as succeeding shots were affected by the recoil, with the recoil causing the aircraft to pitch. Accurate shooting with the 45-mm cannon was only possible at near maximum speeds. The handling in general of the aircraft depended on which cannon was fitted due to the different weights involved.

Production did not proceed with the Yak-9TK, in part because of the unreliability of the 45-mm cannon and (I suspect) because the VYa-23 23-mm cannon was needed for the vitally important Il-2. Although the Yak-9TK did not go into production, the armament fit of the 23-mm cannon and two 20-mm cannons was later used on the Yak-9UT (discussed previously), which did go into production.

Yak-9U VK-105PF-2

Yakovlev was, of course, interested in keeping the Yak-9 competitive with the German fighters being introduced in the latter part of the war. To this end, he developed the Yak-9U VK-105PF-2, which was based upon the Yak-9T airframe and was powered by the VK-105PF-2. The VK-105PF-2 (designated the M-105PF-2 until April 1944) was more powerful at low altitudes than the M-105PF engine that was then powering the Yak-9 production examples. In addition to the different engine, the Yak-9U VK-105PF-2 featured individual ejector-type exhaust stubs that generated a small amount of thrust. A plywood covering on the aft fuselage replaced the fabric covering of the Yak-9T to decrease drag; this plywood covering was also used on the Yak-9U VK-107A (the aircraft that made the Yak-9U VK-105PF-2 redundant). The aircraft was designed to carry a variety of guns in the nose, including the VYa-23 23-mm cannon with sixty rounds along with two UBS machine guns with 170 rounds each, a B-20 20-mm cannon with two UBS, or a NS-37 37-mm cannon along with one UBS machine gun.

The single prototype of the Yak-9U VK-105PF-2 was built in November 1943 and underwent manufacturer's (factory or OKB) tests in December. NII VVS (state) testing was undertaken from 2 January to 11 March 1944. The tests revealed that the aircraft had good performance, with a top speed of 385 mph (620 kph) at 12,631 feet (3,850m). In a combat turn, it had similar performance to that of the Bf 109G-10, the fastest version of the Bf 109G, with a top speed of over 420 mph (676 kph).

Although it was recommended that the changes made to the Yak-9U VK-105PF-2 be introduced to the production Yak-9s, this did not occur. It was probably considered that the Yak-9U VK-105PF-2 was something of a stopgap until the Yak-9U could be fitted with the more powerful VK-107A engine, and only one example of the Yak-9U VK-105PF-2 was built.

Yak-9UV

The Yak-9UV was a dual-control trainer version based upon the Yak-9U airframe, with development starting in fall 1944. It incorporated the long continuous canopy covering the two seats as used on the Yak-9V. The armament was reduced to one B-20M ('M' for *Motor* ('Motor-mounted')) 20-mm cannon in the nose with 100 rounds. Z.82 built the single prototype of the Yak-9UV in June 1945. Testing by the NII VVS went from 10 July through to 12 October 1945. The handling was found to be similar to that of the standard single-seat Yak-9U.

Although the flight tests of the Yak-9UV were satisfactory, the decision was made not to produce the Yak-9UV as the Soviets were moving towards jet-powered aircraft and a jet-powered advanced trainer was what was needed, and until then, the mass-produced Yak-9V would suffice.

Combat Tactics

As with the Yak-1 and most other wartime Soviet fighters, the Yak-9s tried to engage the German fighters in horizontal turning battles, where they usually had an edge. However, with the Yak-9, the Yakovlev fighters were finally able to engage on at least equal terms with the Germans in vertical manoeuvring, especially with the Fw 190, where the Germans had once held the clear edge. The Yak-9U was superior to any German fighter at low altitudes, in speed, horizontal manoeuvring, and vertical manoeuvring. Due to these disadvantages, German pilots were warned not to engage the Yak-9U in combat at low altitudes—high praise indeed.

Combat Use

The Yak-9 was in continuous use by the Soviets from its combat debut at Stalingrad in late 1942 throughout the Manchurian Offensive, even seeing use in the Korean War with the North Korean Air Force.

Stalingrad

The Yak-9 first saw combat use during the Battle of Stalingrad in 1942, being initially used in the second half of December 1942 during the Soviet reduction of the *Kessel*. They entered service with the 42nd IAP. The original series Yak-9s, with the two fuel tanks, were used.

Battle of the Kuban and the Crimea

Yak-9 pilot Il'ya Vasil'evich Shmelyov enjoyed considerable success in fighting over the Blue Line in the Taman Peninsula, shooting down ten aircraft as a member of the 4th IAP.

Kursk (Operation Citadel)

It was during the Battle of Kursk in July 1943 that the problem with fabric separation on the wings first manifested itself with the Yak-9s. This problem, which was caused by a substandard adhesive, was fixed by teams from the Yakovlev OKB, who modified the Yak-9s in the field to strengthen the wings and the fabric covering.

The powerfully armed Yak-9T, with its NS-37 37-mm cannon, first saw combat use during the Battle of Kursk. Thirty-four early production Yak-9Ts were tested operationally with various regiments of the 273rd IAD and 14th Stalingradskiy GvIAP from 5 July (the start of the battle) to 6 August 1943 with the 16th VA. Here it proved to be a potent air-to-air weapon. In seventy-eight air battles, flying alongside Yak-1s, Yak-7Bs, and normally armed Yak-9s, the Yak-9Ts were credited with forty-nine enemy aircraft (or fifty-five aircraft according to one source) for a loss of twelve Yak-9Ts.

It should be noted that in its initial combat trials the Yak-9T was used as an air-to-air fighter, not a ground attack aircraft. However, in the immediate aftermath of Operation Citadel, when the Soviets counter-attacked in the north around Oryol, Yak-9Ts were used in the ground attack role. Although normally used quite successfully as a fighter, the Yak-9Ts were pressed into the ground attack role due to the lack of Il-2s. In the ground attack role, the Yak-9Ts' large 37-mm cannon proved very useful, even being capable of destroying lightly armoured vehicles, such as armoured personnel carriers and light tanks.

Yak-9Ds were used for service trials with the 18th and 20th GvIAPs from the beginning of the Soviet offensive at Oryol. The Yak-9Ds were used to provide cover for attack aircraft supporting the Soviet troops. The Yak-9Ds operated at heights of 656–1,312 feet (200–400 m) to provide close cover for the Il-2s.

Ukrainian Operations in 1943–44

It was a busy day for the Yak-9Ts of the 812th IAP on 25 September 1943. In the Melitopol region of southern Ukraine, Yak-9Ts struck against twenty Ju 87s escorted by Bf 109s. Two Ju 87s and two Bf 109s were downed. The same day, a group of Yak-9Ts over Tokmak attacked several Ju 88s, downing two. Yak-9Ts under the command of Capt. I. Popov attacked some Ju 87s, downing one of them. The day had not ended when Yak-9Ts under the command of I. V. Fedorov were running low on fuel when they encountered fifty-four He 111s escorted by Bf 109s. Using their large 37-mm cannons, the Yak-9Ts attacked the He 111s head-on, downing three of the bombers. A fourth damaged He 111 was downed by Fedorov. The powerful cannon blew the wing off of the He 111. During this day, one Soviet fighter was shot down, and the pilot A. Mashenkin was captured. The total for the day for the 812th IAP was thirteen German aircraft, with only the one loss.

Operation Bagration (The Destruction of Army Group Centre)

Twelve Yak-9s from the 18th GvIAP, on 26 June 1944, commanded by V. I. Zapaskin attacked nine Ju 88s escorted by sixteen Fw 190s. By the time the combat was over, three of the Ju 88s and two of the Fw 190s were claimed as kills.

Balkan Campaign (1944)

Based out of Bari, in 1944, Yak-9DDs were used to support the partisans in Yugoslavia, for example, escorting USAAF C-47 Skytrain (Dakota) transports as they made supply drops to the partisans. Twelve Yak-9DDs were used for this, flying 155 sorties without incident. The Yak-9DDs were also used to escort USAAF B-17 Flying Fortress and B-24 Liberator bombers on their non-stop 'Shuttle Raid' ('Operation Frantic') missions between Bari and bases in the Soviet Union, such as Poltava in Ukraine, bombing the Romanian oilfields along the way.

Baltic Campaign (1944–45)

One pilot who enjoyed success in the Yak-9 during operations in the Baltic States in 1944 was Maj. I. V. Shmelyov, late of the Blue Line in the Taman Peninsula, who flying over Riga, the capital of Latvia, downed nine enemy aircraft, which gave him a total by this time of twenty-nine individual kills and fifteen shared kills in 350 sorties and seventy-seven air combats.

The Yak-9K, with its 45-mm nose-mounted cannon, saw action over the Baltic states. On 27 August 1944, a Yak-9K from the 812th IAP managed to sneak up on a Fw 190 from JG 54 during an air battle over Lithuania, where he blew the enemy aircraft's wing off with one shell.

The 4th IAP had fought across Poland and into the Baltic States, now equipped with Yak-9Ts. From late 1944 into 1945, it flew over the Courland Peninsula (Kurland) in Latvia and over East Prussia. On 16 February 1945, at Tukums-Libau (Liepāja) in Latvia, while flying escort for Il-2s, the Yak-9Ts encountered Fw 190s. Two Fw 190s were shot down, one of which was flown by the fourth highest-scoring ace of the Luftwaffe, Otto Kittel, who had 267 confirmed kills.

Berlin Strategic Offensive Operation (Battle of Berlin)

The Yak-9DD was tested in combat by the 368th IAP and the 334th IAD of the 3rd VA from 9 March to 25 April 1945, which received forty examples of this aircraft (before 16 April 1945, the start of the Battle of Berlin, these missions would have been part of the Vistula to Oder Operation). They were used in Germany, in places such as East Prussia, Stettin (on the Baltic coast), and Berlin. Forty Yak-9DDs were used in these military trials. The Yak-9DD was used mainly as escort fighters for the Pe-2 and Tu-2 bombers at low altitudes. It was not entirely successful in this role, at least with the Tu-2, as its maximum speed was insufficiently more than the speedy Tu-2 to

Yak-9M of the Red Banner (Baltic) Fleet in 1944. (*Viktor Kulikov's collection*)

be able to escort it efficiently. Since these bombers were operating against the front edges of the German's defences, the Yak-9DD did not have the chance to exploit its long-range capabilities as it would have had in deep-penetration missions.

The Yak-9U saw its first action over the skies of Germany in 1945. On 30 April 1945 (the day of Hitler's death), V. V. Isayev from the 42nd GvIAP downed a Fw 190 over Berlin.

It was during the Battle of Berlin that a Yak-9T flown by V. A. Yegorov of the 402nd IAP downed a Me 262 jet fighter.

Manchurian Strategic Offensive Operation

Some of the last air battles of the Second World War involved Yak-9s. On 15 August 1945, ten Yak-9s of the 19th IAP of the Pacific Fleet encountered two Mitsubishi J2M Raiden ('Jack') fighters and downed one of them. On the same day, twelve Yak-9s encountered two other Raidens and shot one of them down. On 16 August 1945, a Yak-9 of the Northern Pacific Fleet was shot down over Sakhalin Island as what was probably the last Soviet fighter to be lost to enemy action during the Second World War.

Yak-9 in Detail

The following description generally applies to all production Yak-9s, especially those with the M-105PF engine. Differences between variants will be noted where appropriate.

General Description

The Yak-9 was a single-engined single-seat cantilever monoplane fighter with an enclosed cockpit and a retractable main landing gear and tailwheel. The aircraft was usually of mixed construction with a steel tube fuselage structure, usually covered in metal, plywood, and fabric, metal tailplanes, and normally mixed-structure wings covered in plywood.

Fuselage

The fuselage structure was similar to the earlier Yakovlev fighters, featuring a steel tube framework, this framework being covered in metal panels on the forward fuselage, which was normally covered by plywood and fabric on the aft fuselage. The top of the rear fuselage was covered in plywood, while the side and bottom were covered in fabric. On the Yak-9U, the rear fuselage was completely covered in a plywood skin, as with the Yak-3. One difference between the fuselage framework of the Yak-9 and that of the Yak-1 was that the engine mount was no longer integral with the steel tube framework, but it was a separate structure that was now bolted to the aft framework, as with the Yak-7. The fuselage cross-section was similar to that of other Yakovlev fighters, being like a 'D' turned over on its flat side.

All the Yak-9s had a cut-down rear fuselage to accommodate the all-around vision bubble-top cockpit canopy first introduced on the Yak-1B and also used on the last Yak-7Bs and all of the Yak-3s. The canopy could be jettisoned in an emergency from the Yak-9M on. The pilot's seat consisted of a steel armoured back, and a fibre 'bucket'

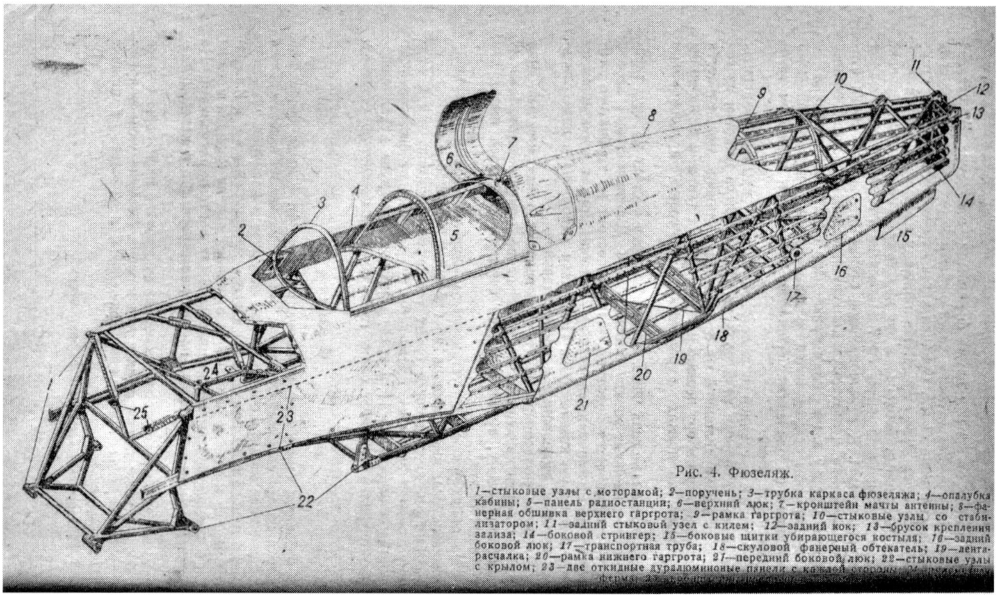

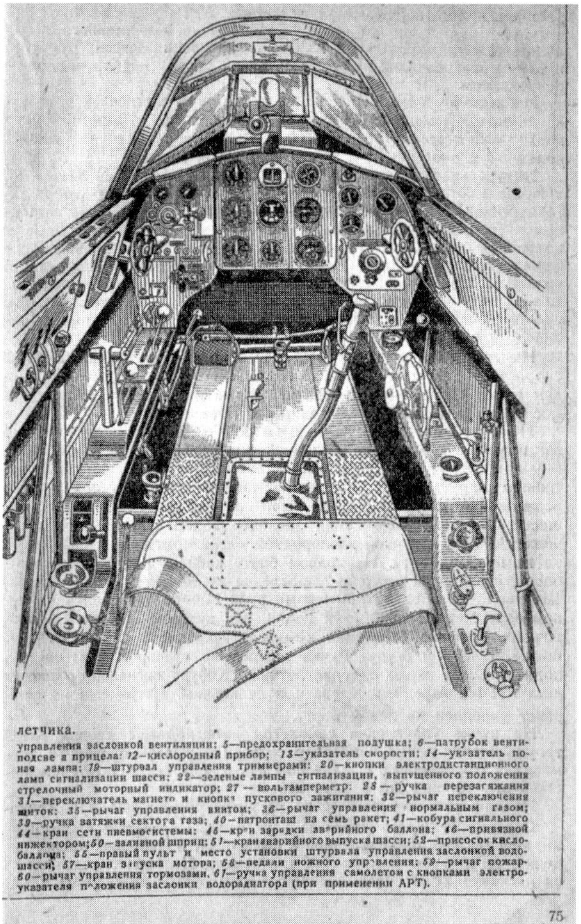

Above: Yak-9 M-105 fuselage structure. Note the hatch for the small compartment aft of the cockpit. (*Yak-9 M-105 Technical Manual*)

Left: Yak-9 M-105 cockpit. (*Yak-9 M-105 Technical Manual*) (whose height was adjustable on the ground). The floor was wooden and attached to the steel tube framework. The cabin could be ventilated through an opening under the windscreen, which, when opened, allowed air to enter the cockpit through a pipe located above the instrument panel. To assist with rear vision, a hinged mirror was attached to the upper frame of the canopy.

There were two main types of fuselages used on the Yak-9s, differing by the placement of the cockpit. The first type used the cockpit position as used on the Yak-1, Yak-7, and Yak-3. The second type adopted a more aft position for the cockpit, with the cockpit moved back 1.31 feet (400 mm). This was initially done on the Yak-9T to give more room to fit the large 37-mm cannon and was also used on the Yak-9K with its 45-mm cannon. However, this position improved the centre of gravity, flight stability, and ground handling (including landing); it was even adopted on later Yak-9s, which did not have the 37-mm or 45-mm cannon, such as the Yak-9M and the Yak-9U.

Wings

One major external difference between the Yak-7 and the Yak-9 was in the wings. The Yak-9 featured more angular wingtips than the rounded wingtips of the Yak-7, these wingtips being extended to accommodate leading-edge slats, which in the event were never fitted (it was felt they were not needed). Another major difference which did not show externally was in the wing structure: The Yak-7 had all-wooden wings, with a wooden structure covered in plywood. The Yak-9 featured two metal spars (as used on the Yak-7D), which were both lighter and stronger than the wooden spars of the earlier Yakovlev fighters, although the wings were still covered in wood, with puttied fabric over the wood to cover the panel lines. In addition, the wings now housed four fuel tanks on most Yak-9s (there were two in the original Yak-9 series and eight in the Yak-9DD), as opposed to the two installed in the Yak-7's wings, the tanks being accommodated between metal ribs. The stringers were made out of pine slats. There was a total of thirty-eight ribs. Like earlier Yakovlev fighters, the wing was constructed as a single-piece unit, which was attached to the fuselage during production.

As with the Yak-1 and Yak-7, the wings were of a Clark YH aerofoil, with 15 per cent thickness at the root and 8 per cent thickness at the wingtip, as with the Yak-7. The single-piece wing was attached to the fuselage at six points.

Tailplanes

Similar to the Yak-7, the Yak-9 featured metal tail surfaces, with the fixed surfaces being covered in dural aluminium alloy over a metal structure and the moveable control surfaces being covered in fabric over a dural structure. The fin and the stabilisers both featured twin-spar construction. The ribs and stringers were made of sheet duralumin.

Engine

The engine used on most Yak-9s was the Klimov M-105 (VK-105) twelve-cylinder vee-type liquid-cooled inline engine, the same engine that was used on the Yak-1, the Yak-3, and the Yak-7. The version used on most Yak-9s was the boosted M-105PF, with 1,260 hp at maximum power rating. Some variants switched to the more powerful M-105PF-2 (VK-105PF-2) with 1,240 hp at take-off and 1,290 hp at its maximum power rating. Late war and post-war Yak-9s (such as the Yak-9U and Yak-9P) were equipped with the similar but more powerful Klimov VK-107A engine of 1,600 hp.

The engine could be started either mechanically by a Hucks starter (fitted onto the dog at the end of the propeller) or pneumatically. The Yak-9D had the VISh-61P metal three-bladed constant-speed propeller (used on earlier Yakovlev variants such as the Yak-7), while the Yak-9T and Yak-9M had the VISh-105SV metal three-bladed constant-speed propeller. The constant-speed VISh-61P propeller featured a R-7A speed controller. An ART-41 regulator automatically controlled the water temperature on the Yak-9M.

Fuel System

Most Yak-9s featured four main fuel tanks, housed in the wings, with a small service tank in the middle of the under-fuselage. These four main tanks gave the Yak-9 more range than the Yak-7 (or the Yak-1 and Yak-3) with its two main fuel tanks. The early Yak-9s featured only two fuel tanks in the wings. The Yak-9DD featured eight fuel tanks in the wings, which gave it the greatest range of the production Great Patriotic War Yakovlev fighters. Detachable metal panels, usually four, covered the tanks on the bottom of the wings.

The fuel tanks themselves were of welded AMTsM aluminium, but these could be substituted with fibre tanks. The fibre tanks had clean-edged holes when punctured, while the metal tanks had holes which could bend outwards, which might prevent the self-sealing layer from properly sealing. The tanks featured the neutral gas fire protection system widely used on Soviet aircraft during the war. As with the Yak-1 and Yak-7, external fuel gauges were located on top of the inner part of the wings, which indicated how much fuel was left in the tanks. Fuel tank caps were also located on top of the wings.

Controls

Most of the moveable control surfaces of the Yak-9 were of a dural structure, with a canvas covering, the exception being the underwing flaps, which were of all-metal construction. The control surfaces were mechanically operated by push-pull rods for the ailerons and elevators and by wires for the rudder. Both elevators had trim tabs that were operated by a wheel located on the port side of the cockpit. The rudder had a duralumin tube at the front and featured a fixed integral trim tab. The ailerons and elevators consisted of tubular spars and stamped ribs. The Schrenk-type flaps were pneumatically operated. As with most of the Yakovlev fighters, the control column was of the columnar 'joystick' type, and this column controlled the ailerons and elevators via rods and pulleys. Foot pedals, which were adjustable to two positions, controlled the rudder via cables.

The ailerons were Frise-type ailerons, with both ailerons fitted with fixed dural trim tabs that extended back from the trailing edge. The ailerons could move up to a greater degree than they moved down.

Landing Gear

The main landing gear on the Yak-9 was fully retractable, retracting inwards, giving the Yak-9 a wide stance (as with the other Yakovlev fighters). The landing gear legs were covered by a single door, and small doors were attached to the wing under surface, which covered the outer part of the wheels when the landing gear was retracted, with these small doors retracting mechanically. There was a small rod, mechanically connected to the landing gear, which indicated the position of the main landing gear; when the rod was up, the landing gear was down, when the rod was down, the landing gear was retracted. The tailwheel was also retractable and was covered by twin doors, one on each side. Sometimes, the tailwheel was locked in the down position in the field, with the doors permanently closed.

Radio Equipment

The standard radio on the Yak-9 was the RSI-4 unit for receiving and the RSI-3bis for transmitting. Not all Yak-9s, especially early versions, were fitted with both units, with many aircraft only being equipped with the RSI-4 receiver. Most of the Yak-9s had antenna masts located immediately behind the canopy, with a bifurcated line running from the top of the mast to two attachment points on the tail fin. Early versions, such as the original series Yak-9 and the Yak-9D, had antenna masts that went straight up from the fuselage. Later Yak-9 versions—such as the Yak-9K, the Yak-9M, and the Yak-9T—had a mast that was slanted forward. The Yak-9U had a single line running directly from the rear canopy to the tail fin, there being no antenna mast. This was done to streamline the aircraft.

Preserved Yak-9U at Monino museum. (*Viktor Kulikov's collection*)

Fixed Armament

Most Yak-9s were equipped with a single ShVAK MP-20 20-mm cannon mounted between the engine cylinder banks to fire through the propeller spinner and with a single UBS machine gun mounted on the port side of the top of the engine cowling. This was one fewer machine gun than the Yak-7 had carried, which was for weight reasons. The 20-mm cannon normally had 120 rounds and the UBS machine gun 200 rounds. The links and shell casings for the machine guns were collected in a box behind the front wing spar. The links for the cannon were collected on the starboard side of the cannon, while shell casings were collected with the machine gun shell casings. The machine gun and the cannon were both reloaded pneumatically.

As the pilots had expressed some displeasure with the normal gun armament of the Yak-9, finding it to a certain extent weak for use against the sturdy German aircraft, heavier options were tried and produced. The most notable example was the Yak-9T, which was fitted with the very powerful NS-37 37-mm cannon firing through the nose, the port UBS being retained for aiming purposes. This cannon was equipped with thirty to thirty-two rounds. An even heavier armament was featured by the Yak-9K, which was equipped with the extremely potent NS-45 45-mm cannon and was even capable of knocking out German tanks. It carried twenty-nine rounds. Only a small trial batch of Yak-9Ks was manufactured, but it proved to be deadly in combat against both Axis air targets and ground targets. The Yak-9UT, based upon the Yak-9U, was equipped with a NS-23 23-mm cannon firing through the spinner and two B-20S 20-mm cannons mounted on top of the cowling. As with the Yak-9K, only a small number were produced, but as with the Yak-9K, these proved deadly in combat with this heavy armament. Amazingly, after the war, one Yak-9 was fitted with a 57-mm cannon in the nose, but perhaps not surprisingly, the installation was not a success because of the massive recoil of this large cannon.

Disposable Armament

Unlike the early Yak-1s and Yak-7s, the Yak-9 does not appear to have carried rockets in service, although it was capable of carrying small bombs under the wings, with the maximum load probably being 441 lb (200 kg) as with earlier Yakovlevs, and in the Yak-9B version, it was capable of carrying up to 882 lb (400 kg) of bombs internally in a small bomb bay behind the pilot.

Yak-9B dropping a bomb in 1944. (*Viktor Kulikov's collection*)

Colour and Markings

The Yak-9 first saw service in late 1942, and these aircraft were painted in the black/green scheme specified at that time—AMT-6 Black and AMT-4 Green over AMT-7 Blue. Most Yak-9s would have been painted in the two-grey fighter scheme of AMT-11 Grey-Blue and AMT-12 Dark Grey over AMT-7 Blue, which was officially adopted in autumn 1943. Some late war Yak-9s were painted in a single grey colour topside, probably AMT-11 Grey-Blue over AMT-7 Blue. If painted in the black/green scheme, it is probable that the 1940-style black-outlined red star would have been carried. A plain red star may also have been carried in place of the black-outlined star. If painted in the two-grey scheme, the 1943-style red star would have been used. Examples of the Yak-9 with the black/green and two-grey schemes can be seen in the colour plates section. The white winter camouflage does not appear to have been commonly used on the Yak-9.

Yak-3

There were two main ways to improve the performance of the Yakovlev fighters (which methods were not mutually exclusive); one was to increase the power of the engine, as seen with versions that were equipped with the M-106, M-107A (VK-107A), or VK-108 engines, and the other was to lighten the aircraft to take full advantage of the horsepower available from the M-105 (VK-105).

The Yak-3 resulted from a successful effort to lighten the Yak-1 airframe, and by the end of the war, the Yak-3 was the lightest of the front-line fighters in use by the major powers, topping out at less than 6,000 lb (2,722 kg). By comparison, the North American P-51D Mustang had a maximum take-off weight of 12,100 lb (5,488 kg). Remarkably, the loaded weight of the Yak-3—5,935 lb (2,692 kg)—was less than the empty weight of the P-51D—7,635 lb (3,463 kg). The Yak-3 was one of the outstanding fighters of the last year of the war, and it excelled in low-altitude combat against the German fighters.

Yak-1M

The development of the Yak-1 which led to the Yak-3 was this lightened version of the Yak-1. Design of the Yak-1M, also known as the *Moskit* or 'Mosquito' (which happened to be the nickname for the light bomber versions of the UT-1 trainer, also built by Yakovlev), started in fall 1942. Part of the impetus for a lightened Yak-1 came from the appearance of an improved Bf 109 fighter over Stalingrad in 1942—the Bf 109G. Unlike the Bf 109F, which featured the Daimler-Benz DB-601 engine, the Bf 109G was equipped with the more powerful DB-605 engine, which enabled it to outfly any Soviet fighters at the time.

The first version of the Yak-1M was finished on 15 February 1943. The Yak-1M featured a ShVAK MP-20 20-mm cannon in the nose, and one UBS machine gun mounted on top of the cowling. It differed from the production Yak-1 mainly in the wing, which was smaller in span, 30.18 feet (9.2 m), compared to 32.81 feet (10 m) and area, being reduced by 24.76 sq. feet (2.3 m^2) to 159.31 sq. feet (14.8 m^2)

from 184.07 sq. feet (17.1 m^2). The Yak-1M featured metal wing spars replacing the wooden spars for a lighter structure. The tail area was also reduced, although the fixed tailplanes remained wooden.

The new aircraft was fitted with four fuel tanks in the wings, as opposed to the two tanks of the production Yak-1 (the production Yak-3 reverted to two tanks). The engine used was the M-105P with a VISh-61P propeller. The oil cooler intake was relocated from the nose to the wing roots, making for a smooth outline to the nose, similar to that of the Yak-9U. The bubble-top canopy of the Yak-1B was used. The water radiator, an OP-492 (replacing the earlier OP-203), was more recessed into the fuselage, resulting in a lower profile for the fairing, which increased the streamlining of the aircraft. The aircraft was also 507 lb (230 kg) lighter than a standard production Yak-1 of that time (the Yak-1B).

Factory tests were conducted from 28 February to 7 June 1943, and the state tests ran from 7 June to 4 July 1943, with additional tests run on 21–22 July 1943. During tests, the aircraft showed good performance, with a speed at sea level of 339 mph (545 kph) and a top speed of 393 mph (632 kph) at 14,600 feet (4,450 m). The 360-degree turn time was an impressive seventeen seconds. The aircraft had good handling, but some deficiencies were noted.

After the state acceptance trials, changes were made to the first prototype. The four exhausts per side, inherited from the Yak-1, were changed to six exhausts per side, with each cylinder having its own exhaust stub. The supercharger intake was moved from the wing roots to under the nose, so the nose once again had an under-nose scoop, as with the production Yak-1s, but it was more streamlined and moved further aft of the spinner.

The second prototype of the Yak-1M, known as the *Dooblyor*, featured modifications to correct some of the deficiencies noted in the first Yak-1M, such as insufficient engine cooling and the lack of a radio. The supercharger intake was moved from the nose back to the wing roots, and the smooth nose profile of the first Yak-1M re-appeared; this streamlined nose would be characteristic for all the inline-engined Yak-3s that followed. This smooth nose improved the streamlining of the aircraft, which improved the speed. The engine was the boosted M-105PF-2, which had a maximum rating of 1,290 hp. The propeller was a VISh-105SV-01 with cuffed blades at the roots. The fuel capacity was increased from 63.4 gal (240 l) to 70.01 gal (265 l). The pilot's armour protection was improved, and the fabric covering of the rear fuselage was replaced by 2-mm-thick plywood. The all-round vision cockpit canopy was now jettisonable. The armament differed in that the ShVAK cannon was replaced by a lightweight ShA-20M 20-mm cannon, and two UBS machine guns were now fitted. The simple mechanical VV-1 gunsight of the first Yak-1M was replaced by the PBP-1A reflector-type collimator gunsight. There was no radio antenna mast, but an RSI-4 receiver was installed. The Yak-1M *Dooblyor* was in effect the prototype Yak-3.

The aircraft was completed on 9 September 1943, and the factory tests took place from 20–30 September 1943, flown by the chief OKB test pilot P. Ya. Fedrovi, with the state tests running from 6–15 October 1943, flown by test pilot Afanasiy G. Proshakov. The quickness with which the tests were conducted was an indication of

Yak-1M *Dooblyor* in 1943. Note the small intake located a small distance behind the propeller spinner. (*Viktor Kulikov's collection*)

the quality and maturity of the new fighter, and in comparative tests the fighter was found to be at least the equal of the fighters in use on the Eastern Front, both Soviet and German. Even the Bf 109, which excelled in vertical manoeuvring, was found to be inferior to the Yak-1M in comparative tests. The *Dooblyor* improved on the first Yak-1M's performance, with a speed at sea level of 354 mph (570 kph) and 405 mph (651 kph) at 14,108 feet (4,300 m). A combat turn gained 4,199 feet (1,280), and a full 360-degree turn could be executed in sixteen–seventeen seconds.

The Yak-1M in its *Dooblyor* configuration was approved for production on 26 October 1943 as the 'Yak-3', this being the second time this designation had been used (the first time was for the experimental I-30, described further on, another example of the Soviet penchant for reusing designations).

Yak-3 VK-105PF-2 (M-105PF-2)

This was the main production version of the Yak-3 and like the Yak-1M *Dooblyor* was fitted with the Klimov VK-105PF-2 (M-105PF-2) engine. It did not have any special designation, other than sometimes being referred to as the 'Yak-3 M-105PF-2' in the Soviet custom of naming aircraft by their engine type. The first production Yak-3 was completed on 1 March 1944, and it flew for the initial time on 3 March 1944. The aircraft was produced at both Z.31 in Tbilisi, where it replaced the LaGG-3, and at Z.292 in Saratov, where it replaced the Yak-1B on the production lines. A total of 4,797 Yak-3s of all versions were produced, including post-war examples. The first regiment to receive the Yak-3 for combat evaluation was the 91st IAP of the 2nd VA (Air Army) in June and July 1944.

Early Yak-3 in flight. (*San Diego Air and Space Museum, Wikimedia*)

Yak-3: Early Version

The first 197 Yak-3s produced featured an armament of one ShVAK MP-20 20-mm cannon with 125 rounds, instead of the ShA-20M 20-mm cannon of the Yak-1M *Dooblyor*, and one UBS machine gun on the port side of the cowling (as with the Yak-1B and Yak-9), with 175 rounds, in place of the two UBS machine guns of the *Dooblyor*. These first Yak-3s still featured the plywood and fabric covering of the Yak-1 for the rear fuselage.

The aircraft displayed a somewhat inferior performance to the *Dooblyor*, with a speed at sea level of 346 mph (557 kph) and a top speed of 391 mph (630 kph) at 12,759 feet (3,900 m), compared to the 354 mph (570 kph) at sea level and a top speed of 405 mph (651 kph) for the Yak-1M *Dooblyor*. This drop in performance from prototypes to production aircraft was common for Soviet aircraft due to the increased equipment (and weight) carried by operational machines and the generally poorer fit and finish of the hastily built production aircraft compared to the carefully built (sometimes hand-built) and maintained prototypes. However, the production machines were found to have good handling qualities like the *Dooblyor*.

Although the aircraft was considered a good aircraft, there were still problems, such as the wrap-around one-piece windscreen causing distortions for forward vision and use of the gunsight, a stiff landing gear that made landing a rather bumpy ride, and the armoured seat back that was uncomfortable for the pilot. As was usual with Soviet wartime aircraft, these issues were to be dealt with as production continued on the aircraft. There was a war on, and the Soviets were not inclined to stop production to make relatively small (or in some cases even fairly large) changes to aircraft.

YAK-3: STANDARD VERSION

After the early Yak-3s, the armament was increased with the addition of an extra UBS machine gun in the upper cowling on the starboard side, which gave the Yak-3 an armament of one ShVAK MP-20 20-mm cannon firing through the propeller spinner and two UBS 12.7-mm machine guns mounted in the upper engine cowling. This gave the Yak-3 more firepower than most Yak-9s, which featured the ShVAK MP-20 20-mm cannon but only one UBS heavy machine gun. The rear fuselage covering was changed from a plywood covering on top with fabric on the sides to an all-plywood covering. This improved the streamlining and lowered the drag. The aircraft carried a total fuel load of 97.74 gal (370 l) in two main fuel tanks in the wings, with a third small tank in the fuselage. The engine was the VK-105PF-2 with a maximum rating of 1,290 hp, and the propeller was a VISh-105SV-01. The oil cooler and the supercharger intakes were in the wing roots, and the water radiator was located under the fuselage at the midway point, with the radiator being partially sunk into the fuselage to lessen the profile of the radiator housing and improve the streamlining as with the Yak-1M. The landing gear and the wings were increased in strength over those of the *Dooblyor*.

The performance of this version of the Yak-3 increased somewhat over that of the early version. Tests showed that the performance of production aircraft differed from each other, with the best results coming from a production aircraft from Z.31 at Tbilisi. It was accepted that aircraft from Z.31 had a better production standard than those from Z.292 in Saratov. A Z.31 aircraft, tested in April 1944, had a speed at sea level of 354 mph (570 kph) and a top speed of 409 mph (658 kph) at 13,615 feet (4,150 m), which compared quite favourably with the *Dooblyor*, the sea level speed being the same and the top speed being slightly higher for the production aircraft. The horizontal turn time had degraded, however, with the normal 360-degree turn time for a production Yak-3 being twenty-one seconds compared to the sixteen–seventeen seconds for the *Dooblyor* and seventeen seconds for the first Yak-1M. This was probably due to the increased weight of the production aircraft, but it was still considered to be an acceptable turn rate.

The aircraft was found to be easy to master by pilots, and according to Gen Zakharov, the pilots of the Normandie-Niemen unit (who were experienced pilots, and who had flown the Yak-1, the Yak-3's immediate 'ancestor') mastered the Yak-3 in only three to five hours.

Yak-3 VK-107A ('Yak-3U')

As had been done with the Yak-9 (as the Yak-9U VK-107A), it was decided to re-engine the Yak-3 with the powerful but troubled VK-107A engine. It was also decided to fit the Yak-3 with metal wings, with the end goal being an all-metal Yak-3 VK-107A. This was part of the Soviet move towards using more metal in their aircraft, made possible in part by Lend-Lease aluminium, the metal replacing the traditional wooden parts. The cockpit was moved back 1.31 feet (400 mm) as with the later versions of the Yak-9 (Yak-9DD, Yak-9M, and Yak-9U). The VK-107A engine was fitted with a VISh-107LO propeller. The armament for the prototypes was two Berezin B-20S 20-mm cannons in the upper cowling with 120 rounds each. There was no gun firing through the spinner. Two prototypes were built—the No. 1 and the *Dooblyor* in January 1944.

Left: Early Yak-3s of the Moscow PVO. The nearest aircraft is a La-5FN. (*Viktor Kulikov's collection*)

Below: Normandie-Niemen Yak-3 in flight. The stars appear to have a silver outline, while the aircraft number could be blue. (*Viktor Kulikov's collection*)

Yak-3 VK-107A prototype in 1945. The aircraft appears to be painted in silver, with a large red band extending back from the red spinner. (*Viktor Kulikov's collection*)

Yak-3 VK-107A in 1945. Note the very high lower camouflage demarcation lines. (*Viktor Kulikov's collection*)

Factory tests on the first prototype were conducted from 15 April to 20 November 1944 by test pilot Fedorov. At sea level, the maximum speed was 380 mph (611 kph) and reached 447 mph (720 kph) at 18,865 feet (5,750 m). Tests showed the aircraft needed strengthening, and there were problems with the propeller. The engine also tended to overheat. The *Dooblyor* underwent state tests from 7 February to 15 May 1944 and from 13 July to 29 August 1944. In total, there were forty-four test flights, and although the tests were not completed, work continued on the Yak-3 VK-107A because of its perceived promise.

Although the Yak-3 VK-107A was mainly a post-war aircraft, a few were used by the 897th IAP, commanded by Pavel Petrovich Karavay, during the Great Patriotic War. Circumventing normal procedures, this IAP took the aircraft directly from the factory at Tbilisi (Z.31). In one of these aircraft, Karavay downed a Bf 109 on 23 March 1945 over Mor in Hungary. He downed another Bf 109 on 22 April 1945 over Lake Balaton, also in Hungary. In addition to the 897th IAP, the 5th GvIAP received Yak-3 VK-107As in early April 1945 to replace their La-5s, but they found them to be so unreliable because of their engines that they went back to their Lavochkin fighters.

During 1945–46, all-metal Yak-3 VK-107As were built with the plywood covering of the fuselage replaced by *elektron*, a magnesium metal alloy. The fin and fixed stabilisers were of all-metal structure and metal covering. The rudder was also of all-metal construction with a metal covering. The armament was now a B-20M 20-mm cannon fitted to fire through the propeller and one B-20S 20-mm cannon with 120 rounds, mounted on the port side of the cowling. The radio was the RSI-6.

In the end, only forty-eight Yak-3 VK-107As with metal wings were built by Z.31 by 1946, mainly post-war, because of continuing problems with the engine and the greater ease with which the similarly powered Yak-9U could accommodate the necessary changes to improve the VK-107A. Please note that the Yak-3 VK-107A is often referred to in Western references as the 'Yak-3U'; this is incorrect and properly refers only to the experimental M-82 (ASh-82FN)-equipped Yak-3 ('Yak-3U M-82', described further on).

Yak-3P

In common with the other Yakovlev fighters, the OKB worked on increasing the offensive firepower of the Yak-3. The 'P' in the Yak-3P's designation stood for *Puschenniy*, or 'Cannon(-armed)', as the armament consisted solely of cannons, the machine guns being dispensed with. The cannons consisted of the B-20M 20-mm cannon with 120 rounds for the nose-mounted cannon and two B-20S 20-mm cannons with 130 rounds for the upper cowling cannons. The weight of fire was 7.76 lb/sec (3.52 kg/sec). The gun recharging was changed from mechanical to pneumatic. In addition, the RSI-4A radio was replaced by a RSI-6M radio.

The modifications to two Yak-3s for the all-cannon armament were carried out pursuant to a GKO order dated 29 December 1944. The aircraft underwent state tests from 23 March to 4 April 1945 (one source has 9 April 1945), with the test pilot being V. G. Ivanov. In comparison to other aircraft, the weight of fire was as follows; for the Yak-3P it was 7.76 lb/sec (3.52 kg/sec), the Fw 190A-8 had 7.58 lb/sec (3.44 kg/sec), and the P-39 Airacobra had 7.01 lb/sec (3.18 kg/sec). The recoil effect was found to be insignificant. The aircraft passed its state tests, and it was decided to produce all-new Yak-3s with the all-cannon armament.

From April 1945 to the middle of 1946, 596 Yak-3Ps were built at Z.292 and Z.31. From 1 August 1945, all the Yak-3 VK-105PF-2s were built as Yak-3Ps with the all-cannon armament. It does not appear that any Yak-3Ps saw combat.

Yak-3: Experimental Versions

Yak-3 VK-108

The Yak-3 VK-107A was not the only attempt to fit the Yak-3 with a more powerful Klimov engine than the VK-105 (M-105). The similar but even more powerful VK-108 was fitted to what was essentially a Yak-3 VK-107A airframe, the VK-108 having a maximum rating of 1,850 hp. This installation was characterised by four rows of exhausts (two rows were also on top of the cowling) as opposed to just the two rows on the sides of the cowling of other Yakovlev fighters. The front of the cowling also had 'bumps' to accommodate the larger cylinders of the VK-108 (somewhat as with the Griffon-powered Spitfire fighters). A VISh-107LT-5 propeller replaced the VISh-107SV-1. The armament was changed to a single NS-23 23-mm cannon firing through the propeller spinner, equipped with sixty rounds. The ailerons were covered in metal instead of fabric, and the pilot was given an armoured headrest instead of the armour glass behind the seat. With these and other changes, the flight weight was now 6,385 lb (2,896 kg).

The Yak-3 VK-108 was built at the Yakovlev OKB from 1 August to 1 October 1944 and underwent its factory tests from 7 October 1944 to 8 March 1945. The first flight took place on 19 December 1944, piloted by Viktor L. Rastorguyev. The factory

Yak-3 VK-108 in late 1944 or early 1945. Note the polished unpainted propeller blades. (*Viktor Kulikov's collection*)

tests took so long due to the temperamental nature of the experimental VK-108 engine. Nonetheless, on 21 December 1944, without armament or a full fuel load, the Yak-3 VK-108 attained a maximum speed of 463 mph (745 kph) at 20,636 feet (6,290 m). This was the highest speed ever attained by a pure piston-engined Soviet aircraft. Despite the impressive performance, there were continuing problems with the VK-108 engine, which included smoking and shaking, and the engine ran 'hot', with over-heating being a problem. The engine was replaced after the 21 December flight, and the next flight did not take place until 8 March 1945, after which tests were discontinued because of continuing issues with the VK-108 engine. The aircraft apparently never underwent any state tests.

This was not the end of the Yak-3 VK-108, however, as another aircraft was built with this engine from 1 August to 1 November 1944 at the Yakovlev OKB. The only difference between this aircraft and the first Yak-3 VK-108 was with the armament. In place of the single NS-23 23-mm cannon, this aircraft was armed with two B-20S 20-mm cannons. This aircraft did not prove any more successful than the first Yak-3 VK-108, and although an NKAP order dated 28 March 1946 authorised the construction of three new Yak-3 VK-108s, only this one additional aircraft was actually built.

In the end, the Yak-3 VK-108 was not produced because of the experimental nature of the VK-108, which would have needed much more work to make it into a service-worthy engine, and the need for Yakovlev to start concentrating on jet-powered aircraft for the post-war VVS.

Yak-3 with Laminar Wings

Just as a Yak-7 had been tested with laminar wings (the Yak-7L), a Yak-3 was experimentally fitted with laminar wings. The laminar wings would be less drag-inducing than the normal profile wings. The project was assigned to Oleg Konstantinovich Antonov (1906–84), who would become famous after the war as a designer of transport aircraft. A standard Yak-3 was modified, with only the rib profiles being changed, the basic planform of the wing remaining unchanged, although the wing root leading edges were extended. The armament was a NS-23 23-mm cannon in the nose with two UBS machine guns on top of the cowling. Unfortunately, there is no record of the aircraft's testing nor information regarding its ultimate disposition.

Yak-3PD

A Yak-3 (c/n 1012-43) was taken from Z.292 and was modified for high-altitude flight as the Yak-3PD. The aircraft was now equipped with a new VK-105PD (originally M-105PD) engine with the Dollezhal E-100 two-stage supercharger. The supercharger intake fairing was fitted under the wing-fuselage junction. This aircraft was armed with a single NS-23 23-mm cannon equipped with sixty rounds, firing through the propeller. The wingspan was increased over that of the production Yak-3 by 1.97 feet (0.6 m), which led to an increase in wing area of 5.38 sq. feet (0.5 m^2). It is unclear from the record if the VK-105PV-equipped Yak-3, described below, also had the longer wings. On 18 February 1945, the propeller was changed to the experimental VISh-105TL-2 with a 9.84-foot (3-m) diameter.

This Yak-3 with the VK-105PD was tested at the LII from 23 February to 3 May 1945 (the Great Patriotic War ended on 9 May 1945). After further revisions, including the addition of the VK-105PV engine, the aircraft was tested at the LII in June and July 1945, flown by the test pilot I. I. Shuneiko. On 26 June 1945, this aircraft achieved a top speed of 441 mph (710 kph) at 36,089 feet (11,000 m). A height of 43,635 feet (13,300 m) was achieved on 6 July. These were remarkable figures for a Soviet piston-engined aircraft. The aircraft was still able to manoeuvre normally at altitudes of from 36,089 feet (11,000 m) to 41,011 feet (12,500 m).

Yak-3PV (Yak-3PD)

Yakovlev's efforts to create a high-altitude fighter did not stop with the Yak-9PD. The Yak-3 airframe also 'got the treatment', being fitted with the high-altitude VK-105PV engine, in addition to the VK-105PD, as described above. The design of a high-altitude interceptor version of the Yak-3 began in the spring of 1944. Besides the VK-105PV engine, the armament was to be reduced to one lightweight 20-mm cannon equipped with 150 rounds firing through the spinner, although the armament fitted appears to have been a single NS-23 23-mm cannon.

The aircraft was completed on 28 September 1944, this being a production Yak-3 with c/n 4419 taken from Z.292 and with the VK-105PV added from 20 to 28 September. The aircraft was equipped with a VISh-105TL-2 propeller. The aircraft's weight was lightened from 5,919 lb (2,685 kg) to 5,904 lb (2,678 kg). Factory (OKB) tests were conducted on this aircraft from 29 September to 7 October 1944 by the test pilot V. L. Rastorguyev. In six flights conducted from 3 to 7 October 1944, the aircraft achieved a speed at sea level of 344 mph (554 kph) and a top speed of 408 mph (656 kph) at 18,127 feet (5,525 m). It appears that at some point, this aircraft was re-engined with the VK-105PD. It appears that at this time, the armament fit was a single NS-23 cannon.

Neither the original Yak-3PD nor the Yak-3PV were produced due to the unreliability of the VK-105PV and VK-105PD engines and the imminent arrival of the first of the jet-powered fighters, but the Yak-3PD re-engined with the VK-105PV did continue to fly at the LII until 1947, where it was used to gather information about the performance of engine radiators at high altitudes.

Yak-3RD

The Yak-7 had been fitted with ramjets under the wings as a means of boosting performance for short periods, as the Yak-7PRVD. The Yak-3RD followed this example, but this time, a single rocket engine was fitted in the tail as a means of enhancing the speed for short durations or 'bursts of speed'. The tail installation avoided the drag of the underwing-mounted ramjets of the Yak-7PRVD. The engine to be fitted was the RD-1 liquid-propellant rocket engine of 661 lb thrust designed by Valentin P. Glushko. The RD-1 engine could deliver its maximum thrust for three minutes. The aircraft carried 110 lb (50 kg) of kerosene and 441 lb (200 kg) of oxidiser in two wing tanks. The 'RD' in the aircraft's name stood for *Raketniy Dvigatel'*, or 'Rocket Engine'—a reasonable enough designation. The Yak-3RD was

Yak-3RD in 1945. The rocket outlet at the back is covered by a streamlined fairing here. (*Viktor Kulikov's collection*)

fitted with only a single NS-23 23-mm cannon mounted to fire through the propeller, being equipped with sixty rounds. The piston engine was the VK-105PF-2.

The rocket was installed in the tail with a removable streamlined metal tail cone fairing covering it when it was not to be used. The rudder was shorter to accommodate the engine, and had increased chord, while the elevators were cut away slightly at the base. Both the elevators and the ailerons were now covered in metal. The cockpit was lower in height by some 2.76 inches (70 mm) for better streamlining.

The aircraft was completed in December 1944 and underwent its factory tests from 22 December 1944 to 15 May 1945 at the LII. The test pilot was V. L. Rastorguyev. The aircraft showed impressive performance with the rocket working. A speed of 486 mph (782 kph) at 25,591 feet (7,800 m) was recorded on 11 May 1945. There were problems with the electrical ignition of the rocket, so chemical ignition was substituted instead, the new booster rocket with the chemical ignition having the designation of RD-1KhZ.

The aircraft was to participate in the 1945 Aviation Day Display on 18 August when disaster struck. On 16 August, the aircraft crashed, killing the pilot V. L. Rastorguyev. The aircraft entered into a dive from which it did not recover. The cause was thought to be either a problem with the pilot (perhaps he was overcome by fumes) or the elevators. As the aircraft appeared to be trying to recover from the dive before it crashed, the first cause seems the more probable. By this time, V. L. Rastorguyev had flown twenty-six flights on the Yak-3RD. A replacement aircraft was not constructed.

With the appearance of jet-powered aircraft, reaction-boosted piston-engined fighters became redundant, and work on the Yak-3RD was stopped.

Yak-3T

As with the Yak-7-37, and the Yak-9T, a Yak-3 was fitted with a 37-mm cannon, in this case, the lightweight Nudelman N-37 37-mm cannon with twenty-five rounds. Additionally, the Yak-3T carried two B-20S 20-mm cannons in the upper cowling with 100 rounds apiece. The 37-mm cannon was fitted with a large muzzle brake that

Yak-3T in January 1945. Notice the muzzle brake on the cannon barrel and the unpainted propeller blades. The two-piece main landing gear doors, like those of the Yak-1, can be seen well. (*Viktor Kulikov's collection*)

dissipated up to 75 per cent of the recoil. As with the Yak-9T, the cockpit was moved aft 1.31 feet (400 mm). The VK-105PF-2 engine was fitted with an experimental VISh-105L-28 propeller, and the fuel load and armour were reduced to lower the aircraft's weight.

The Yak-3T was modified from a production Yak-3 and was completed on 8 January 1945. The factory tests were conducted from 19 to 31 January 1945 with V. L. Rastorguyev and M. I. Ivanov as the test pilots. State tests at the NII VVS were conducted from 17 February to 27 April 1945 with Leonid M. Kuvshinov as the test pilot. The weight of fire was an impressive 12.68 lb/sec (5.75 kg/sec). Up to four rounds could be fired by the 37-mm cannon with no effect upon the aim. The 20-mm cannons could be fired for eight to ten rounds without disturbing the aim.

Defects such as the engine malfunctioning and problems with the B-20S mount were detected, and the aircraft was modified to try and alleviate these issues. The modifications were finished by 21 May 1945. New tests were conducted from 24 May to 2 June 1945 with M. I. Ivanov as the test pilot. A total of twelve flights were conducted. Despite the modifications, problems persisted with the engine.

Due to the end of the war and continuing problems with the engine and the presence of the similarly armed but much less troublesome Yak-9UT, production was not proceeded with.

Yak-3U M-82

As with the Yak-7 and the LaGG-3 (which led to the La-5 series), it was decided to fit the Shvetsov M-82 (ASh-82) radial engine to the Yak-3—in this case, the boosted ASh-82FN (M-82FN) version—to provide the Yak-3 with more power. In keeping with the Soviet late war move towards all-metal aircraft, it was to be of all-metal construction.

The first prototype still featured mixed-construction wings but replaced the wooden tail of the Yak-3 with a metal-structured tail, as on the Yak-9 (and Yak-7). Along with the ASh-82FN, a VISh-105V4 propeller was fitted. The wingspan was increased from 30.18 feet (9.2 m) to 30.84 feet (9.4 m), and the wings were shifted forward 8.62 inches (219 mm). The cockpit was raised 3.31 inches (84 mm) to increase visibility for the pilot, and the fuel tanks were changed from metal to soft, flexible tanks. The armament was comprised of two B-20S 20-mm cannons with 120 rounds each. Despite being heavier than the Yak-3 VK-105PF-2 by 249 lb (113 kg) in terms of flight weight, the Yak-3U was lighter than the Yak-3 VK-107A by 423 lb (192 kg) and the La-7 by 1,043 lb (473 kg).

The aircraft was built from 20 January 1945 and completed on 23 April 1945, with the first flight taking place on 12 May 1945, with P. Ya. Fedrovi as the test pilot. The factory testing continued to 9 June 1945. A top speed of 424 mph (682 kph) was attained at an altitude of 19,685 feet (6,000 m).

After the conclusion of the factory tests, the Yak-3U was returned to the factory for modifications. The rebuilt prototype replaced the mixed construction wings with all-metal wings, but the fuselage was still of composite construction. The modifications were completed by 25 September 1945. By this time, the Second World War had ended, so further testing was stopped.

Although the radial-engine installation was considered quite successful, and the resulting aircraft showed good performance, production was not proceeded with since there was no real need for the aircraft as the inline-engined Yakovlevs and the radial-engined Lavochkin fighters fulfilled the needs of the VVS. It did, however, help pave the way for the Yak-11 'Mule', which was equipped with the ASh-21 radial engine (a bit like half of an ASh-82 engine) and was based upon the Yak-3 airframe. The Yak-11 became a heavily used primary trainer post-war with quite a few different air forces, including the Soviet Air Force.

Combat Tactics

With small, light, and very manoeuvrable aircraft such as the Yak-3, Soviet tactics consisted of manoeuvring with the enemy, trying to turn inside the enemy aircraft to get into close contact, then using their few heavy calibre guns in the nose to down the aircraft with a few bursts.

With the later wartime Soviet aircraft such as the La-5FN, La-7, Yak-9U, and the Yak-3, not only were the Soviet aircraft superior in horizontal manoeuvring at low altitudes, but they also bettered the German aircraft in vertical manoeuvring, something which the German aircraft had been masters of earlier in the Great Patriotic War. In addition, as they were optimised for fighting at lower altitudes, with engines that were designed for high output at such altitudes, the Soviet aircraft were faster at these heights than the German fighters, such as the Bf 109 and the Fw 190 (with the possible exception of the Fw 190A-8 on maximum boost). Due to its higher speed and better manoeuvring at low altitudes, the Yak-3 bettered any German fighter at these altitudes. The main area where German fighters maintained their superiority was in a dive as their well-streamlined and heavier aircraft could dive better than the lightweight Soviet fighters. The German fighters also generally, although not always, had heavier gun armaments.

Combat Use

Although it did not see substantial use until the middle of 1944, the Yak-3 was used heavily from then until the end of the Manchurian Offensive in August 1945. Along with the La-7, and the Yak-9U, it was the most formidable Soviet-built fighter in the last year of the war and was at least the equal of any Axis piston-engined fighters it faced in combat, especially at low altitudes.

Kursk (Operation Citadel)

Pre-production Yak-3s first saw use at the end of Operation Citadel. This was even before the aircraft had finished its state tests. The pilots were enthusiastic about the new aircraft's handling, finding it light and easy to control and felt it gave them a fighter to match the Bf 109s and Fw 190s of the Germans. However, it was found to have faults, such as tricky low-speed handling, especially during landing, when it could drop a wing if the landing speed fell too low. Ground loops were also not uncommon with pilots not experienced with the Yak-3, although it must have taken a very ham-fisted pilot indeed to ground loop an aircraft with wide-track landing gear such as the Yak-3. Due to these and other shortcomings, the Yak-3 did not enter into large-scale service until the middle of 1944.

Ukrainian Operations in 1944

The 91st IAP of the 2nd VA (Air Army) was the first regiment to receive the production Yak-3. It took part in operations in June and July 1944 against Lvov (L'viv) in Ukraine in the Lvov-Sandomir operation. More than 40 per cent of the pilots were inexperienced, so this was no elite Guards unit. After a month and a half of fighting, the regiment had completed 430 sorties, during the course of which it claimed twenty-three Axis aircraft for the loss of only two Yak-3s. This result was probably exaggerated, but it was clear from the experiences of this unit that no German aircraft, neither the Bf 109 nor the Fw 190, could match the Yak-3 in low-altitude air combat. It was said that German pilots were warned not to engage at low altitudes any Soviet inline-engined fighters without under-nose air intakes; this sage advice also applied to the equally deadly Yak-9U.

Some deficiencies came to light, such as the relatively short flight time of the Yak-3 due to its fairly low fuel capacity. This limited its ability to perform 'free hunt' operations, which became more common in the last year of the war as the gradual disappearance of the Luftwaffe over the Eastern Front freed up fighters from their escort and support duties to perform other functions. However, there were other fighters, such as the Yak-9D, which could perform these 'free hunt' operations, which involved not just searching for enemy aircraft, but also bombing the enemy behind the front lines, which the Yak-3 was incapable of as it could not carry bombs. A much

Normandie-Niemen Yak-3s. Note the Cross of Lorraine on the tail of the nearest aircraft, a symbol of the Free French forces. (*Viktor Kulikov's collection*)

more serious problem was that the plywood skinning could become detached from the upper wing while pulling out from a high-speed dive, with disastrous consequences. This could be avoided by not entering into dangerous flight regimes, such as pulling out too quickly from a fast dive. Whatever its issues, the manoeuvrability and speed of the Yak-3 found great favour with Soviet pilots, and it proved itself in combat as a deadly fighter, especially at low altitudes.

When the 39th Army of the 3rd Byelorussian Front began an operation towards Tilsit (Sovyetsk) in East Prussia on 6 October, the Normandie-Niemen regiment covered the Soviet troops. The most successful day for the regiment in the entire war occurred on 16 October 1944. On this day, twenty-three pilots flew combat missions, and it is recorded that each claimed at least one victory. Some 110 sorties were flown, fifty-nine of which were bomber escort missions. Ten combats occurred, with thirty German aircraft claimed downed—specifically sixteen Fw 190s, nine Bf 109s, and five Ju 87s. No Normandie-Niemen pilots were lost. These results may very well be exaggerated, but by this time, experienced pilots flying the Yak-3 would have enjoyed a large advantage over the Bf 109s and Fw 190s of the increasingly depleted Luftwaffe, with their increasingly inexperienced pilots.

Operations over the Balkans

It was while flying over Yugoslavia on 7 November 1944 that the Yak-3s of the 866th and 659th IAPs were involved in a rather bizarre incidence of 'friendly-fire'. Due to a navigational error, USAAF P-38s of the 82nd Fighter Group attacked a Soviet armoured column north-west of Belgrade, the capital of Yugoslavia. They strafed the troops, and a Soviet general was killed. Before the situation could be sorted out, Yak-3s were sent to attack the P-38s, succeeding in downing three or four aircraft for the loss of three Yak-3s. Inappropriately, many years later, American aviation artist Keith Ferris (a fine artist) chose to commemorate this event, apparently celebrating this as an early victory of the Americans over their eventual Cold War foe, instead of recognising it for the tragic mistake (on the part of the Americans) that it was. As a personal aside, I find it very unfortunate that all too often Cold War and anti-Communist prejudices have entered into analyses of the Soviet war effort during the Second World War.

Operations Over East Prussia

No account of the Yak-3's combat operations would be complete without mentioning the activities of this aircraft with the famous Normandie-Niemen regiment. The regiment received twenty Yak-3s directly from the factory on 13 August 1944. Having flown the Yak-1B and Yak-9, it did not take long for the regiment to master their new aircraft. However, tragedy soon struck the regiment when the Yak-3 of pilot Bertrand lost a piece of its right wing during a dive—a result of the wing's weakness during some types of dives. The aircraft crashed into the ground and the pilot was killed. This took place west of Gumbinnen (Gusev), East Prussia.

Over East Prussia, on 1 February 1945, ace Nikolaiy Grigor'evich Pinchuk (twenty-two victories by war's end) and his wingman were attacked by some late-model Bf 109s at 13,000 feet (3,962 m). The Yak-3s were able to manoeuvre the Bf 109s to a lower altitude, where the Yak-3s held the advantage, and each pilot shot down one of these fighters.

Berlin Strategic Offensive Operation (Battle of Berlin)

During April 1945, a Yak-3 of the 7th GvIAD flown by ace Arseniy Vasilyevich Vorozheykin (forty-six victories during the Second World War) was able to shoot down an Ar 234 jet-powered German bomber over Berlin. However, the kill was not officially recorded as the Ar 234's crash was obscured by the clouds of smoke that continually covered the German capital by this time.

Manchurian Strategic Offensive Operation

The 611th IAP was transferred from Europe to the Far East and took part in the Manchurian Campaign. As it found the Japanese presence in the air lacking, most of its missions consisted of reconnaissance and ground support, where it would have relied upon its gun armament as it was not equipped to carry rockets or bombs. These were the last Yak-3s to see any combat of any type.

Yak-3 in Detail

The following description details a typical production Great Patriotic War Yak-3 VK-105PF-2. Differences with other variants will be noted.

General Description

The Yak-3 was a single-engined single-seat cantilever monoplane fighter with an enclosed all-around vision cockpit and retractable main landing gear and tailwheel.

The aircraft was of mixed construction with a steel tube fuselage structure, covered in metal and plywood, wooden fixed tailplanes with fabric-covered metal structure control surfaces, and mixed-structure wings covered in plywood.

Fuselage

The fuselage structure was similar to the earlier Yakovlev fighters, featuring a steel tube framework, this framework being covered in metal panels on the forward fuselage, and plywood on the aft fuselage. The cross-section was the same as these earlier fighters. As with the Yak-1, the engine mount was integral with the fuselage framework, which helped to keep the aircraft lighter than if the engine mount was separate, as it was with the Yak-7 and Yak-9. The top of the rear fuselage was covered in plywood, while the sides and bottom were covered in fabric on the earliest Yak-3s, with all other Great Patriotic War Yak-3s having a 2-mm-thick plywood covering on the rear fuselage. All the Yak-3s had the cut-down rear fuselage to accommodate the all-around vision bubble-top cockpit canopy first introduced on the Yak-1B and also used on the last Yak-7Bs and all the Yak-9s. The canopy did not feature a flat armoured windscreen as with the Yak-9, but instead had a wrap-around unarmoured windscreen, which although streamlined, did cause some distortion to the pilot's vision.

Preserved Yak-3 showing hinged access panels under the cockpit canopy. All production Yakovlev wartime fighters had these access panels, which made maintenance easier. (*Viktor Kulikov's collection*)

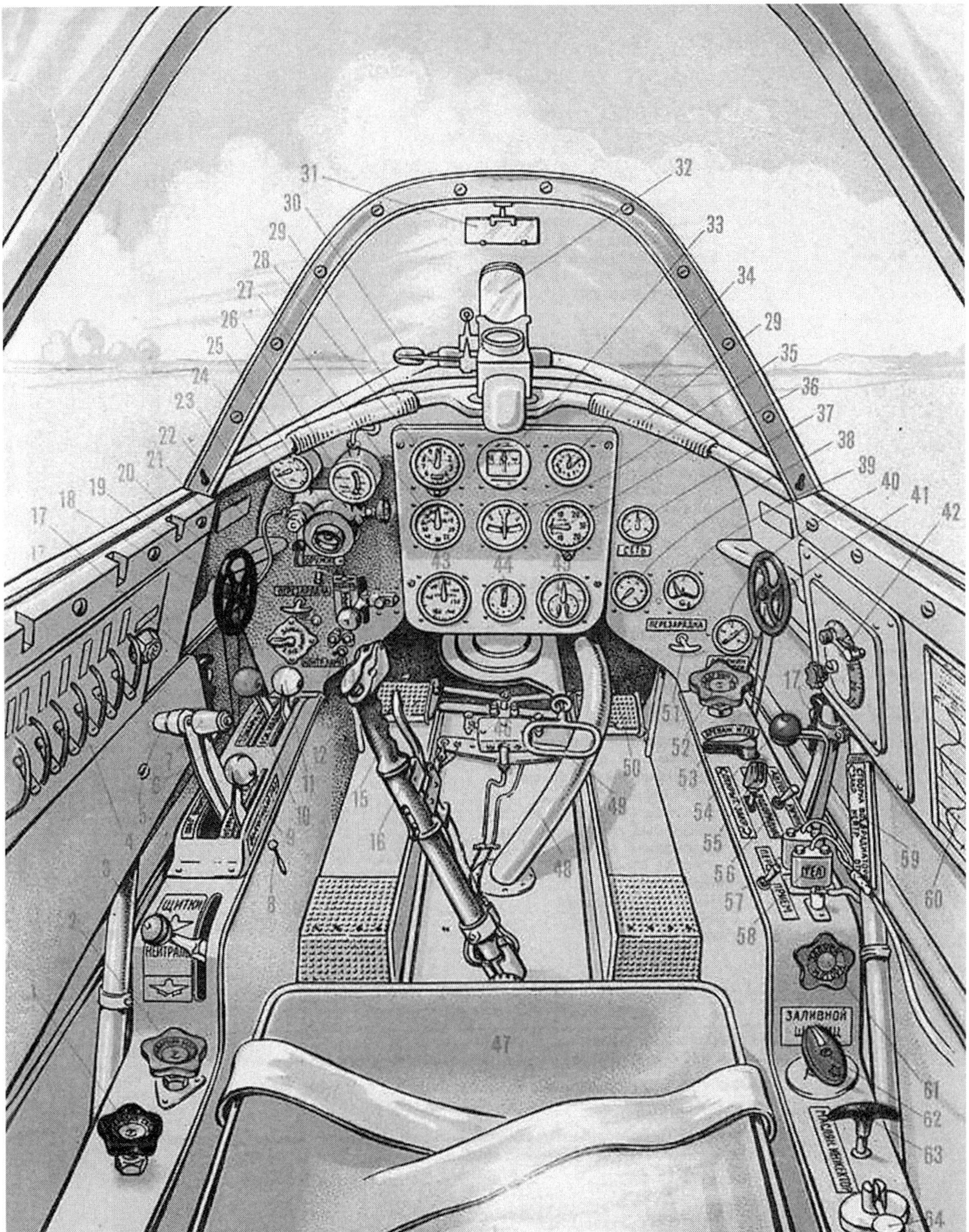

Yak-3 cockpit. (*Yak-3 Flight Manual*)

The instrument panel of preserved Yak-3. (*Viktor Kulikov's collection*)

Wings

The wings on the Yak-3 were of mixed construction, with two metal wing spars, wooden ribs, and wooden stringers all covered in plywood, which was then covered in doped fabric for a smooth finish. The wooden skin was riveted to the metal wing structure. Although smaller in span and area than the Yak-1, the Yak-3 wings featured the rounded wingtips of the Yak-1 and Yak-7, as opposed to the angular wingtips of the Yak-9. In contrast to the single-piece wings of earlier Yakovlev fighters, those of the Yak-3 were constructed in two parts and joined in the middle. This made replacing a damaged wing easier.

The wings were of a Clark YH aerofoil, with 14 per cent thickness at the root and 7 per cent thickness at the wingtip, compared to 15 per cent and 8 per cent respectively for the Yak-7 and Yak-9 (the Yak-1 had a chord of 15 per cent and 7 per cent). This made the wings not only smaller than the other Yakovlev fighters but also thinner, which helped make them lighter and more streamlined.

Tailplanes

As with the Yak-1, the Yak-3 featured mixed-construction tail surfaces, with the fixed surfaces being covered in plywood over a wooden structure, and the moveable control surfaces being covered in fabric over a dural structure. The fixed fin, which was integral with the fuselage, and the single-piece horizontal stabiliser were of a two-spar wooden structure. The experimental Yak-3U M-82 had tail surfaces of all-metal construction, as with the Yak-9.

Engine

The engine on the vast majority of Yak-3s was the Klimov VK-105PF-2 (M-105PF-2) twelve-cylinder vee-type liquid-cooled engine that developed 1,290 hp at its maximum rating. The engine drove a metal VISh-105SV-01 three-bladed constant-speed propeller. Some late and post-war Yak-3s were equipped with the similar but more powerful Klimov VK-107A engine (the same engine fitted to the Yak-9U), with 1,600 hp at its maximum output, but these Yak-3s were only produced in small quantity because of the continuing unreliability of this engine. The oil cooler and the supercharger intakes were in the wing roots, and the water radiator was located under the mid-fuselage in a semi-submerged installation.

Fuel System

The fuel system consisted of two main tanks in the wings, with a small service tank in the middle of the under-fuselage. The total fuel load was 97.74 gal (370 l). As with the other wartime Yakovlev fighters, detachable metal panels covered the tanks on the bottom of the wings. On the Yak-3, there were only two metal panels—one on each side. As with previous Yakovlev fighters, external fuel gauges were located on top of the inner portion of the wings, which indicated how much fuel was left in the tanks. Fuel tank caps were also located on top of the wings.

Controls

Most of the moveable control surfaces of the Yak-3 were of a dural structure, with a fabric covering, the exception being the underwing Schrenk-type flaps, which were all-metal. The 'joystick' type control column controlled the Frise-type ailerons and elevators, and twin rudder pedals controlled the rudder. The control surfaces were activated by push-pull rods for the ailerons and elevators and by wires for the rudder. The flaps were pneumatically operated. Although pneumatic systems were not as reliable as hydraulic systems, they were lighter, which was of paramount importance with the Yak-3.

Landing Gear

The main landing gear of the Yak-3 was similar to those of the Yak-1, with the main wheels 'trapped' against the doors with the wheel axles, which pointed outward towards the gear doors. The upper part of the main gear doors was attached to the wing, while the lower part was attached to the landing gear strut. The outer part of the wheels was covered by small doors that were attached to the underside of the wings, spring-loaded, and retracted mechanically. The landing gear themselves were retracted pneumatically and retracted into the wings ahead of the front wing spar. The tailwheel was fully retractable and was enclosed by two doors (as on the Yak-9), one on each side, which retracted inwards, the tailwheel retracting backwards. The tailwheel was equipped with an automatic locking mechanism which assisted ground handling, and which had been influenced by German designs of such a mechanism. The landing gear was operated pneumatically.

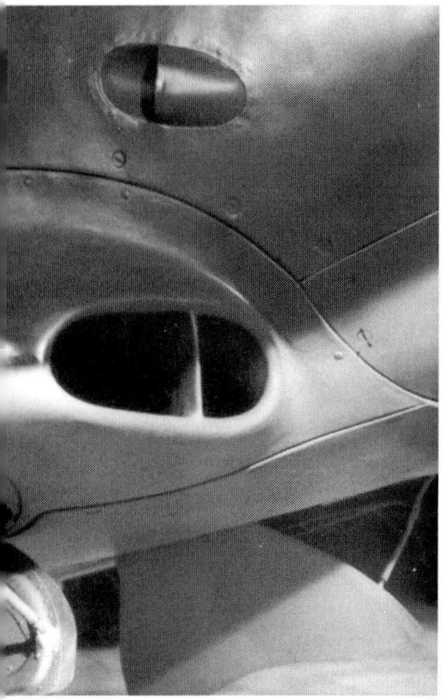

Above left: Bifurcated wing root air intake of preserved Yak-3. (*Viktor Kulikov's collection*)

Above right: The engine cowling of preserved Yak-3. (*Viktor Kulikov's collection*)

Below: Water radiator intake of preserved Yak-3. The bulges in front of the intake are retractable heat outlets for the engine (the Yak-9U also featured these). (*Viktor Kulikov's collection*)

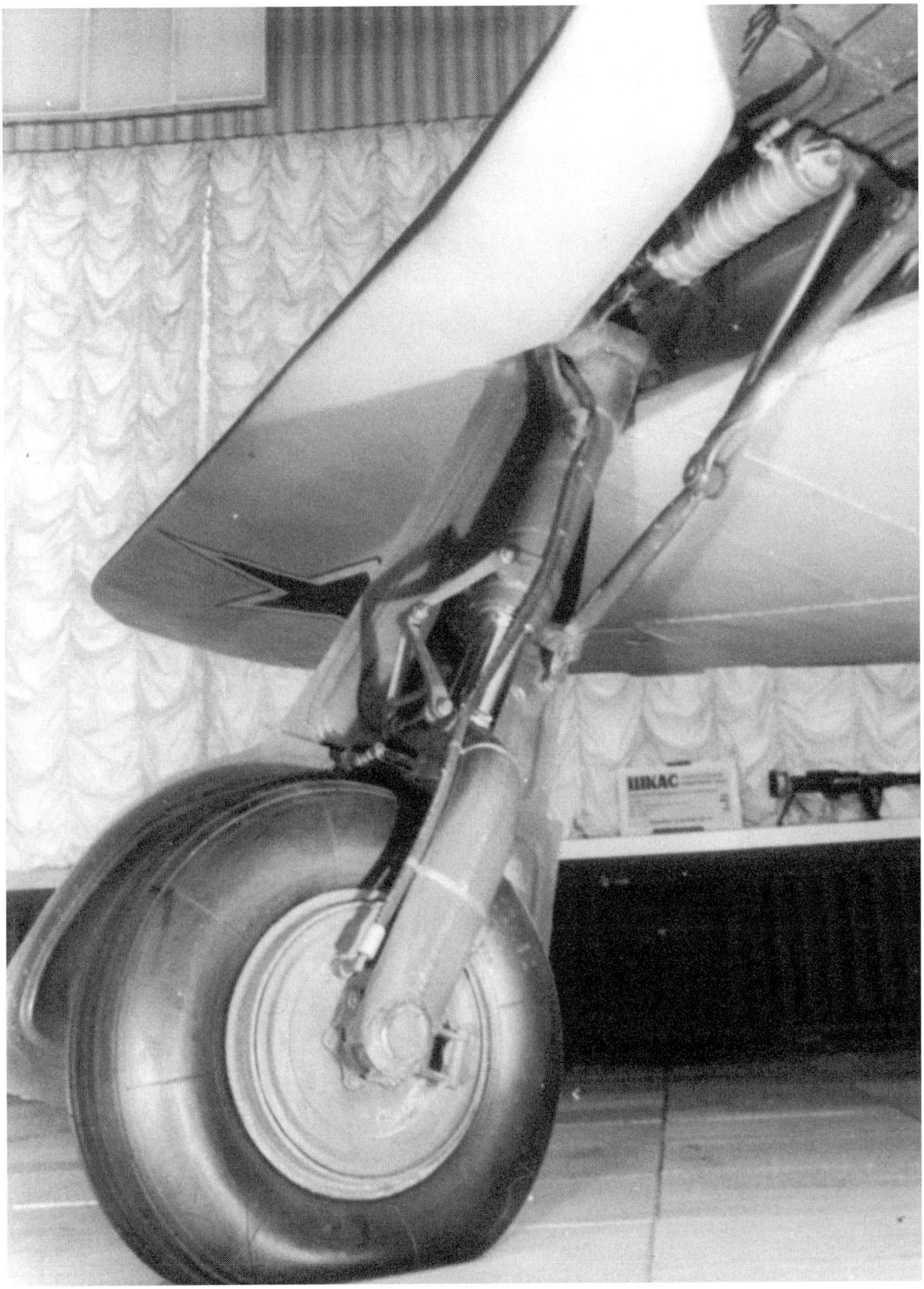

Starboard main landing gear of preserved Yak-3. (*Viktor Kulikov's collection*)

Preserved Yak-3 from the front. (*Viktor Kulikov's collection*)

Radio Equipment

All the production Yak-3s had the RSI-4 receiver, with half also being equipped with the RSI-3 transmitter. As with the Yak-9U, there was no antenna mast, as the radio line was attached directly to the front of the fin and ran to the rear canopy, where a line then connected it to the radio. The mainly post-war Yak-3P had a RSI-6M replacing the RSI-4.

Fixed Armament

The armament for most production Great Patriotic War Yak-3s was a ShVAK MP-20 20-mm cannon firing through the spinner with 120 rounds and two synchronised UBS 12.7-mm machine guns mounted on top of the engine cowling to fire through the propeller disc with 150 rounds each. This was the same armament fit that had characterised the Yak-7B and the Yak-9U. The earliest Yak-3s had only one UBS machine gun along with the 20-mm cannon, which was the standard fit on the Yak-9. After the war, more powerful armaments were tested, including the B-20 20-mm cannon, the N-37 37-mm cannon, and the N-45 45-mm cannon. The Yak-3P had three B-20 20-mm cannons with 120 rounds for the B-20M nose cannon and 130 rounds for the cowling-mounted B-20S cannons.

Disposable Armament

Unlike the other Yakovlev fighters, the Yak-3 was not equipped to carry either underwing rockets or bombs. When used in the ground attack role (as being a Soviet aircraft it inevitably was), it relied solely upon its gun armament for strafing ground targets.

Colour and Markings

During the Second World War, the Yak-3s were normally painted in the two-grey fighter scheme with AMT-11 Grey-Blue and AMT-12 Dark Grey topside over AMT-7 Blue underside (no production aircraft were painted in the earlier black/ green scheme). Some late war examples were painted AMT-11 Grey-Blue overall topside. The star insignia used was of the '1943' type. As with all Soviet fighters, personal and unit markings were not uncommon. For example, the unit marking of the Normandie-Niemen regiment was a white lightning bolt on the fuselage, as can be seen on one of the profiles in the colour plates section.

Experimental Yakovlev Single-Engined Fighters

The response from Yakovlev for the request from the Soviet government in 1939 for new modern fighters was met not just with the I-26 (which became the Yak-1) and the I-27 (which became the UTI-26, or Yak-7), but with the I-28 (Yak-5) and the I-30—related but different designs. The I-29 designation was used for an unrelated fighter design, described in the Experimental Fighters section, which was based upon the Yak-2 light bomber.

I-28 (Yak-5)

In addition to the I-26 design for a frontal fighter, Yakovlev also proposed a high-altitude fighter designated the I-28. This aircraft used the M-105PD engine of 1,160 hp, which was equipped with a V. A. Dollezhal-designed supercharger for high-altitude operation. The 'Yak-5' designation was also used on another Yakovlev design, but this was an experimental trainer based upon the UT-2 that did not go into production. The I-28 was the first of the Yakovlev fighters to be optimised for high-altitude flight and should not be confused with the Yatsenko I-28.

The I-28 was very similar to the I-26, but perhaps counterintuitively for a high-altitude aircraft, it featured shorter wings than the I-26, with leading-edge slats (31.96 feet (9.74m) to 32.81 feet (10 m)). The wings featured somewhat angular wingtips, which were very similar to those of the Yak-9. The tailplanes were of all-metal structure (as they would be on the Yak-7 and Yak-9), whereas on the I-26, the fixed portions were wooden. The aircraft was fitted with a RSI-3 radio. The fixed armament was the same as the I-26, with one ShVAK MP-20 20-mm cannon firing through the spinner with 120 rounds and two ShKAS machine guns mounted on top of the engine cowling with 750 rounds.

One major difference with the I-26 was the engine fitted was the experimental M-105PD fitted with the Dollezhal E-100 supercharger. The M-105PD was a better high-altitude engine compared to the standard M-105P of the Yak-1 (the production version of the I-26). Its first supercharger height was at 7,710 feet (2,350 m), compared to the 6,562 feet (2,000 m) of the M-105P, and the second height was at 21,522 feet (6,650 m) to 13,123 feet (4,000 m), which was a considerable improvement in height.

The aircraft flew for the first time on 1 December 1940. This first flight was not a success as the engine shook, smoked, and leaked oil. The aircraft had to be landed in a dead-stick (engine-off) landing after only twenty minutes of flight. Nonetheless, the sole I-28 did show a rather impressive top speed of 404 mph (650 kph) during testing. It also showed a high service ceiling of 39,370 feet (12,000 m). Despite the top speed and high service ceiling, the aircraft did not go into production because of problems with the M-105PD engine.

The aircraft was fitted with a new M-105PD engine and transferred to the LII, where it was tested until the end of 1942 to try and improve the engine, but with no great success. Development continued on the M-105PD engine and high-altitude Yakovlev fighters, and both the Yak-7PD (experimentally) and the Yak-9PD (operationally) were fitted with this engine.

I-30 (Yak-3: First Use of this Designation)

As the final Yakovlev design proposed in 1939, the I-30 was offered as a 'heavy' fighter, featuring powerful armament and a different wing design from the I-26. This aircraft, with its heavy armament, would be capable of intercepting and downing multi-engine bombers. The wing featured dihedral on the outer portion and also accommodated 20-mm cannons in the inner portion of this outer wing. The total armament was three ShVAK 20-mm cannons (one being in the nose) and two ShKAS machine guns mounted on top of the nose. The wings on the first I-30 (the I-30-1) were of all-metal construction, with a metal covering, except for the fabric-covered ailerons, and leading-edge slats were fitted. The tailplanes were of all-metal structure, with the control surfaces being fabric-covered. The fuselage structure was similar to most Yakovlev fighters, with a metal tubular structure with metal panels on the front portion, plywood on the top of the rear fuselage, and fabric covering

Yakovlev I-30 in 1941. (*Viktor Kulikov's collection*)

elsewhere. Originally, a M-105P with a supercharger was fitted, but this suffered from breakdowns and was replaced by a M-105P without the supercharger in 1941. The engine bearing structure was different from that used on the Yak-1, which, together with the new wings, made the I-30 a largely different aeroplane from the Yak-1 despite the similarity in outward appearance.

The I-30-2 *Dooblyor* differed from the first prototype by having wooden outer wings, instead of the all-metal wings of the I-30-1. The armament remained the same.

Although a decision was made to produce the I-30 as the 'Yak-3', with metal wings, none were ever built beyond the two prototypes, the reason being that the Yakovlev OKB was too preoccupied with the production of the Yak-1 to spend time and resources on the I-30. Another reason for not producing the mostly metal I-30/Yak-3 was the shortage of suitable metals in the wartime Soviet Union. In the end, the 'Yak-3' designation was reused for the production version of the lightened development of the Yak-1, the Yak-1M.

Conclusion

The Yakovlev fighters were the most heavily produced Soviet fighters of the Second World War, with over 30,000 being produced during the war. The Yak-1, the first Yakovlev fighter, was the best of the three new fighters the Soviets possessed at the beginning of the Great Patriotic War (the others being the LaGG-3 and the MiG-3). It was a somewhat immature aircraft at first, but the basic airframe was developed in succeeding models until the excellent Yak-9U and Yak-3 went into service in 1944. The Yak-7 was an interesting aircraft in being a fighter redesigned into a trainer that was then redesigned back into a fighter. The Yak-9 was the most versatile fighter that the Soviets possessed, and the Yak-3 was the lightest dedicated fighter at the end of the Second World War, as well as one of the best, excelling at dogfighting. Together with the Yak-9U and the La-7, it was unmatched by any Axis aircraft at low altitudes.

The Yakovlev fighters were used from the very beginning of the Great Patriotic War until the end of the Second World War, continuing in Soviet and foreign use for some years after the war, as well as being developed into a post-war trainer (the Yak-11 'Mule') and even jet-powered fighters (the Yak-15 and Yak-17 'Feather'). With the Lavochkin fighters, they were responsible for wresting control of the air away from the Luftwaffe, and their importance to the Red Air Force can hardly be overstated. Along with the Il-2 attack bomber, and the Pe-2 light bomber, the Yakovlev fighters were the most important aeroplanes in the Soviet aerial arsenal, both numerically and in terms of overall effect.

Yakovlev Fighter Specifications

N.B. Metric measurements are in parentheses				
Type	I-26-1	Yak-1	Yak-1B	Yak-7A
Year	1940	1941	1943	1941
Engine	M-105P	M-105P	M-105P	M-105P
Max. Power (Horsepower)	1,100	1,100	1,100	1,100
Fixed Armament	2 × ShKAS 7.62-mm, 3 × UBS 12.7-mm machine guns	2 × ShKAS 7.62-mm machine guns, 1 × ShVAK MP-20 20-mm cannon	1 × UBS 12.7-mm machine gun, 1 × ShVAK MP-20 20-mm cannon	2 × ShKAS 7.62-mm machine guns, 1 × ShVAK MP-20 20-mm cannon
Disposable Armament	N/A	6 × RS-82 Rockets	N/A	6 × RS-82 Rockets
Length—feet (m)	27.89 (8.5)	27.89 (8.5)	27.89 (8.5)	27.89 (8.5)
Wingspan—feet (m)	32.81 (10)	32.81 (10)	32.81 (10)	32.81 (10)
Weight (Empty)—lb (kg)	4,409 (2,000)	5,176 (2,348)	5,055 (2,293)	5,401 (2,450)
Weight (Loaded)—lb (kg)	5,732 (2,600)	6,277 (2,847)	6,314 (2,864)	6,471 (2,935)
Max. Speed at Sea Level—mph (kph)	301 (485)	304 (490)	335 (539)	308 (495)
Top Speed—mph (kph)	373 (600)	359 (577)	379 (610)	355 (571)
Range—miles (km)	-	435 (700)	548 (882)	400 (643)
Service Ceiling—feet (m)	36,581 (11,150)	34,449 (10,500)	29,528 (9,000)	31,168 (9,500)
Turn Time (sec)	24-25 (for I-26-2)	19	17-18	21-22

Yak-7B	Yak-9	Yak-9D	Yak-9T	Yak-9U	Yak-3
1942	1942	1943	1943	1944	1944
M-105PF	M-105PF	M-105PF	M-105PF	VK-107A (M-107A)	VK-105PF-2 (M-105PF-2)
1,260	1,260	1,260	1,260	1,600	1,290 (YG/airwar. ru – 1,240)
2 × UBS 12.7-mm machine guns, 1 × ShVAK MP-20 20-mm cannon	1 × UBS 12.7-mm machine gun, 1 × ShVAK MP-20 20-mm cannon	1 × UBS 12.7-mm machine gun, 1 × ShVAK MP-20 20-mm cannon	1 × UBS 12.7-mm machine gun, 1 × NS-37 37-mm cannon	2 × UBS 12.7-mm machine guns, 1 × ShVAK MP-20 20-mm cannon	2 × UBS 12.7-mm machine guns, 1 × ShVAK MP-20 20-mm cannon
6 × RS-82 Rockets (on early aircraft) and 2 × 220-lb (100-kg) bombs	N/A	N/A	N/A	N/A	N/A
27.89 (8.5)	27.89 (8.5)	27.89 (8.5)	28.41 (8.66)	28.05 (8.55)	27.89 (8.5)
32.81 (10)	31.96 (9.74)	31.96 (9.74)	31.96 (9.74)	31.96 (9.74)	30.18 (9.2)
5,467 (2,480)	4,850 (2,200)	5,181 (2,350)	5,267 (2,389)	5,461 (2,477)	4,691 (2,128)
6,636 (3,010)	6,327 (2,870)	6,872 (3,117)	6,429 (2,916)	7,064 (3,204)	5,725 (2,597)
319 (514)	323 (520)	332 (535)	319 (514)	357 (575)	352 (567)
354 (570)	372 (599)	367 (591)	359 (577)	418 (672)	397 (640)
401 (645)	590 (950)	845 (1,360)	457 (735)	419 (675)	403 (648)
32,480 (9,900)	36,417 (11,100)	29,856 (9,100)	32,808 (10,000)	34,941 (10,650)	34,121 (10,400)
19	16-17	20	18-19	20	21

7
Twin-Engined Fighters

Although several twin-engined fighter designs were tested shortly before and during the Second World War by the Soviets, none of these designs went into production (these experimental designs are described further on in the Experimental Fighters section). The only twin-engined Soviet fighter to go into production during the war was the Pe-3, a development of the Pe-2 dive-bomber, which had itself started life as a twin-engined high-altitude fighter. Some twin-engined Douglas A-20 Boston light bombers were used in combat as night-fighters, but these were American-built Lend-Lease aircraft.

Petlyakov

Since the Pe-2 dive-bomber had been developed from a fighter, the experimental VI-100 high-altitude fighter, it was perhaps inevitable that the Pe-2 itself would be modified back into a fighter. This heavy fighter version was designated as the 'Pe-3'. In addition to the purpose-built Pe-3 fighter, a small number of Pe-2 bombers were modified for use as night-fighters.

Pe-2

This twin-engined aircraft, designed by Vladimir Mikhailovich Petlyakov (1891–1942), was originally a high-altitude fighter project, designated as the '100' and designed, like Andrey Tupolev's Tu-2 ('103' or 'ANT-58), while Petlyakov was still under NKVD detention in a *sharashka* (TsKB-29). As the VI-100, it first flew on 22 December 1939. However, what the VVS desired and felt it needed at the time was a modern dive-bomber (the VVS had seen the success of the German Ju 87 in Western Europe), not a high-altitude fighter. The VVS already had the MiG-1 high-altitude fighter being developed, which would be able to handle any high-flying attackers. In addition, the Soviets had purchased and examined the twin-engined Ju 88 in 1940, which was capable of dive-bombing and were impressed enough to want a twin-engined

Pe-2 (or Pe-3) with Gneys (Gneiss) radar. Note the aerials on the wings and the nose. (*Viktor Kulikov's collection*)

dive-bomber of their own. Therefore, the Pe-2, as it was named from 1942, was redesigned from a fighter into a dive-bomber.

First entering service in 1940, the Pe-2 was used throughout the Great Patriotic War as a dive-bomber, level bomber, reconnaissance aircraft, and ground attack aircraft. Even after the entry into service of the Tu-2 twin-engined tactical bomber, it continued to be used as a dive-bomber as it was found to be more suitable for that role than the Tu-2, which had originally been designed and built with that capability (having also been influenced by the Ju 88).

Equipped with the *Gneys* ('Gneiss') radar, a few Pe-2s were used as night-fighters in the second half of the Great Patriotic War. They were used by the PVO for protection against Axis bombers. It is doubtful if they saw much action.

Pe-2I (1941)

The first attempt to convert the Pe-2 design back into a fighter involved the Pe-2I, where the 'I' stood for *Istrebitel'*, or 'Fighter'. At the end of August 1941 Z.22 began converting a Pe-2 into this experimental fighter. In addition to the normal nose armament of one UBK 12.7-mm machine guns and two ShKAS machine guns, two ShVAK 20-mm cannons were installed in the bomb bay. One UBT machine gun in a ventral fairing comprised the defensive armament. The aircraft was a two-seater and like the Pe-3 had no dive brakes. The aircraft had a maximum speed of 336 mph (540 kph), and a service ceiling of 31,168 feet (9,500 m). The aircraft did not go into production and this first Pe-2I remained a one-off. The second aircraft to have the 'Pe-2I' designation was an improved Pe-2 bomber and went into very limited production in 1945.

Pe-2VI

This aircraft was intended as a high-altitude fighter version of the Pe-2, for which the Pe-2 had been originally designed, as the VI-100, before being redesigned as a dive-bomber. This redesign was under the control of Aleksandr I. Putilov. The Petlyakov OKB received the go-ahead to construct this version in December 1942. As with many Soviet high-altitude fighters of the GPW, the Pe-2VI was equipped with the M-105PD engines. It was also equipped with a pressurised cabin. This cabin did not perform well in tests. The Pe-2VI achieved a top speed of 351 mph (565 kph) and had a service ceiling of 36,089 feet (11,000 m). Due to problems with the cabin and the M-105PD engines, production did not take place on the Pe-2VI, and apparently only three were completed. Most importantly, during 1943, the continued production and improvement of the Pe-2 were far more pressing issues at this time for A. I. Putilov to attend to.

Pe-3

The Pe-3 was a heavy fighter developed from the Pe-2 dive-bomber, described above. Unlike the VI-100 fighter, from which the Pe-2 was developed, the Pe-3 was not optimised for the high-altitude role, but it was rather intended as a general-purpose long-range heavy fighter. In this respect, it was similar to the British Bristol Beaufighter and the German Bf 110 twin-engined fighters. Unlike the British and German twin-engined fighters, only a relatively small number of Pe-3s of all types were produced, 360 in total.

When produced as a fighter, the Pe-2 was given the designation of 'Pe-3' (odd numbers being used for fighters). Although built as a fighter, it still retained some of the bombing capability of the Pe-2 and was often used as a bomber, despite its reduced

Early Pe-3 undergoing trials in Moscow in September 1941. Note the slat on the leading edge of the wing and the solid nose. (*Viktor Kulikov's collection*)

bomb load compared to the Pe-2 (it no longer carried the fuselage bomb bay, this space now being occupied by a fuel tank). The nacelle bomb bays remained. It was also frequently used as a reconnaissance aircraft alongside the Pe-2.

The circumstances of the Pe-3's genesis was rather remarkable. The Soviets felt they needed a twin-engined fighter, something along the lines of the German Bf 110, an aircraft they had examined in great detail before the Great Patriotic War. They also felt that due to the necessity to get this aircraft into production as quickly as possible (a war was raging), it needed to be based upon an existing design. An obvious choice was the Pe-2, which had originally been designed as a fighter (the VI-100). The GKO issued a decree on 2 August 1941 for Petlyakov to create this new fighter, with the prototype ready for delivery by 6 August 1941. Amazingly, Petlyakov was able to suitably modify a Pe-2 into the Pe-3 within this timeframe, and this aircraft was flown for the first time on 7 August 1941, by Maj. Fyodorov. On 8 August 1941, NII VVS test pilot Col. Vasiliy Andreyevich Stepanchonok (1901–1943) completed the manufacturer's tests, and the Pe-3 was submitted for state testing. This must have set some sort of record for accelerated development and testing of an aircraft, even in the wartime Soviet Union.

Among the changes made to the Pe-3 as compared to the Pe-2 was the deletion of the radio-operator/gunner, leaving a two-member crew. As a result, the ventral gondola and the rear-firing machine gun were deleted. The gunner position behind the pilot was retained and manned by the radio-operator. As with the Pe-2, this position initially used a manually operated gun that was later replaced by a powered turret (in the Pe-3bis). This manually operated gun was a ShKAS machine gun.

Pe-3bis

This variant of the Pe-3 was an effort to upgrade the aircraft, especially in regards to its gun armament. One of the main complaints about the Pe-3 was the relatively light forward-firing armament in the nose. It had a fixed armament of only one ShVAK 20-mm cannon and one ShKAS 7.62-mm machine gun, compared to the much more powerful fixed armament of two 20-mm cannons and four 7.92-mm machine guns with the equivalent Bf 110.

Interestingly, part of the impetus for the changes that resulted in the Pe-3bis resulted from a letter written by a squadron commander named Capt. Zhatkov and sent to Secretary of the Council of People's Commissars Georgiy Maksimilianovich Malenkov (1902–88). In this remarkable letter, Capt. Zhatkov complained about the armament, stating the need for ShVAK cannons in the nose and the replacement of the defensive ShKAS of the navigator with a UBT machine gun. Capt. Zhatkov's criticisms, and those of other pilots, were taken to heart, and the Petlyakov OKB made changes in September 1941 to a Pe-3 to modify it into what became the Pe-3bis. This modified aircraft was tested in September and October 1941.

One of the main changes between the Pe-3bis and the earlier Pe-3s was the provision of a VUB-1 rotating turret with a UBT heavy machine gun, which greatly improved the defensive armament. The nose was now equipped with two UBK machine guns and one ShVAK 20-mm cannon. The wings were now equipped with leading-edge slats to improve take-off and landing characteristics, which were never the Pe-2/Pe-3's

Pe-3bis from Z.39 in April 1942. (*Viktor Kulikov's collection*)

greatest strength. Although a bit slower than the Pe-3 because of a slightly greater weight, the Pe-3bis handled better.

The first production Pe-3bis (20 aircraft) entered service with the 9th BBAP (light bomber air regiment) in June 1942. The Pe-3bis were then sent to the 2nd, 4th and 40th separate long-range reconnaissance regiments. Several aircraft were received by the 9th Reconnaissance Squadron, and later were used by the 1st and 39th Air Regiments of the VVS. According to reviews from the front, many pilots felt that the Pe-3bis was a better aircraft than the standard Pe-2. With the AVMF, the largest number of Pe-3bis (no more than a dozen) were sent to the 65th Aviation Regiment. These aircraft served from 1942 until the end of the Great Patriotic War. Some were equipped with radar and served as night-fighters. It is not clear from the record if they served in the Manchurian Campaign. The Pe-3s, both the Pe-3 and the Pe-3bis, apparently saw greater use as a bomber than as a fighter, an indication of the Soviet Union's bias, or at best, indifference, towards twin-engined fighters.

Pe-3M

This experimental version of the Pe-3 was developed in 1944 by Vladimir Mikhailovich Myasishchev (1902–1978), who had taken over the Petlyakov OKB's control upon the death of Vladimir Petlyakov in an aeroplane crash in 1942. It was the final version of the Pe-3. It was characterised by a revised armament: the rearward-firing ShKAS was removed, two ShVAK 20-mm cannons were fitted in the nose, and it also carried three UBS 12.7-mm machine guns. In addition, two of the DAG-10 grenade dispensers, which launched grenades to the rear for defensive purposes, were also fitted. The engines were VK-105PFs. The maximum speed was 339 mph (545 kph), and the service ceiling was 31,168 feet (9,500 m). Despite good flight characteristics, the aircraft was not produced in series, and only one was built.

Conclusion

Unlike other Second World War combatants, twin-engined fighters were not heavily used in the Soviet Union, with the purpose-built Pe-3 seeing more use as a bomber and reconnaissance aircraft than as a heavy or long-range fighter or night-fighter. The other twin-engined fighter designs that were flown and tested during the war did not even enter production. The Soviets preferred their fighters to be small, single-engined, and manoeuvrable. A benefit of single-engined fighters was that they were smaller, used less raw materials, and could be built in larger quantities than twin-engined fighters. Building these twin-engined fighters would have taken resources from their single-engined fighters, and the Soviets were reluctant to do anything that disturbed the production of their single-engined fighters. The disparity in importance between the two types of aircraft for the Soviets can be seen in the production numbers; 360 Pe-3 twin-engined fighters were built, compared to over 22,000 Lavochkin single-engined fighters, and over 36,000 Yakovlev single-engined fighters.

Since the main role of the Soviet fighter was to support the front-line troops and provide cover for the aircraft that provided the troops with ground support, they were normally based near the front lines and range was not normally a great concern, and there was thus little need for a long-range twin-engined fighter. As the long-range bombers operated mainly at night, there was little necessity for twin-engined escort fighters. The few radar-equipped twin-engined night-fighters that were used by the Soviets consisted of modified Pe-2s, Pe-3s, and American-built A-20s, and the Soviets had no purpose-built night-fighter designs.

Twin-Engined Fighter Specifications

N.B. Metric measurements are in parentheses				
Type	VI-100	Pe-2 Gneys (Gneiss)	Pe-3	Pe-3bis
Year	1940	1943	1941	1942
Engine	2 × M-105PD	2 × M-105PD	2 × M-105R	2 × M-105RA
Max. Power (Horsepower)	1,160	1,160	1,100	1,100
Gun Armament	2 × ShKAS 7.62-mm machine guns, 2 × ShVAK KP-20 20-mm cannons	1 × UBK 12.7-mm machine gun, 2 × ShVAK KP-20 20-mm cannons, defensive armament of 1 × ShKAS 7.62-mm machine gun, and 1 × UBT 12.7-mm machine gun	2 x UBK 12.7-mm machine gun, defensive armament of 2 × ShKAS 7.62-mm machine guns	2 x UBK 12.7-mm machine gun, 1 × ShVAK SP-20 20-mm cannons, defensive armament of 1 × ShKAS 7.62-mm machine gun, and 1 × UBT 12.7-mm machine gun

Disposable Armament	2,205 lb (1,000 kg) of bombs	1,543 lb (700 kg) of bombs	1,543 lb (700 kg) of bombs	4 × RS-82 rockets, 2 x RS-132, 1,543 lb (700 kg) of bombs
Length—feet (m)	41.63 (12.69)	41.57 (12.67)	41.57 (12.67)	41.57 (12.67)
Wing span—feet (m)	56.27 (17.15)	56.20 (17.13)	56.20 (17.13)	56.20 (17.13)
Weight (Empty)—lb (kg)	11,402 (5,172)	12,721 (5,770)	12,632 (5,730)	12,820 (5,815)
Weight (Loaded)—lb (kg)	16,006 (7,260)	17,053 (7,735)	17,328 (7,860)	17,350 (7,870)
Max. Speed at Sea Level—mph (kph)	283 (455)	282 (454)	275 (442)	272 (438)
Top Speed—mph (kph)	332 (535)	336 (540)	332 (535)	329 (530)
Range—miles (km)	870 (1,400)	1,305 (2,100)	1,336 (2,150)	1,243 (2,000)
Service Ceiling—feet (m)	40,026 (12,200)	31,168 (9,500)	28,215 (8,600)	28,871 (8,800)
Turn Time (sec)	-	29.5 (for Pe-2 Series 110)	-	35.1

8

Colours and Markings in General

I have discussed the camouflage and insignia used for particular aircraft. In this section, I shall give a more comprehensive summary of Soviet colours and markings as they applied to Second World War aircraft.

Pre-War

During the late 1930s, Soviet aircraft were normally painted in a light grey—AE-9 gloss light grey and/or a silver finish, AII aluminium, or in the case of all-metal aircraft, they were sometimes left in a natural metal finish. However, none of the operational Soviet fighters in the late 1930s were all-metal. On aircraft such as the I-15bis and the I-153, which had both metal and fabric covering, the metal areas were painted light grey, and the fabric-covered areas were painted silver (or aluminium). Some aircraft, such as the I-16 were painted in a green colour, AII *3* Green. This colour would have been over light grey/silver under surfaces. Many of these aircraft retained their pre-war colours into the Second World War and even the Great Patriotic War.

Khalkhin-Gol

An interesting exception to the normal pre-war paint schemes occurred in the Battle of the Khalkhin-Gol. In this conflict, some light grey, silver, or natural metal-finished aircraft, such as the I-153, had green painted onto them as *ad hoc* field-applied camouflage. This camouflage consisted of irregular markings, such as 'squiggles' or 'blotches' of green paint, applied directly over the light grey, silver, or metal finish on the topside of these aircraft. The paint used was apparently the '3B' green paint. Some of these aircraft, both fighters and bombers (such as I-153s and Tupolev SBs), still retained this scheme into the early part of the Great Patriotic War.

Crash-landed I-153 at the Khalkhin-Gol in 1939. This aircraft shows very well the field-applied green lines that were painted over the standard aluminium and grey paint. (*Viktor Kulikov's collection*)

Early Second World War

In May 1940, a directive ordered that Soviet military aircraft should be finished with a green topside over a blue underside. The green utilised on the upper surfaces of the fighters was AII *3* (Green—where 'II' is the Roman numeral for '2' and the *3* is actually the Cyrillic letter representing 'Z' for *Zashchitniy*, or 'Protective (Colour)' in Russian). The blue utilised for the under surfaces was AII Blue (Sv.gol.—*Svetlo Goluboi* or 'Light Blue' in Russian). The red stars were to be outlined in black and consisted of stars on the fuselage, and the tops and bottoms of the wings. Instead of being repainted in blue, evidently, some aircraft retained the underside colour(s) they had originally been painted in, such as light grey and/or silver. Some aircraft with this scheme can be seen in the colour plates section.

This directive was not followed immediately, and the pre-war schemes of light grey and aluminium continued to be used on some aircraft such as the I-153 into the early period of the Great Patriotic War. As mentioned previously, some aircraft still retained their field-applied green mottling or squiggle sover light grey/silver camouflage from the Khalkhin-Gol conflict.

Great Patriotic War: Early to Mid-War

Despite opinions to the contrary, Soviet wartime camouflage was actually quite simple. It was not the conceptual 'minefield' that some in the West still suppose it to be. Only a handful of colours were used (unlike Luftwaffe colours, where no one today seems to be able to even agree on what colour RLM 83 was, for example). These Soviet paints were applied in patterns that generally complied with the officially decreed patterns. If the Soviets were not as uniform in their application of camouflage patterns as RAF fighters were, for example, they certainly did not have an 'anything goes' attitude, as is commonly supposed. Another misconception is that non-aircraft paints were regularly used; with only a few very rare exceptions, specifically manufactured aviation paints were used for VVS aircraft.

The standard early Great Patriotic War camouflage for wooden and mixed-construction aircraft was black (AMT-6 in Soviet parlance) and green (normally AMT-4, but also A-19f and AII *3*) over blue (AMT-7 Blue, which seems to have been the standard underside paint for all fighters). These colours were applied to all types of Soviet combat aircraft. The topside was painted with alternating bands of black and green, although the application of these bands varied from aircraft type to aircraft type (and sometimes from aircraft to aircraft for a given type, especially early in the Great Patriotic War). Colour profiles of aircraft with this scheme can be seen in the colour plates section.

The brown and green schemes, seen on many colour profiles for Great Patriotic War fighters, especially in older books and profiles, were actually black and green (AMT-6 Black and AMT-4 Green), and the brown colour that often appears in these colour profiles (and in plastic kit instructions) is a misinterpretation of wartime photographs.

The AMT nitrocellulose lacquers were normally a matte to satiny finish when first applied, which would have then weathered to a more matte finish.

In the initial part of the Great Patriotic War, fighters, which were of mixed construction or wooden aircraft, such as the Yakovlev and Lavochkin fighters, were still painted in AII Blue and AII *3* Green. These colours were soon changed to AMT lacquers, such as AMT-6 Black and AMT-4 Green over AMT-7 Blue.

One change made to aircraft after the beginning of the Great Patriotic War was that propellers were painted overall black. Before the Great Patriotic War, these had been left in their natural metal, with only two-thirds or so of the inner part of the propeller blades painted in black to prevent the pilot from being blinded by the sunlight reflecting off the shiny metal blades. The blades were painted overall black during the war as a safety measure and to prevent the bare metal blades from reflecting the sunlight while on the ground or in the air, possibly attracting the unwelcome attention of marauding German aircraft. Soviet-built aircraft did not have yellow propeller tips, unlike British and American aeroplanes during the Second World War.

During the winter, a temporary white finish was sometimes used, called distemper paint or MK-7, which was normally a mixture of white chalk powder and casein glue, with the 'MK' standing for *Melo-kleyevaya Kraska* or 'Chalk-glue Paint'. This was sometimes applied over the normal or 'summer' camouflage (Russian historian Mikhail Orlov sometimes refers to this as 'spring' camouflage). Here is where the situation gets a bit more complicated. There seem to have been no real standards as to how the white was applied; it varied from aircraft to aircraft and regiment to regiment (and quite possibly within the regiment itself). Although it was common to see the white applied to the entire topside, especially with factory-applied winter camouflage, this was by no means always done in the field, and if done, it was done with varying results. Sometimes, the white was applied evenly (especially if it was applied at the factory with an airgun); sometimes, it was applied unevenly in the field with a brush.

At times you will see a patchy white camouflage on the nose—in these instances, it is possible that the use of the tarpaulins may have worn off some of the temporary white finish. Sometimes, white tarpaulins were also placed on the wings, which negated the need for MK-7 on the wings also, at least as far as camouflaging the aeroplane on the ground. Early in the war, with the very real threat of intruding Axis aircraft attacking airfields, the winter camouflage served not only to protect the aeroplane while flying at low altitudes, but also to provide camouflage when it was parked on the ground.

The white covering was applied evenly with an airgun at the factory, whereas at other times, the white was applied roughly, sometimes with a brush, with the summer camouflage showing through in many places. It is also possible that when first applied, the white overcoat was relatively pristine (again, especially with factory-applied winter camouflage), but the undercoat showed through more as time went on and the aircraft became more weathered, with the temporary white paint wearing or washing off. Profiles of winter-camouflaged aircraft can be seen in the colour plates section.

Great Patriotic War: Mid- to Late-War

The black/green scheme was superseded by the two-grey 'fighter' scheme of AMT-11 Grey-Blue and AMT-12 Dark Grey topside over AMT-7 Blue underside. This change was made from September 1943 on. This scheme can be seen in the colour plates section.

White distemper paint (MK-7) was applied over the summer camouflage in the winter of 1942–43 and the winter of 1943–44, but not the winter of 1944–45, when this practice seems to have been abandoned.

As the concentration of Soviet aircraft grew, identification markings became more important to keep track of the aircraft from different units as they flew together in massed formations. Thus, for example, fighters sprouted stripes on the fuselage, the wings, coloured fins and rudders, and distinctively coloured spinners and cowlings, all in an effort to distinguish their particular unit (or even place within that unit, such as which flight in a *polk*, with the different flights having differently coloured spinners, for example). As the Luftwaffe was scarcely to be seen anymore late in the Great Patriotic War, attack while on the ground was no longer a concern for the Red Air Force. Therefore, Soviet fighters became more colourful as control and identification in the air increased in importance with the large formations that these aircraft were now flying in. This lack of Luftwaffe fighters also explains the abandoning of winter camouflage after the winter of 1943–44 as the extra effort in applying (and removing) the white distemper paint was no longer justified in the late war period.

Insignia

The standard Red Air Force insignia was the red star, which had been in use since the Russian Civil War of 1918–22. According to a May 1940 directive (for aircraft with a green upper surface), red stars with a black outline were specified to be applied in six positions—the fuselage and lower and upper wing surfaces. The usage of these black-outlined stars persisted long into the Great Patriotic War, especially on certain aircraft types such as the Lavochkin fighters, although no stars were applied to the upper wings after the beginning of the Great Patriotic War (those that were present were usually fairly quickly painted over).

A June 1941 directive (for aircraft with the black/green camouflage scheme) did not specify any border—stars were supposed to be borderless with this scheme. Factories did generally follow this as an instruction, but in operational units, white, black, or silver borders, were added to make the stars more visible against the black/green background. Stars were not painted on the upper wings. In addition, there would normally be stars on the rudder and the fuselage. The 1940-style black-bordered stars were still applied in some factories, appearing on fighters well into 1943.

From September 1943, for aircraft with the two-grey scheme, stars with a white border and a thin red outline around it were specified. This directive has been followed to the present day. These stars—called 'Victory Stars' by at least one source, although perhaps more properly referred to as '1943' stars, since that is when they went into effect—still appear on modern Russian aircraft.

The so-called 'Kremlin Star' (a 'relief' star in two shades of red to give it a three-dimensional effect, mimicking the stars mounted over the Kremlin, hence the name) was something of a decorative element applied by units to individual aeroplanes; it was like a personal marking. Strangely, the Kremlin Star was not necessarily applied to all the positions on a single aircraft; for example, it might be used only on the fuselage and not on the wings. The different types of stars can be seen on the aircraft profiles in the colour plates section.

Aircraft (Tactical) Numbers

Most Soviet warplanes, in the ADD (Long-Range Aviation), AVMF, PVO, and VVS bore some sort of tactical or aircraft number, known as a *bort*, on the tail, fuselage, or, much more rarely, both. The numbers were typically red, white, or blue (or a combination of these colours), were normally one or two digits (although three-digit *borts* were seen), and the style and font varied from regiment to regiment. Sometimes, the numbers had a border around them. These numbers were not applied at the factory, but in the field by the regiments. Although you will see it in colour profiles, yellow was rarely used during the Great Patriotic War as this was the Axis identification colour. Yellow borts were seen applied on aircraft early in the Great Patriotic War, but this practice was soon discontinued because of the possibility of misidentification with Axis aircraft. Yellow, however, was commonly used before the Great Patriotic War for the *borts*, for example, during the Winter War. Examples of the different styles of borts can be seen in the colour plates section.

Personal Markings

There does not seem to have been any specific official prohibition against the use of personal markings on ADD, AVMF, PVO, and VVS aircraft, and these were common on Soviet fighters and other Soviet aircraft during the Second World War, especially during the Great Patriotic War. Animals were commonly used as markings. Erotic themes such as nude or semi-nude pin-ups were not used, and supernatural or religious themes do not seem to have been used either. One exception to this was the use of a coat of arms featuring St George slaying the dragon; this was the traditional coat of arms for Moscow and was no doubt also seen as an analogy for the Soviet Union (St George) defeating Nazi Germany (the dragon). This was made more explicit with the markings on General Georgiy Nefyodovich Zakharov's (1908-96) Yak-3 aircraft, where 'St George' was dressed as a Soviet general (apparently General Zakharov himself), fighting a snake (in place of the dragon) with Nazi Propaganda Minister (Paul) Joseph Goebbels' (1897–1945) head.

Common markings were patriotic slogans such as *Za Rodinu!* ('For the Motherland!') or *Za Stalina!* ('For Stalin!'), as examples. Animals—such as lions, bears, and eagles—were common. Examples can be found in the colour plates section.

Kill markings were normally represented by small red stars, not the German-style crosses (*Balkenkreuz*, 'Balkan Cross' in German) seen on Western Allied aircraft; any use of German insignia or symbols was discouraged unless it was in a clearly derogatory way—for example, an eagle clutching a broken swastika in its talons. An exception was the French-manned Normandie-Niemen unit, which, in the Western European style, represented its kills with the German *Balkenkreuz*.

A special type of aeroplane was the presentation aircraft. This was presented to a pilot who had distinguished himself in combat, and it might even be inscribed with the pilot's name. It also often had an inscription stating who the donor was, whether a *kolkhoz* (collective farm), a *komsomolets* (a Communist youth organisation), or even an individual who had purchased it. Part of the responsibility of flying a presentation machine was that the pilot had to periodically write to the donor, thanking them and informing them of the deeds he had performed in it (contrary to popular belief, most of the men and women in the wartime Soviet military were literate).

9

Soviet Second World War Fighter Specifications

N.B. Metric measurements are in parentheses				
Type	I-16 *tip* 24	MiG-3	LaGG-3 Series 35	La-5FN
Year	1939	1941	1942	1943
Engine	M-63	AM-35A	M-105PF	M-82FN
Max. Power (Horsepower)	1,100	1,350	1,260	1,850
Fixed Armament	4 × ShKAS 7.62-mm machine guns	2 × ShKAS 7.62-mm, 1 × UBS 12.7-mm	1 × UBS 12.7-mm, 1 × ShVAK MP-20 20-mm cannon	2 × ShVAK SP-20 20-mm cannons
Disposable Armament	6 × RS-82 Rockets	6 × RS-82 Rockets, or 485 lb (220 kg) of bombs	6 × RS-82 or RS-132 Rockets, 2 × 110 lb (50 kg) bombs	2 × 110 lb (50 kg) bombs
Length—feet (m)	20.01 (6.1)	27.07 (8.25)	28.9 (8.81)	28.45 (8.672)
Wingspan—feet (m)	29.53 (9)	33.46 (10.2)	32.15 (9.8)	32.15 (9.8)
Weight (Empty)—lb (kg)	3,049 (1,383)	5,950 (2,699)	5,357 (2,430)	6,235 (2,828)
Weight (Loaded)—lb (kg)	4,149 (1,882)	7,385 (3,350)	6,967 (3,160)	7,407 (3,360)

La-7	Yak-1B	Yak-3	Yak-7B	Yak-9T	Yak-9U
1944	1943	1944	1942	1943	1944
M-82FN	M-105P	VK-105PF-2 (M-105PF-2)	M-105PF	M-105PF	VK-107A (M-107A)
1,850	1,100	1,280 (YG/airwar. ru – 1,240)	1,260	1,260	1,600
2 × ShVAK SP-20 20-mm cannons (from 1945, 3 × Berezin B-20 20-mm cannons)	1 × UBS 12.7-mm machine gun, 1 × ShVAK MP-20 20-mm cannon	2 × UBS 12.7-mm machine guns, 1 × ShVAK MP-20 20-mm cannon	2 × UBS 12.7-mm machine guns, 1 × ShVAK MP-20 20-mm cannon	1 × UBS 12.7-mm machine gun, 1 × NS-37 37-mm cannon	2 × UBS 12.7-mm machine guns, 1 × ShVAK MP-20 20-mm cannon
2 × 110 lb (50 kg) bombs	N/A	N/A	6 × RS-82 Rockets (on early aircraft) and 2 × 220-lb (100-kg) bombs	N/A	N/A
29.21 (8.9)	27.89 (8.5)	27.89 (8.5)	27.89 (8.5)	28.41 (8.66)	28.05 (8.55)
32.15 (9.8)	32.81 (10)	30.18 (9.2)	32.81 (10)	31.96 (9.74)	31.96 (9.74)
-	5,055 (2,293)	4,691 (2,128)	5,467 (2,480)	5,267 (2,389)	5,461 (2,477)
7,496 (3,400)	6,314 (2,864)	5,725 (2,597)	6,636 (3,010)	6,429 (2,916)	7,064 (3,204)

Weight (Maximum) —lb (kg)	-	-	-	7,474 (3,390)
Max. Speed at Sea Level—mph (kph)	255 (410)	314 (505)	310 (499)	362 (583)
Top Speed—mph (kph)	304 (489)	398 (640)	352 (566)	394 (634)
Range—miles (km)	273 (440)	777 (1,250)	565 (910)	360 (579)
Service Ceiling—feet (m)	31,824 (9,700)	39,370 (12,000)	32,808 (10,000)	31,168 (9,501) (one source has 35,000 feet (10,688))
Turn Time (sec)	17-18	25.5	21.9	19

-	-	-	-	-	
381 (613)	335 (539)	352 (567)	319 (514)	319 (514)	357 (575)
409 (658)	379 (610)	397 (640)	354 (570)	359 (577)	418 (672)
413 (665)	548 (882)	403 (648)	401 (645)	457 (735)	419 (675)
37,000 (11,278)	29,528 (9,000)	34,121 (10,400)	32,480 (9,900)	32,808 (10,000)	34,941 (10,650)
19	17-18	21	19	18-19	20

10

Non-Soviet Second World War Fighter Specifications

Type	Bf 109G-6	Fw 190F-8	Hawker Hurricane Mk.IIC	Spitfire Mk.IXe
Year	1943	1944	1942	1943
Engine	DB 605A-1	BMW 801 D-2	Rolls-Royce Merlin XX	Rolls-Royce Merlin 66
Max. Power (Horsepower)	1,455	2,100	1,185	1,720
Fixed Armament	2 × MG 131 13-mm machine guns, 1 × MG 151/20 20-mm cannon	2 × MG 131 13-mm machine guns, 2 × MG 151/20 E 20-mm cannons	4 × Hispano II 20-mm cannons	2 × Browning M2 50-calibre machine guns, 2 × Hispano II 20-mm cannons
Disposable Armament	551 lb of bombs (250 kg)	2,646 lb of bombs (1,200 kg)	500 lb of bombs (227 kg)	1,000 lb of bombs (454 kg)
Length—feet (m)	29.36 (8.95)	29.53 (9)	32.25 (9.83)	31.08 (9.47)
Wing span—feet (m)	32.56 (9.925)	34.48 (10.51)	40 (12.19)	32.5 (9.91)
Weight (Empty)—lb (kg)	4,954 (2,247)	7,330 (3,325)	5,745 (2,606)	5,090 (2,309)
Weight (Loaded)—lb (kg)	6,940 (3,148)	-	7,670 (3,479)	7,400 (3,357)
Weight (Maximum) —lb (kg)	7,496 (3,400)	10,858 (4,925)	8,710 (3,951)	-
Max. Speed at Sea Level—mph (kph)	326 (524) for Bf 109G-2	317 (510) for Fw 190A-4	-	-
Top Speed—mph (kph)	398 (640)	395 (635)	340 (547)	404 (650)
Range—miles (km)	621 (1,000 with drop tank)	466 (750)	600 (966)	980 (ferry range) (1,577)
Service Ceiling—feet (m)	39,370 (12,000)	34,777 (10,600)	36,000 (10,973)	42,500 (12,954)
Turn Time (sec)	21	22-23 for Fw 190A-4	17	18

P-51D Mustang	P-47D-30 Thunderbolt	A6M2 Zero	Macchi MC.202
1944	1944	1942	1942
Packard V-1650-7 (licence-built Rolls-Royce Merlin)	P&W R-2800-59B Double Wasp	Nakajima NK1C Sakae-12	Alfa Romeo RA.1000 R.C.41-I Monsone (licence-built DB 601A)
1,720	2,600	940	1,159
6 × Browning M2 50-calibre machine guns	8 × Browning M2 50-calibre machine guns	2 × Type 97 7.7-mm machine guns, 2 × Type 99-1 20-mm cannons	2 × Breda-SAFAT 7.7-mm machine guns, 2 × Breda-SAFAT 12.7-mm machine guns
2,000 lb? of bombs (907 kg)	2,500 lb of bombs (1,134 kg)	550 lb of bombs (249 kg)	353 lb of bombs (160 kg)
32.25 (9.83)	36.08 (11)	29.72 (9.06)	29.04 (8.85)
37 (11.28)	40.75 (12.42)	39.37 (12)	34.71 (10.58)
7,635 (3,463)	10,000 (4,536)	3,704 (1,680)	5,492 (2,491)
9,200 (4,173)	12,731 (5,775)	6,164 (2,796)	6,457 (2,929)
12,100 (5,488)	17,500 (7,938)	-	-
-	-	-	-
437 (703)	433 (697)	332 (534)	373 (600)
1,650 with drop tanks (2,655)	800 (combat range) (1,287) 1,800 (ferry range) (2,897)	1,929 (3,104)	475 (765)
41,900 (12,771)	43,000 (13,106)	32,808 (10,000)	37,730 (11,500)
21	24	17.7	20

11

Experimental Fighters

Below are descriptions of some of the most interesting and important experimental Soviet fighters designed or tested during the Second World War, including a few notable projects that were never built. Belying the Soviets' reputation for conservative or derivative aircraft design, some of these designs were very innovative. Although a few of these fighters were produced in small numbers, and some even saw combat, none went into large-scale production or service.

Bereznyak-Isayev BI-1

Aleksander Yakovlevich Bereznyak (1912–74) and Aleksei Mikhailovich Isayev (1908–71) designed one of the first reaction-powered fighters in the world with the BI-1, powered by rockets designed by the engineer Dushkin. The design was built by the Bolkhovitinov OKB (OKB-239).

Five prototypes were approved for construction, with the first unpowered flight occurring on 10 September 1941, with Boris M. Kudrin as the pilot. The first powered flight took place on 15 May 1942, with Grigoriy Y. Bakchivandzhi at the controls. The aircraft was a low-wing monoplane of all-wooden construction, with an enclosed cockpit for the pilot, a retractable tailwheel landing gear, and an armament of two ShVAK cannons in the upper nose. The strut-braced horizontal tailplane featured small end plates that were introduced to improve stability. The BI-1 was very light in weight, with a take-off weight of only 3,638 lb (1,650 kg). The fuel consisted of kerosene and red, fuming nitric acid (which was as unpleasant and dangerous as it sounds). The aircraft was designed to have a top speed of 559 mph (900 kph), although it does not appear from the record that it ever achieved this, with a top speed of approximately 500 mph (805 kph) being achieved by the third prototype on 27 March 1943. Unfortunately, the pilot, G. Y. Bakchivandzhi, crashed and was killed during this flight. Despite the crash, testing continued on the surviving aircraft, although no production ensued.

If not for the disruption caused by the German invasion, this aircraft might have become the first rocket-powered aircraft to go into production (as it was, the Second World War German Me 163 fighter was the only rocket-powered aircraft to ever go into production).

Bisnovat

In 1938, the engineer Matus Ruvimovich Bisnovat (1905–77) was assigned an OKB to design and construct an aeroplane to test high-speed wing aerofoils. The result of this was the SK (and SK-2).

SK (SK-1)

Looking very much like a racing aircraft, with its flush canopy and very aerodynamically clean lines, this aeroplane was intended as a test aircraft to examine the properties of different types of wings at high speed. The designation 'SK' stood for *Skorostnoiy Krylo* (meaning 'High-speed Wing'). The flush canopy had a windshield that hinged upward, and the pilot was provided with a raising seat to give him better vision for take-off and landing, both the windshield and seat being hydraulically powered. The windshield was lowered down for high-speed flight. The aircraft was of all-metal construction, and all the landing gear were fully retractable and enclosed with doors, with the main landing gear retracting inwards. The engine was a M-105 of 1,100 hp.

The aircraft was first flown on 15 February 1940 by the TsAGI test pilot G. M. Shiyanov, equipped with skis. The aircraft was expected to have a top speed of 441 mph (710 kph). Since this was the manufacturer's estimate, and prototype aircraft are seldom able to meet these usually overly optimistic estimates, it is improbable that the SK ever reached this speed. The highest speed recorded was 359 mph (577 kph). Gunston has the top speed being 421 mph (678 kph). The flight characteristics, including handling on the SK, were good enough, and its performance impressive enough that it was decided to build a fighter version of the aircraft, which became the 'SK-2'. The SK was then apparently retroactively re-designated as the 'SK-1'.

SK-2

In order to improve the pilot's vision, this was basically the SK fitted with a conventional raised canopy and a larger vertical tail for use as a high-speed fighter. These changes increased drag, but definitely improved the pilot's very limited vision in flight on the SK and stability. Nonetheless, with his aft-mounted cockpit and a long inline engine in front of him, the pilot still did not have a very good view for take-offs and landings.

The aircraft was first flown on 10 November 1940 by G. M. Shiyanov, and during testing, it achieved a top speed of 410 mph (660 kph) at 16,076 feet (4,900 m). This was an impressive top speed for the time. The SK-2 was tested at the LII during the winter of 1940–41. The two UBS machine guns that were intended to be used may have never been fitted to the SK-2 (Yefim Gordon seems to indicate that they were

Bisnovat SK-2 in winter 1940–41. (*Viktor Kulikov's collection*)

fitted, however). As fighter aircraft such as the LaGG-3, MiG-1/3, and Yak-1 were already nearing or even in production by late 1940, there was little need for the SK-2, despite its impressive speed, and the aircraft did not go into production.

Borovkov-Florov

The young aircraft engineers Aleksey Andreyovich Borovkov (1903–?) and Ilya Florentyevich Florov designed a series of remarkable little biplane fighters, which, although never going into production, probably represented the pinnacle of biplane fighter design in the form of the I-207/4, the last of their designs. Their OKB was created in early 1936 to transform their design ideas into actual aircraft.

'7211'

This aircraft was designed as a biplane with a minimum of bracing, making it as aerodynamically clean as possible. To this end, it featured equal-span cantilever aluminium upper and lower wings, which required no interplane struts, the only wing struts being those which connected the upper wing to the top of the fuselage. The front of the fuselage was metal, the rear portion being of a wooden monocoque structure, while the tailplanes, including the very small, almost vestigial fin, were metal. The rudder was metal-framed, and fabric-covered like the rest of the control surfaces and, unlike the fin, was rather substantial. The engine, powering a three-bladed metal propeller, was a Tumanskiy (Tumanskiy, Sergeiy Konstantovish (1901–1973) M-85 radial engine (a licence-built French Gnome-Rhône 14K). The main landing gear was fixed and spatted, with a bracing strut between the two spats. The pilot sat well aft in an enclosed cockpit just in front of the fin, the canopy sliding on rails to the front.

The '7211' first flew on 23 May 1937. The aircraft had a horizontal 360-degree turn rate of fourteen seconds, which was more than the I-15, but better than the I-16. The state trials began on 21 (or 22) June 1937, but unfortunately, this first state flight (the twenty-fourth overall for the '7211') ended in a crash, in which the test pilot E. Y. Preman died. Despite this, the authorities were impressed enough with the aeroplane to plan to produce it, and eventually, it was decided to build the I-207 prototypes, which were developed from the '7211'.

I-207

With the success of such biplane fighters during the Spanish Civil War as the Fiat CR.32 and the Polikarpov I-15, the Soviets—even in the latter part of the 1930s—were not prepared to give up on the biplane. The I-153 and the Borovkov-Florov I-207 were not entirely successful efforts to update the biplane and keep it as a viable option in an age of monoplanes.

Based upon the pre-war '7211', there were at least four I-207 prototypes built (although sources differ on the exact number), which were the same in featuring equal span cantilever all-metal wings, a metal forward fuselage coupled with a wooden rear fuselage, and metal tailplanes, all as with the '7211'. The tiny, fixed fin of the '7211' was also retained, as was the aft-mounted cockpit just in front of the fin, although this was now open on all but one of the I-207 prototypes. The only struts were those that braced the upper wing to the fuselage.

The first two prototypes featured a fixed, cantilever spatted main landing gear like that of the '7211', except without the connecting strut. The cockpit was open, unlike the enclosed cockpit on the '7211'. The first prototype (I-207/1) featured a M-62 engine in a very small diameter cowling, which necessitated bulges to cover the ends of the engine cylinders. The second prototype (I-207/2) featured a smooth NACA cowling, without the bulges, enclosing a M-63.

The third and fourth prototypes were fitted with fully retractable main landing gear, with the fourth prototype also featuring an enclosed cockpit. For such a small aircraft, it had good bomb-carrying capabilities, with the third prototype (I-207/3) able to carry one FAB-250 551-lb (250-kg) bomb under each wing for a total bomb load of 1,102 lb (500 kg). The fourth prototype, or I-207/4, featured the M-63R engine in a more streamlined installation than the third prototype (I-207/3, also powered by a M-63), in addition to an enclosed cockpit for the pilot. The M-63R had an extended shaft that allowed for better streamlining of the cowling on the I-207/4, also known as the 'I-209'. The I-207/4 prototype had a top speed of 322 mph (518 kph), which was surpassed among biplane fighters only by the DB 601A-powered version of the Italian Cr.42, the experimental Cr.42DB with a top speed of 326 mph (525 kph).

Unlike the I-153, the I-207 did not go into production and only the prototypes were built as the time of the biplane was clearly past, although one at least reportedly saw some combat early in the Great Patriotic War. The I-207 may have also seen action in the Winter War with Finland, but this remains unconfirmed.

Borovkov-Florov I-207 no. 3 prototype in 1940. Note the narrow track of the fully retractable main landing gear. (*Viktor Kulikov's collection*)

Gorbunov I-105

This aircraft, developed by Vladimir P. Gorbunov, one of the original designers of the LaGG-3, was a final effort to update the LaGG-3. As this was a development of the LaGG-3, it is described in the Lavochkin fighter section.

Grushin GR-1 (IDS)

The Soviets had been impressed by the Bf 110 twin-engined heavy fighter they had purchased from the Germans in 1940, and the GR-1 was something of the Soviet equivalent to this German aircraft, being intended as a long-range escort fighter. Designed by Pyotr Dimitrievich Grushin (1906–93), like the Bf 110, the GR-1 was of all-metal construction and featured twin fins and rudders. The fixed armament consisted of four ShKAS and two ShVAKs, similar to the fixed armament on the Bf 110. Bombs of up to 1,102 lb (500 kg) could be carried in an internal bomb bay (which the Bf 110 did not possess). The GR-1 was powered by two 1,400-hp AM-37 inline engines. Unlike the Bf 110, the GR-1 was a single-seater, with no second crewman/rear gunner. Although the aircraft was built, it never flew as when the train on which it was being despatched to the east was attacked by German aircraft, the single prototype was destroyed. In the turmoil of the early part of the Great Patriotic War, a replacement prototype and further development were not proceeded with.

Gudkov

One of the designers who had worked on the LaGG-3, Mikhail I. Gudkov also worked on two other fighters—one a derivative of the LaGG-3 and the other a completely original design.

Gu-37 (Gu-1)

In many ways, this was the Soviet analogue to the American Bell P-39 Airacobra, which served with some distinction with the Soviet Union. Like that aircraft, the Gudkov Gu-37 featured a retractable tricycle landing gear, a mid-mounted engine, and a heavy cannon in the nose (the '37' in the designation referring to the calibre of this cannon, a Taubin 37-mm cannon). Unlike the P-39, the Gu-37 featured a mainly wooden airframe, with the wings (except for the metal centre-section spars), the rear fuselage, and the tailplanes being of wooden construction. The forward part of the fuselage was a welded steel tube structure, covered by aluminium alloy plates. The armament consisted of the Taubin 37-mm cannon and six ShKAS machine guns mounted in the fuselage and the wings.

Unfortunately, on its first flight on 12 June 1943, after a long take-off run, the Gu-37 reached an altitude of about 600 feet (183 m), stalled, and crashed into the ground, killing the famous test pilot Aleksey I. Nikashin (he had flown the I-301, the prototype of the LaGG-3). Some have speculated that the wings were too small. After this crash, development was halted.

Gu-82

Since this was a re-engined LaGG-3, now fitted with the M-82 engine, see the Lavochkin fighter section for a description of this aeroplane. Although engined with the M-82 like the La-5, it was a somewhat different aircraft from what became the La-5.

Ilyushin

Although mainly noted for his work pre-war and during the Second World War on bombers and attack aircraft such as the Il-2 assault aircraft and the Il-4 (DB-3F) bomber, Sergeiy Ilyushin designed two fighters during the Second World War, the Il-1 and the Il-2I. Post-war, Ilyushin mainly produced transport aircraft.

Il-1

Even though the Il-2I fighter development had not proved a success (see below), the Ilyushin bureau created one more armoured fighter—the Il-1, although Sergeiy Ilyushin himself was apparently dubious of its utility. This was a heavily armoured single-seater, with a smaller, more streamlined shape than the Il-2, and was without the rear gunner. It was constructed completely of metal, and like the second Il-8 prototype shturmovik, it featured landing gear that rotated through nearly 90 degrees to retract directly into the wings, rather than into the underwing nacelles of the Il-2. In appearance, it resembled a smaller version of this second variant of the Il-8 shturmovik.

Although the Il-1 was much faster than the Il-2I, having a top speed of around 380 mph (612 kph), it was still considered to be too slow to engage in air-to-air combat with the new German types. It did provide a basis for the Il-2's replacement, however, and with a rear gunner added to the basic design and redesigned wings, it appeared as the Il-10 shturmovik, which at first was simply known as the two-seat Il-1 attack aircraft. The Il-10 entered production and eventually replaced the Il-2 in Soviet service.

Il-2I

During the futile attempt by the Luftwaffe to keep the besieged garrison at Stalingrad supplied in the winter of 1942–43, the Il-2 found itself used as an ad hoc fighter against the bombers and transports that were being used to ferry and drop supplies. Earlier, the Il-2 had been used against transports successfully re-supplying the German troops surrounded north of Moscow at Demyansk, which had become encircled during the Soviet Winter Counteroffensive of 1941–42.

The Il-2 enjoyed some success in this role, especially against slow aeroplanes, such as the Junkers Ju 52 transport. It also proved very deadly during the early part of the Great Patriotic War against the Luftwaffe's single-engined battlefield reconnaissance aeroplane, the Hs 126, whose single rifle-calibre defensive gun was useless against the heavily armoured Il-2 and was too slow to outrun the Shturmovik. These successes, at least in part, led to the idea to adapt the Il-2 into an armoured, single-seat fighter. A two-seater, possibly an arrow, was taken from the production lines and modified into a single-seater, now armed with only two VYa-23 23-mm cannons in the wings.

One source mentions that it went into production with about fifty made in an all-metal form with the arrow wings, although I have never seen any photographic evidence for this, nor solid confirmation from other sources. However, one VVS veteran mentions in an interview flying a Shturmovik that sounds very much like the Il-2I, and this late in the war. In any event, It is questionable if it ever saw (much) service as it was considered too slow to be an effective fighter, having a top speed that was only marginally better than the two-seater versions, being too slow even to catch some of the Luftwaffe bombers, such as the Ju 88 and Do 217, much less German fighters. Interestingly, the idea of an armoured fighter was resurrected with the Il-1 single-seater (described above), which was then developed into the Il-2's replacement, the two-seater Il-10.

TsKB-54 (DB-3)

One of the problems with long-range bombers was providing protection on their long-range missions. The bombers possessed defensive armament, but this was often found lacking in combat. Normal fighters did not possess the range to escort the bombers to and from their targets. A seemingly obvious solution was to modify some of the long-range bombers into heavily armed escort fighters (a type of aeroplane that before the war had been called a 'cruiser').

Armed with more defensive weapons than the normal bomber versions, these aircraft would have the range to keep up with and the armament to protect the bombers from attacks by enemy fighters. That was the theory, anyway, and Ilyushin tried out this concept with the TsKB-54, a modification of the DB-3. Interestingly, this idea was also tried out by the USAAF in the form of the YB-40, a modified B-17 Flying Fortress that featured even more heavy armament than that already heavily armed aeroplane. Unfortunately for the USAAF, it met with the same problems and had the same success (or lack thereof) as the TsKB-54.

TsKB-54-I

This first heavy escort version was modified from one of the first DB-3s from Z.18 in Voronezh. One of its interesting features was the provision for a remote-controlled ShKAS machine gun mounted in a streamlined pod on a pylon under the fuselage, which had a 240-degree range of movement in the horizontal plane. The normal ventral position was also retained. The nose and dorsal turret now featured ShVAK 20-mm cannons.

TsKB-54-II

This was an improved escort version, modified from a newer airframe from the 1939 production run. One difference between it and the TsKB-54-I was the installation of gun blisters on each side of the fuselage, the blisters featuring ShKAS machine guns. Unlike the TsKB-54-I, it did not feature the remote-controlled gun installation under the fuselage, which had been found to cause handling problems when moved. The standard ventral position was also removed. The dorsal turret and nose installations were given new gunsights.

Due to the added weight of the additional gun armament, the TsKB-54-II was actually heavier and slower than the bomber version. Due to this, it could not keep up with the bomber version in flight, which made it useless as an escort fighter. The concept was therefore dropped.

Mikoyan-Gurevich

Although known mainly for the MiG-3 during the Second World War, the MiG OKB designed a number of other fighters during the war, both single and twin-engined. None, however, went into large-scale production, although at least one type, the I-210 (MiG-9), did see combat.

DIS-200 (T, MiG-5)

Intended as a fighter and ground attack aircraft, this aeroplane resembled the GR-1 (described previously) in general appearance. This is not surprising since P. D. Grushin headed the MiG OKB division (or 'brigade') responsible for designing the DIS. This aircraft competed against the GR-1, TIS, and the Ta-3. It was of a mixed metal and wooden construction and was powered by two Mikulin AM-37 inline engines. The armament consisted of a VYa-23 23-mm cannon in a fairing under the nose and two Berezin UB machine guns in the centre-section leading edge, with four ShKAS above them.

Mikoyan-Gurevich DIS-200 (MiG-5) in 1941. (*Viktor Kulikov's collection*)

The aircraft first flew on 6 November 1941 with A. I. Zhukov at the controls. The top speed recorded was 379 mph (610 kph) at 22,310 feet (6,800 m). Due to the decision not to produce the AM-37 engine, work on the DIS-200 'T' was stopped in 1942.

DIS-200 with M-82 (IT, MiG-5)

With the unavailability of the AM-37, the basic DIS-200 design was changed to take M-82 radial engines. This aircraft differed mainly from the original DIS-200 prototype in the provision for the M-82 radial engines, which required a redesign of the engine nacelles. The aircraft also featured a somewhat different armament of two VYa-23 cannons in an under-nose pod (the DIS-200 T had featured a similar pod with only one cannon) and four Berezin UB machine guns in the wing root. The aircraft was fitted with a streamlined cone at the back that opened up into a dive brake as with some versions of the German Do 217.

The DIS IT first flew on 28 January 1943 with Viktor N. Savkin at the controls. During testing, it achieved a top speed of 375 mph (604 kph). On 12 May 1943, the NKAP stopped development, perhaps as by this time the M-82 engines were fully committed to the La-5 and Tu-2 aircraft.

I-210 M-82A (MiG-3 M-82A, IKh, MiG-9, Izdeliye 65)

Not to be confused with the immediate post-war jet fighter of the same designation, 'MiG-9', this aircraft was a heavily redesigned MiG-3 equipped with the M-82A (ASh-82A) engine. In appearance, it closely resembled the I-185 of the Polikarpov OKB, with which it was in competition.

Mikoyan-Gurevich I-210 (MiG-9 M-82) in 1942. (*Viktor Kulikov's collection*)

Though the wings and tailplanes resembled those of the inline-engined MiG-3, the fuselage had to be redesigned to accommodate the larger diameter of the radial engine, as opposed to the relatively slim AM-35 inline engine of the standard MiG-3. The wings were moved back 3.94 inches (100 mm) and leading-edge slats fitted to improve manoeuvrability. The resulting aircraft was a rather handsome, clean design, with the radial engine enclosed in a close-fitting cowling, featuring a large spinner to help with the streamlining. The aircraft was to have three UBS guns mounted on the cowling, with two ShKAS guns also fitted. It appears that the ShKAS guns were not initially fitted but were fitted to the three aircraft that saw combat in 1943-44.

The I-210 was first flown on 23 July 1941 by M. I. Martselyuk according to Gordon, but Gunston has the first flight as 2 January 1942 by V. Ye. Golofastov. In spite of its good looks, the I-210's performance was found to be rather disappointing. It had a top speed of 351 mph (565 kph) at best, with its top speed at the NII VVS being 336 mph (540 kph) at 16,404 feet (5,000 m). The top speed was supposed to be 391 mph (630 kph) at 21,325 feet (6,500 m). The greater cross-section of the fuselage increased the drag, as well as poor sealing of the engine cowling. In addition to its disappointing top speed, compared to the MiG-3 the service ceiling dropped from 37,730 feet (11,500 m) on the MiG-3 to only 28,543 feet (8,700 m) on the I-210. The manoeuvrability, despite the addition of the leading-edge slats, was found to be overall less than that of the MiG-3. Due to its mediocre performance, the decision was made not to produce the I-210.

Nevertheless, the I-210 or MiG-9 did see combat. In June 1942, three were sent to the 34th IAP of the 1st IAK, a PVO unit on the Kalinin Front, where they served until 27 October 1942 when they were returned to the MiG OKB for work on the engines. At least four of the five MiG-9s that were built were sent to front-line units, where they saw combat service, with three of them seeing service into 1944 with the 260th Mixed

Aviation Division of the 7th Air Army of the Karelian Front. These may have been the three aircraft that had seen combat previously in 1942. That they used an airframe similar to that of the MiG-3 and a production engine, the M-82, no doubt made it possible to maintain them and keep them serviceable, despite being experimental aircraft.

I-211 (MiG-9Ye)

The I-211 was a further development and refinement of the I-210, now more optimised for high-altitude flight, and more thoroughly redesigned to accommodate an improved M-82 engine (the M-82A of the I-210 was replaced with a boosted M-82FN of 1,850 hp) with an extensively modified fuselage smoothly fairing in the rather bulky radial engine. The cockpit was moved aft and the tail was moved forward. There were two ShVAKs mounted above the engine, as on the La-5, and the engine now featured La-5-type cooling flaps.

The first flight was on 18 December 1942, piloted by V. Ye. Golofastov. The top speed was 416 mph (670 kph) with a service ceiling of 37,073 feet (11,300 m) It was found to be a good aircraft that could outperform other Soviet fighters, but there was no spare production capacity, so there was no large-scale production (that the La-5 likewise used the M-82 engine and was already in large-scale production also no doubt figured in the decision). Gunston claims that ten were built as a service trial batch, and were used at the Kalinin Front from September 1943, although Gordon states that only one prototype was built, even though there were plans to build ten pre-production examples for operational tests.

I-220 (A, MiG-11)

The appearance of high-altitude German aircraft, such as the Ju 86P bomber, which could overfly the Soviet Union (including Moscow) with impunity, was a subject of concern for the Soviets, and they looked for interceptors to counteract these aircraft. Even before this, the MiG OKB responded to a specific early 1941 request for high-altitude interceptors with the I-220, also known in the OKB as the 'A', with the 'service' designation of 'MiG-11'.

Although the aircraft bore a family resemblance to the MiG-3, it was essentially a new aircraft. It was intended that the Mikulin AM-39 be installed as its powerplant, but this was not available at the time, so initially, the AM-38F (used by the Il-2) was installed. The aircraft was of mixed construction, with all-metal inner wings, metal wing spars, and wooden-covered outer wings. The fuselage was of mixed construction also, with a wooden centre section and an all-metal tail. The pilot was provided with a pressurised cockpit and the aircraft was very well-armed with four synchronised ShVAK cannons mounted around the engine cowling.

The I-220 was first flown in July 1943 by Yakimov. The second prototype was flown by I. I. Shelnest in September 1944. The long time between the first flights of the prototypes would indicate that there were significant changes made between the two aircraft. During testing, the I-220 showed a maximum speed of 433 mph (697 kph) and a service ceiling of 36,089 feet (11,000 m). However, by 1944, the threat of high-flying German aircraft over the Soviet Union had disappeared, so no production ensued.

Mikoyan-Gurevich I-211 M-82F (MiG-9Ye) in 1943. (*Viktor Kulikov's collection*)

Mikoyan-Gurevich I-220 AM-38F in 1943–44. The AM-38F was the same engine used on the Il-2. (*Viktor Kulikov's collection*)

I-221 (2A, MiG-7)

Similar in appearance to the I-220, the I-221 had longer-span wings and was of all-metal construction. The aircraft was armed with two ShVAK cannons and was powered by a Mikulin AM-39A engine with a TKB-2 turbo-supercharger mounted on the starboard side. Although this aircraft (and the I-222 and 1-224) was given the designation 'MiG-7', it should not be confused with the earlier 'MiG-7' (MiG-3 with AM-37, *Izdeliye* 72), which was a MiG-3 with an AM-37 engine installed. As has been noted before, re-use of designations was not unknown with Soviet aircraft.

The aircraft was flown for the first time on 2 December 1943 by the test pilot Zhuravlyev. On an early flight, a connecting rod broke, and the pilot was forced to bail out. The top speed was 428 mph (689 kph) and the service ceiling was a very impressive 47,572 feet (14,500 m). There was no production as further development was continued on subsequent MiG high-altitude interceptors.

I-222 (3A, MiG-7)

Another of the MiG OKB's high-altitude interceptors, the I-222 strongly resembled the I-221 in plan and was fitted with a Shchyerbakov-designed pressurised cabin similar to those fitted experimentally to the I-153 and I-16 fighters. Unlike the I-221, the I-222 featured a wooden structure for the rear fuselage and outer wings. The engine was an AM-39B-1 fitted with a TKB-300B turbo-supercharger on the port side. As with the I-221, two ShVAKs were carried. The vertical tail was larger than that fitted to the I-220 and I-221, and the rear fuselage was slightly cut-down to give the pilot a better view aft.

The I-222 flew for the first time on 7 May 1944 piloted by A. I. Zhukov. At some point in the testing, the aircraft was fitted with a large, four-bladed propeller, which was rare for Soviet aircraft at this time. The top speed was 429 mph (691 kph) and the service ceiling was 47,572 feet (14,500 m), figures which were almost identical to those of the I-221.

I-224 (4A, MiG-7)

The final aircraft in the series of MiG-designed Great Patriotic War high-altitude interceptors, this aircraft differed from the I-222 in featuring a higher-thrust version of that aircraft's four-bladed propeller. Like the I-222, it was equipped with two ShVAK cannons, and it also featured that aircraft's lowered rear fuselage and all-round vision cockpit canopy.

The aircraft flew for the first time on 20 October 1944 (or 16 September 1944, sources differ), piloted by Aleksey P. Yakimov. Testing showed that both the range and service ceiling were less than those for the I-222. The top speed was 431 mph (693 kph) and the service ceiling was 46,260 feet (14,100 m).

The I-224 continued to be developed into 1946, when development was stopped, probably because the new jet fighters had made it redundant.

I-225 (5A)

Unlike the previous series of MiGs, which had been optimised for high-altitude flight, the I-225 was optimised for medium-altitude flight. The engine was the AM-42, the same 2,000-hp-class engine that powered the Il-10 shturmovik, and the engine was

Mikoyan-Gurevich I-224 in 1944. The aircraft appears to be painted in a grey over blue camouflage. (*Viktor Kulikov's collection*)

Mikoyan-Gurevich I-225 in 1944. The propellor blades appear to be unpainted. (*Viktor Kulikov's collection*)

now equipped with a TK-300B turbo-supercharger on the starboard side. The overall planform was similar to the I-221/I-222, but with shorter span wings, and a smaller vertical tail like that of the I-220. There were two prototypes built, both equipped with four ShVAKs (Yefim Gordon has the guns as four SSh-20s), with the first prototype fitted with the AM-42B engine and the second prototype fitted with the AM-42FB. Both aircraft were fitted with three-bladed propellers. The first prototype was rebuilt from the second I-220.

The first prototype flew on 21 July 1944, flown by test pilot A. P. Yakimov. The second prototype flew on 14 March 1944. The top speed was 451 mph (726 kph), making it one of the fastest Soviet piston-engined aircraft, and the service ceiling was 41,339 feet (12,600 m). Despite the impressive performance, there was no production.

I-230 (MiG-3U, D, MiG-3D)

The I-230 was essentially an effort to improve the MiG-3 with better aerodynamics and a more powerful engine, the experimental Mikulin AM-39 inline engine. As it was, the MiG-3's AM-35A was used instead. There were many changes from the MiG-3, including a mainly metal wing with all-metal spars. The fuselage, by contrast, was mainly wooden, whereas in the MiG-3 it was about half and half, being all-metal to the end of the cockpit, with the rear fuselage being wooden. The I-230 also featured revised landing gear and a new cockpit canopy. The armament was now two ShVAKs mounted above the engine on the upper cowling, as with the La-5. The resulting changes were such that they resulted in a significantly different aeroplane from the MiG-3, despite having the same service designation of 'MiG-3' ('MiG-3U', or 'MiG-3D'). That this aircraft retained the MiG-3 designation, despite being very different from the normal production MiG-3, while the La-7 received a different designation from the very similar late La-5FN is due to the vagaries of Soviet aircraft designations. By this point, the observant reader should be well aware of the caprices of Soviet aviation nomenclature.

The I-230 was first flown on 11 August 1942. The top speed was 410 mph (660 kph) and the service ceiling was 37,730 feet (11,500 m). As the AM-35A was no longer being produced, large-scale production of the I-230 was impossible, although a pre-series batch of five aircraft was built, and four of these saw action on the Kalinin Front with a PVO unit. In PVO service, it was known as the MiG-3U, the 'U' standing for *Ulushchenniy* (meaning 'Improved').

I-231 (2D)

Similar to the I-230, the I-231 was equipped with the AM-39A, which had been originally intended for the I-230. The rear fuselage reverted to the type used on the MiG-3.

It was initially flown in February 1943 by Yu. A. Antipov (Yefim Gordon has the first flight on 19 October 1943 by Viktor N. Savkin; perhaps the first date was for the OKB tests, and the second date related to the state tests). The aircraft had an impressive top speed of 439 mph (707 kph) at 23,294 feet (7,100 m) and a service ceiling of 37,402 feet (11,400 m). There was no production as again there was no excess production capacity, and the AM-39 engine did not go into production.

Mikoyan-Gurevich I-231 in 1943. (*Viktor Kulikov's collection*)

I-250 (MiG-13)

The appearance of jet-powered fighters in the Luftwaffe was met with considerable alarm in Soviet military circles as none of their piston-engined fighters had a performance anywhere near that of such aircraft as the Me 262. As a stopgap measure until all-jet fighters could be developed, the Soviets developed mixed-powered aircraft, which utilised a piston engine as its main powerplant, with the piston engine also providing power to a compressor for a rudimentary jet engine, a so-called 'motorjet'. Two different mixed-powered motorjet aircraft were built, the I-250, sometimes known as the 'MiG-13' (which was to have been its service designation) and the Su-5.

The I-250 was a rather stubby-looking little aeroplane, with a VK-107 engine driving a three-bladed propeller and the compressor for the motorjet, which exhausted through a nozzle at the tail, closed by clamshell doors. The aircraft was of all-metal construction and featured an armament of three B-20 20-mm cannons. The cockpit was situated well aft towards the tail, which must have given the pilot a poor view on take-off and landing. The main landing gear was somewhat unusual in having the wheels levered forward. The tailwheel on the prototype retracted into a fairing under the outlet nozzle for the motorjet. The initial flight was on 3 March 1945. A maximum speed of 513 mph (825 kph) was achieved. Two prototypes were built.

Despite the loss of the first prototype on 5 July 1945, it was decided to build a small batch for military trials. Sources differ, but from eight to fifty may have been produced and used by the Baltic Fleet until perhaps as late as 1950 (Gunston and the Soviet aircraft designer and historian Vadim B. Shavrov state 1948).

Mikoyan-Gurevich I-250 (MiG-13) in 1945. The deepness of the fuselage is caused by the necessity to house the duct for the motorjet in the rear. (*Viktor Kulikov's collection*)

Moskalyev SAM-13

Designed by Aleksandr Sergeyevich Moskalyev, and possibly inspired by the Dutch Fokker D.XXIII fighter, the SAM-13, like the D.XXIII, was a 'push-pull' design with two engines on the central fuselage pod, one mounted as a tractor engine on the front and one engine mounted on the back as a pusher engine. This had the advantage of giving the aircraft the power of two engines without the drag or the asymmetrical power should one engine stop. Like the D.XXIII, the SAM-13 also featured a retractable tricycle landing gear, one of the first to be used in the Soviet Union. Unlike the mainly metal (on the proposed production version) D.XXIII, the SAM-13 was almost completely of wooden construction and was much smaller, with a 25.75-foot (7.85-m) length (Gordon has 7.68 m (25.2 feet)) and a 23.95-foot (7.3-m) wingspan. The D.XXIII had a length of 33.46 feet (10.2 m), and the wooden wings were of 37.73 feet (11.5 m) in span. The engines were MV-6s, licence-built air-cooled inline Renault engines of 220 hp.

The SAM-13 first flew in late 1940. It was tested at the LII during spring 1941 by the famous test pilot Mark L. Gallai. During testing, the aircraft reached a top speed of 423 mph (680 kph) at 13,123 feet (4,000 m). Despite the promising performance, the invasion by Germany and subsequent destruction of the prototype halted all further development.

Nikitin-Shevchenko

In the 1930s, the VVS faced the same question that dogged other air forces at the time—which was better: the monoplane with its superior speed or the biplane with its superior handling and manoeuvrability? In a truly inventive attempt to solve this question, two Soviet designers decided to combine the two. These engineers—Vasiliy Vasilyevich Nikitin and Nikitin's test pilot Vladimir Vasilyevich Shevchenko (also spelt 'Shyevchyenko')—came up with an ingenious solution. Nikitin had built sporting aircraft and an analogue to the U-2/Po-2 called the 'NV-5' or 'U-5' and a one-off development of the NV-5 called the Lsh. For the development of their ideas regarding fighters, OKB-30 was organised in the middle of 1939 to put these ideas into practice.

IS-1

The first result was the remarkable Nikitin-Shevchenko IS-1 ('IS' for *Istrebitel' Skladnoiy*, meaning 'Folding Fighter', although it was also understood that 'IS' could stand for 'Iosef Stalin'). This aeroplane had a retractable lower wing in what was one of the first variable-geometry aircraft. The concept was relatively simple. The aircraft would take off as a biplane, preserving the biplane's ease of handling for take-off (and landing), then the lower wing, along with the main landing gear, would retract into recesses on the sides of the fuselage and the underside of the upper wing. Once in the air, the aircraft would continue flying as a cantilever high-wing monoplane, with the high speed of a modern monoplane. Before landing, the lower wing and landing gear would again be lowered, and the aircraft would land as a biplane.

The aircraft was of all-metal construction, with both steel and dural components, with the control surfaces being fabric-covered. The armament consisted of two ShKAS machine guns in each upper wing. The engine was the M-63 of 900 hp, the same engine that powered later versions of the I-153 and I-16. The aircraft flew for the first time on 6 November 1940. In tests, the IS-1 showed a top speed of 281 mph (453 kph), which was only very marginally better than that of the I-153 at 280 mph (451 kph). Development was stopped in favour of the improved IS-2.

Nikitin-Shevchenko IS-1 in 1940. (*Viktor Kulikov's collection*)

IS-2

Even though the wing retraction of the IS-1 had worked well in testing, the aircraft's performance was found lacking. In response to this, the improved IS-2 was built, which had a more powerful engine, the M-88 of 1,100 hp, in a more streamlined cowling with a large spinner, had cantilever horizontal tailplanes replacing the strut-braced units of the IS-1, and featured a retractable tailwheel. All this was done to squeeze more performance out of the basic design. The IS-2 also featured heavier armament, with the outer two of the ShKAS 7.62-mm (30-calibre) machine guns being replaced by UBS 12.7-mm (50-calibre) machine guns. The vertical tailplane was changed in shape, becoming more circular. Like the IS-1, the IS-2 was of all-metal construction (a photograph appears to show that some of the rear fuselage was fabric-covered). The OKB estimated the top speed would be 365 mph (588 kph). The aircraft was ready for testing by January 1941.

As with the IS-1, the retracting wing mechanism worked flawlessly. Although the official reason given for halting development was the inadequate performance of the IS-2, I strongly suspect other factors were at work. Despite the wing retraction mechanism working well under test conditions, where it was carefully attended to by expert mechanics, the situation would have been different in service conditions. It was especially clear that keeping the mechanism working in the chaotic conditions of a wartime environment would have been rather daunting. In addition, combat damage to the wing retraction gear might well be catastrophic, with only the wing on one side extending, for example. Although the concept had proven to be workable, it was not practical for a warplane, and further testing on the IS-2 stopped; it only flew four test flights.

Nikitin-Shevchenko IS-2 in 1941. (*Viktor Kulikov's collection*)

IS-3 (Project)

No information is now available on this projected version, although it may have featured a more powerful engine than the IS-2 in order to increase the performance.

IS-4 (Project)

In a further development of the retracting wing concept, this aeroplane would have featured a tricycle landing gear, a more powerful engine than the IS-1 and IS-2 (an AM-120 or AM-37 inline), and an enclosed cockpit. It would have featured two ShVAK 20-mm cannons (or two UBS) and four (or two) ShKAS 7.62-mm machine guns. It never went further than the drawing board as the practical problems of the retracting wing concept became apparent.

Pashinin I-21 (IP-21)

The designer immediately below Nikolaiy Polikarpov in the Polikarpov OKB, Mikhail Mikhailovich Pashinin (1902–73), designed this clean monoplane in response to the VVS's call for modern monoplane fighters. The resulting design was a streamlined and modern-looking monoplane fighter, with a cut-down rear fuselage and all-round vision canopy, which would eventually become standard on Soviet fighters. The aircraft was powered by a M-105P of 1,100 hp, featuring a fixed armament of one ShVAK 20-mm cannon and two ShKAS 7.62-mm machine guns.

The first prototype flew on 21 May 1940 (Gordon has 11 June 1940 by P. Fokin). The I-21 showed a top speed of 356 mph (573 kph) at 16,404 feet (5,000 m). Although it showed a respectable top speed, the I-21 also exhibited handling problems, suffering from instability, and had a high landing speed.

The second prototype was submitted for state trials in December 1940. The third prototype's initial flight was on 5 April 1941. The single ShVAK 20-mm cannon was replaced by a Baburin-Taubin BT-23 23-mm cannon. Production was not proceeded with as the LaGG-3, MiG-3, and Yak-1 were already in production.

Pashinin I-21, third prototype, in 1941. (*Viktor Kulikov's collection*)

Polikarpov

Although best known for his I-15 series of biplanes and his I-16 monoplane, Nikolaiy Polikarpov also designed new aircraft before and during the Second World War, before his death in 1944 of stomach cancer. None of these, unlike the I-15 and I-16 series, ever went into mass production. Part of the problem was that for various reasons, not all related to the aircraft designs, several test pilots, including the famous test pilots Valeriy Chkalov and Vasiliy Stepanchonok, died testing Polikarpov's wartime prototype fighter aircraft. The death of Valeriy Chkalov, a favourite of Stalin, proved particularly troublesome for Polikarpov.

I-170 (Project)

A development of the I-153, this aircraft would have featured an all-wooden fuselage replacing the steel tube structure of the I-153. In addition, it would have had tapered wings as opposed to the parallel-sided wings of the I-153, and the radial engine would have been replaced by a Klimov M-106 inline engine.

Design of the aircraft was started in the summer of 1939, but Polikarpov lost much of his engineering staff to the Mikoyan OKB during the year, and the project was eventually abandoned. The loss of these individuals may well have been due to Stalin's antipathy towards Polikarpov, explained more fully below.

I-180

A development of the I-16, the I-180 featured a longer fuselage, a more powerful engine, and completely redesigned all-metal wings, including metal covering, though the fuselage retained the wooden structure of the I-16. Although the cockpit was normally open on the prototypes, the third example was tested with an aft sliding canopy, which was intended for use on the production examples. The engine was the 960-hp Tumanskiy M-88 radial engine. Four ShKAS machine guns were carried, with two in the cowling and two in the wing centre section, equipped with 200 rounds apiece. The I-180 was also designed to carry 441 lb (200 kg) of bombs.

Still lacking armament and with its landing gear locked down, the prototype made its first flight on 15 December 1938. Unfortunately, while on its landing approach, the engine failed and the aircraft crashed, mortally injuring the famous test pilot Valeriy Chkalov. This was to have far-reaching consequences as Chkalov was a personal favourite of Stalin and the most famous and lionised pilot in the Soviet Union at the time. Due to this crash, Dmitriy Lyudvigovich Tomashevich, Polikarpov's deputy at the time, was arrested and imprisoned, although since Polikarpov himself had not given his permission for the flight, he was not personally punished, officially at least.

Despite the crashes, continued testing showed the I-180 to be manoeuvrable, faster, and more stable than the I-16. It was decided to put the I-180 into production.

Ten production examples of the I-180, with open cockpits, were produced before production was stopped, and these aircraft never saw active service, being instead used for various tests. It is indeed possible, even likely, that Josef Stalin never forgave Polikarpov for the I-180 killing his favourite pilot, Valeriy Chkalov, and was from then

Polikarpov I-180, third prototype, in 1940. This aircraft has an enclosed cockpit, unlike most of the I-180s. (*Viktor Kulikov's collection*)

on prejudiced against Polikarpov and his designs; Stalin was not one to forgive nor forget. One source opines that Stalin was not biased against Nikolaiy Polikarpov due to Chkalov's death as he still allowed Polikarpov to design aircraft, but it is rather telling that none of these designs ever went into production, even the highly regarded I-185 fighter. After the very small production run of the I-180 (ten aircraft), until Polikarpov's death on 30 July 1944, not a single new Polikarpov design left the production lines.

I-185

Built to the same specification which produced the I-210 M-82A (Mig-9), the I-185 also featured a radial engine and clean lines. It was similar in construction and layout to the I-16 and I-180, featuring a wooden fuselage combined with metal wings and horizontal tailplanes with a metal covering over the metal structure (as with the I-180). The engine intended for the production version was the experimental Shvetsov M-71 radial engine (initially, the Tumanskiy M-90 was planned), and the I-185 was armed with three ShVAK 20-mm cannons arrayed around the cowling with 100 rounds apiece. All the landing gear were retractable and covered by doors, and the pilot was provided with an enclosed cockpit, with an aft-sliding canopy very similar to that used by the I-210. In appearance, the I-185 resembled both the I-210 and the La-5, also radial-engined fighters built in the same time period.

The first prototype was equipped with a Shvetsov M-81 engine of 1,200 hp, but only one brief take-off and landing (on 11 January 1941) was attempted. This aircraft was later re-engined with the much more powerful M-71, of 2,000 hp. The second prototype, completed at the end of 1940, was equipped with a M-82A of 1,600 hp and had three ShVAK 20-mm cannons fitted. It began OKB tests in May 1941. Compared to the M-71-equipped I-185, the front section of the fuselage was smaller in diameter due to the smaller size of the M-82A compared to the M-71.

Three (or four) prototypes were used for service trials beginning November 1942 at the Rzhev Salient west of Moscow, but they were forbidden to fly over German-

Polikarpov I-185 with M-71 engine in 1941. (*Viktor Kulikov's collection*)

controlled territory. Two sorties were flown where the I-185s protected a P-40 Kittyhawk flying a reconnaissance mission. On another sortie, a free hunt over Soviet territory, it was recorded that a German aircraft was damaged or destroyed by the pilot Borovykh. These sorties took place from 9 December 1942 to 12 January 1943.

Pilots who flew the aircraft considered it to be the best fighter then available to the Soviet Union, perhaps in the world. In comparison with the performance of the LaGG-3, MiG-3, Yak-7B, P-39, Spitfire Mk Vb, Bf 109F, and the He 100, the I-185 was judged to be superior. For a time, it appeared that this outstanding aircraft would enter production at Z.81. In April 1942, the M-71 *Etalon* was built and tested by the Polikarpov OKB beginning on 10 June 1942. It was submitted for NII VVS trials on 18 November 1942. The sea-level speed was an impressive 373 mph (600 kph), with a top speed of 404 mph (650 kph). In a combat turn, the aircraft gained 4,921 feet (1,500 m). However, on 5 April 1943, test pilot Vasiliy Stepanchonok died in a crash while attempting a dead-stick (engine-out) landing. The carburettor had become clogged, causing the engine to stall at low altitudes. This crash may have been the proverbial 'last straw' when it came to the production of the I-185.

Due to various circumstances, such as using much more aluminium than the mostly wooden La-5 and the non-production of the M-71 engine, the aircraft was never produced. A. S. Yakovlev, who some believe had strong, even undue influence with Stalin in aviation matters, understandably did not want his fighters displaced by Polikarpov fighters and may have influenced Stalin in his decision not to produce the I-185. One of the reasons given was the supposedly short range of the I-185, but other fighters with shorter ranges were in production or were later produced. Despite the non-availability of the M-71 engine, if Stalin had wished for the I-185 to be produced, the M-82 could have been used, even if it meant fewer M-82s were available for use by the La-5, or production of the La-5 could have even been stopped and the La-5 replaced by the I-185 (which would then have been designated the 'Po-15').

Polikarpov I-185 with M-82A engine in 1941 Note the highly polished metal propeller blades. (*Viktor Kulikov's collection*)

In all probability, Stalin's prejudice against Polikarpov entered into the decision not to proceed with production, despite the excellent characteristics displayed by the aircraft and the high praise it received from its pilots. Another very important factor was the reluctance of the Soviets to do anything that might interfere with the production of other established fighters as the Soviets had to continually replenish their heavy losses at the front. The Polikarpov I-185 is one of those interesting 'might-have-beens' of aeronautical history.

I-190

The I-190 was a development of the I-153, featuring a more powerful engine, and was cleaned up aerodynamically in an effort to generate more speed from the basic biplane design. It had become apparent that the I-153 was about as fast as it was ever going to be, despite increases in engine power, absent some significant redesign. The I-190 was the result of this redesign.

The I-190 featured cantilever horizontal tailplanes, a forward-retracting tailwheel, and plywood-covered wooden wings (as opposed to fabric-covered), all to create a more aerodynamically clean airframe. In addition, the cowling was better streamlined and featured a large spinner for improved aerodynamics. The lower wings were approximately the same span as the I-153's but were of a broader chord and carried ailerons. The upper wings retained the same size and shape as on the I-153 and had similar ailerons, but as with the lower wings, the upper wings were covered in 1.5-mm thick plywood as opposed to the fabric-covered wings of the I-153. The I-190 still featured an open cockpit, the gull-wing, I-shaped interplane struts, and wire-bracing between the upper and lower wings of the I-153. The retractable main landing gear was also similar between the two aircraft.

The first I-190 prototype flew for the initial time on 30 December 1939 by test pilot A. I. Zhukov, utilising a ski undercarriage. The aircraft featured a 1,100-hp

Polikarpov I-190 in 1940. The aircraft is in an overall light grey finish often used on Soviet aircraft prototypes. (*Viktor Kulikov's collection*)

Tumanskiy M-88V engine driving a three-bladed propeller and was armed with four ShKAS machine guns (it was also supposed to have two ShVAK 20-mm cannons but evidently these were never fitted).

During the testing of the I-190, different propellers were used, and the cowling, was elongated like the I-180 cowling to provide better aerodynamics. Originally, the aircraft had a direct-drive M-88 engine, but this was replaced by a geared M-88R after an accident in April 1940, with this M-88R eventually being replaced with a M-88A engine. Despite the considerable efforts at improving the aerodynamics (and performance) of the I-153 design, the I-190 proved to have an insufficient performance advantage over that aircraft, displaying a top speed of 303 mph (488 kph) at 16,404 feet (5,000 m) as compared to the 280 mph (451 kph) of the I-153. It was intended that the aircraft should have a maximum speed of 311 mph (500 kph).

After the crash of the first prototype on 13 February 1941, flown by test pilot Ulyakhin (he was uninjured, but the aircraft was badly damaged), all further development was discontinued on the I-190. The partially built second prototype, which was to have a pressurised cockpit (with an enclosed canopy) and a turbo-supercharger, was not completed; Bill Gunston states that it was completed with a ducted spinner like that planned for the I-195 and had the pressurised cabin. It was designated as the I-190GK, where the 'GK' stood for *s Ghermeticheskoy Kabinoy*, meaning 'Hermetic Cabin'.

I-195 (Project)

Polikarpov made one final effort to create a biplane fighter—the I-195. This design was even more streamlined than the I-190, featuring a larger ducted spinner that blended smoothly with the cowling and an enclosed pressurised cockpit, though Yefim

Gordon states it was unpressurised. Although the upper wings were still to be braced by I struts to the lower wings, with the gull-winged configuration being preserved, there was to be no wire bracing, and the tailplanes were cantilever. It was also to have had the 1,500-hp Tumanskiy M-90 engine, which was projected to give it a top speed of 367 mph (590 kph, although Gunston has 580 kph (360 mph)). The fixed armament would have comprised two ShVAK 20-mm cannons and two 12.7-mm (50-calibre) machine guns, as well as a disposable armament of 551 lb (250 kg) of bombs. However, Polikarpov realised that the time of the biplane was passed, and the I-195 apparently never progressed beyond the design phase, although Gunston states that it was partially built. In any case, it was neither completed nor flown.

ITP (M, M-1)

First designed in 1940, this cannon-armed single-engined fighter did not first fly until 23 February 1942 because of the disruptions caused by the German invasion in 1941. The name stood for *Istrebitel' Tyazhyoliy Pushechniy*, meaning 'Heavy Cannon(-armed) Fighter', as in a cannon-armed heavy fighter. It was intended for both fighter and ground attack duties and was heavily armed with a ShK37 37-mm cannon firing through the spinner and two ShVAK 20-mm cannons mounted on the cowling. Alternatively, the 37-mm cannon could be replaced by a 20-mm cannon. It was of mixed construction with a wooden fuselage and metal wings. The engine was the Klimov M-107P of 1,400 hp.

It first flew, piloted by A. I. Nikashin, on 23 February 1942. The top speed was 407 mph (655 kph) at 20,669 feet (6,300 m) according to Gunston, yet according to Gordon, the performance was not determined. The tests were not completed because of problems with the engine, a recurrent theme with M-107-equipped aircraft. The M-107 was replaced with a M-107A and the 37-mm cannon was replaced with a 20-mm cannon. The aircraft ended up being used for static tests (which is why, according to Yefim Gordon, the performance was never determined).

Polikarpov ITP (M-1) in 1942. (*Viktor Kulikov's collection*)

M-2

Similar to the ITP (M-1), the M-2 was equipped first with an AM-37, which proved unreliable, then an AM-39A engine. It was equipped with three ShVAK 20-mm cannons.

The M-2 first flew on 23 November 1943, with Nikolay V. Gavrilov at the controls. With the AM-39A engine, the top speed was 404 mph (650 kph) at 8,202 feet (2,500 m). It was tested into June 1944, but no production resulted as the Polikarpov OKB was winding down after the death of its chief designer, Nikolaiy Polikarpov. It was also not produced because there were already aircraft in production with similar performance.

TIS (A)

This very clean twin-engined monoplane aircraft was designed as an escort fighter, especially for the TB-7 (Pe-8) four-engined heavy bomber. The 'TIS' stood for *Tyazhyoliy Istrebitel' Soprovozhdeniya*, meaning 'Heavy Fighter Escort'. The 'A' was apparently an internal OKB designation for 'Aircraft A'. It was of all-metal construction and included a rear gunner (a radio-operator/gunner). The armament consisted of four ShKAS machine guns in the nose, two ShVAK 20-mm cannons in the wing roots according to Gunston (Gordon has two 37-mm cannons), and an upper and lower ShKAS for the radio-operator/gunner (the upper gun was on a TSS mounting). The aircraft was powered by twin AM-37 inline engines of 1,400 hp. Like the Grushin GR-1, the TIS was something of an analogue to the German Bf 110, even featuring a very similar forward-firing armament.

The aircraft first flew in September 1941, piloted by N. V. Gavrilov. The top speed was recorded as 345 mph (555 kph) at 19,029 feet (5,800 m). As the AM-37 engine did not go into production, it was decided to build a second prototype with AM-39 engines, although in the event, this aircraft flew with the AM-38F as the TIS (MA), described below.

Polikarpov TIS (A) in 1941. (*Viktor Kulikov's collection*)

TIS (MA)

A development of the TIS, this aircraft had taller vertical tails, an AM-38F (the engine used on the Il-2) instead of the AM-37 engines or the unavailable AM-39, and a heavier armament. The armament now consisted of two UBK heavy 12.7-mm (0.50-calibre) machine guns in the nose, two Sh-37 37-mm cannons in the wing roots, a NS-45 45-mm cannon in an under-fuselage gondola (Gordon has two 45-mm cannons in the wing roots), and one ShKAS for the radio-operator/gunner in a VUB-1 turret replacing the earlier TSS mount (the ventral gun position of the TIS was deleted). The 'MA' in the designation stood for *Mnogotsyelevoiy A*, meaning 'Multi-role A' (from the designation 'Aircraft A').

Flight testing was done by N. V. Gavrilov from June to September 1944. The aircraft crashed on 16 September 1944 and was not rebuilt as Polikarpov had died by then and his OKB was being run down. The top speed was 332 mph (535 kph), with a service ceiling of 21,654 feet (6,600 m).

Sil'vanskiy I-220 (IS)

Designed by Aleksandr Vasilyevich Sil'vanskiy (1915–1978), this small aircraft resembled the I-16, although it certainly did not enjoy that aircraft's success. This aircraft was also known as the 'IS', for *Istrebitel' Silvanskovo*, meaning 'Silvanskiy Fighter'. It was a clean single-engined monoplane with retractable landing gear and an enclosed cockpit. Power was provided by a M-88 engine, although Yefim Gordon has a M-87A of 950 hp being used. The aircraft's structure was similar to that of its lookalike, the I-16.

Due to a design error, there was very little clearance between the propeller tips and the ground. Sil'vanskiy took the rather interesting expedience of cropping 3.94 inches (100 mm) off the propeller tips. After this was done, the aircraft was transferred to

Polikarpov TIS (MA) in 1944. (*Viktor Kulikov's collection*)

the LII for flight testing. Unfortunately, the propeller cropping had a disastrous effect upon performance, and the I-220 could barely take off. At full power, an unfortunate pilot (perhaps the TsAGI test pilot Sergey Korzinshchikov) was able to fly the aircraft up to 984 feet (300 m), at which point the aircraft was about to stall. The aircraft was successfully landed but never flew again, and in a rather telling statement on his designing abilities, Sil'vanskiy was banned from further aircraft design.

Sukhoi

Even though the OKB of Pavel Osipovich Sukhoi (1895–1975) was to enjoy great success post-war with its jet-powered fighters, fighter-bombers, and light bombers, during the Second World War, none of its fighters proceeded beyond the prototype phase. Before the Second World War, Pavel Sukhoi had worked under Andrey Tupolev, for whom he had designed the all-metal I-4 sesquiplane fighter in the late 1920s, and the all-metal I-14 monoplane fighter (a competitor to the I-16), which had retractable landing gear and was built in small numbers. In addition, he designed the mixed construction Su-2 light bomber, which was in production until 1942 and saw heavy service during the first two years of the Great Patriotic War. During the war, Sukhoi designed the single-engined Su-6 (which also led to the Su-7 fighter), an unsuccessful competitor to the Il-2 Shturmovik, and the twin-engined Su-8 shturmovik, which also did not go into production. In addition, he designed two related fighter aircraft, neither of which went into production, the Su-1 and the Su-3, as well as the mixed-power fighter, the Su-5.

Su-1 (I-135, I-330)

Designed as a high-altitude fighter, this single-engined single-seat aircraft was of mixed construction with a mainly wooden fuselage, metal wings, and metal horizontal tailplanes (resembling the Su-2 bomber in its construction). The fuselage featured fairly extensive metal sheathing to protect the wooden components from the exhaust of the semi-externally mounted TK-2 turbo-superchargers, one on each side. The main landing gear rotated to lie flat in the wings in the manner of the American Curtiss P-40 Warhawk (or 'Tomahawk' as it was called in Soviet service). The tailwheel retracted aft and was covered by doors, with the tyre partially protruding. The pilot was accommodated in a raised unpressurised cockpit, which however did not feature an all-around vison canopy, having a metal fairing in the back instead of clear glazing. The engine was a M-105P with two TK-2 turbo-superchargers. The armament comprised two ShVAK 20-mm cannons and two ShKAS 7.62-mm machine guns mounted in the engine's upper cowling.

The prototype first flew on 15 June 1940. Testing revealed problems with the reliability of the TK-2s; it reached a notable top speed of 398 mph (641 kph) at 32,808 feet (10,000 m). The Su-1 had a service ceiling of 41,011 feet (12,500 m). Despite this impressive performance, the Su-1 was superseded by the very similar Su-3, in part because the Su-1 was damaged when the Sukhoi OKB was evacuated from Podlipki (north-east of Moscow) to Molotov (Perm) in autumn 1941.

Sukhoi Su-1 in 1940. Note the large semi-external turbo-supercharger on the side of the engine. (*Viktor Kulikov's collection*)

Su-3 (I-135, I-360)

Although appearing almost identical to the Su-1 and featuring similar construction, the Su-3 differed in featuring a wing with a reduced span and with a different aerofoil. When the flight tests were finally conducted in March 1942, the Su-3 reached a top speed of 396 mph (638 kph), very slightly less than the Su-1 but still impressive. The Su-3 had a service ceiling of 39,042 feet (11,900 m). However, a resolution of the Council of People's Commissars dated 16 April 1941 had already stopped further development of the Su-1 and Su-3 apparently due to the unavailability (and unreliability when available) of the TK-2 superchargers, so no production ensued.

Su-5 (I-107)

This mixed-power aircraft was designed to the same specification that resulted in the I-250 (MiG-13), and like that aircraft, it utilised a piston engine that also powered via a driveshaft a small VRDK motorjet engine exhausting through the tail. The Su-5 was of all-metal construction. As with the I-250, it was a rather rotund aircraft, necessary on both aircraft to accommodate the large duct leading to the combustion chamber of the motorjet. The Su-5 utilised conventional retractable tailwheel landing gear.

The aircraft flew for the first time on 6 April 1945. Unlike the I-250, which went into very limited production, the Su-5 was not produced, with only one being built and flown. It did, however, achieve a top speed of 503 mph (809.5 kph) (one source has 493 mph) with its motorjet engaged, no mean achievement for a mainly piston-engined design.

Su-7

Based on the Su-6 shturmovik, this rather ungainly-looking single-engined fighter was of composite construction, with a wooden fuselage, an all-metal centre section for the wings,

Sukhoi Su-3 in 1942. (*Viktor Kulikov's collection*)

Sukhoi Su-5 in 1945. Note the rotund fuselage, made necessary by the ducting for the motorjet (as with the I-250/MiG-13). (*Viktor Kulikov's collection*)

metal tailplanes, and metal-sparred wooden-covered outer wings. Like the Su-1 and Su-3, there was extensive metal sheathing on the fuselage sides to protect the airframe from the supercharger exhaust. The engine was to be the M-71F radial engine equipped with TK-3 turbo-superchargers as the Su-7 was designed to be a high-altitude fighter. This engine was to drive a four-bladed propeller. When the M-71F was not produced, the engine was to be replaced with the M-82 (ASh-82FN), which powered the La-5 fighter. However, with this less powerful engine (1,850 hp compared to the 2,000 hp for the M-71F), the projected performance fell well short of expectations with a top speed of only 348 mph (560 kph) at 20,669 feet (6,300 m), and this version of the Su-7 remained apparently unbuilt. YG has this aircraft flying with the M-82 engine only, at least in 1943, but other sources seem to indicate this aircraft was not built by this time. Gunston has this aircraft being completed in late 1943, but other sources have it being built in 1944.

In an effort to give it more power for possible use as a high-altitude interceptor, the Su-7 design was now to be equipped with various versions of the RD rockets in the tail, with testing starting in late 1944. The aircraft was duly built, but the RDs were very unreliable, and there was scorching of the paint from the turbo-superchargers, and the Su-7 was not considered a viable fighter even with this additional powerplant despite the marked improvement in performance, with the top speed increased by 57 mph (91 kph) from the projected top speed of the M-82-only design. Development was discontinued, with testing ending in mid-December 1945 on the single prototype.

The history of the Su-7 is somewhat murky, and given the passage of time and the relative obscurity and unimportance of this experimental aircraft, it is probable that it will remain so.

Sukhoi Su-7 in 1945. There is extensive metal sheeting on the fuselage to protect it from the exhaust of the turbo-supercharger. Of interest is the elongated tail fairing, which protected the rocket engine. (*Viktor Kulikov's collection*)

Tairov

Vsevelod Konstantinovich Tairov (?–1941) had worked as a designer for Nikolaiy Polikarpov. His OKB was set up to build a twin-engined fighter for the Red Air Force. The fighters were built at Z.43. Unfortunately, Tairov was killed in a crash in December 1941 while travelling between Moscow and Kuibyshev. With his death, his OKB was shut down.

Ta-1 (OKO-6)

Built to a specification for a twin-engined escort fighter, this aircraft was in competition with the GR-1, the MiG DIS, and the Polikarpov TIS. Like those aircraft, it was a clean, modern, twin-engined monoplane. The Tairov design resulted from an effort to make the most streamlined twin-engined aircraft possible for use as a fighter and also as a ground attack aircraft. Towards this end, it featured short wings and a small-diameter oval-section fuselage, which contrasted with the large cowlings necessary to enclose the Tumanskiy M-88 1,000-hp radial engines. The propellers rotated in opposite directions to counteract the effect of torque.

The heavy armament consisted of two Berezin UB 12.7-mm machine guns in the upper nose (Gordon has two ShKAS) and four ShVAK 20-mm cannons in the forward part of the lower fuselage, and the single pilot was protected by armour in both front and back. The aircraft was mainly of metal aluminium alloy construction, with a wooden rear fuselage, and a single fin and rudder.

The aircraft flew for the first time on 31 December 1939, with this aircraft being tested at the LII until the middle of 1940. It had a top speed of 352 mph (567 kph) at 24,770 feet (7,550 m). It displayed stability problems which were addressed in the second prototype, the OKO-6bis.

OKO-6bis

An improved version of the Ta-1 was built, known as the 'OKO-6bis'. It differed from the Ta-1 in featuring a longer fuselage and endplates at the ends of the longer span horizontal tailplanes, at first retaining a central fin, though this was later deleted. These changes were made to improve longitudinal stability. The M-88 engines now both rotated to the left.

The TsAGI (LII) tests started in January 1941, with the aircraft piloted by A. Yemel'yanov. The top speed was 367 mph (590 kph) at 23,130 feet (7,050 m). The aircraft crashed on 14 January 1941 when one of the engines failed.

Ta-3 (OKO-6bis)

A third prototype was built—apparently, a rebuild of the Ta-1—with the wings increased in span. It was originally still designated as the OKO-6bis before being redesignated the 'Ta-3'. Unlike the Ta-1, the propellers on the Ta-3 rotated in the same direction as on the OKO-6bis. The engines were now M-89s, of 1,300 hp each. The Ta-3 carried the same armament as the Ta-1, but it could carry an alternative armament of two ShKAS, two ShVAK, and a 37-mm cannon. The top speed was 360 mph (580 kph) at 23,294 feet (7,100 m).

In the end, although a promising design with a powerful armament, the Ta-3 (and its competitors) did not go into production. The VVS simply did not feel the need for twin-engined fighters, instead preferring single-engined designs, which were simpler and easier to produce in large numbers and met the tactical needs of the VVS. The death of Vsevelod Tairov in late 1941 also deprived the Tairov OKB of its chief designer, sealing the fate of the Ta-3.

Ta-3bis

In one last attempt at creating a fighter fit for production, the Ta-3 was rebuilt as the Ta-3bis. The outer wings were now made of *elektron*, a magnesium alloy. The fuel tankage was increased and the wing dihedral decreased. If the aircraft had gone into production, the M-89s could have been replaced by M-82s, but as described above, the VVS was no longer interested in (single-seat) twin-engined fighters.

Tikhonravov I-302P

The BI-1 was not the only rocket-powered interceptor designed and built during the Second World War. The other all-rocket interceptor was the I-302. Design started in 1940 when designer Mikhail Klavdievich Tikhonravov (1900–74) of the RNII decided he could make a fighter with a rocket in the tail and ramjets under the wings.

It was decided to not use the ramjets, and the I-302 was changed to a rocket-powered only interceptor. The aircraft was tested as a glider as the I-302P in 1943, but it never flew under rocket power as the rockets were never made available and the project was abandoned.

Tomashevich '110'

Designed in the same *sharashka* (TsKB-29) in which Andrey Tupolev and Vladimir Petlyakov were imprisoned, this design of Dmitry Ludvigovich Tomashevich (1899–1974) was for a single-engined, single-seat fighter. Tomashevich found himself imprisoned for the crash of the first prototype of the Polikarpov I-180 (he was Polikarpov's deputy at the time), which had cost the life of the famous test pilot, Valeriy Chkalov.

As the new design came from the '110' department of the *sharashka*, it was designated as the '110' (in the same way that Petlyakov's fighter was designated as the VI-100, as it came from the '100' department). The '110' was equipped with the powerful new Klimov M-107 engine. To provide the necessary cooling for this temperamental new engine, the '110' featured a very large under nose radiator, rather like later versions of the Curtiss P-40.

The '110' was of mainly metal construction, with a steel tube forward fuselage, and metal wings and horizontal tailplanes of aluminium alloy (dural) construction, with the control surfaces being fabric covered. Only the rear fuselage was of wooden construction. It featured a fairly heavy armament, consisting of a 20-mm cannon firing

Tomashevich I-110, the first aircraft to be equipped with the Klimov M-107 (VK-107) engine, in 1942. (*Viktor Kulikov's collection*)

through the spinner, two 12.7-mm machine guns mounted on the top of the engine cowling, and two 7.62-mm machine guns in the wings, although Gordon has these 7.62-mm guns mounted above the cowling.

The first flight of the '110' occurred at the end of 1942. The top speed was recorded as 379 mph (610 kph) at 20,341 feet (6,200 m), with a service ceiling of 32,808 feet (10,000 m). The climb rate was poor as the aircraft was overweight. It was not produced as its performance was not superior to that of aircraft that were already in production.

Although it was not put into production, the '110' was nevertheless a significant aircraft in being the first design to be powered by the new M-107 engine, which would go on to power later versions of the Yak-9 fighters (the Yak-9U and Yak-9P). The long and arduous process of making the M-107 a viable engine for production aircraft started with the '110'.

Yakovlev I-29 (BB-22IS)

Yakovlev designed a high-speed twin-engined aircraft (the 'Ya-22') that could be used for various purposes, such as a high-speed light bomber (the 'BB-22'), reconnaissance aircraft, and as a fighter. The fighter version received the 'I-29' designation, were the 'I' stood for *Istrebitel'* meaning 'Fighter' (literally in Russian 'Destroyer'). It was designed as an escort fighter with two ShVAK 20-mm cannons under the fuselage and increased fuel, according to Bill Gunston, who has it as being flown by Pyotr M. Stefanovskiy in early 1941, although another source has it flying as early as February 1939. It was apparently similar in appearance to the Ya-22, not the later Yak-4 light bomber.

Unlike the reconnaissance and light bomber versions of the Ya-22 (the Yak-2, and Yak-4), the I-29 was neither produced nor used in combat. Its existence has even been questioned, as the records are not very clear nor voluminous on this aircraft.

Yatsenko I-28

Designed by Vladimir Panfilovich Yatsenko, the I-28 was a low-wing cantilever monoplane of modern configuration, with an enclosed cockpit and inwards retracting main landing gear, the tailwheel also being retractable. The wings had a reverse gull-winged inner section and the pilot was positioned aft of the wing, which with the large radial engine, must have adversely affected his view on take-off and landing.

Like the LaGG-3, the I-28 was of almost completely wooden construction, with only the engine and the front fuselage covered in metal but differed in featuring a radial engine instead of the LaGG-3's inline M-105. The first prototype had a Tumanskiy M-87A engine of 950 hp, while the second prototype had a Tumanskiy M-88 of 1,000 hp. The armament consisted of two ShKAS 7.62-mm and two ShVAK 12.7-mm machine guns (the 12.7-mm ShVAK was the basis for the ShVAK 20-mm cannon).

The first prototype of the I-28 was tested from 1 June 1939 to 4 July 1939 by P. M. Stefanovskiy. The top speed was 339 mph (545 kph) at 19,685 feet (6,000 m). The second prototype was tested from 20 April 1940 to 15 May 1940 by Aleksey G. Kubyshkin. The top speed was 352 mph (566 kph) at 22,966 feet (7,000 m), which was a respectable top speed given the relatively low-powered M-88 engine (1,000 hp). Five further aircraft were built but these did not go into service and development of the I-28 was halted in June 1940.

The I-28 was the fourth aircraft to be built in response to the 1939 Soviet requirement for a modern fighter, and the only one of the four that did not go into mass production, the three aircraft designs that were produced being the LaGG-3, the MiG-3, and the Yak-1 fighters. It was considered that these other designs were more advanced (presumably making them more amenable to continued development).

Yatsenko I-28 in 1939. (*Viktor Kulikov's collection*)

12
Experimental Fighter Specifications

N.B. Metric measurements are in parentheses			
Type	I-28 – first Prototype	I-180 No. 2	I-185 M-71
Year	1939	1939	1942
Engine	M-87A	M-87B	M-71
Max. Power (Horsepower)	950	950	2,000
Fixed Armament	2 × ShKAS 7.62-mm machine guns, 2 × ShVAK 12.7-mm machine guns	4 × ShKAS 7.62-mm machine guns	3 × ShVAK SP-20 20-mm cannons
Disposable Armament	N/A	441 lb (200 kg) of bombs	8 RS-82 Rockets, 1,102 lb (500 kg) of bombs
Length—feet (m)	28.02 (8.54)	22.28 (6.79)	25.10 (7.65)
Wingspan—feet (m)	31.5 (9.6)	32.97 (10.05)	32.12 (9.79)
Weight (Empty)—lb (kg)	-	4,453 (2,020)	6,274 (2,846)
Weight (Loaded)—lb (kg)	5,864 (2,660)	4,938 (2,240)	7,716 (3,500)
Max. Speed at Sea Level—mph (kph)	256 (412)	254 (408)	345 (556)
Top Speed—mph (kph)	339 (545)	336 (540)	391 (630)
Range—miles (km)	-	497 (800)	519 (835)
Service Ceiling—feet (m)	34,121 (10,400)	33,629 (10,250)	-
Turn Time (sec)	-	21	-

I-222	IS-2	TIS (A)
1944	1942	1941
AM-39B-1	M-88	2 × AM-37
1,500	1,100	1,400
2 × ShVAK SP-20 20-mm cannons	2 × ShKAS 7.62-mm machine guns, 2 × UBS 12.7-mm machine guns	6 × ShKAS machine guns, 2 × 37-mm cannons
N/A	N/A	-
31.51 (9.603)	23.29 (7.1) (or 24.15 (7.36) according to Gunston)	38.39 (11.7)
42.65 (13.0)	28.22 (8.6)	50.85 (15.5)
6,982 (3,167)	-	12,787 (28,191)
8,356 (3,790)	6,195 (2,810)	17,284 (7,840)
-	291 (468)	304 (490)
424 or 429 (682 or 691)	Estimated – 365 (588)	345 (555)
621 (1,000)	-	1,069 (1,720)
47,572 (14,500)	36,089 (11,000)	35,433 (10,800)
-	-	-

13
Concluding Thoughts

At the beginning of the Second World War, the Soviet Union was equipped with obsolescent aircraft such as the Polikarpov biplane fighters the I-15bis and I-153 as well as the early 1930s design, the Polikarpov I-16 monoplane (very advanced when introduced in 1934, but obsolescent by 1939). Although the I-153 and I-16 performed well enough in the Khalkhin-Gol conflict in 1939, by the Winter War with the Finnish in 1939–40 against more modern aircraft, it was clear that they were outdated. By the beginning of the Great Patriotic War in mid-1941, these aircraft were hopelessly outclassed by German aircraft such as the Bf 109E and Bf 109F, and even the twin-engined Bf 110. The entry into service on the Eastern Front in 1942 of the fast, tough, and heavily armed Fw 190 and the enhanced Bf 109G-2 did not improve matters for the Soviets.

The Soviets had realised even before the beginning of the Second World War that their fighter force urgently needed modernising, and by the start of Operation Barbarossa on 22 June 1941, three new modern fighters were entering service—the LaGG-3, the MiG-3, and the Yak-1. Although the high-altitude MiG-3 was a dead-end in an air war that was fought largely at low altitudes, the LaGG-3 and Yak-1 were developed into aircraft that eventually equalled, then bettered the Luftwaffe fighters, with aircraft such as the La-5FN, La-7, Yak-3, and Yak-9U.

At the beginning of the Great Patriotic War, the Soviet Union was faced with a perfect storm that threatened to overwhelm their air forces. The effects of the military purges of the late 1930s had deprived them of many experienced commanders and pilots, the slowness in bringing modern aircraft into production left them with large numbers of obsolete fighters still in front-line service, and the limited number of new modern fighters they had were flown by pilots with little experience in them. Add to that the presence of large numbers of poorly-trained pilots resulting from the rapid expansion of the Red Air Force in 1940 and 1941 and an experienced and well-equipped foe in the Luftwaffe, and the results were predictable—for at least the first six months of the war, the Soviets suffered huge casualties with their aircraft both on the ground and in the air. The situation would improve, but that was little solace to the many hundreds of pilots who perished in those terrible (to the Soviets) first months of the war.

For at least the initial two years of the Great Patriotic War, the Soviets were also hindered by the lack of radios in their aircraft. This affected their ability to communicate in the air, with the commander having to use hand signals and wing movements to indicate to his pilots his intentions. This meant the pilots in his formation had to fly closely together to see the signals, which limited their flexibility. The lack of radios also made communication with the ground impossible. This problem was gradually resolved as the war went on and more fighters were equipped first with a receiver and then with two-way radios (receiver and transmitter), enabling better communication in the air and with ground forces, but it is true that avionics (aviation electronics) were never the Soviets' strength.

A persistent problem with Soviet fighters—and indeed all Soviet-built aircraft during the war—was the very frequently poor quality of the workmanship. Fit and finish were lacking due to the constant demand for more aircraft and the often-inexperienced workers that constructed them (the experienced workers were in the military). As the war went on, this state of affairs improved somewhat as the Soviet leadership, both political and aviation, realised that their aircraft were not built to high standards and made some efforts to improve this situation. The workers also became more experienced as the war continued.

One factor that mitigated against this poor construction was that many of these sub-par aircraft coming from the production lines were extensively refitted (or even rebuilt) at the PARMs (the field aircraft repair workshops) before they were ever released to front-line units. Ironically, some of the experienced workers who would have been in the production lines if not for the war were now serving in these PARMs. In a way, the final finishing of the aircraft was just moved from the factory to the PARMs.

A lack the Soviets never really solved, at least for fighters, was the development of a dependable high-powered inline engine. The Klimov M-107/VK-107, although powerful at 1,600 hp, was never a reliable engine, certainly not during the Second World War. The large (1,940-lb) and powerful (1,770-hp) Mikulin AM-38F engine was desperately needed for the Il-2 ground attack aircraft and therefore not available for use in fighter aircraft. Despite this, the inline-engined Yakovlev fighters were able to flourish due to their small size and light weight, allowing them to take full advantage of the relatively low-powered (1,290-hp, maximum), but light (1,323 lb in the M-105PF) Klimov M-105 engines available to them.

The Soviets were able to make a virtue out of necessity; these small aircraft, necessary because of the low power of the Soviet inline engines, preserved precious resources and were also highly manoeuvrable. This is a tribute to wartime Soviet ingenuity in the face of technological problems. In addition, the Soviets were able to develop a powerful and successful radial engine in the Shvetsov M-82/ASh-82 (1,850 hp in its M-82FN/ASh-82FN version), which allowed the mediocre LaGG-3 to be developed into the good La-5 and superb La-7 fighters.

Another lack the Soviets never properly solved was creating reliable turbo-superchargers for use with high-altitude aircraft. This was not for lack of trying as even biplane fighters before the Great Patriotic War such as the I-15bis and I-153 had been fitted with both turbo-superchargers and pressurised cockpits for high-altitude flying. Although aircraft such as the La-7TK, Yak-7PD, and Yak-9PD were tested (and in the case of the La-7TK and Yak-9PD even produced in very small numbers), they proved unreliable due to unreliable engines and turbo-superchargers and incapable of intercepting high-flying German aircraft. Fortunately for the Soviets, this problem did not become a serious one as German high-altitude overflights of cities such as Leningrad and Moscow were never too common, and after 1943, they ceased altogether.

It should be mentioned that as the war continued, the Soviets received increasing amounts of aluminium from American Lend-Lease shipments. This enabled the Soviets to use more aluminium in the design and construction of their fighters. The Yak-9 and Yak-3 had metal wing spars where the earlier Yak-1 and Yak-7 had wooden wing spars. The same situation existed with the Lavochkin fighters, where the increased availability of aluminium allowed the later examples of the La-5FN and all of the La-7s to have metal wing spars as opposed to the wooden wings spars of the earlier Lavochkin fighters. This increased use of aluminium in the structure of Soviet fighters allowed them to be lighter, stronger, and more durable. Nonetheless, the Soviet-built single-engined fighters of the Great Patriotic War were still of largely wooden or mixed construction, out of necessity. All-metal single-engined fighters such as the Yak-9P and La-9 had to wait for the post-war period.

One interesting note about German and Soviet aircraft is the differing amount they improved during the Great Patriotic War. Even discounting the clearly obsolete early war Polikarpov fighters, the Soviet fighters greatly improved as the war progressed. The La-7 was a vast improvement over the early war LaGG-3, and the Yak-9U and Yak-3 were also greatly improved over the earlier Yak-1. While the German aircraft inexorably increased in weight, the Soviets were better able to keep the weight of their aircraft down and make their aircraft lighter in some cases, notably the Yak-3.

The German aircraft were not improved as dramatically as the Soviet aircraft during the Great Patriotic War at least in part because they did not need to improve as much as the Soviet aircraft; there was much more room for improvement with the Soviet fighters. This is one reason why the Bf 109 saw much less improvement for most of the Great Patriotic War; the Bf 109 had seen most of its improvement—from the Bf 109A through the Bf 109F—before the Great Patriotic War had even started.

The difference between the Bf 109F and its development, the Bf 109G, was in the area of engine development (a more powerful engine) and heavier armament and armour, which did not confer better manoeuvrability or handling on these later Bf 109s. Indeed, many German pilots felt that from a flying aspect, the Bf 109F was the best handling of the Bf 109s and a better dogfighter than the Bf 109G, although the Bf 109G was better-armed and armoured, and some of the Bf 109Gs were considerably faster. The last version of the Bf 109 to see action during the war, the Bf 109K-4, a sort of rationalised late-model Bf 109G, was very fast, with a top speed of 452 mph (727 kph), but it came too late in the war to make any difference.

One area where the Bf 109 did not improve nearly as much as Soviet aircraft was in the area of the pilot's visibility. Although some later Bf 109Gs did have improved visibility, with the less heavily framed 'Erla Haube' canopy, and with armour glass replacing the solid metal headrest, it did not match the all-around visibility of Soviet fighters such as later Yak-1s and Yak-7s, the Yak-9 and Yak-3, the La-5F and La-5FN, and the La-7, with their bubble-type canopies. The Fw 190, on the other hand, had always featured all-around visibility, which was only improved with the 'blown' canopies of some of the Fw 109Fs, Gs, and later As.

The later radial-engined Fw 190As and Fw 190Fs and Gs had little (if any) advantage in terms of handling and manoeuvrability on the earlier Fw 190As, which had first seen combat in 1942 on the Eastern Front. The late-war Fw 190s were better-armed and armoured than the earlier Fw 190s, but this made them heavier and less manoeuvrable. The inline-engined developments, such as the Fw 190D and the Ta 152, like the Bf 109K arrived too late to be of benefit. It was almost as if German piston-engined aircraft development had peaked too early in the war, and the Soviets were given time to catch up and, with their last fighters, even exceed the German piston-engined fighters.

It may also be that there was a certain amount of complacency with the Germans as their fighters were so clearly superior to the Soviet fighters at the start of the Great Patriotic War that they felt little need to radically improve or replace them, believing that incremental improvements were enough. They may have also felt that the 'sub-human' Soviets simply could not make aircraft well enough to match theirs. The Soviets were not allowed the luxury of such contentment. Another factor may be that the Germans believed that their efforts should be devoted towards developing and building their jet fighters, such as the Me 262—efforts that might have been better used in the short term to improve the now obsolete (in German eyes) piston-engined fighters. With no jet fighters to develop or build, this did not happen to the Soviets.

As far as the Eastern Front was concerned, the Germans should have been concentrating on developing and producing fighters that were better at low altitude to combat the Soviets. However, the Germans faced a conundrum the Soviets did not; they were fighting a two-front war with differing requirements. German fighters had to perform well at high altitude to combat the high-flying Western Allied bombers and escort fighters. The Soviets were faced with no such problem; they could concentrate on making their aircraft excel at low-altitude flight, and by the end of the war, they had bettered the German fighters at low-altitude combat.

It is true that as the war progressed, there were increasing numbers of American and British Lend-Lease fighters in service with the Soviets, which eased the production burden on the Soviet Union. Nevertheless, these aircraft were always very much in the minority in the VVS, AVMF, ADD, and PVO. The most numerous of the Lend-Lease fighters was the Bell P-39 Airacobra, of which 4,952 were used by the Soviet Union. This compares with the 22,422 Lavochkin fighters and 35,096 Yakovlev fighters that were built from 1940–45.

Without getting into the old argument about how vital Lend-Lease may have been to Soviet victory, the Soviets won the air war against the Axis mainly using Soviet-built aircraft. Some 14,093 Lend-Lease fighters were used by the Soviet Union during the Second World War, although 2,400 of these were Bell P-63 Kingcobras, which did not see action during the Great Patriotic War; if this number is subtracted, the number of Lend-Lease fighters becomes 11,693. This number of 11,693 can be compared to the number of Soviet fighters built from 1941 through the first six months of 1945—58,513. This means that of the 70,476 fighters available to the Soviets during the Great Patriotic War, some 16.6 per cent, were Lend-Lease fighters—a not inconsiderable percentage, but still greatly in the minority.

The Soviets were also able to achieve air superiority in 1944 and air dominance in 1945 partly because of the withdrawal of most German dedicated fighters from the Eastern Front to combat the growing presence of the Anglo-American strategic bombing campaign in Western and Central Europe (the Combined Bomber Offensive). The gradual achievement of air superiority by the Soviets can be seen by the increasing number of sorties flown before loss (this includes all Soviet aircraft, not just fighters): 1941—1:32 (one loss for every thirty-two sorties), 1943—1:72, and 1945—1:165. For the Germans, the situation was the reverse: 1942—1:25.5, 1943—1:22.5, and 1945—1:11.

The Germans' increasingly crippling lack of fuel contributed to the inability of the Luftwaffe to even win back air parity with the Soviets, who had also suffered from lack of fuel, but this Soviet lack was alleviated by Lend-Lease supplies from the United States. Soviet air superiority was also achieved partly by the presence in 1944 and 1945 of such qualitatively superior Soviet fighters as the La-7, the Yak-3, and the Yak-9U. It has long been believed by some in the West (and by some 'revisionists' even in Russia), no doubt in the West coloured by old anti-Soviet Cold War prejudices, that the Soviets prevailed in the air because of the great quantity of aircraft they built, overpowering the Germans by sheer numbers. However, the facts would appear to be somewhat different. Although the Soviet air industry did out-produce the Germans throughout the war, by 1944, their new fighters, such as the La-7, Yak-3, and Yak-9U, were also better fighters at low altitudes than the German fighters they faced. By 1944, the Soviet Union had come a very long way indeed from the collection of obsolete fighters, and immature modern fighters with which they had faced the Germans at the start of the Great Patriotic War.

APPENDIX I

Ordnance

Fighter aircraft are not of much use without weapons, so below is a discussion of some of the guns, rockets, and bombs carried by Soviet fighters during the Second World War.

Guns

The main rifle-calibre weapon used in the Soviet Union on aircraft during the Second World War was the Shpitalniy-Komaritskiy ShKAS 7.62-mm (30-calibre) rapid-fire machine gun, which featured a revolving magazine. These guns were used both in moveable and fixed installations. Although they sometimes jammed, they had an extremely high rate of fire—1,800 rpm for the unsynchronised version and 1,600 rpm for the synchronised version. However, it was this high rate of fire that caused them to jam. Most fighters used the synchronised version. An 'Ultra-ShKAS' was even developed, with a maximum rate of fire of 3,000 rpm, but this gun jammed too readily and did not go into large-scale use.

The main aerial heavy machine gun used by the Soviets during the war was the Berezin UB 12.7-mm (50-calibre) machine gun. Like the ShKAS, this gun was used in both moveable (the UBT, the 'T' standing for *Turel*, or 'Turret') used on shturmoviks and bombers) and fixed (the UBK and UBS (used on fighters) versions, the UBS being synchronised to fire through the revolving propeller ('S' for *Sinkhronizovanniy* or 'Synchronised') and the wing-mounted UBK ('K' for *Krylo* or 'Wing') being unsynchronised. Soviet fighters normally used the synchronised UBS.

One trend that occurred as the war progressed was the smaller-calibre ShKAS machine guns were replaced by the larger, more powerful UB machine guns on fighters. This was done as the smaller-calibre guns were sometimes found to be lacking in power against the sturdily built and well-armoured German aircraft. Even so, there were continuing (no doubt carefully worded) complaints about the firepower of some aircraft, such as the La-5 and La-7 with their armament of two 20-mm cannons (a few late-war La-7s had three 20-mm cannons). This was not a problem with the Yak-9T, with its huge and potent NS-37 37-mm cannon, however, which was capable of destroying a single-engined fighter with one shell or crippling a twin-engined bomber.

There were two aerial cannons that were widely used by the Soviets during the war—the Shpitalniy-Vladimirov ShVAK 20-mm cannon and the Volkov-Yartsev VYa-23 23-mm cannon. The ShVAK was used in both moveable (TP-20: 'T' for *Turel* or 'Turret') and fixed installations (MP-20 for a motor-mount and KP-20 for a wing-mount), although only in fixed positions on production fighters, while the VYa-23 was used only in fixed installations. A limited number of fighters were equipped with the VYa-23 firing through the spinner, such as a few LaGG-3s and Yak-9s, but the vast majority of VYa-23s were used as wing-mounted weapons on most of the Il-2s, which had first priority on these powerful cannons.

Rockets

The Soviets initially used aerial rockets as air-to-air weapons, seeing their first combat use in the Battle of the Khalkhin-Gol. The rockets used were RS-82 rockets. Being unguided, they were none too accurate, and they soon found use mainly as ground attack weapons, being fitted to many aircraft during the Second World War, such as the LaGG-3 and the Yak-1 when they were being used as fighter-bombers. The larger RS-132 (the number referring to the diameter of the rocket in millimetres) was also used widely in the Great Patriotic War, although it was mainly used by the Il-2. The rockets were normally carried on unstreamlined RO-82 rocket rails.

The RS-82 and RS-132 rockets were armour-piercing projectiles, although these were supplemented from spring 1942 by the more effective armour-piercing RB-82 and RB-132 rockets. From later in 1942, M-8 (82-mm) and M-13 (132-mm) rockets were also fitted, which were developments of the RS-82 and RS-132 rockets respectively. The ROFS-132 was a powerful fragmentation rocket that was apparently mainly used by the Il-2.

Bombs

Some Soviet fighters were capable of carrying relatively small bombs. A typical bomb would be the FAB-100 general purpose aviation bomb of 220 lb (100 kg). Smaller bombs could also be accommodated, such as the FAB-50 (110 lb (50 kg)). The bombs would normally be carried under the wings. PTAB anti-tank bomblets could be carried internally on the Yak-9B, in place of the usual FAB bombs, but this was soon stopped because of some premature explosions. The Pe-3bis, developed from the Pe-2 bomber, could carry bombs internally in its nacelle bomb bays.

APPENDIX II

Soviet Fighter Doctrine During the Second World War

The main duty of Red Air Force fighters, such as the La-5 and Yak-9, was to support Red Army ground forces, mainly by protecting the low-flying bombers and attack aircraft (shturmoviks) that supported the troops and to fly patrols above the troops. As such, these aircraft were based near the front line (as part of 'Frontal Aviation'), flying and fighting at low altitudes, normally under 16,404 feet (5,000 m). Fighters were also used to protect high-value targets, such as cities and factories. These aircraft were used as interceptors to attack any enemy aircraft approaching these targets. From 1942, these fighters were not a part of the Red Air Force, but they were a part of the PVO Strany, a separate service from the VVS. Free hunts, whereby fighters went in search of aerial prey, were rare until the final year of the war.

Soviet Fighter Tactics

Unlike American and, to an extent, German aircraft, which relied upon 'boom and zoom' or high-energy tactics, whereby an aircraft utilised its superior speed (and diving ability) to make multiple attacks against a target, Soviet tactics relied upon manoeuvrability and surprise. Soviet fighters used their manoeuvrability in both the horizontal and (later in the war) vertical planes to place themselves behind their prey, where it could be despatched by a few rounds at close range from the cannons and heavy machine guns mounted in the noses of their aircraft. As stated in *Bf 109E/F vs Yak-1/7: Eastern Front 1941–42* by Khazanov and Medved (p. 73): 'According to different assessments, 50 to 70 per cent of all aircraft shot down were hit during surprise attacks, when the attacker opened fire at a range of about 50–70m (55–77yd) [156–231 feet]'.

Soviet aircraft were designed to keep the wings free of guns, making the wings smaller and lighter and the aircraft lighter and more manoeuvrable. Cannons were fitted to the nose, synchronised to fire through the propeller blades on the La-5 and La-7, actually firing through the propeller spinner on the LaGG-3 and Yakovlev fighters. Machine guns were mounted on top of the engine cowlings on the LaGG-3 and Yakovlev fighters. Heavy 12.7-mm (50-calibre) machine guns replaced rifle-calibre guns of 7.62 mm (30 calibre) as the war progressed. For example, the twin 7.62-mm (30-calibre) ShKAS machine guns of the Yak-1 at the beginning of the Great Patriotic War (1941) were replaced by two 12.7-mm (50-calibre) UBS machine guns for the Yak-3 and Yak-9U of 1944.

The two most important missions for Soviet fighters were providing close escort and protection for ground attack aircraft, such as the Il-2, and light bombers, such as the Pe-2, and patrolling over the front lines (it was considered important to Soviet morale for the ground soldiers to see VVS aircraft above them). As such, they were not as free as German aircraft to engage in 'free-flight' or 'free-hunting', attacking targets of opportunity, such as Soviet airfields, at the time of their choosing, and under conditions that favoured them. The Germans would also have some of their fighters 'sweep' the area in front of their bombers, while only some of their fighters were flying loose escort.

German tactics were more offensive in nature, aggressively searching for the enemy, while the Soviet tactics were more defensive in nature, waiting for the enemy to come to them. The Soviet fighters were closely tied to protecting Soviet assets, while the German fighters had more flexibility to find the enemy and destroy him. Sometimes the Soviets patrolled a certain sector, which they were forbidden to leave; the Germans had no such limitations. The Soviets early in the war also flew in close 'vee' formations, while the Germans flew in the more flexible *schwarm*. This was partly out of necessity as often lacking radios, the Soviet fighters had to stay close to their leader to see any hand signals for flight commands. The Germans, always being equipped with full radios (receiver/transmitter) had no such limitations.

The Soviets did not have the same culture of the 'aerial knight', steadily increasing his kills, as the Germans did, where individual success was so highly valued. The Soviets, at least partly due to Communism, had more of a 'collective' mind-set, where what was stressed was overall unit success not individual success (not that this was not also important, especially to the pilots). To the Soviet fighter pilots, what was important was protecting their bombers and shturmoviks, not shooting down large numbers of enemy aircraft. If you protected all your shturmoviks but did not shoot down any German aircraft, that was a successful mission. If you shot down some German aircraft but lost some of your shturmoviks, that was not considered a successful mission. For the Germans, the most important factor was downing enemy aircraft; if you shot down more of their aircraft than you lost, that was a successful mission. Due at least partially to these differences (but also due in large part to better training, aircraft, and experience for the German pilots), Soviet pilots suffered greater losses than the Luftwaffe pilots, especially during the first two years of the war, and these tactics make the Germans' huge individual kill claims more believable.

One Soviet tactic that surprised the Axis forces was the use of the *taran*—ramming attack. These attacks often occurred when the Soviet fighter pilot had run out of ammunition and had no other means of downing an enemy aircraft. The pilot might ram the aircraft with one of his wingtips or get close enough to damage the enemy aircraft's tail surfaces with his propeller. These were not meant as suicide attacks, and many pilots who attempted these attacks survived, either to successfully bail out or land their damaged aircraft. The Germans had not seen such tactics employed in the West, and their use in the East came as an unpleasant surprise and a reminder that the war in the East was, as Hitler himself had said, a different kind of war.

The tide in the aerial war finally began to irreversibly turn in 1943, with the introduction of improved Lavochkins, such as the La-5F and the La-5FN with their boosted engines and developed Yakovlevs such as the heavily armed Yak-9T. These fighters, with well-trained pilots, proved to be the equal of the German fighters, even in vertical manoeuvring, and proved faster at lower altitudes, where most of the fighting took place. This allowed the Soviet fighters to match the Germans in tactics as no longer could the German pilots rely solely on speed and superior vertical manoeuvring. Now, victory in the air was up to the individual skill of the pilots.

Later in the war, as the Luftwaffe's strength waned, Soviet fighters had more flexibility to engage in free hunt tactics, and their loss rates were reduced, while those of the Luftwaffe's grew. This change in the loss rate was also due to the increasing ability and experience of Soviet pilots, compared to the inexperience and poor training of the early war period. The average Luftwaffe pilot's training and experience, on the other hand, worsened as the war progressed, due to the increasing lack of fuel for training, and the need to quickly replace their pilot losses, in a kind of vicious circle.

By 1944, with the introduction of the La-7, the Yak-3, and the Yak-9U, the German fighters had finally met more than their match. Not only were these aircraft faster at low altitudes—especially the La-7 (except against the Fw 190A-8, which with boost was faster than all but the La-7 at sea level)—but they more than matched the German fighters in vertical manoeuvrability. The situation had become dire enough for the Germans that their pilots were reportedly warned not to engage in-line engined fighters without under-nose radiators, which applied to the Yak-3 and Yak-9U. With better fighters, better pilots than earlier in the war, and the increasing numbers of German fighters pulled from the Eastern Front to combat Western aircraft, the Soviets gained air superiority during 1944, which they increased to air dominance during 1945. The air war had come full circle; it was as if the Red Air Force had changed places with the Luftwaffe.

German Fighter Tactics

Early in the Great Patriotic War, although the Red Air Force had a quantitative advantage over the German fighters, the German fighters had a large qualitative edge over the Soviet fighters. Most of the Soviet fighters were obsolete Polikarpov biplanes and monoplanes, which when facing the Bf 109F, the main German fighter in 1941, were facing the best fighter aircraft in the world. Although less manoeuvrable in the horizontal plane than the Polikarpov fighters, the Bf 109F was much faster and was much better in vertical manoeuvring, and the Germans took advantage of these superior qualities in their tactics. Rather than engage the Soviet pilots in turning contests, the Germans used their abilities in 'boom and zoom' fighting; they would dive down on the Soviets, then climb away to begin their attack again. They had the advantage that if they were in trouble, they could always use their greater speed to fly away from the combat.

The situation for the Soviets improved somewhat with the introduction in 1941 of increasing numbers of modern fighters such as the LaGG-3, MiG-3, and Yak-1. Both the LaGG-3 and MiG-3 were quite inferior to the Bf 109, especially the Bf 109F, due to their lack of greater speed (at lower altitudes for the MiG-3) and vertical manoeuvrability, in which the Bf 109F excelled. The Yak-1 was considered the best of this troika of fighters because it was more manoeuvrable and handled better than the LaGG-3 and MiG-3, but it was still inferior to the Bf 109F in speed and vertical manoeuvrability.

Even when more modern Soviet fighters such as the Yak-1 became commonplace in 1942, the Germans still maintained an edge in speed, vertical manoeuvrability, and usually firepower. Their basic formation of the four-aircraft *schwarm* was tactically more flexible than the three-aircraft 'vee' still in common use with the Soviets. The Germans better understood the value of having their aircraft fly at different altitudes, with one flight above the other. It took time for the Soviets to adopt the tactic of these 'layered' flights, where one set of fighters would provide close cover for the bombers and shturmoviks, and the second set would fly much higher, which enabled them to dive on any enemy fighters attacking the Soviet aircraft below. This tactic was adopted by the Soviets in 1943. The German fighters also did not fly as close an escort for their bombers, relying on the bombers' guns for close-in defence against the Soviets. Considering the relatively weak defensive armament of many German bombers, this may not have always been the best tactic, especially against the Yak-9T, which could destroy a bomber with a single shell from its 37-mm cannon.

The German pilots were still much better-trained in 1942, and their pilots were better able to use their aircraft's strengths and exploit the enemy's weaknesses. It was not until the disappearance of most MiG-3s from front-line duties in 1942, and the introduction of new versions of Lavochkin and Yakovlev fighters such as the La-5 and the Yak-9 in late 1942 did the situation really improve for the Soviets. With these two fighters, the Soviets were approaching parity with the Bf 109G-2 and the Fw 190A (both introduced in 1942), but the German fighters still had the edge, even if it had narrowed somewhat.

Another difference with Soviet tactics was instead of always flying escort for their bombers and dive-bombers, the Germans would use some fighters to fly ahead, to look for enemy fighters and clear the way for their bombers. They were given a flexibility that Soviet pilots could only dream of. German fighters often engaged in 'free-hunting', in which they went in search of targets of opportunity, choosing tactical situations that favoured them, such as attacking Soviet formations from a higher altitude or attacking Soviet fighters at their airfields.

One tactic that was used by the Fw 190s was to engage in head-on attacks against Soviet fighters. The Fw 190 had heavy armament, and these tactics proved successful. The appearance of the Yak-9T in 1943, with its massive 37-mm cannon in the nose, helped to stop these attacks since the Yak-9T was almost impossible to distinguish from other Yakovlev fighters head-on, and just one hit from a 37-mm shell would definitely ruin the Fw 190 pilot's day.

By the end of the Great Patriotic War, when most of the German fighter aircraft facing the Soviets were fighter-bomber versions of the Fw 190 flown by ex-attack aircraft pilots, their main tactic consisted of trying to fly away when faced with Soviet fighter opposition. Diving down and with their engine-boosting engaged, the Fw 190s could outrun even the La-5FN at low levels, although the La-7 was another matter, being just able to overtake and fight them. Once the La-7s had reached the Fw 190s, they were relatively easy prey for the La-7, especially since most of the La-7s were flown by elite Guards units.

APPENDIX III

Soviet Fighter Organisation During the Second World War

The basic unit of Soviet fighters was the *polk* ('regiment'). The *polks* were first formed in 1938; they varied in size with time and the availability of fighter aircraft. The *polk* itself was made up of different *eskadrilya* ('squadron(s)'). Originally, a *polk* consisted of four to five squadrons, for up to seventy-seven aircraft. In August 1941, the fighter *polk* was changed to three squadrons of ten aircraft each, with two 'command' aircraft (reserve aircraft) for a total of thirty-two aircraft, as the larger formations were found to be difficult to control in combat, especially by the inexperienced aircraft commanders who filled the VVS at this time. Due to this lack of control and the heavy losses at the beginning of the Great Patriotic War, the *polk* formation was changed to two squadrons for a total of twenty aircraft very soon after they had been changed to thirty-two aircraft.

By spring 1943, fighter *polks* consisted of three squadrons with nine aircraft each with four to five aircraft in reserve for a total of thirty-one to thirty-two aircraft. This was then changed to thirty-four aircraft in three ten-aircraft squadrons with four reserve aircraft. By the end of 1943, the fighter *polk* consisted of three squadrons with twelve aircraft each and four reserve aircraft for a total of forty aircraft.

The wartime *eskadrilya* was made up of *zveno* ('flight(s)'), the number of which changed over time. Originally, the squadron had been made up of different numbers of three-aircraft units. The change from the three-aircraft formation to the four-aircraft formation was made in September through November 1942. The *zveno* was made up of two *pari* (Russian plural of *para* or 'pair'). At the ultimate level, two individual aircraft made up a *para*, with a lead pilot and a wingman. The *zveno* was based upon the wartime Luftwaffe 'Finger-four' formation (*Schwarm*), which gave more flexibility than the pre-war three-aircraft 'vee' formation. The flexibility came from the looser formation, comprised of two units (the unit being the *para* for the Soviets).

From 20 August 1941, the squadron was to be composed of nine aircraft—three three-aircraft units. By the middle of 1943, this had changed to ten aircraft composed of two flights and a pair. By the end of 1943, the fighter squadron consisted of twelve aircraft composed of three flights.

The air brigade, consisting of three or four squadrons, was the main tactical unit of the VVS until the period from 1938–40, when they were abolished.

The first air divisions were formed in the second part of 1940 due to the experience of the Winter War and analyses of the air fighting in Western Europe at the beginning of the Second World War. These reforms were instituted by the then head of the VVS, Pavel Zhigarev. Aviation divisions could consist of up to 350 aircraft in from three to six regiments. There were fighter-only divisions and mixed divisions, made up of shturmoviks and fighters or bombers and fighters. The air divisions replaced the air brigades as the main tactical unit of the VVS during the Second World War.

Air corps had been formed as early as 1933. The number of aircraft varied from 120 to 270 aircraft (the lower number than with air divisions is probably due to the fact that the air corps often consisted at least partly of bombers, which were present in lower numbers than fighters). In 1941. fighter air divisions were created for air defence, with two or three air divisions.

The first air armies, as part of the large-scale reorganisation of the VVS by General Novikov, were created in 1942. There was only one fighter air army created—the 1st Fighter Air Army.

Reorganisation During 1942 (The Novikov Reforms)

General (Marshal from 17 March 1943) Aleksandr Novikov, who had replaced Pavel Zhigarev in April 1942 as head of the VVS, initiated far-reaching reforms during the spring of 1942, utilising the lessons learned during the hard fighting against the Germans. Far from moving away from the long-standing mission of the VVS to support the Red Army, the VVS was reorganised to become even more efficient and responsive to the needs of the Red Army's ground forces, which included using their fighter assets more efficiently.

One of the most important reforms effected by General Novikov was the creation of 'Air Armies' (or *VA* for *Vozdushnaya Armiya* or 'Air Army' in Russian). The aerial forces under the command of the Western Front were grouped together and became the 1st Air Army on 5 May 1942 by order of Stalin himself. The advantage of the air armies was that they were under centralised VVS control and could be switched quickly from one front to the other, as needed, thus giving the VVS operational flexibility in countering the Germans. This was more effective than sending smaller units piecemeal to different areas of the front. During May through June 1942 seven more air armies were formed; by the end of the summer ten had been formed. Most of the air armies were mixed, with fighters and bombers and/or shturmoviks.

The air army's commander worked in close concert with the frontal commander of whichever front they were assigned to. This enabled the resources of the air army, or VA, to be used wherever the frontal commander needed them and ensured good cooperation between the air units and the ground units they were supporting. At the air division and air regiment (*polk*) level, an effort was made to make the units homogeneous, comprised of one aircraft, such as the Pe-2 in bomber units. Where implemented, this improved efficiency in the supply and maintenance of these units, as only one type of aircraft now had to be supplied and maintained. However, as described in the section on Yakovlev fighters, this was often not the case, especially early in the war, where Yak-1s served alongside Yak-7s in the same regiments, for example. Nonetheless, as the war went on, even these units became more homogeneous.

At first, the VAs had only five to eight air divisions attached to them. This was increased to eighteen air divisions, although some VAs had only thirteen air divisions attached. By late 1944, there were sixteen VAs, with thirty-seven air corps and 170 air divisions comprised of sixty-three fighter, fifty-five bomber, fifty shturmovik, and two composite air divisions.

An air corps comprised two air divisions, with 120–170 aircraft per corp. Initially, in 1942, some of the air divisions consisted of two polks per division. By late 1943, most air divisions had switched to three polks, with 100–120 aircraft.

The air armies proved to be so effective that by 1945, there were seventeen of these air armies on the Eastern Front, composed of 175 air divisions.

One improvement to Soviet aircraft, in general, was the provision of two-way radios for all aircraft as the war progressed; in the early part of the Second World War, only some aircraft were fitted with this equipment, and some aircraft lacked radios altogether. Radios enabled aircraft to keep in close contact with the ground forces, and with each other in the air, an important consideration with the increasingly large formations the Soviets flew in as the war continued.

APPENDIX IV

Soviet Fighter Pilot Training

Note: much of the following discussion on training is based upon the research of Khazanov and Medved in their fine book *Bf 109E/F vs Yak-1/7: Eastern Front 1941–42* (pp. 45–50).

Like many items concerning aircraft during the Great Patriotic War, Soviet fighter pilot training went from being a rather haphazard affair in its early days to an efficient and productive system by the later stages of the conflict.

Before Barbarossa, pilot training was a relatively leisurely and selective process: each candidate was carefully examined with regards to his health, political views, and education (both general and aviation-related). Candidates who met the requirements were then enrolled in the *Osoavhiakhim* Flying Club or a Special Air Force School. The Flying Club course took a complete year to finish. Training took place on the reliable and tractable U-2 (Po-2) biplane, which in these pre-war years was still a simple trainer and utility aircraft and not the night-time nuisance bomber it later became in the Great Patriotic War.

Before 1940, graduation carried with it an automatic rank of junior lieutenant. This changed in 1940, when it was decided that graduates would be given the rank of Sergeant and would not become Lieutenants until three years after their studies were completed. This change was not surprisingly unpopular with the pilots.

Unfortunately for the Soviets, the unusually harsh winter of 1940-41 negatively affected pilot training by limiting the number of flights. In addition, the aircraft the new pilots were expected to master were new and immature monoplane fighters, such as the LaGG-3, MiG-3, and Yak-1, which did not have the relatively easy handling of the I-15bis and I-153 biplane fighters, to which some of the pilots were accustomed. It was many of these inadequately trained pilots, flying unfamiliar and difficult aircraft, who fell victim to the Luftwaffe in such great numbers in the opening months of the Great Patriotic War.

Remarkably, the VVS did not suffer a shortage of pilots after these terrible losses; quite the opposite happened, as the Luftwaffe destroyed so many aircraft in the air and on the ground in those early days of the Great Patriotic War that many Soviet pilots were without aircraft.

In order to improve pilot training, the new commander of the Red Air Force, Aleksandr Novikov, instituted a new training programme on 16 October 1942, whereby pilot graduates were to once again be given the rank of junior lieutenant after the completion of at least nine months of training.

One of the most important elements of the training system was the Auxiliary Aviation Regiments ('ZAPs', from *Zapasnoy Aviatsionniy Polk*: 'Reserve Air Regiment'), which served to train new pilots and re-equip regiments that had been pulled from the front lines to refit and reform. The new pilots were part of the reformation of these decimated regiments. In addition, the ZAPs trained already experienced pilots to fly new types of aircraft. The ZAPs also tried to ensure that new pilots sent to the front-line units had at least some training in actual combat aircraft, as opposed to dedicated training aircraft.

A change that helped the aircraft units of the Soviet Union was adopted in June 1943. Previously, when units were understrength, the entire regiment was sent to the back to re-equip and reform. A new unit, with inexperienced pilots, was then sent to take its place on the front lines, so the experience of the withdrawn units was lost. Now, individual pilots were trained by the ZAPs to fill the vacancies, and front-line regiments remained and were replenished where they were, thus maintaining their experience and integrity.

During the final eighteen months of the war, the training of pilots was extended to an entire year, with the total hours of a new pilot destined for a front-line unit now in excess of 100 hours. This was in marked contrast to the first few months of the war, when some pilots were thrown into battle with as little as ten hours' flying time.

The Germans noticed the improvement in the Soviet pilots' ability—the high-scoring ace Gunther Rall (1918–2009, credited with 275 kills), for one, as quoted in *La-5/7 vs Fw 190: Eastern Front 1942–45*, p. 50):

> They learned unbelievably quickly. Already by the middle of 1943 their tactics were close to matching those of the Luftwaffe, and modern Yakovlev and Lavochkin fighters started to appear—both powerful, agile aircraft. I tried repeatedly to better different types of La-5s and Yak-9s in horizontal manoeuvres in my Bf 109G, but this proved to be practically impossible, even when the throttle was pushed forward against the stop.

The Soviet pilots' kill ratios were also on an upwards trajectory. During the Battle of Stalingrad (mid-1942 to early 1943), the Soviets were lucky to achieve parity with the Germans in kills and usually lagged behind. Yet by 1944 and 1945, some La-5/La-7 units were claiming kill ratios of 10:1. Even though exaggerated, these kill ratios indicate how far Soviet pilots (and their aircraft) had come since the grim days of 1941.

Kill Confirmation

How many aircraft a specific side or pilot shot down at any given time is often a heated topic. Discussion is often fraught with political overtones that have little or nothing to do with the actual combat situation, such as reported American aerial losses during the Korean War (1950–53) when many shot-down American aircraft were recorded as lost to other causes, such as flak or mechanical failures. Even looking at total losses of aircraft does not give a true picture of combat losses, as air forces may have claimed their combat losses as non-combat losses for propaganda purposes (as with American aircraft during the Korean War), and amid the 'fog of war', inaccurate observations are often made. In addition, total losses include aircraft lost in accidents, sometimes far from the front, which may account for a substantial number of aircraft, as it did for the Soviets in the Great Patriotic War, where many aircraft were lost during training.

A few historians have been sceptical of the huge claims of the German aces during the Second World War, especially on the Eastern Front, where a handful of pilots claimed kill totals several times that of the highest-scoring aces of any other nation. For the purposes of full disclosure, I admit to being one of those sceptics. The Luftwaffe, like most air forces, had rigorous standards for victory confirmation, and there was good reason to get an accurate count of the enemy aircraft actually destroyed; this was a direct reflection of the effectiveness of pilots, their training, aircraft, and tactics, as well as the abilities of the enemy. Knowing how many enemy aircraft were destroyed in a certain sector of the front also aided in the assessment of enemy forces and allocation of aerial assets.

Yet, as an example, it seems almost inconceivable to me that one man, Erich Alfred Hartmann (1922–99), actually shot down 352 enemy aircraft during the Second World War. This is his confirmed total; his claimed total must have been even higher. I have seen other estimates that put his actual number of downed aircraft at something closer to 100 aircraft, which to me seems altogether more plausible. I have read many explanations for how these so-called *Experten* ('Experts' in German) were able to rack up their enormous kill totals, but I still find myself somewhat less than convinced.

The Luftwaffe were just as much a part of Nazi society as the SS at the time, no doubt under the same intense propaganda pressures. Indeed, the head of the Luftwaffe, *Reichsmarshall* Hermann Wilhelm Göring (1893–1946), was Adolf Hitler's chief deputy. As the Germans' war effort began to crumble, and the Luftwaffe's efforts to stop the Anglo-American Combined Bomber Offensive proved ineffective, one straw Göring could continue to clutch was the (apparent) continuing success of his *Experten* on the Eastern Front. That young men like Erich Hartmann were caught up in the adulation and the need for ever-increasing scores is certainly understandable. They may have been happy to consider every Soviet aircraft that started to put out smoke and fly away during combat a certain kill; they may well have believed their huge scores—in essence, they may have believed their own press clippings. We will never know for certain. In addition, as *Experten* such as Erich Hartmann tallied up these huge kill claims, instead of their claims being more heavily scrutinised, they were more likely to be rubber-stamped. I doubt that anybody wanted to be known as the lowly *Unteroffizier* Luftwaffe clerk who was questioning the claims of the 'Blond Knight of Germany'.

I find it easier to believe the more modest claims of the Soviets. A pilot is far more likely to have shot down fifty-one aircraft than 301. This is not to say there was no exaggeration on the part of the Soviets—Stalin's regime was certainly no stranger to propaganda. There undoubtedly was some inflation of the figures, but it does not seem to me to have been to nearly the same extent as with the Germans.

German Kill Confirmation

The kill had to be witnessed by someone other than the pilot—for instance, ground observers—or caught on the gun-camera film. The kill itself had to be either the destruction of the aircraft in the air or a bail-out of the pilot. If these criteria were not met, the claim was supposed to be disallowed. These were the official criteria.

Soviet Kill Confirmation

At least two other pilots, ground troops, or partisans had to have witnessed the kill in order for the pilot to make a claim. This claim was then to be examined by both an NKVD (Soviet political and military police) officer and the squadron intelligence officer. If the evidence was considered adequate, the kill would usually then be confirmed by the regimental commander. Again, these were the official criteria.

APPENDIX V

Top Soviet Fighter Aces (Pilots with Fifty or More Kills)

Note: The names of the aces are written in the traditional Russian style, with the family name first, then the given name and the patronymic (which was based upon the father's name).

Name	Individual Kills	Shared Kills	Fate	Comments	Awards/Titles	Sorties	Combats
Kozhedub Ivan Nikitovich	62	-	Survived war	Top Allied ace: downed two American P-51Ds when they attacked him in friendly fire incident; downed a Me 262 in 1945	Three times a Hero of the Soviet Union	330	120
Pokryshkin Aleksandr Ivanovich	59	-	Survived war	Noted air tactician; at least 5 kills were recorded on the MiG-3	Three times a Hero of the Soviet Union	560	156
Gulayev Nikolaiy Dmitriyevich	57	3	Survived war	Post-war he became a Colonel-General in the VVS	Twice a Hero of the Soviet Union	248	69
Rechkalov Grigoriy Andreyevich	56	5	Survived war	Post-war he became a Major-General in the VVS	Twice a Hero of the Soviet Union	450	122
Yevstigneyev Kirill Alekseyevich	53	3	Survived war	Post-war he became a Major-General in the VVS	Twice a Hero of the Soviet Union	283	109
Vorozheykin Arseniy Vasilyevich	52	13	Survived war	Post-war he became a Major-General in the VVS	Twice a Hero of the Soviet Union	300	90
Glinka Dmitriy Borisovich	50	-	Survived war	Born in Ukraine. His brother, Boris, was also a multiple ace (29 + 2 shared)	Twice a Hero of the Soviet Union	300	90

Ivan Nikitovich Kozhedub in his La-5F. (*Viktor Kulikov's collection*)

One item to note is the prevalence of Russian names on this list; most of the pilots in the VVS were ethnic Russians. However, the top ace, Ivan Kozhedub, was an ethnic Ukrainian, born in Ukraine, and he achieved all his kills on fighters designed by Semyon Lavochkin, a Jew, which serves as a reminder that the Soviet war effort was not a 'Russians-only' endeavour.

Another item to note is that different sources have different numbers for the pilots' scores. For example, some sources have Nikolaiy Gulayev as the fourth highest-scoring ace with fifty-five kills to Grigoriy Rechkalov's fifty-six kills. Note also that all these pilots survived the war.

Some 810 Hero of the Soviet Union titles were awarded to fighter pilots. Sixty-one pilots were awarded this title twice, while only Ivan Kozhedub and Aleksandr Pokryshkin, the number one and number two Soviet aces respectively, were awarded it three times.

APPENDIX VI

Production Figures

Production figures for Soviet aircraft are sometimes incomplete, and figures from different sources often differ. The difference is usually not great and could be attributable to whether the sources include such items as experimental aircraft, pre-production aircraft, or service trials aircraft. I have attempted to use numbers from what I consider to be the most accurate sources available to me, although I have at times included different figures where the data come from equally reliable sources.

Lavochkin

LaGG-3

Year	1941	1942	1943	1944
Number Produced	2,463	2,771 (or 2,736)	1,294 (or 1,065)	215
			Grand Total	6,514 (or 6,479)

Production Notes

Fifty-four or sixty-five LaGG-3s were produced by Z.23 in 1941. Some 2,771 (or 2,736) LaGG-3s were built in 1942, more than in any other year. *Zavod* 21 produced both LaGG-3s and La-5s in 1942.

The total production of the LaGG-3 according to one source was 6,528. Another source has the total number at 6,493, broken down by year as 1941—2,463, 1942—2,736, 1943—1,065, and 1944—215. A Z.165 at Rostov-on-Don (Rostov-na-Donu), not otherwise known to this author, is mentioned, although it is not clear if it ever produced any LaGG-3s.

La-5FNs on the production line. It was just this sort of mass production that ruined the Germans' chances of defeating the Soviet Union. (*Viktor Kulikov's collection*)

La-5

Zavod	1942	1943	1944	Zavod Total
21	1,107	4,619	3,503	9,229
31	22	5	N/A	27
99	N/A	184	102	286
381	N/A	240	221	461
Yearly Total	1,129	5,048	3,826	
			Grand Total	10,003

Production Notes

Production of the La-5 started in 1942 at Z.21 in Gor'kiy. Some 1,129 high-back La-5s had been produced by the end of 1942. Z. 21 built 1,107 and Z.31 built twenty-two. The first La-5F left Z.21 in May 1943. The first La-5FN left Z.21 in March 1943.

The La-5FN and La-7 were produced in parallel from April 1944 until La-5FN production was ended in November 1944. When the last La-5FN left the assembly line, the total of all La-5 variants produced was 10,003 (one source has 9,985, another has 10,002, and yet another 10,013; using the figures of my preferred source, the total number I have come up with is 10,003; as you can see, the difference in the totals is rather insignificant).

La-7

Zavod	1944	1945	1946	Zavod Total
21	1,558	2,799 (includes 205 La-7UTIs)	430 (includes 377 La-7UTIs)	4,787
99	40	210	N/A	250
381	638	660	N/A	1,298
Yearly Total	2,236	3,669	430	
			Grand Total:	6,335

Production Notes

Going by the figures in these tables, the total number of Lavochkin wartime fighters produced, from the LaGG-3 in 1941 to the La-7 in 1946, is 22,852 aircraft. Again, different sources give slightly different figures, but this number is a reasonable estimate for total production of all of the Great Patriotic War Lavochkins.

MiG-3

Zavod	1940	1941	1942	Zavod Total
1	20	3,122		3,142
OKB-155			30	30
Total	20	3,122	30	
			Grand Total:	3,172

Production Notes

As can be seen from the table, nearly all of the MiG-3s were produced at *Zavod* 1 in Moscow. In 1942, OKB-155 (the Mikoyan-Gurevich Design Bureau), also in Moscow, completed thirty additional aircraft from components produced elsewhere. These were the last MiG-3s produced. By 1942, *Zavod* 1 had already been evacuated from Moscow to Kuibyshev on the upper Don and was producing Il-2s. Apparently, the figure of 3,172 does not include the 100 MiG-1s, which were produced at Z.1 in 1940.

Polikarpov

I-5

Zavod	1931	1932	1933	1934	Zavod Total
1	66	76			142
21		10	321	330	661
Yearly Total	66	96	321	330	
				Grand Total	803

Production Notes

The production of the I-5 started at Z.1 in Moscow, then shifted to Z.21 in Nizhniy-Novgorod (soon renamed to 'Gor'kiy", which it would be known as throughout the Second World War; it has since be renamed back to Nizhniy-Novgorod).

I-15bis

Zavod	1937	1938	1939
1 & 21	-	-	-
		Grand Total:	2,408

Production Notes

The I-15bis was produced at both *Zavodi* 1 and 21, but the records do not separate production by zavod or year. Only the total number produced has been recorded in the sources I have researched, although these sources do seem to agree on the total number produced—2,408.

I-153

Zavod	1939	1940	1941	
1	1,011	2,362	64	
			Grand Total:	3,437

Production Notes

All the I-153s were produced by Z.1 in Moscow. This factory then switched to production of the MiG-1/MiG-3 fighters.

I-16

Zavod	1934	1935	1936	1937	1938	1939	1940	1941	1942	Zavod Total
21		527	902	1,881	1,070	1,571	2,207	336		8,494
39	50	4	4							58
153				6	105	264	503	423		1,301
458								356	83	439
Yearly Total	50	531	906	1,887	1,175	1,835	2,710	1,115	83	
									Grand Total	10,292

Production Notes

The I-16 was by far the most heavily-produced fighter of the inter-war period (1919–1939), with 6,384 produced from 1934–39, production not ending until 1942. The great majority of the I-16s were produced at Z.21 at Gor'kiy (Nizhniy-Novgorod), although significant numbers were also produced at Z.153 in Novosibirsk and Z.458 in Rostov-on-Don (Rostov-na-Donu). The aircraft produced at Z.458 were apparently all of the UTI-4 trainer version.

Yakovlev

Yak-1

Zavod	1940	1941	1942	1943	1944	Zavod Total
301	48	69				117
292	16	1,212	3,474	2,720	1,128	8,550
Yearly Total	64	1,281	3,474	2,720	1,128	
					Grand Total	8,667

PRODUCTION NOTES

The majority of the Yak-1s were produced at Z.292 in Saratov, with only a few produced at Z.301 in Moscow due to the evacuation of factories from Moscow in late 1941. Improved versions of the Yak-1 (the Yak-1B) continued in production after the introduction of the Yak-7 in 1941 and the Yak-9 in 1942. On 23 June 1943, Z.292 was bombed and heavily damaged, but by 29 June 1943, production had resumed amid the ruins of the burned-out factory. The Yak-1B continued in production into June 1944 at Z.292, when they were replaced on the production line by the Yak-3, itself a development of the Yak-1.

Yak-3

Type	Zavod	1944	1945	1946	Total by Type by Zavod
Yak-3 VK-105PF-2	31	498	462		960
	292	1,682	1,918	240	3,840
Yak-3 VK-107A	31			48	48
Yearly Total		2,180	2,380	288	
				Grand Total	4,848

PRODUCTION NOTES

The aircraft produced at Z.31 at Tbilisi were widely considered to be of better finish and quality than those produced at Z.292 at Saratov, even though the majority of Yak-3s were produced at Z.292.

Yak-7

Type	Zavod	1941	1942	1943	1944	Total by Type by Zavod
Yak-7UTI	301	186				186
Other Yak-7s	153	21	2,211	2,656		4,888
	82		215	640	465	1,320
	21		5			5
Yearly Total		207	2,431	3,296	465	
					Grand Total	6,399

Production Notes

As seen in the above table, the majority of the Yak-7s were produced by the huge Z.153 in Novosibirsk, in Siberia. Z.82 switched over to production of the Yak-7's successor, the Yak-9, in the middle of 1944, when production of the Yak-7 ended. Z.301 in Moscow ended production of the Yak-7 (Yak-7UTI) in 1941, with the evacuation of factories to the east. It was noted that the Yak-7s built at Z.153 were of better quality than those built at Z.82.

Yak-9

Type	Zavod	1942	1943	1944	1945	1946	1947	1948	Total by Type
Yak-9 M-105	153	59	1,761	5,808	2,721	321	175		
	166		721	481					12,047
Yak-9U VK-107	156			50	838	2			
	166		11	1,119	1,084				
	82			373	444				3,921
Yak-9P VK-107A	153					30	522	249	801
Yearly Total		59	2,493	7,458	4,643	353	697	249	
								Grand Total	16,769

Production Notes

It can be seen that the majority of Yak-9s were produced at Z.153 in Novosibirsk while a substantial number were produced at Z.82 in Moscow (Tushino), where it had replaced the Yak-7, and at Z.166 in Omsk.

The Yak-9P was produced entirely in the post-war period but is included here for completeness. Including post-war production, a total of 36,683 Yakovlev fighters were produced from 1940–48, with 32,051 being produced during the war. A further 4,635 Yak-3s and Yak-9s were produced after the war.

APPENDIX VII

Fighter Production During the Great Patriotic War for Germany and the Soviet Union

	1941	1942	1943	1944	1945 (first 6 months)	Total
Soviet Union	7,086	9,924	14,590	17,913	~9,000	~58,513
Germany	3,744	5,358	10,059	24,981	5,732	49,874

As can be seen from the table above, although Soviet fighter production exceeded German production during the Great Patriotic War, it did not do so by a huge margin. The greatest percentage difference was during 1942, when the fighting was especially intense and the Soviets suffered large aerial losses (although still less than in 1941) so had to make good those losses, producing nearly twice as many fighters as the Germans. However, in 1944, Soviet fighter production was actually less than that of the Germans, who initiated their Emergency Fighter Programme (*Jagernotprogramm*) on 3 July 1944, part of which involved the cessation of production of any aircraft except fighters. If the 6,634 Fw 190s built as fighter-bombers/ground attack aircraft are added, then the number of German fighters grows to 56,508, which comes close to the Soviet total of 58,513. When the German jet fighter total of 1,493 is added, the German total becomes 58,001, nearly the same as the Soviet total. It must be remembered, though, that most jet fighters did not see any combat, and even fewer saw combat on the Eastern Front.

This table does not contain the Western Allied-built Lend-Lease fighters, which was 14,093, or 11, 693, which is minus the 2,400 P-63 Kingcobras, which were not used in the Great Patriotic War. With these added to the Soviet total, it is 70,017 for the Great Patriotic War. However, the table does not contain those fighters built by Germany's allies, such as Italy (whose fighters were mostly used in the West), which produced 3,355, which when added to the German total gives 61,356. These two totals—70,017 fighters for the Soviet Union as compared to 61,356 (at least) for the Axis—gives the Soviet Union a considerable advantage, especially considering the large numbers of Axis aircraft fighting in the West, but numbers alone do not explain the Soviet victory over Germany and the Axis forces, at least in the air. The Germans outproduced the Soviet Union in fighter aircraft in 1944 (although many of these fighters would have been used in the West), but this did not stop the Soviets from firmly and irrevocably establishing air superiority that year. The La-7, Yak-3, and Yak-9U were all introduced in 1944, so quality matched quantity for the Soviets.

APPENDIX VIII

Total Fighter Combat Losses During the Great Patriotic War

	1941	1942	1943	1944	1945	Total
German	568 (Eastern Front only)	1,029	2,896 (1,099 on Eastern front)	2,855 (losses through June, records partially lost)	Records lacking	21,452 (includes non-combat loses, on all fronts)
Soviet	5,100	4,400	5,600	4,100	1,500	20,700

The above losses are for fighters lost in combat. The numbers for the Soviets include not just the VVS, but the AVMF and the PVO. Not surprisingly, the Soviets lost very heavily in the first six months of the Great Patriotic War. If extended out to a whole year, the losses could have been over 10,000 fighter aircraft lost in combat. The costliest year overall was 1943. This high loss can be accounted for by the change in the war itself; up until 1943, the Soviets had mainly been on the defensive. In 1943, they went on the offensive on all fronts, in Ukraine (after the Battle of Kursk), at Leningrad, and in the central part of the Soviet Union, in central Russian and the eastern edge of Byelorussia. These great offensives put any chance of German victory out of reach, but they came at a high cost to the Soviets in both ground and aerial casualties. By 1943, the Soviets were able to absorb these casualties, with their aircraft production having fully recovered from the evacuations of 1941 and 1942, and their now more effective training programme providing new pilots for the front (although these pilots were still not nearly as well-trained as the German pilots). The Germans, on the other hand, could not absorb nor sustain their casualties.

Still, it is clear from the records on both sides that the Soviet Union lost more fighter aircraft in combat than Germany during the Great Patriotic War (the German numbers above include losses in the West). What is not clear is if the Germans counted Fw 190 fighter-bombers as fighter losses or ground attack losses, which were counted separately. If counted with ground attack losses, the Fw 190 fighter-bomber losses would nudge the German fighter losses up a bit if included with those. The total losses for the Germans, including non-fighter and non-combat losses on the Eastern Front, was 52,850 aircraft; for the Soviets, it was 106,400, or slightly more than twice the German aircraft losses.

One aspect of the total losses of aircraft for the Soviets was the high number that were lost due to non-combat causes; one source (*Soviet Casualties and Combat Losses in the Twentieth Century*, G. F. Krivosheev, from which the above Soviet loss figures are taken) has 60,300. This was for all aircraft; for fighters, the non-combat losses were 26,100, as compared to their combat losses of 20,700. Many of these aircraft were lost in accidents of various sorts, including very numerous training casualties. This may seem like a large number, but both sides suffered many non-combat aircraft losses.

Bibliography

Internet Resources

Note: Some of the sites listed below are in Russian, but there are online translating tools that should allow you to read them, if you cannot read Russian.

vvs.hobbyvista.com: Modelling the Aircraft of the Soviet VVS—this was a worthwhile site for making VVS models. It contains some useful information, although its articles on colour are controversial and should not be taken for gospel. This site is now moribund and the forum portion is no longer functioning, but the reference articles are still up as of the time of writing (2021).

www.airaces.ru: a very useful Russian language site that contains much information about Soviet aeroplanes, including production figures.

www.airfield.narod.ru: This site is dedicated to the Yakovlev OKB. Although not just limited to Yakovlev's wartime fighters, it contains some good information about these aircraft.

www.airpages.ru: This site is not only about Soviet aircraft, but as a Russian site it does contain a great deal of material about Soviet aeroplanes of the Second World War. It has both a Russian language and an English language option, but the Russian language option is more exhaustive in its coverage, although the English language version is expanding. The English language version contains some interesting information, such as drawings, photographs, and performance figures (as does the Russian language version). The site contains primary source materials, such as wartime orders and reports. A very useful site.

www.airwar.ru: An excellent resource for aviation-related material of all eras, and not just for Soviet aircraft. It has much textual information on Great Patriotic War fighters, and also has many plans, drawings, and photographs of these aircraft. In Russian, although an incomplete English version is available.

www.arcforums.com: Not specifically for the VVS, but contains threads and posts regarding VVS aircraft.

www.britmodeller.com: A good site for modelling in general, containing some threads and posts concerning Soviet aircraft, some by this very author.

www.iremember.ru: A site that has interviews with veterans of the Great Patriotic War. The interviews are available in both Russian and English. This site is recommended not just for aviation historians, but also for anyone interested in the experiences of Soviet military men and women during the Great Patriotic War.

www.massimotessitori.altervista.org/sovietwarplanes/pages/: An excellent website for all things VVS and run by the illustrator of my books on the Il-2 Shturmovik and wartime

Lavochkin fighters, Massimo Tessitori. Highly recommended for all those interested in Soviet Great Patriotic War aircraft and has accurate representations of the colour schemes that they wore. This site should also be of great interest for the plastic modeller of VVS aeroplanes. It includes low-resolution versions of some of the colour profiles in this book. It has an excellent section on the MiG-3, which is not surprising as Mr. Tessitori wrote a book on this aircraft.

www.redbanner.co.uk: The successor site to Modelling the Aircraft of the Soviet VVS. The same comments about the old site generally apply to this site.

www.ScaleModels.ru: A very good site for reference material on VVS aircraft, including the Soviet wartime fighters and kits. In Russian with automatic English translation available (with all the interesting translation artefacts and peculiarities that entails).

Published Works

057 Samolot Mysliwski La-7 (Warsaw: Wydawnictwo Minsterstwa Obrony Narodewej, 1979)

Gordon, Y., *Red Star Volume 10: Lavochkin Piston-Engined Fighters* (Hinckley: Midland Publishing, 2003)

Gordon, Y., *Soviet Air Power in World War* 2 (Hinckley: Ian Allen Publishing Ltd, 2008)

Gordon, Y. and Khazanov, D., *Soviet Combat Aircraft of the Second World War: Single-Engined Fighters*, Vol. 1 (Hinckley: Midland Publishing, 1998)

Gordon, Y. and Dexter, K., *Mikoyan's Piston-Engined Fighters* (Hinckley: Midland Publishing, 2003)

Gordon, Y. and Dexter, K., *Polikarpov's Biplane Fighters* (Hinckley: Midland Publishing, 2002)

Gordon, Y. and Dexter, K., *Polikarpov's I-16 Fighter: Its Forerunners and Progeny* (Hinckley: Midland Publishing, 2001)

Gordon, Y., Komissarov, S., and Komissarov, D., *Famous Russian Aircraft, Ilyushin Il-2/Il-10* (Hinckley: Midland Publishing, 2010)

Gordon, Y., Komissarov, S., and Komissarov, D., *Yakovlev Fighters of World War Two* (Manchester: Hikoki Publications Ltd, 2015)

Green, W., *War Planes of the Second World War—Fighters*, Vol. 3 (Garden City: Doubleday & Company, 1971)

Gunston, B. and Gordon, Y., *MiG Aircraft Since 1937*, (London: Putnam Aeronautical Books, 1998)

Gunston, B. and Gordon, Y., *Yakovlev Aircraft Since 1924*, (London: Putnam Aeronautical Books, 1997)

I-153 M-62 Technical Manual (Moscow: TsAGI, 1940)

I-16 M-63 Technical Manual (Moscow: Oborongiz, 1941)

I-301 Technical Manual (Moscow: 1940)

Khazanov, D. and Medved, A., *La-5/7 vs FW 190: Eastern Front 1942–45* (Botley: Osprey Publishing, 2011)

Khazanov, D. and Medved, A., *MiG-3 Aces of World War 2* (Botley: Osprey Publishing, 2012)

Kotel'nikov [Kotelnikov], V., *Istrebitel' MiG-3—Aviakollektsia*, (Moscow: Modelist-Konstruktor, 2015)

Kotelnikov [Kotel'nikov], V., Russian Piston Aero Engines (Ramsbury: The Crowood Press Ltd., 2005)

Kotelnikov [Kotel'nikov], V., Orlov, M., and Yakubovich, N., *Wydawnictwo Militaria. #249. LaGG-3* (Warsaw: Wydawnictwo 'MILITARIA', 2006)

Kotel'nikov, V., Orlov, M., and Yakubovich, N., *La-7—Aviakollektsia* (Moscow: Modelist-Konstruktor, 2003)

Krivosheev, Colonel-General G., *Soviet Casualties and Combat Losses in The Twentieth Century* (London: Greenhill, 1997)

La-5 Flight Manual (Moscow: Ministry of Defence, 1943)
La-7 Technical Manual (Moscow: Ministry of Defence, 1945)
LaGG-3 Flight Manual (Moscow: Ministry of Defence, 1943)
Legendariye Samolyeti Yak-1 No 75 (Moscow: DeAgostini, 2013)
Legendariye Samolyeti Yak-7 No 79 (Moscow: DeAgostini, 2013)
Legendariye Samolyeti Yak-9 No 1 (Moscow: DeAgostini, 2011)
Leonard, H., *Encyclopaedia of Soviet Fighters 1939-1951* (Paris: Histoire & Collections, 2005)
Leonard, H., 'Les chasseurs Lavochkine', *Aérojournal*, 20 (2015)
Liss, W., *Profile Publications Nr 149: The Lavochkin La-5 & 7* (Leatherhead: Profile Publications, 1967)
Maslov, M., *Istrebitel' I-15bis* (Moscow; RUSAVIA, 2003)
Maslov, M., *Istrebitel' I-16* (Moscow: M-Hobby, 1997)
Maslov, M., *Istrebitel' I-16* (Moscow: 'Yauza', 'Kollektsiya', 'Eksmo', 2008)
Memo to the Pilot on the Use of the Yak-7 (B) Aircraft with the M105PF Engine (Moscow, Leningrad: Office of the Naval Publishing House NKVF USSR, 1945)
Moore, J. N., *Il-2 Shturmovik: Red Avenger* (Stroud: Fonthill Media, 2015)
Moore, J. N., *Lavochkin Fighters of the Second World War* (Stroud: Fonthill Media, 2016)
Moore, J. N., *Soviet Bombers of the Second World War* (Stroud: Fonthill Media, 2019)
Mellinger, G., *Osprey—Aircraft of the Aces 56—LaGG & Lavochkin Aces of World War 2* (Botley, Oxford: Osprey Publishing, 2003)
Orlov, M., *Aviakollektsia—Soviet VVS Colours 1941–1945* (Moscow: Modelist-Konstruktor, 2008)
Stapfer, H., *La 5/7 Fighters in action—Aircraft Number 169* (Carrolton: Squadron/Signal Publications, 1998)
Stapfer, H., *LaGG Fighters in action—Aircraft Number 163* (Carrolton: Squadron/Signal Publications, 1996)
Stapfer, H., *Polikarpov Fighters in action Pt. 1—Aircraft Number 157* (Carrolton: Squadron/Signal Publications, Inc., 1995)
Stapfer, H., *Polikarpov Fighters in action Pt. 2—Aircraft Number 162* (Carrolton: Squadron/Signal Publications, Inc., 1996)
Vestsik, M. and Vrany, J., *Lavockin La-5: MBI* (Prague: MBI)
Vestsik, M. and Vrany, J., *Lavockin La-7: MBI* (Prague: MBI)
Yak-1 Technical Manual (Moscow: Ministry of Defence, 1942)
Yak-9 Technical Manual (Moscow: Ministry of Defence, 1944)
Yakubovich, N., *Istrebitel' La-5* (Moscow; Yauza, Kollektsiya, Eksmo, 2008)
Yakubovich, N., *Istrebitel' Yak-9* (Moscow; Yauza, Kollektsiya, Eksmo, 2008)
Yakubovich, N., *Yak-3 Istrebitel' "Pobeda"* (Moscow; Yauza, Kollektsiya, Eksmo, 2011)

Magazines

Voiyna v Vozdukhe volumes 32–34)
Voiyna v Vozdukhe volumes 68–70)

Index